MECHADEMIA 4

War/Time

Mechademia
An Annual Forum for Anime, Manga, and Fan Arts

FRENCHY LUNNING, EDITOR

Mechademia is a series of books published by the University of Minnesota Press devoted to creative and critical work on anime, manga, and the fan arts. Linked through their specific but complex aesthetic, anime, manga, and the fan arts have influenced a wide array of contemporary and historical culture through design, art, film, and gaming. This series seeks to examine, discuss, theorize, and reveal this unique style through its historic Japanese origins and its ubiquitous global presence manifested in popular and gallery culture. Each book is organized around a particular narrative aspect of anime and manga; these themes are sufficiently provocative and broad in interpretation to allow for creative and insightful investigations of this global artistic phenomenon.

Mechademia 1 *Emerging Worlds of Anime and Manga*
Mechademia 2 *Networks of Desire*
Mechademia 3 *Limits of the Human*
Mechademia 4 *War/Time*

MECHADEMIA 4

War/Time

Frenchy Lunning, Editor

UNIVERSITY OF MINNESOTA PRESS MINNEAPOLIS · LONDON

http://www.mechademia.org

Spot illustrations by Joshua Eull

"Ninja, Hidden Christians, and the Two Ferreiras: On Endō Shūsaku and Yamada Fūtarō" was previously published as "Futari no Fereira: Yamada Fūtarō ron," in Takayuki Tatsumi, *Nihon henryū-bungaku* (Japanese slipstream literature) (Tokyo: Shinchōsha, 1998).

Published by the University of Minnesota Press
111 Third Avenue South, Suite 290
Minneapolis, MN 55401-2520
http://www.upress.umn.edu

ISSN: 1934-2489
ISBN: 978-0-8166-6749-9

Printed in the United States of America on acid-free paper

The University of Minnesota is an equal-opportunity educator and employer.

20 19 18 17 16 15 14 13 12 11 10 09   10 9 8 7 6 5 4 3 2 1

Mechademia Editorial Staff

Contents

Mobilization/Domestication

Review and Commentary

Preface

THOMAS LAMARRE

WAR/TIME

In advanced consumer societies, we are used to thinking of war as a disruption of the normal state of affairs, as an irruption of irrational violence and destruction into an otherwise peaceful condition. Because we associate our peace with exhausting yet safety-enhanced cycles of production and consumption, we have become accustomed to thinking of war as the opposite of productivity—war as destruction in opposition to production, war as something different from the everyday violence of our workaday lives, which happens at a distance, in other places and times, seen on screens. We are liable to acknowledge that war makes for profits, that there are and always have been war profiteers, but we are unlikely to grasp how the increasingly fragile prosperity of the United States and its client states might be predicated upon war, because we still think war in opposition to peace, prosperity, productivity.

But there are arguments for, and demonstrations of, a state of affairs in which war constitutes the very ground of our productivity and prosperity. Chalmers Johnson, for instance, argues that the United States economy (and thus that of its client states) has become a form of military Keynesianism, in which "the making and selling of weaponry has become our way of life."[1] Simply put, war-related technologies and military bases are a major worldwide employer and growth industry, and a highly regulated one at that. On a related tack, Naomi Klein's discussions of disaster capitalism have shown how contemporary American-articulated global capitalism deliberately builds disaster into the business of producing of wealth. War and natural disasters do not disrupt the cycles of production and consumption but on the contrary spur them.[2] If Johnson and Klein are right, this military-driven economy and disaster capitalism have material limits, which are already visible on the horizon in the deepening ecological and economic crises of this destruction-centered productivity.

Maybe this is why so many of our entertainments dwell on apocalypse, Armageddon, genocide, and the Holocaust—not merely because we delight in spectacles of mayhem and destruction but also because we long to discover the material limit of this current state of affairs and to find something new in its ruination. But the imagination typically falters on the verge of apocalypse, as if it is not entirely possible or desirable to dispense with the current state of affairs, not quite yet, for maybe we continue to hold out hope for its sustainability.

Michel Foucault's writings on war put a different, somewhat alarming twist on such problems. He inverted Karl von Clausewitz's dictum that war is only a branch of political activity, to challenge any residual commitment to the idea that war happens only when politics fails. Foucault suggested instead that war is the permanent basis of all modern institutions of power. Where our received wisdom posits war as a disruption of the normally peaceful order of things, Foucault saw that, in modern times, the implementation of various fields of rationality had made for a situation in which "society must be defended." Consequently, not only is war the basis for modern institutions of power but also, conversely, war becomes a technology of social control.

Like any modality or technology of social control, war too has its dream. Foucault offered this vision: "Historians of ideas usually attribute the dream of a perfect society to the philosophers and jurists of the eighteenth century; but there was also the military dream of society; its fundamental reference was not to the state of nature but to the meticulously subordinated cogs of a machine, not to the primal social contract but to permanent coercions, not to fundamental rights but to indefinitely progressive forms of training, not to the general will but to automatic docility."[3]

Today, as neoconservative regimes and neoliberal corporate interests readily dispense with or easily bypass the social contract (constitutions, parliaments, basic rights to peaceful protest, etc.) and the utopian aspirations associated with them, and as we find ourselves caught up in indefinitely progressive forms of training (retooling ourselves to implement the next generations and latest wrinkles in information and communications technologies), it seems as if we are already living the military dream of society, preternaturally fascinated with our relation to mechanisms that appear, at least initially, to be postmechanistic (cyborgs, thinking computers, sentient robots, swarm intelligence) yet that frequently betray a profound commitment to mechanistic philosophies, fragmenting and dispersing them, reinscribing them in the guise of deconstructing them. Such cyber-entities are not postmechanistic in the sense of coming after or moving beyond the mechanistic; they are postmechanistic in the sense that the modern technological condition finally appears as irrevocable as it is indefensible and unlivable.

Such an evocation of Johnson's, Klein's, and Foucault's perspective on the contemporary situation may appear unduly bleak and pessimistic to some readers, for it implies that today we can no longer afford to think of society or productivity or prosperity apart from war, to the point that war and everyday life are inseparable, and both our daily time or temporality and our historical moment are conditioned in war. Yet, if we take Johnson, Klein, or Foucault at their word despite their differences in emphasis, we must also acknowledge a gap implicit in this condition—which is not wartime but *war/time*, not an equation of war and the everyday but a self-propelling operative condition in which war acts as a control on the everyday time of orderly social productivity, while that everyday time spurs the spread of war, of its technologies (weapons) and its networks (bases). The project of this volume is to locate, explore, and critically inhabit the gap implicit in war/time wherever it appears.

Because the emphasis of this volume is on manga, anime, and associated fan activities, and thus on Japan, the war/time gap will appear in distinctive locations and modalities. Across a number of the essays, for instance, appears an emphasis on the Japanese experience of World War II and on the legacy of Japanese empire and militarism. The essays grouped under the rubric "Legacies of Sovereignty" look at the relation between national sovereignty and war in very different ways. Here questions arise about the agency of manga artists in the context of the wartime mobilization of artists to produce military propaganda (Rei Okamoto Inouye), about the internalization of military modes of behavior in children, as critically exposed in Takahata Isao's *Grave of the Fireflies* (Wendy Goldberg), and about how temporality of Japanese colonialism and its historical moment reappears in ShinKai Makoto's *The Place Promised in Our Early Days* (Gavin Walker). The different emphases in these essays merit close attention: where Goldberg finds in animation a thoroughly effective critique of blind patriotism, Inouye's account poses questions about how manga art, in its resistance to commodification, entered fully into wartime nationalism. In other words, in its resistance to temporality of mechanical reproduction that had come to characterize everyday life in the 1930s, manga art actively bridged the gap between war and everyday life. Walker goes even further, showing how the war/time gap turns into an affective loop in ShinKai Makoto's animation, evoking colonial conflict only to channel it into an affectively closed system of sovereign identity.

The essays under the heading "Control Room" look at relations between war and technologies of social control. Tom Looser demonstrates how the experience of war becomes the foundational logic of contemporary political and social life in the works of Oshii Mamoru, stressing the importance of the production of worlds in which death no longer serves as an operative limit for the imagination of political risk and social conflict. Mark Anderson directs attention to Oshii Mamoru's presentation in *Patlabor 2* of how postwar politics thoroughly compromised Japanese sovereignty, stressing how Oshii's films, even if they remain overtly committed to the logic of sovereignty, invite us to think media not as a realm of representation but as a theater of operations. Looking first at *Neon Genesis Evangelion,* Christophe Thouny's essay explores how the destructiveness of war (apocalypse) becomes an everyday reality, which, in the context of *Densha otoko,* he links to communication technologies (connectivity). Between apocalypse and connectivity, between war and the everyday temporalities of communications, emerges a distinctive spatiotemporal configuration, which Thouny dubs the waiting room. Michael Fisch also examines the role of war in *Densha otoko,* beginning with metaphors of war only to discover that such metaphors depend on technologically generated intervals or spacing, which link the space of the train (the mobilization of commuters) to the spectacle of war (the media mobilization of the populace). In sum, across this group of essays, the war/time gap is associated with media spaces that allow war to act as social control, while everyday life, as life, loses its capacity to place a limit on conflict. The result is a proliferation of quasi-apocalyptic space-times or control rooms.

Dennis Washburn emphasizes in his discussion of video games and media convergence how the ubiquity and simultaneity of media networks have radically transformed the experience of space and time and thus of history and memory. Rather than a total eradication of history and memory, however, Washburn looks for new formats for storytelling in which gameplay implies different modalities of time and memory, particularly in *Final Fantasy X.* In contrast, Michael Dylan Foster finds familiar modalities of nostalgia and commemoration in the context of contradictions that have arisen around the transformation of manga artist Mizuki Shigeru's hometown into a tourist memorial dedicated to his works, their critique of war, and to forgotten patterns of everyday life. Sheng-mei Ma's essay looks at how different manga writers have sought to come to terms with the trauma of Japan's defeat in World War II. Here, too, we see an analytic effort to insert a gap between war and temporality, between military destruction and everyday life. But, where fading memory and nostalgia imply some manner of psychological separation or cognitive distance, trauma implies an eternally present injury, prone to displacement and reenactment—as characterized in manga writer Kobayashi Yoshinori's notorious defense of war.

As a mode of regulated difference, genre complicates questions about the gap between wartime and everyday temporality. In particular, in war and combat genres, the dynamics of battle must be continually renewed, at once familiar yet subtly different from past and future instances. Zília Papp, for instance, traces various versions of *Yōkai daisensō*, showing how master genre bender Miike Takashi exploits genre conventions to political ends very different from those of his predecessors. At the same time, as Takayuki Tatsumi demonstrates, genres are frequently formed transnationally. Tatsumi explores how the cultural misunderstanding inherent in transnational interactions allows genre to go beyond regulated difference or the repetition of the same, suggesting that the transnational dynamics of the ninja genre result in hybridization, both at the level of human and machine, and at the level of cultures. Similarly, Rebecca Suter is interested in how the figure of the girl knight serves to challenge received genre expectations about the relations between war and gender identity. The explorations of generic difference in the essays under the heading "Genre Violence" thus stand in stark contrast to previous essays that stressed war as a technology of social control. They bring forth a moment or site of "deregulation" within generic repetition. Where many of the prior essays see such moments or sites as those where control finds its material point of leverage, these essays affirm the generativity of cultural production, stressing in effect the force of everyday novelty over social mechanisms.

The final group of essays, "Mobilization/Domestication," explores the interaction of wartime mobilization and cultural domestication. Christine Marran takes up the manga adaptation of Numa Shōzō's famous novel, *Human Cattle Yapoo,* in which the Western domestication of Japan, especially as configured in the postwar American Occupation of Japan but also in the experience of Japanese wartime mobilization, is displaced onto the sadomasochistic paradigm of white women cruelly engineering yellow men for their greater pleasure. Here, as Marran points out, the pleasure of domination and submission make for a feedback loop between racial domestication and imperial mobilization. Marco Pellitteri looks at giant robots in Japanese animations as symbolic of Japan's relation to the United States. Significantly, he finds that Japanese and American warriors tend to join forces to combat alien invaders. In other words, the peace between, or reconciliation of, Japan and the United States is frequently predicated upon total war, which appears as the condition for social harmony. Finally, highlighting the class warfare implicit in Kobayashi Yoshinori's apologia for Japanese militarization, Mark Driscoll considers the possibility for countermobilization in the face of the ascendancy and apparent victory of neoconservative agenda. Popular culture, he demonstrates, presents possibilities for countermobilizations based in everyday consumption, particularly when power disparities such as between classes become visible. Driscoll thus acknowledges the stakes implicit in all these studies of war/time in the context of Japanese manga, animation, and popular culture: can such forms of expression open the gap where wartime enacts social control of everyday life and culture, inviting fans and fan communities to consider the politics inherent in their practices, spurring new movements of countermemory, counterhistory, and countermobilization?

....

Notes

1. Chalmers Johnson and Tom Engelhardt, "A Tomdispatch Interview with Chalmers Johnson, Pt. 2," at http://www.tomdispatch.com (accessed March 22, 2006).

2. For an overview of the key ideas that later appear in the book *Shock Doctrine* (Toronto: Knopf Canada, 2007), see Naomi Klein, "The Rise of Disaster Capitalism," *The Nation,* May 2, 2005.

3. Michel Foucault, *Discipline and Punish: The Birth of the Prison,* trans. Alan Sheridan (New York: Pantheon Books, 1977), 169.

Legacies of Sovereignty

GAVIN WALKER

The Filmic Time of Coloniality: On Shinkai Makoto's *The Place Promised in Our Early Days*

In 2004, Shinkai Makoto's major film-length feature, *The Place Promised in Our Early Days* (*Kumo no mukō, yakusoku no basho*) was released, solidifying the position of his work as that of a decidedly new generation, one stemming neither from the older big-budget cinematic style of Miyazaki nor the previous generation's anime studio system, symbolized by Gainax. Shinkai debuted as a quintessentially digital-age auteur with his entirely self-created 2001 short film *Voices of a Distant Star* (*Hoshi no koe*), perhaps the most concentrated expression of this new aesthetic regime, which came to be known as "*sekai-kei*" (literally, "world-style").

The Place Promised in Our Early Days (hereafter *PPED*) is in a doubled sense a *Zeitgeist* film: on the one hand, its success, its sensibility, its conditions of production, and its visual register make it a production representative of a distinctive shift in the archetypal anime feature; on the other hand its narrative structure places it in direct linkage to the recent boom of "alternative history" films and the politics of the field of significations implicit to this boom. But more specifically, I argue that *PPED* is itself a vehicle for something else, an expressive device for the question of coloniality, one in which we can read the problem not only of the historical memory and meaning of the colonial system but also its field of epistemological effects in relation to the contemporary shifts occurring in the ostensibly "postcolonial" system of nation-states today. In its visual politics as much as its narrative arc, *PPED* is a lens through which the temporality of colonialism and the writing of history intertwine and overlap in a dense recoding of the present.

The backdrop to the narrative of the film proceeds from an alternative, but not unthinkable, history: in the decades following World War II, Japan is jointly occupied and, in 1973, divided into northern and southern portions: in the north by the "Union," and in the south, by the United States.[1] Subsequently, the south shifts from an exclusively U.S.-occupied territory to an "Alliance" of the American and Japanese governments—conflict with the Union is impending, and at the climax of *PPED*, war breaks out between them. The Union controls Ezo, what would be contemporary Hokkaido, while the Alliance governs the rest of modern-day Japan, south of the Tsugaru Strait. From the film's vantage point, Ezo is a site of mystery, and the Union is a closed and enigmatic society left largely undepicted. Dominating all is the immense Tower, which generates matter from parallel universes in the area surrounding it. Built by the Union on the southern edge of Ezo, it stretches far into the sky and is seemingly visible throughout southern Japan. It serves as a focal point both of the narrative and of the specular field of the film.

We are introduced to three middle-school students in modern-day Aomori: friends Fujisawa Hiroki and Shirakawa Takuya, as well as their classmate and mutual object of desire Sawatari Sayuri. The two boys, who are fascinated by the Tower in Ezo, are constructing an airplane in their spare time, with which they hope to fly across the Tsugaru Strait toward the Tower. Sayuri, who discovers this, becomes a third member of their group, and they promise each other that in the future they will achieve this dream. As the narrative shifts to years later, Hiroki is a depressed student in Tokyo, living alone and daydreaming of his love for Sayuri, while Takuya is a precocious military scientist at the Aomori Army College, studying the bizarre effects of the Tower in Ezo and the parallel universes it generates. Sayuri, meanwhile, has slipped into a coma—it turns out that her condition is directly related to the strange Tower. Eventually, Hiroki learns of Sayuri's fate, and plans to fly her to the Tower, their "promised place" from childhood, believing that contact with the Tower will wake her up. Takuya, now also involved in the reunification guerrilla movement known as the Uilta Liberation Front, persuades Hiroki to fly their childhood plane, carrying Sayuri, to the Tower, now understood to be a Union weapon, and destroy it with a single missile. On the eve of war between North and South, Hiroki accomplishes his

mission, reviving Sayuri, and destroying the Tower in Ezo.

From the outset of the film, division is the essential trope through
which the narrative proceeds—the division of time into the time of the audience and initial narrative voice-over
from the time of the storyline proper,

THROUGH THE RECURRENT THEME
OF DIVISION, *PPED* SHOWS US A
SERIES OF INTERCONNECTED
PROBLEMATICS ESSENTIAL TO
GRASPING THE QUESTION OF
COLONIALITY AND THE POSITION
OF THE NATION-STATE TODAY.

the division of the country into north and south, the division of families as a
result of this national division, the division between the three protagonists
of the story from the holistic group of their childhood, the division between
city and countryside, between "official" space and "private" space, between
the time of the romantic encounter and the time of the world, and so forth.
Through the recurrent theme of division, *PPED* shows us a series of interconnected problematics essential to grasping the question of coloniality and the
position of the nation-state today. The film can be read as itself a "parallel
universe," in which the mutually reliant and reinforcing nature of imperial
and ethnic nationalisms is incarnated in a disjunct *present,* rather than in a
fantasy of return to the past or as a projection of the future. I would like to
draw attention to the strong potentiality and prescience of Shinkai's "postcolonial" scenario, which richly portrays the contours of the epistemic ordering
mechanisms of coloniality and their provenance. Naoki Sakai has delivered an
essential summation of the question of what we mean by the postcolonial:

> It would be better to avoid the sense in which the term "postcolonial" is
> broadly used today to mean "after the colonial system" or "what follows the
> colonial system in chronological order." This "post-" is "post factum," that is,
> "post-" in the sense of a situation that is "too late," irreparable (*torikaeshi ga
> tsukanai*), or irredeemable. Thought from the postcolonial viewpoint, the char-
> acteristic of being the colonizer is not an accidentally attributable supplemen-
> tal situation to the identity of being Japanese, but rather its essential situa-
> tion. The history of colonialism is sealed into the identity of being Japanese by
> means of this irreparability, and thus having been the colonizer is essentially
> included in being Japanese. It is the fact of this irreparable history that con-
> structs the identity called "Japanese," and thus in fact it is the *present existence*
> (*genzon*) of this history of colonialism that is precisely the postcolonial.[2]

In this sense, the colony itself is a fundamentally retrospective condition,
which is possible only through postcoloniality as a projection back toward

the past. During the actual existence of the colonial system, coloniality itself is not established—it cannot be represented to itself as a colony but only as something else. The colony is consequently something like a testing ground or a research-and-development organ for its own aftermath, when its conditions have been established, for the technologies of government of the nation-state. Thus the nation-state, and the position of belonging to it as a national citizen, are conditions enabled not through the chronological overcoming of coloniality but rather through its establishment. It is in this sense that the postcolonial is a type of "continuity in discontinuity," a circuit of regulation and control that only comes to function as the primary level of power relations after the colonial system has become a retrospective reality. Thus, coloniality is a machine whose parts are assembled in the colony, but which comes to function as a unitary circuit only, paradoxically, in the postcolonial present. We can identify this functioning as a kind of general "coloniality of power," which "allows us to understand the diachronic density and the constant rearticulation of colonial difference even today, in a world governed by information and communication, and by a global colonialism not located in any particular nation-state."[3]

In such a situation, it is necessary to hold ourselves immanent to the decisive meaning of what Sakai has called the "present existence of the history of colonialism." Shinkai's image of the split of Japan through a North–South "division system"[4] is not only a clear allusion to the history of defeat and occupation in the Japanese context but also something that alerts us to a general split of the nation-state itself, or more broadly, a split of our "being national": it reimages or retrospectively reveals how the colonial system was not an aberration or deviation but rather is *an essential and internal* element of the nation-state *at present*.

In the time of the film, in the fact that it is neither a fantasy of the future nor the retrospective projection of an imagined past but rather a parallel present, *PPED* explicates to us something crucial in this respect: it is necessary to examine the history of colonialism, the effects of coloniality today, and the role of "being national" in oneself, in the structure of the single person's immediate existence. The objective system is grasped by the individual subjectively, producing an otherness not external to the sense of self but rather internal to it. It is this division of internal/external, private/official, or individual/world which recurrently expresses the aesthetic of the film, and in which, I argue, we can see the affective drive of the contemporary time of coloniality.

At the beginning of the story, Takuya and Hiroki wait at their local train station after school, chatting about their upcoming summer vacation, and their part-time job at a munitions factory supplying the U.S. military. As they prepare to board the train, the frame pans upward, exposing the incredible size of the Tower in Ezo, visually bifurcating the backdrop of the sky, (Figure 1) colored red by the setting sun. In this shot, we see the Tower as an integral part of the natural expanse, an ordering focal point of the film's specular logic. In marked contrast, the figure of Hiroki and the lines of the train share our camera-gaze: small, rooted to the ground, and gazing upward to emphasize the differentiation of scale. As our view pans toward the top of the Tower, Hiroki's disembodied voice-over tells us, "We admired two things—one was our classmate Sawatari Sayuri, and the other was the Tower."

In the sense that Sayuri represents everything close, nearby, and intimate, the Tower symbolizes precisely the inverse: distance, the foreign, the artificial and mysterious. In this early moment of *PPED*, the aesthetic sensibility of what has come to be called the *sekai-kei* style is visibly rendered.

"*Sekai-kei*" emerged in the early part of the 2000s as a vague catchall phrase for a certain shared aesthetic surfacing in the subcultural arts of anime, manga, and games. Although a universally agreed-on definition of what precisely constitutes *sekai-kei* does not exist, it tends to be used to denote a particular type of aesthetic register reliant on the structure of the romance story as the foreground for a type of world-historical, interplanetary, or international conflict. Within this style, the overwhelming emphasis is on a bittersweet nostalgia, often mobilized through the disjunction of the linear temporality of a romantic

FIGURE 1. The Tower in Ezo visually bifurcates the backdrop of the sky. From Shinkai Makoto's major film-length feature *The Place Promised in Our Early Days* (2004, *Kumo no mukō, yakusoku no basho*).

relationship—flashback, flash-forward, and multiple timelines coexisting in one filmic situation are the primary narrative devices.

The romance is invariably cast in a kind of parallelism to war, the earth, the nation, and so on, and this parallelism is the usual lever for the operation of nostalgia: through the juxtaposition of imagined or daydreamed past possibilities or lost hopes within the relationship, the positions in conflict are thrown into relief. Filmically, this style tends toward macro-aestheticization at all times: extradiegetic music and a visual aesthetics of contrasting scale are formalized features. Through the juxtaposition of hallmarks of intimacy and closeness—smallness, slowness, lightness, taciturnity, the silhouette, the sweet memory, touch, the vanishing moment—with the hallmarks of "the world" and distance—bigness, speed, heaviness, multivocality, endless differentiation, immensity, monumentality, world-time (in contrast to the time of sociality), and so forth—the tendency toward aestheticism, contemplation, and the parallelism of individual and world is constantly rearticulated. Landscape, and its relation to the individual, is a recurrent image employed in Shinkai's films, a visual configuration in which this parallelism of contrasting scale is constantly put forward.

But equally important to the *sekai-kei* style is the affective level at which this relation of individual and world operates. "World" here is not only "the" world but also "my" world. Thus, there is a constant emphasis in *PPED* on the enclosed, small, internal, psychic spaces of the individual life as one "world." The tendency toward this mentality, that is, toward flirtation with a certain solipsism, can be considered a quintessentially post-Fordist phenomenon, into which most of the younger generation in the "advanced" industrialized countries are thoroughly inculcated. On one hand, the boundaries of the world are both more diffuse in terms of the latticed networks of information, communication, commonality of the image, synchronization of everyday time, and so forth. Simultaneously, the scale of the world itself is infinitesimally smaller, mirroring the shrinking nature of the commodity unit and its increasing concentration. Hence, the world is both enormous and immediately at hand, and the position of the self is increasingly "global" in its cross-fertilized contamination.

At the same time, the means of access to "the" world are increasingly mediated by a new, dense array of technologies—most importantly, the sociality on which we had come to rely for our earlier notions of individual and world are largely being replaced. For example, I might relate to an increasingly vast number of people, from a series of distant locations, with a bewildering amount of information, opinion, and affect, but I relate to them through the mobile phone, through the two-dimensional screen of the computer, and so forth. Consequently, an essential element of the *sekai-kei* aesthetic could be considered a new discovery of "world"—in other words, the world and all of its vast scale, its overwhelming openness, is also contained in this "cramped space" implied by the miniaturization of the object today. The perfect example of this can be seen at the beginning of Shinkai's debut film, *Voices of a Distant Star,* when the protagonist's voice is overlaid on the opening of the film: she dials a number on her mobile phone while her voice tells us, "There is a word—'world.' Until I was in middle-school, I thought that 'world' just meant somewhere that my cell-phone signal reached."

But what Shinkai's films, and *PPED* in particular, demonstrate is not that "world" is discovered as an autonomous, distant field outside consciousness but rather that the world is understood as a ubiquitous connective tissue related to the formation of an "I." It is possible to discover in *sekai-kei* productions a merely solipsistic, isolated, fearful sociality in which "world" comes to signify everything from which one must escape. But it is also possible, and, I would argue, more suggestive, to see in *PPED* and its aesthetic counterparts an identification of a kind of "general intellect," an increasingly socialized knowledge involved in the constant figuration of the world and its history (Figure 2).

In *PPED*, as Hiroki, Takuya, and Sayuri walk back to their local train station, Hiroki narrates their transition from childhood. As the train pulls away

FIGURE 2. "...but in those days, I felt that the smells of the night wafting into the train, the trust I had in my friend, and the hint of Sayuri that lingered in the air were everything in the world" (*sekai no subete*). From Shinkai Makoto, *The Place Promised in Our Early Days.*

from the station, Hiroki stares out of the window of the train and says, "Just close by, the world and history were changing, but in those days, I felt that the smells of the night wafting into the train, the trust I had in my friend, and the hint of Sayuri that lingered in the air, were everything in the world (*sekai no subete*)." This parallel of monumentality ("the" world and "history") and miniaturization (the relation of I and you as another world) again shows us the degree to which "world" here is a bundle of significations, a vehicle both of everything absolutely external as well as a series of internal affective judgments through which there is a common logic connecting them along a chain of meaning or identification, also called "world."

We have, throughout *PPED*, a mobilization of "world" as a contested, unstable object which is more than anything identifiable solely through its creation as a unifying aesthetic—in a sense, the film demonstrates and relies on a notion of the thickness of world as a material-semiotic field.[5] Thus, *sekai-kei,* rather than necessarily being a reactionary retreat from the responsibility and burden of historical memory, could be read as having precisely the opposite set of potentialities at work. Because it breaks down the density of "world" as a concept toward "world" as a name for a series of malleable affective registers, *sekai-kei* admits and images the world and history as figuration; that is, it shows that *the making* of a world and its history *is* that world and its history. Thus it comes as no surprise that in *PPED* the question of writing, rewriting, and overwriting, or "coding," is key. But as we will see, while *PPED* raises a series of decisive questions about our contemporary moment, not only in its narrative and associated "world" but also in its visual logic, the film itself is resolved in the final analysis through an evasion of the problems it itself articulates.

As mentioned at the beginning of this essay, *PPED* is not a futural projection nor a reimagined past—rather it is, in keeping with its diegetic narrative, itself a type of parallel present, a "remix" of contemporaneity. It is itself a "world," and it is this that distinguishes it as representative of a new type of creation within the anime sphere—as a work, the traditional contours of *PPED* as a "story" or "plot" are significantly less important than its "world." To a certain extent this is what Azuma Hiroki, among others, has referred to as "manga-anime realism" (*manga-animeteki rearizumu*)—*PPED* is a work that rests on a world that is found only as a figuration on Shinkai Makoto's hard drive, a new type of realism whose "reality" is itself a feedback loop for its own "world."[6] But this problematic is not merely worth considering in terms of the formal conditions of production of *PPED* but also as a part of its internal logic and as something that we could say is "theorized" by the film's narrative itself.

As Takuya goes on to work as a scientist in the Alliance's top-secret research division dedicated to reconnaissance and investigation of the Tower in Ezo, we are given an increasing amount of information about its powers. The Tower, it turns out, is a device intimately related to dreams. When Takuya and his coworker (and new romantic interest) Maki visit the munitions factory where Takuya and Hiroki once worked, she explains: "our world hides all these different possibilities, things that could have been,

> PPED IS A WORK THAT RESTS ON A WORLD THAT IS FOUND ONLY AS A FIGURATION ON SHINKAI MAKOTO'S HARD DRIVE.

inside our dreams—we call these 'parallel worlds' (heikō sekai) or 'branch universes' (bunkyūchū)." Just prior to this, we have learned that a certain Ekusun Tsukinoe, a famous Union scientist who proved the existence of "parallel worlds," was responsible for the design and supervised the construction of the Tower. In the area surrounding the Tower, there is a space of "completely different matter," itself composed of "different universes," and between the world in which PPED takes place and the areas around the Tower, there is a constant ebb and flow of "spatial displacements with these parallel worlds." That is, the Tower is to a certain extent a spatial concretization of the dreamspaces of all the people around it. It is not simply that the Tower produces these "parallel worlds"; rather, these worlds are internal features of all organisms' brain patterns—hence the research unit to which Takuya belongs is known as the "Brain Science Unit." The importance of this research is visually confirmed by the presence of the U.S. National Security Agency at their laboratory—the potential power of this technology stems from its use to predict future historical outcomes. However, these future outcomes are not grasped by examining a field of possibilities across linear, chronological time and computing their likelihood. Instead, PPED tells us that the "future" is predicted, or more accurately, identified, by seeing in these "parallel worlds" the results of an actual future. In other words, the ability to grasp the past, or indeed the ability to understand the future, occurs through the conceptual overlapping of another disjunct temporality on the present—to a certain extent in PPED, there is no time other than the present, a type of "eternal now" that is stretched, elongated, and retracted through its imbrication with other parallel presents, an endless oscillation from one present to another and back.

Hiroki and Sayuri, who has been in a coma for three years since their "promise" to go to the Tower, dream of each other. Their parallel interior worlds overlap—and when Hiroki encounters Sayuri in his dreams, that is, when he encounters "her" within "himself," he remarks that the experience was "more real than reality" or "more present than the present" ("*genjitsu yori mo genjitsu rashii*"). As Sayuri's dreams shift in the wake of seeing Hiroki in her ostensibly "private" internal space, the Tower begins to inscribe its parallel realities over the existing material world surrounding it. The "Brain Science Team" are frantically scrambling to prevent the "real" material world from being swallowed up by this widening "parallel world," and, as the circle of "overwritten" matter widens (Figure 3), the chief scientist Tomizawa asks himself, "Do they mean to rewrite the world?" ("*Sekai o kakikaeru tsumori na no ka?*").

The Tower is "rewriting" the world, "rewriting" history, and destabilizing the facticity of *this* present, by recoding it with the endless possibilities of the parallel presents occurring in conjunction with that of *PPED*'s narrative. Thus, we can see the equivalent occurring on the internal level of the narrative as is occurring for the audience watching, with respect to the temporality of *PPED*. In this sense, the film can also be read as itself depicting the development of an animated cinematic logic essential to the affective structures implied by computerization, digitalization, immaterialization, and so forth. That is, particularly in its expressive functions, *PPED* is exemplary of the transition between what Paul Virilio called extensive and intensive time.

What is increasingly being replaced through digitalization, the instaneity of computerization and automation, is the logic of extensive time, which "worked at deepening the wholeness of infinitely great time," articulated in the chronological order of "past, present, and future." In its place is increasingly a kind of "intensive time," no longer marshaled across the tenses, but

FIGURE 3. The Tower begins to inscribe its parallel realities over the existing material world surrounding it. From Shinkai Makoto, *The Place Promised in Our Early Days.*

in the "real time" and "delayed time" of the image.[7] This is explicated in *PPED* precisely through the Tower as the point of mediation of "real time" and its displacement. The displacement occurring around the Tower is not a shift of the past into the future,

or vice versa, so much as it is an intensification and compression of the "real time" of the narrative with other presents, including that of the audience.

One of the widely remarked-on techniques employed in *PPED* is Shinkai's use of the photograph as a reference point. Scenes in the film would be essentially drawn "on top" of photographic images of Aomori in a new type of digital overwriting or refiguration. That is, the processes of imagination at work in this type of visuality stem not from the imagining of "new" worlds (as in the older "extensive" form of science fiction) but rather from a new type of sensibility in its *sekai-kei* inflection, that is, science fiction as remix or paralleling of the present. In just the same way as the Tower rewrites or recodes the space of the "world," so Shinkai rewrites the space of "Japan" by recoding the visual register of Aomori and Tokyo. Azuma for instance remarks, "When I first saw [Shinkai's] *Hoshi no koe,* I thought, this is something completely different from anime thus far. This isn't a moving image, it's something more like a collection of still images that happen to be moving."[8] That is, there is a strange doubled system of visual referentiality operating in *PPED* (as well as in *Hoshi no koe*)—the still image overlaps with the audience's "real time," and is imbricated with the audience's sense of spatiality, but when the image begins to move, it does not move in this "real" time but in a displaced, parallel trajectory, thus visually "theorizing" for the audience the immanent possibility of multiple directions in the present.

Through the graphic superimposition, tracing, and doubling of the audience's "real time" and space with the "parallel world" of the animated image, *PPED* itself is constituted as a perfect symbolization of the supersession of extensive time/extensive space with intensive time and, by extension, a direct emphasis on history and memory as continual creation. The rewriting or redrawing of the contours of history is an articulatory act of re-outlining, redrawing the boundaries of the space of the world itself, an endless, improvised figuration in an unstable, partially determined present that is increasingly evident and visible in contemporary cognitive capitalism.

PPED articulates the "present" nature of coloniality, the temporality of the constant creation of the "here," and the new direct productive capacity of affect, gesture, and so forth. By displacing and dislocating the conceptual architecture of "our" present into another present in which the same materials are divergently organized, the film itself becomes an image of "the geopolitical postcolonial situation" that serves "as something like a paradigm for the thought of history itself as figuration, figuring something out with 'chunks of the real.'"[9] That is, its strength as a creation lies not in its prescriptive capacity for reflection but in the way it performatively puts into question our inherited organization of history.

Hiroki boards a train for his home of Aomori, in preparation for his mission to fly to the Tower with Sayuri, and as we see him on the train, reading Miyazawa Kenji's *Spring and Asura* (*Haru to shura*), we hear in a voiceover Okabe stating to his comrades in the Uilta Liberation Front: "It's now clear that the Tower is a weapon—over the past twenty-five years, it has become a symbol of every aspect of daily life: the nation-state, war, ethnicity, despair, and longing. But the one constant is that everyone sees it as something unreachable, something that can't be changed. As long as they do, this world won't change either." The Tower is reflected in the glass of the train, and in our screens we see again the doubling effect of the present in *PPED*—the superimposition of the young man reading a classic of "our" modernity in a vehicle that is a recognizable technological innovation of "our" history, on top of which is overlaid the Tower, the symbolic ordering mechanism of "his" present (Figure 4). In this sense, Shinkai's film can be read as a replication and dislocation device for us, a way to see a series of still images, snapshots, and movements of the operation of contingency in our present, the presents within the self that are endlessly vanishing and emerging.

PPED, in this sense, *structurally* articulates the coloniality of the present and its irreversible location in "me" but, on the level of its narrative, in the end reveals itself as an evasion of history, predicated on a denial and unwillingness to confront situatedness or positionality. It is impossible to reverse, repair, or redeem "oneself" from the fact of the history of colonialism—in this sense, it must be said that *PPED* recognizes that "I," as the audience, implicitly acknowledge this in the identification of my present as the time of coloniality. Thus, in the film, the entire question of the linear flow of time, and in particular the traditional linear narrative of the beginning, establishment, and end of the colonial system, is displaced through the fragmenting of the present. Because the form of the film itself is predicated on the understanding that it is *our time* and *us* in which coloniality exists, *PPED* cannot be accused of being an erasure of the history of colonialism. But it does not draw this interrelated network of problems out to its natural conclusion; rather,

FIGURE 4. The doubling effect of the present in *The Place Promised in Our Early Days*: the super-impositions of a man reading "our" modernity, in an innovation of "our" history, overlaid by the Tower, the symbolic ordering mechanism of "his" present.

it can be said that *PPED*, while a mechanism for examining the coloniality of the immediate moment, is nevertheless *devoted to effacing the present, to escaping from confronting it within oneself*. It is never the retrospective linear gaze back toward the moment of colonial violence that is disquieting, instead it is "our" actual present existence that gives us pause. My "self" is precisely the site of the postcolonial in the sense of its irreversibility, an existence it-self always already implicated.

When Hiroki describes Ezo and the Tower early in the film, he suggests that its specular power to generate fantasy stems precisely from the fact that, while it is constantly seen, it is fundamentally unreachable. The Tower is that "place that looks so close, it's like you could reach out and grab it, but you can never actually get to it—we wanted to see it with our own eyes." They thus aim for something impossible, the encounter and conquest of "the Real." Okabe duplicates this with his argument that as long as the Tower remains unreachable as a symbol of war, the nation-state, ethnicity, and so forth, none of these things can be changed themselves. But in *PPED* precisely the opposite happens: the Tower *is* reached by Hiroki and Sayuri, she *is* awak-ened, and they *do* destroy the Tower with a single missile. Thus, at the climax of the film, it is not that "war," "ethnicity," the "nation-state," and so on are confronted and re-figured—they are blown away entirely as constraints pre-cisely by the destruction of the Tower. In this sense, the Tower is not just the externalized concretization of desires, dreams, and so forth, it is within the film something inside "me," the colonizer, in which the signifying chain of "responsibilities," "guilt," and so forth exceed me and come to, in a sense, control me, and that one wants desperately to be rid of. Thus, as the Tower explodes in a massive conflagration (Figure 5), Hiroki and Sayuri float in the blue sky in the airplane of their childhood dreams and Hiroki says, in a voiceover and thus not to Sayuri *but to the audience,* "We've lost our promised place in this world, but now our lives can begin."

Here is the real dream of *PPED*—that there is within me a detectable kernel that symbolizes the position of being the colonizer or the oppressor that can be externalized and destroyed, so that one might begin again, free of guilt and shame. Thus the destruction of the Tower is not so much a utopian act for a new world as it is a concentration of the desire to be free of one's own irredeemable positionality, free of the need to ask "on what is the 'fact' of my immediate existence predicated?" *PPED* confronts directly the most essential problem of "responsibility," it confronts the fact that "my" identity already contains the irreversible time of being the colonizer. In the face of this fact, *PPED* essentially narrates in its form its own "dream of the universe"— the fantasy of being able to start over, to find a new moment of departure wherein there is neither "place" nor "position" as such, but rather an endless and untethered subjectivity predicated on nothing more than the individual's self-positing. This incredible fear of positionality in *PPED* thus can show us a great deal about the function of the "coloniality of power" today, not to mention the operations of contemporary capitalism that rely on it.

FIGURE 5. The Tower explodes in a massive conflagration, and Hiroki and Sayuri float in the airplane of their childhood: "We've lost our promised place in this world, but now our lives can begin." From Shinkai Makoto, *The Place Promised in Our Early Days.*

It could be argued that at the climax of the film the nation has achieved reunification through the destruction of the Tower, the foremost constraint and symbolic placeholder for the border and division, in direct parallel with the reunification of Sayuri and Hiroki. But, problematically, Sayuri realizes upon reunification that she has lost her memory, her psychic life reduced to immediate experience without the intervening grid of historical memory, and thus her love for Hiroki will vanish in tandem with the Tower. This decisive concluding gesture within the *sekai-kei* aesthetic—this parallel reunification, or indeed the reunification of the nation on the basis of the reunification of separated young lovers albeit at the expense of the past—should seem to strike a bittersweet note, but in fact it is precisely the opposite. This loss of memory is the ultimate triumph, the fantasy of integration into a new holism in which historical memory and the experience of trauma are eliminated, the fantasy of reversibility and escape.

The Place Promised in Our Early Days retreats from its own possibilities, in that it acknowledges the only partially determined nature of the national community, the space for figuration that its need for constant reproduction establishes. Instead of confronting this irredeemable position of "I" and "we," the film resolves itself in discovering a means of being entirely free from *the present*, that is to say, of being entirely free from oneself. But it is not possible to simply encounter the sorrow of the history of oppression by countering it, or "overcoming" it—it is not possible to "demarcate" oneself from racism, from the history of colonialism, and so forth, such that I can discover a new, untainted position from which I can relieve myself of the burden *of being myself*: "the only choice is the choice between the terrifying contaminations it assigns. Even if all forms of complicity are not equivalent, they are *irreducible*."[10] The unreachable place of *The Place Promised in Our Early Days* is not the diegetic split of north and south but rather the split within the place where the "I" can come to be, from which escape is impossible—a new politics and new sociality able to grasp and respond to the contemporary "coloniality of power" can emerge only to the extent that we hold ourselves immanent to the complicity and irreversibility contained in the formation of this "I."

....

Notes

In revising this essay for publication, I would like to mention my gratitude for Thomas Lamarre's advice, suggestions, and incisive critical reading of the essay. I also benefited from discussions with Naoki Sakai, Christopher Ahn, and Noriaki Hoshino and would like to thank the reviewers for *Mechademia*. All translations from languages other than English are my own unless otherwise indicated.

1. It bears pointing out that in the defeat and occupation of Japan, this split division between the Soviet Union and United States was a concrete possibility, which resulted in the annexation of Sakhalin by the Soviet Union. The "actuality" of this process, however, can be continuously seen in the existence of the divided Korean peninsula.

2. Naoki Sakai, *Nihon/eizō/Beikoku: Kyōkan no kyōdōtai to teikokuteki kokuminshugi* (Japan/image/America: The community of sympathy and imperial nationalism) (Tokyo: Seidosha, 2007), 294–95; my italics. It goes without saying that this formulation is not limited to the case of the putative unity "Japan" but is a general condition of the form of belonging to the nation-state.

3. Walter Mignolo, "Capitalismo y geopolítica del conocimiento," in *Modernidades coloniales: otros pasados, historias presentes,* ed. Saurabh Dube, Ishita Banerjee Dube, and Walter Mignolo (Mexico City: El Colegio de México, 2004), 248. The term "coloniality of power" is associated with the work of Aníbal Quijano.

4. The concept of "division system" was put forward by Paek Nakchōng in the 1970s to describe the system of mutual reliance between the governments of North Korea, South Korea, and the United States on the field of effects generated by the division of the Korean peninsula; that is, he points not merely to the violence of "division" itself but to its solidification into a continuously self-reproducing "system." Among his many publications on this subject, see, in English, "Habermas on National Unification in Germany and Korea," *New Left Review* 219 (September/October 1996): 14–22; "Coloniality in Korea and a South Korean Project for Overcoming Modernity," *Interventions* 2, no. 1 (2000): 73–86.

5. This phrase is taken from Donna Haraway: see *How Like a Leaf* (London: Routledge, 2000), 107. Also see on this point her well-known "Situated Knowledges: The Science Question in Feminism and the Privilege of Partial Perspective," in *Simians, Cyborgs, and Women: The Reinvention of Nature* (London: Routledge, 1991), 183–201.

6. See the discussion between Shinkai Makoto, the critic Azuma Hiroki, and the manga creator Nishijima Daisuke, "Sekai kara, motto tōku e" (Far from the world) originally published in *Hajō genron* (Speech waves), September 2004. Reprinted in Azuma Hiroki et al., *Kontentsu no shisō* (Thinking content) (Tokyo: Seidosha, 2007): 34–35. See also Azuma's extended discussion of this question in *Gēmuteki rearizumu no tanjō: Dōbutsuka suru posutomodan 2* (A birth of gamelike realism: animalizing postmodernity 2) (Tokyo: Kōdansha, 2007).

7. Paul Virilio, *The Vision Machine,* trans. Julie Rose (London: The British Film Institute and Bloomington: Indiana University Press, 1994), 66–72.

8. Shinkai, Azuma, and Nishijima, "Sekai kara, motto tōku e," 23.

9. Gayatri Spivak, *A Critique of Postcolonial Reason: Toward a History of the Vanishing Present* (Cambridge, Mass.: Harvard University Press, 1999), 62–63.

10. Jacques Derrida, *Of Spirit: Heidegger and the Question,* trans. Geoffrey Bennington and Rachel Bowlby (Chicago: University of Chicago Press, 1991), 40.

REI OKAMOTO INOUYE

Theorizing Manga: Nationalism and Discourse on the Role of Wartime Manga

During the 1920s and '30s, Japan underwent an unprecedented expansion of its modern institutions. A mass culture emerged and media consumption expanded. As Japan's total war system intensified in the 1930s, the field of manga, one of the emerging visual media of the time, witnessed the rise and fall of the proletarian movement, the dominance of "*nansensu*" (nonsense) as a popular genre, and the increasing presence of war, whether physically or ideologically. This was also the period when cartoonists began theorizing about the nature of manga. After the Japan–China War broke out in 1937, discourse on the role of manga and cartoonists appeared as a response to Japan's wartime mobilization.

A close study of the discourse on the status of manga as expressed by cartoonists themselves reveals that, by defining manga as an ideal medium for conveying nationalism, cartoonists played an active role as agents of the war. They did not simply submit to state thought control in order to continue drawing manga. Rather, in the course of this theorization, they attempted to "recover" the artistic quality of manga from being merely a commodity of consumerism, as was the case with *nansensu* manga. This recovery was articulated by, for instance, the former proletarian cartoonist Katō Etsurō. This discourse reflected the ambiguity inherent in the nature of manga as a hybrid of the visual and the verbal, as well as its marginalized identity as a subgenre of painting. The various desires and ideals of Japanese cartoonists regarding the future of the medium were subtly and intricately manifested in this discourse.

> BY DEFINING MANGA AS AN IDEAL MEDIUM FOR CONVEYING NATIONALISM, CARTOONISTS PLAYED AN ACTIVE ROLE AS AGENTS OF THE WAR.

The discourse that connected war and manga began appearing in humor magazines—such as *Karikare* (Caricare),[1] *Osaka pakku* (Osaka Puck), *Manga ōkoku* (Manga kingdom), *Manga no kuni* (The country of manga), and *Manga*—as well as in monographs on manga after the Japan–China War broke out in 1937. The discussion continued until near the end of World War II. The discourse asserted that manga is important as a powerful agent of wartime propaganda; that in order to correct society's perception of manga as "lowbrow," cartoonists need to become more aware of the urgency of the current wartime situation; and that cartoonists should seriously study manga and improve their skills so that a "new type of cartoonist" would emerge.

A GENEALOGY OF PREWAR DISCOURSE ON THE ROLE OF MANGA

During the Sino-Japanese War (1894–1895) and Russo-Japanese War (1904–1905), the popularity of "*nishikie*" (multicolored woodblock prints) was briefly revived, even though woodblock printing was gradually being replaced by lithography. During these international wars that brought Japan victories, *nishikie* manga (then called *ponchi*)[2] portrayed war as a colorful, visual spectacle and aroused patriotism among an enthusiastic mass audience.[3]

Discourse on manga—such as criticism and theory—first appeared in the late Meiji period (1868–1912). It was also around this time when the term "manga" started to mean "caricature." Manga scholar Miyamoto Hirohito has shown how manga as a subgenre of fine arts came to be formed in the late Meiji through the early Taishō periods (1912–1926). Miyamoto points out that, in the course of this process, the historical view of manga that traced its roots to *Chōjūgiga* (Scrolls of frolicking animals) of the twelfth century was "reinvented" in the modern period.[4] Various critiques of individual manga works and humor magazines originated at about the same time.

The first issue of *Hōsun*, an art magazine that began serialization in 1907,

THE FIRST CARTOONISTS
ORGANIZATION, TOKYO MANGAKAI
(TOKYO MANGA ASSOCIATION), WAS
ESTABLISHED IN 1915 AND HELPED
POPULARIZE THE TERM "MANGA."

contained the first installment of artist Yamamoto Kanae's three-part essay on contemporary humorous and satirical arts.[5] Manga had not yet acquired the contemporary meanings of "caricature," "cartoons," and so on. Yamamoto's early contribution was his attempt to theorize the characteristics of comic art by defining humorous art (*kokkeiga*) and satirical art (*fūshiga*). Yamamoto explained the distinction between *kokkeiga* and *fūshiga* as follows: while *kokkeiga* is lighthearted in nature and avoids direct criticism, *fūshiga* must have elements of criticism. *Fūshiga* could be humorous but no *kokkeiga* is critical. Thus, *kokkeiga* is usually objective and descriptive, while *fūshiga* is subjective and creative. Stimulation is the life of *fūshiga*. Having made this point, Yamamoto shifted his focus to the more general topic of Japanese art. According to him, the Japanese were not made to entertain profound thoughts because of the climate of Japan. As a result, few great *kokkeiga* or *fūshiga* had been produced. Intriguingly, Yamamoto used the term "manga" to critique Japanese comic art as something ambiguous and of lesser quality than *kokkeiga* and *fūshiga*. He followed his historical overview with a harsh criticism of manga as they were then being serialized in contemporary humor magazines such as *Tokyo pakku* (Tokyo Puck), *Osaka pakku,* and *Jōtō ponchi* (High-class caricatures).

The Taishō period is characterized by cultural and political liberalism. Mass culture, fueled by capitalism, brought modernity to the everyday life of Japanese. In the world of manga, this was the time when some of the earliest professional cartoonists emerged as "manga journalists," a prime example of which would be Okamoto Ippei. The first cartoonists organization, Tokyo Mangakai (Tokyo manga association), was established in 1915 and helped popularize the term "manga."[6] Efforts to situate manga historically began to mature during this time. For example, Ishii Hakutei's "Honchō mangashi" (History of Japanese manga) was a ten-part series of essays published in an art magazine, *Chūō bijutsu* (Central art), between January 1918 and May 1919.[7] This is probably the earliest comprehensive overview of the history of manga. Ishii defined the term "manga" as "the art that is carefree, not regulated by rules, and based on the free observation of mainly human life." He also pointed out that "manga flourishes naturally when a civilization reaches maturity and decadence permeates; therefore, the main focus of the history of manga should be in the Edo period (1603–1867)."[8]

The early Shōwa period (1926–1989) saw publication of monographs and

collected works that studied manga as a mass medium, partly due to a growing publishing industry as encouraged by the birth of mass culture and mass
consumption. Major publications include the ten-volume *Gendai manga tai-
kan* (1928, An overview of contemporary manga) published by Chūō Bijut-
susha, the four-volume *Manga kōza* (1933–34, Lectures on manga) edited by
Nihon Mangakai, *Shin Mangaha Shūdan manga nenkan* (1933, New Cartoonists Faction Group's manga almanac), and so on. Some art magazines, such
as the 1927 *Bijutsu shinron* (New views of art; [vol. 1, no. 2]), published special
issues on manga.

In the latter half of the 1920s, proletarian cartoonists—such as Okamoto
Tōki, Yanase Masamu, Matsushita Fumio, Suyama Keiichi, and Iwamatsu
Jun—began theorizing about the role that manga might play in cultivat-
ing the masses through promoting Marxist ideology. They attempted the
theorization of manga as an effective means of agitation and propaganda
(*ajipuro*).[9] This leftist movement was severely suppressed by the authorities
and withered by the mid-1930s. The year 1933 is generally called "the sea-
son of apostasy" (*tenkō no kisetsu*), as many leftists—voluntarily or not—
denounced Marxism. Jennifer Weisenfeld's study of the radical Japanese art
group Mavo, which made a lasting mark on the 1920s avant-garde art scene,
traced the paths the Mavo artists followed after 1933. This group included
some of the above-mentioned cartoonists: "Some collaborated with the war
effort, directly or indirectly; some were forced to apostatize or were allowed
to work only if they refrained from any controversial activity; and some lived
in self-imposed exile, completely out of the public eye."[10] Several former proletarian cartoonists—for example, Ōta Kōji and Katō Etsurō—went on to
theorize the nature of wartime manga by shifting focus to the New Order and
to how manga could contribute to the war effort.

THE DISCOURSE ON WARTIME MANGA
BEFORE THE PACIFIC WAR, 1937–1941

Soon after the outbreak of the Japan–China War in 1937, the discourse on
manga began to pay attention to the medium's relationship with the war. For
instance, the founding declaration of the Tokyo Manga Institute stated:

> Printed and filmed manga can instantaneously make a million people laugh
> and feel happy. It can also easily achieve the important mission of mass cul-
> tivation through humor, which is often difficult to accomplish. Manga is an

indispensable political and economic weapon, and has grown into a powerful propaganda tool. In addition, it has absolute value as a sincere reflection and record of our time . . . Living under wartime tensions, whether at the war zone or at the home front, our people need enjoyable manga to cleanse their minds. They need them as much as they need food.[11]

Cartoonists Ōta Kōji, Kume Kōichi, Matsushita Ichio, and Onosawa Wataru organized this institute in April 1938. The institute's organ, the monthly magazine *Karikare*, began publication in June of the same year and put out a special issue on "war and manga" as well as several articles on wartime propaganda and the role of manga written by Ōta in 1939 and 1940 (Figure 1).[12]

Ōta and the rest of the coterie were arrested by the Special Higher Police (*tokkō*) in 1941, charged with involvement in "leftist cultural activities," and the magazine was discontinued in June of that year. There appears to be grave disparity between the content of the above-mentioned statement and the fact that the authorities had monitored the action of the coterie as if they were the remnant of the leftist movements that had been suppressed in the early 1930s.[13] Why did this "leftist" magazine *Karikare* make attempts to theorize the role of wartime manga? Was it simply a camouflage of their "leftist cultural activities"? I would argue that theorizing the wartime role of manga did not necessarily contradict their expression of leftist sentiment since they both were earnest undertakings done to elevate the status of manga as a serious and meaningful art. Significantly, this mission of emphasizing the power and usefulness of manga led artists to cultivate the masses by spreading revolutionary ideals as well as by promoting the causes of Imperial Japan.

FIGURE 1. The cover of *Karikare* 2, no. 6 (July 1939), a special issue on war and manga.

For example, in *Karikare*, Ōta touched on the effectiveness of Chinese anti-Japan cartoons that use drastic means of propaganda: "It is necessary to stress domestic propaganda and agitation, though we must not forget that powerful international propaganda (targeted at the enemy or those who remained neutral) has also helped lead this war to victory." He bemoaned the fact that, although

Japanese "manga, too, must take on this task of enforcing propaganda, offering more sophisticated form and more content than [Chinese] cartoons," the only countermeasure the Japanese authority took was to ban the import of Chinese cartoon magazines, mainly published in Shanghai, that condemned Japanese imperialistic aggression. Chinese cartoonists routinely engaged in anti-Japanese propaganda, but, as Ōta pointed out, Japanese manga artists were oblivious to the current situation. Silly "*nansensu* manga are rampant in the domestic market . . . Cartoonists can't grasp the meaning of our holy war and are still drawing vulgar *ponchi*.[14] Superior cartoonists are as needed a weapon as airplanes and tanks."[15] Ōta also discussed an example of wartime propaganda in Europe during World War I, and principles of wartime propaganda that employed the theory of mob psychology. Furthermore, he maintained: "Our country's manga should focus on helping people realize the ideals of the New Order of East Asia, not on 'how to slander others.'" In order to achieve this goal, "an urgent prerequisite is to establish theories of propaganda and to develop [a cartoonists'] organization."[16]

> "CARTOONISTS CAN'T GRASP THE MEANING OF OUR HOLY WAR AND ARE STILL DRAWING VULGAR PONCHI. SUPERIOR CARTOONISTS ARE AS NEEDED A WEAPON AS AIRPLANES AND TANKS."

Kitazawa Rakuten, who founded the full-color, large-format manga magazine *Tokyo pakku* during the Russo-Japanese War and made it the most popular humor magazine of the time, also remarked several times on the topic of war and manga. His essay in the "war and manga" special issue of *Karikare* (July 1939) compared the current situation to that of the Russo-Japanese War and criticized the censorship of manga by the authorities. He first emphasized the potential power of manga: "When the emotions of our nation are uplifted, then the potential of manga can be elevated to its best. It has an immeasurable power to kindle animosity toward the enemy and guide the direction of mass movements." He also maintained, "At this time when we need to unite the will of Japan's subjects, manga is the most effective instrument of all in directly reaching peoples' hearts." He pointed out, however, that state censorship had placed a limit on cartoonists' competence: "Manga hasn't played a large role in the China Incident (*Shina jihen*) because of the complex nature of the current situation, and because of the narrow-minded thought control exerted by the authorities. I do hope that those in power will be generous enough to let cartoonists employ their skill."[17]

At another time, in a *zadankai* (roundtable talk) published in *Manga* in August 1941,[18] Kitazawa again repeatedly complained that the government is ignorant of the importance of manga as an effective propaganda tool: "Politicians have very little understanding of manga . . . [They] should think of ways to make better use of it"; "It's not that complicated. They should have cartoonists create manga in order to boost the morale of Japanese troops and to strengthen the readiness of the home front. Why don't they let us do that? It's totally frustrating"; "It's not that contemporary cartoonists are incapable of contributing; it's that the government doesn't appreciate manga at all. They think that manga is just some funny, goofy, laughable thing . . . Manga has a far more important mission than that."[19]

The foreword in the subsequent September issue of *Manga* further articulated the mission of cartoonists for internal and external propaganda:

> We need to expel the persistent, imperialistic Western culture from China, from Vietnam, and from Thailand, and extend to them our culture based on Japanese ethics . . . We need to emphasize not the evil of the West but the brightness of our culture—as supported by constructive, compassionate, absolute war ideologies. Starting here, we should go on to develop a progressive style. We are already mobilized. We need to follow the imperial army with pens as our weapons. At times we act as a propaganda corps. At other times we should become pacification units. At still other times we ought to participate as journalists, contributing to the culture of war with our continuous criticisms based on ideologies in support of the New Order.[20]

The above examples illustrate that contemporary cartoonists in the late 1930s and early '40s, just before the Pearl Harbor attack, were made aware of the role that manga ought to assume for wartime propaganda and enlightenment, and they demanded that manga be brought into play. Additionally, it often becomes apparent that cartoonists were discontented with their society's disregard for manga's usefulness. It should be further noted that this discourse at the same time expressed discontent directed toward the current state of the manga scene and toward cartoonists themselves. The target of blame was often *nansensu* manga, a genre that became very popular and commercially successful during the 1930s.

When "*ero guro nansensu*" (erotic grotesque nonsense), a global culture with strong American flavor, swept Japan, new genres of manga such as *ero* manga and *nansensu* manga sprang into popularity. Miriam Silverberg situates *ero guro nansensu* within a global context and uses the term in an expansive way to cover the mid-1920s through the early 1940s rather than only the first few years of the 1930s, as has been the case in Japanese scholarship.[21]

Nansensu manga became prevalent in popular magazines such as *Asahi gurafu* (Asahi graph), a large-format visual magazine, and *Shin seinen* (New youth), a high-class entertainment magazine targeted at urban youth. According to Okamoto Ippei, who played the leading role as a professional cartoonist during the Taishō period, *nansensu* manga suggested, as is the case with the English "nonsense," "the trivial, the silly, the insignificant, a joke," with the added "meaning of transcendence and playfulness." It transcends all reality, logic, and living, and corresponds to human "desire in a modern sense" that "seeks for the world of sensational playfulness where one could forget oneself and be delighted."[22] Modern masses in Japan, too, demanded a similar sensibility in manga.

It was particularly significant that young cartoonists whose selling point was *nansensu* manga organized a production group, the Shin Mangaha Shūdan (New Cartoonists Faction Group), in 1932. This innovative collaboration among aspiring cartoonists proved successful and achieved commercial success. Yokoyama Ryūichi was a star cartoonist of the group, for instance. He embodied the *nansensu* manga style and quickly established his popularity. Yokoyama's drawing style was refreshingly simple and playful; unlike his predecessors who heavily used dialog, he depended less on the verbal and more on speedy movements of the characters and visual humor. His most well-known work is the family comic strip *Fuku-chan,* which ran in the daily newspaper *Asahi shinbun* between 1936 and 1944 (Figure 2).

At the same time, criticism of this new genre and its creators became increasingly harsh. Katō Etsurō was probably the most vocal leader of the anti-*nansensu* manga critics. Katō himself had changed his ideological orientation twice in his life: from leftist to ultranationalist in the 1930s, and from ultranationalist to communist after the war.[23] As early as 1934, in an essay in the fourth volume of *Manga kōza,* he asserted that the success of

FIGURE 2. In this installment (August 23, 1941), one of many episodes of wartime children at play, Fuku (the five-year-old protagonist) displays his innovative prowess: he can make gas masks from a broken lantern. This is an example of the pantomime humor Yokoyama excelled at. Yokoyama Ryūichi, "Fuku-chan jissen" (Little Fuku practice), *Asahi shinbun,* August 23, 1941. Reprinted with permission by Yokoyama Takao.

the Shin Mangaha Shūdan is "not the well-deserved success of an art organization but merely the commercial success of a business organization," and that its commercialism "did help acquire a market, but, at the same time, created a decadent atmosphere that is most shameful to an artist, by producing a large body of work purely for commercial reasons."[24] Katō's argument presupposes that manga is art and that its connection to commercialism would degrade its status. This premise that "manga and art are synonyms" is likely a product of the discursive process that began in the late Meiji period. This explanation situated manga as a subgenre of painting, resulting from how the modern fields of literature and fine arts developed separately, divorcing themselves from the word-picture symbiosis commonly used in works of *kusazōshi* (woodblock-printed, illustrated literature) that were popular from the eighteenth century.[25] In the 1930s, when the profession of cartoonist had been well established and the commercialization of the medium accelerated, there emerged a vigorous argument that manga had been corrupted and its more artistic potential should be revisited.

In the same essay, Katō further pronounced that *nansensu* manga is in fact merely an obsolete *ponchi* with a new label, and that its substance is only "a piece of caricature that imposes meaningless laughter on the reader," lacking elements indispensable to "genuine" manga that "enlightens, strengthens, and comforts the masses."[26] As such, Katō was one of the first to criticize severely the Shin Mangaha Shūdan and *nansensu* manga. It is not clear whether his position at this time was that of a proletarian or a nationalist cartoonist, but he probably was already leaning toward the latter since his anti-*nansensu* rhetoric would last until the end of the war. The feud between Katō and the members of the Shin Mangaha Shūdan gradually became worse. We will return to Katō and his theory on war and manga as it was accelerated following the attack on Pearl Harbor in late 1941.

Katō was not alone in arguing that *nansensu* manga was a source of evil that degraded manga in general. As we have seen, Ōta Kōji described *nansensu* manga as "silly" and "vulgar" in *Karikare*. In the first issue of his magazine *Manga ōkoku,* Shimokawa Hekoten, who was known for his *ero* manga, called cartoonists who draw *nansensu* manga "amateurs." According to Shimokawa's typology, the world of manga fell into the following classifications: fascist (Germany and Italy), socialist (Russia and France), and the nonsensical or anti-political (Japan, Great Britain, and the United States). He maintained that, at the time when Japan, Germany, and Italy were forming alliance, it was not acceptable that Japan was caught up only in *nansensu* manga. He further argued that, in Japan, the era when professional cartoonists drew for newspapers was long gone, and that the era when amateur cartoonists drew *nansensu* manga for popular magazines had begun. But now was the time for people to demand better manga than what amateurish *nansensu* manga could produce, a situation in which only truly professional cartoonists could flourish.[27]

Others grieved over the lack of awareness on the part of cartoonists. For instance, a "manga review" page of *Osaka pakku* in November 1941 commented on the recent trend of "so-called light

> ACCORDING TO SHIMOKAWA'S TYPOLOGY, THE WORLD OF MANGA FELL INTO THE FOLLOWING CLASSIFICATIONS: FASCIST (GERMANY AND ITALY), SOCIALIST (RUSSIA AND FRANCE), AND THE NONSENSICAL OR ANTI-POLITICAL (JAPAN, GREAT BRITAIN, AND THE UNITED STATES).

political manga" by cartoonists who had aimlessly drawn *nansensu* manga and children's manga until recently. It pointed out the problem that cartoonists lack awareness and self-examination, which leads to an irresponsible attitude of "opportunism" (*binjōshugi*).[28] In a subsequent issue, the same review page asserted that "today's manga world is 90 percent corrupted," and that very few cartoonists are aware of their own responsibility. Indeed, many do not understand the gravity of their situation, thus allowing "fate to lead the art of Japanese manga to its destruction."[29] Along with these concerns regarding the present situation of the manga world, an emphasis was made on the need to study manga, including a call for cartoonists to improve their skills in order for a "new type of cartoonist" to emerge.

In the 1930s, a number of amateur cartoonists regularly appeared in major magazines as contributors. Accordingly, study manuals and how-to books were targeted at these aspiring amateurs. By the middle of that decade, an increasing number of would-be cartoonists formed local manga clubs in different areas across the nation. Thus, newly established manga institutes and magazines all proposed to train amateurs and inexperienced cartoonists to become "the new type of ideal cartoonist." For example, a 1937 foreword in *Manga no kuni,* a magazine devoted to amateur cartoonists, emphasized the important mission of cartoonists after the outbreak of the Japan–China War: it is not just a dream that cartoonists like Louis Raemakers in the Netherlands, whose caricature led to the downfall of the German Emperor during World War I, could spring up among readers.[30] The above-mentioned founding declaration of the Tokyo Manga Institute in April 1938 also stated: "A new cartoonist who can respond to the demand of the modern world needs to be born."[31] In the first issue of its organ *Karikare,* cartoonist Tomita Tateo argued: "The military is said to have acknowledged the power of manga and is seeking cartoonists who could create powerful manga. However, there are currently no cartoonists who could respond to this calling. There are only lazy opportunists trying to take advantage of the current situation."[32]

These commentaries constantly reminded cartoonists and would-be cartoonists that they must keep working hard at improving their drawing skills and staying informed about the current situation of the war. To them, the present was never good enough. *Nansensu* manga, which remained in vogue even in the early 1940s, was perceived in this discourse as the root of all evil, one that had corrupted the quality and status of manga. The artistic qualities of manga required saving by a new kind of cartoonist. The embodiment of these manga discourse ideals came to mean someone who would be able to elevate the status of manga from a mere commodity of commercialism by making it a superior, powerful, and persuasive expression of war. Manga's savior would have to be someone who could disseminate the ideologies of Imperial Japan and further the cause of their holy war.

KATŌ'S THEORY OF WARTIME MANGA AND A UNIFIED CARTOONISTS ASSOCIATION

As we have seen, the discourse on war and manga just prior to Japan's Pearl Harbor attack in late 1941 represented two sides of the same coin. Criticism of the corruption of the manga world represented by *nansensu* manga was also an embodiment of discontent toward professional cartoonists' obsession with commercialism, unwillingness to progress, and indifference to current affairs (*jikyoku*). The discourse uniformly predicted that this "new type of cartoonist" would emerge from aspiring amateur cartoonists. In spite of the urgent need for such figures, however, it was not clear what the exact qualifications of this new cartoonist would be, except that he be the antithesis of a *nansensu* cartoonist. In the meantime, under the mobilization law of the New Order, the Shin Nippon Mangaka Kyōkai (New Cartoonists Association of Japan) was established to consolidate cartoonists, and its organ, *Manga* magazine, was founded in 1940 despite various oppositions and contradicting opinions among the members. This was the first step to address one of the concerns expressed by the discourse on war and manga: that the state government underestimated the power of manga. Nevertheless, this association fell short of unified efforts to produce effective propaganda because they never reached consensus as to the definition of "desirable manga under the New Order."[33]

Not long after the start of the new integrated cartoonists association, Katō Etsurō left the association and created a separate organization, the Kensetsu Mangakai (Constructive Manga Association), with several other cartoonists who followed him. By then, Katō's relationship

> "MANGA IS AN ART THAT SHOULD WARN OF OR ACTIVELY ATTACK ALL THINGS IN THE WORLD THAT ARE UNJUST, IRRATIONAL, UNNATURAL, OR INCONGRUOUS WITH A WILL OF THE NATION."

with the members of the Shin Mangaha Shūdan, who occupied the central position of the Shin Nippon Mangaka Kyōkai, had deteriorated because of his ongoing criticism of them. With Pearl Harbor and the expansion of the war in the Pacific, Katō published a book, *Shin rinen manga no gihō* (A new philosophy on the techniques of manga), in 1942, as part of the activities of the Kensetsu Mangakai.[34] At this time, Japan was winning a series of battles in the Pacific; and it is here, in this book, that Katō's theorization of manga became directly connected to the war. He submitted a new definition of manga in this treatise: "Manga is an art that should warn of or actively attack all things in the world that are unjust, irrational, unnatural, or incongruous with a will of the nation." Manga is "a perfect integration, a balance of political thought and artistic quality," and can only become a perfected art when it acquires both thought—the ability to observe and to recognize "the unjust, irrational, unnatural, incongruous" in a just and profound way—and artistic quality, which is the ability to most accurately and strongly express what is observed.[35] With this ideal in mind, Katō himself tirelessly produced propaganda manga during the war. He was a regular of *Osaka pakku* (which changed its title to *Manga Nippon* in 1943) (Figure 3) and was in charge of the single-panel manga published daily in *The Japan Times* between 1941 and 1945.

According to Katō, cartoonists since the beginning of the Shōwa period had been extremely "individualistic" and had forgotten their own nationality. Thus, there could not be any real development of a national art. This also explained why the insipid *nansensu* manga, directly imported from America, were allowed to become mainstream, and why several proletarian manga became nothing more than a tool of the international Communist Party.[36] In a section titled "Atarashiki mangaka no ninmu" (The responsibilities of the new cartoonists), Katō spoke to those newcomers who would become the next generation of manga artists. He encouraged them to make every effort to study and to correctly capture the essence of manga as an art form. They were not to forget that manga should not be considered only as a means of earning money (*shokugyōteki shudan*) but should be recognized for its ability to express and propagate important human values.[37]

FIGURE 3. Katō filled the entire cover of *Manga nippon* in December 1944 with innumerable Japanese citizens. All are prepared to fight against their enemies—the United States and Great Britain. The phrase that runs across the cover in red says: "the angry one hundred million will defeat America and England."

In the final chapter of his book, Katō discussed the New Order of manga, asserting that liberalism and individualism have been obstacles to the uniting of cartoonists for the cause of war ever since the China Incident. His rhetoric assumes here an equating of commercialism/utilitarianism and liberalism/individualism. He repeatedly emphasized that they contaminate the cartoonists' consciousness. Not only this, but they became an obstacle that prevented the uniting of cartoonists following the outbreak of war in China. He argued that only the eradication of the liberalism then current among so many would allow for the creation of an "intelligence warfare unit."[38] Katō concluded his book by proposing a blueprint for a unified cartoonists organization: "We artists-cartoonists are soldiers on the propaganda front. This is our calling to fulfill. Grounded in a national, ethnic consciousness, our glorious duty is to unify manga production, which is the most powerful aspect of the propaganda war. We must actively engage ourselves."[39] The unified organization envisioned here was actually proposed as the "Nihon Mangakai" (Japan Cartoonists Association) by three cartoonists, Shimokawa Hekoten, Asō Yutaka, and Shishido Sakō, but was never actualized because it failed to gain support from the members of the Shin Nippon Mangaka Kyōkai.[40]

CONCLUSION: MANGA, WAR, AND THE EMERGENCE OF THE NEW CARTOONIST

In sum, the discourse on war and manga since 1937 embraced cartoonists' various intentions and desires, and assumed a role of urging cartoonists to become agents of the New Order and to produce manga vital to fighting the propaganda war. In this discursive space, a number of operations were intricately entwined: the attempt to purify the impure and ambivalent nature of manga as a mixed medium, the effort to elevate the status of manga by linking its nature as a verbal and visual form with propaganda, the attempt to warn manga against becoming a commodity of commercialism, and a call for cartoonists to awaken to their artistic potential.

In 1943, the Nihon Manga Hōkōkai (Japan Manga Service Association) was created as a "part of the mobilization and simplification of the art industry" by the culture division of the government-controlled Taisei Yokusankai (Imperial Rule Assistance Association). This organization is said to have become "consistently under the total control of the state government."[41] In other words, the cartoonists' will to be mobilized for the cause of the war, as shown in the discourse examined, and the state's needs to fully utilize manga for wartime propaganda finally came together at this moment. This discourse did help prepare cartoonists' active participation in the fascist order, yet the idealized "new cartoonist" who could create manga that integrates thought and art never emerged during the war, since those who actually came to play the central role in producing manga to fight the holy war were the members of the Shin Mangaha Shūdan—such as Yokoyama Ryūichi, Kondō Hidezō (Figure 4), and Sugiura Yukio—who established their status by popularizing *nansensu* manga. Why did *nansensu* manga become a target of criticism and the antithesis of manga that would have been created by the "new type of cartoonist"? This line of argument is consonant with the increasing criticism of the general trend of "*ero guro nansensu*" in wartime Japan. *Nansensu* manga was most closely associated with an all-pervasive American culture

FIGURE 4. "Roosevelt," by Kondō Hidezō, on the cover of *Manga*, February 1943. Kondō, chief editor of the magazine, drew many caricatures of political leaders for the cover during the war. His favorites were Franklin Roosevelt and Winston Churchill, who appeared repeatedly on the cover of the magazine.

that was vigorously attacked and suppressed as decadent and capitalistic during the war years. Even the manga artists who were labeled *nansensu* cartoonists had adjusted their drawing style to be more appropriate for wartime mobilization.

One could also say that the ideal cartoonist as described by the prewar and wartime discourse was prepared during the war and appeared once the fighting ended. For example, Katō Yoshirō, who flourished as the creator of the longest-running newspaper manga *Mappira-kun* (Mr. No Way) after the war,[42] was an active amateur cartoonist who submitted his works to magazines such as *Manga* and *Asahi gurafu,* and often received prize money.[43] It is also known that Tezuka Osamu, who was called "God of manga" in postwar Japan, avidly studied and imitated prewar manga like *Fuku-chan*. Tezuka is said to have created more than three thousand pages of unpublished manga by the end of the war.[44] In *Mechademia 3,* an essay by Ōtsuka Eiji points out that Tezuka's pictorial techniques seen in his patriotic wartime sketch "Shōri no hi made" (Till the Day of Victory) deployed a combination of an anime-style influenced by prewar Disney and the realistic depiction of weaponry influenced by wartime "scientific realism," elements of which were carried forward in his postwar manga.[45] The sudden political shift from fascism to liberalism brought by Japan's defeat in 1945 turned the country's ideological focus from the war to a wider consideration of the various ideological positions of different artists. The hybridity of the medium itself invited a wide range of expression appropriate to the fragmented nature of postmodern culture. Postwar Japan has seen the growing popularity of manga as a monstrous medium whose impure and ambiguous nature—a mixture of word and image—became an engulfing force. This "new type of manga artist" who emerged in Japan after the war made full use of manga in order to convey their ideals, be it Tezuka's humanism or Katō Yoshirō's satire on social hypocrisies and contradictions in the rapidly changing postwar society.

....

Notes

1. This magazine used both *katakana* "*karikare*" and romanized "caricare" ("caricature" in Italian). The *katakana* version was used for the title on the cover.

2. This term originates from Charles Wirgman's humor magazine *Japan Punch* that was started in Yokohama in 1862. For more on this magazine, see Shimizu Isao, *Nihon manga no rekishi* (The history of Japanese manga) (Tokyo: Sanseidō, 1989), 29–52. "*Ponchi*" was popularly used to describe the humorous or satirical combination of words and pictures at the turn of the century, until it was transformed and eventually replaced by a new term, "manga," at the end of the Meiji period. For the process of this transformation, see Miyamoto Hirohito, "The Formation of an Impure Genre—On the Origins of *Manga*," *Review of Japanese Culture and Society* 14 (December 2002): 39–48. His related research on the conceptualizaion of the term "manga" is discussed in "'Manga' gainen no jūsōka katei—kinsei kara kindai ni okeru" (The stratifying process of the notion of "manga": From the early modern age to the modern age), *Bijutsushi* (Journal of the Japan Art History Society) 154 (March 2003): 319–34.

3. Kawasaki-shi Shimin Myūjiamu, ed., *Nihon no manga sanbyakunen-ten kaisetsu zuroku* (Three hundred years of Japanese manga exhibition catalog) (Kawasaki: Kawasaki-shi Shimin Myūjiamu, 1996), 77.

4. Miyamoto, "The Formation of an Impure Genre," 39.

5. Yamamoto Kanae, "Gendai no kokkeiga oyobi fūshiga ni tsuite" (On contemporary humorous and satirical arts), *Hōsun* 1, no. 1 (May 1907): 3; no. 2 (June 1907): 3; no. 3 (July 1907): 3–4. Yamamoto was one of the founders of the magazine, which lasted until 1911 (thirty-five issues). Others who participated in this magazine include Ishii Hakutei, Kosugi Misei, Morita Tsunetomo. They were young *yōga* (Western-style paintings) artists and engravers who were interested in establishing the genre of artistic caricature. See Shimizu, *Nihon manga no rekishi*, 119, 123. This magazine carried a number of works of this kind. A special manga issue of *Hōsun*, February 1909, was an attempt to collect "ideal manga" (note that they use this term). Another unique feature of this issue was that all the texts

other than the announcement, which claimed that "Japanese characters won't remain the mixture of *kana* and *kanji* forever," was romanized. It noted that they "wanted to see how beautiful the pages should look with all-romanized texts."

6. Kawasaki-shi, *Nihon no manga,* 89.

7. Ishii Hakutei, "Honchō mangashi," *Chūō bijutsu* 4, no. 1 (January 1918): 139–42.

8. Ibid., 139.

9. For a firsthand account of the proletarian manga, see Matsuyama Fumio, "Puroretaria manga shōshi" (A short history of proletarian manga), in *Nihon puroretaria bijutsushi* (History of Japanese proletarian art), eds. Okamoto Tōki and Matsuyama Fumio, 103–52 (Tokyo: Zōkeisha, 1972).

10. Jennifer Weisenfeld, *Mavo: Japanese Artists and the Avant-Garde, 1905–1931* (Berkeley and Los Angeles: University of California Press, 2002), 252–53.

11. This declaration was an insert of *Karikare* 1, no. 1 (June 1938). The insert indicates that the institute was founded as a training school for amateur cartoonists.

12. These are: Ōta Kōji, "Sensō to manga joron: Manga no chikara o saininshikiseyo" (Introduction to war and manga: Reconfirm the power of manga), *Karikare* 2, no. 5 (June 1939): 11; Ōta Kōji, "Sensō to manga 2 (War and manga 2)," *Karikare* 2, no. 6 (July 1939): 2; and Ōta Kōji, "Senji senden to manga" (Wartime propaganda and manga), *Karikare* 3, no. 9 (October 1940): 2, 5.

13. Kajii Jun, *Tore, yōchō no jū to pen: Senjika mangashi nōto* (Take the chastening gun and pen: Notes on the history of wartime manga) (Tokyo: Waizu Shuppan, 1999), 176.

14. By this time, the term *ponchi* came to signify manga that are outdated and low quality. See Suyama Keiichi, *Nihon manga hyakunen* (One hundred years of Japanese manga) (Tokyo: Haga Shoten, 1968), 11–19.

15. Ōta, "Sensō to manga joron," 11.

16. Ōta, "Senji senden to manga," 2–3.

17. Kitazawa Rakuten, "Sensō to manga," *Karikare* 2, no. 6 (July 1939): 3.

18. "Rakuten sensei ōi ni kataru" (Master Rakuten holds forth), *Manga,* August 1941, 12–21.

19. Ibid., 19.

20. "Kantōgen" (Foreword), *Manga,* September 1941, 7.

21. Miriam Silverberg, "The Ero Gro [sic] Nonsense of Japanese Modern Times," in *Iwanami kōza kindai Nihon no bunkashi 7: Sōryokusenka no chi to seido* (Iwanami lecture series on modern Japanese cultural history 7: Knowledge and system under total war), eds. Komori Yōichi et al., 61–109 (Tokyo: Iwanami Shoten, 2002).

22. Okamoto Ippei, "Sōron" (General remarks), in *Manga kōza,* vol. 1, ed. Nihon Mangakai (Tokyo: Kensetsusha, 1933), 8–9.

23. Regarding Katō's ideological transformation, see Shimizu, *Manga no rekishi,* 161–64. Also see John Dower, *Embracing Defeat* (New York: W. W. Norton, 1999), 65–73, for how Katō's little booklet published in 1946 captured the Japanese sentiment during the first year of the U.S. occupation. Two years later, Katō joined the communist party.

24. Katō Etsurō, "Gendai Nihon mangadan no tenbō" (A perspective on the contemporary Japanese manga establishment), in *Manga kōza,* vol. 4, ed. Nihon Mangakai (Tokyo: Kensetsusha, 1934), 166–67.

25. Miyamoto, "Formation of an Impure Genre."

26. Katō, "Gendai Nihon," 180–81.

27. *Manga ōkoku,* February 1937, 2.

28. Minatogawa Rokkō, "Manga jihyō: Muri shicha akan" (Manga review: Take it easy), *Osaka pakku,* November 1941, 14–15.

29. Shidōken Mondo, "Manga jihyō: Aru hi no taiwa" (Manga review: An occasional dialogue), *Osaka pakku,* December 1941, 20.

30. "Kokuminteki kensetsu to sōzō no daininen e" (Toward the second year of national foundation and creation), *Manga no kuni,* December 1937, 3.

31. See note 11.

32. *Karikare* 1, no. 3 (August 1938): 7.

33. For the situation surrounding the foundation of the association, see Inoue Yūko, "Senjika no manga: Shintaiseiki ikō no manga to manga dantai" (Wartime manga: Manga and manga groups under the New Order), *Ritsumeikan daigaku jinbunka kenkyūjo kiyō* (Ritsumeikan University Humanities Institute bulletin) 81 (December 2002): 103–33.

34. Katō Etsurō, *Shin rinen manga no gihō* (Tokyo: Geijutsu Gakuin Shuppanbu, 1942). The members of this group published several other books as well. See Shimizu, *Manga no rekishi,* 15–17.

35. Ibid., 15–16.

36. Ibid., 5–6.

37. Ibid., 23.

38. Ibid., 164–65.

39. Ibid., 171.

40. Inoue, "Senjika no manga," 115–17, for details. Cartoonist Kobayashi Takeshi recorded that Katō was actively advocating this organization.

41. Ibid., 117–8.

42. "Okuyami: Katō Yoshirō-san (mangaka) ga kokyū fuzen no tame shikyo" (Obituary: Mr. Katō Yoshirō [manga artist] dies of respiratory deficiency), *Nikkan spotra* (January 2006), http://www5.nikkansports.com/general/obituary/2006/20060106-9416.html (accessed May 5, 2008). According to his obituary, Katō's *Mappira-kun* ran in the evening edition of the daily *Mainichi shinbun* for forty-seven years (1954 to 2001), which makes it Japan's longest-running newspaper manga.

43. Katō Yoshirō, personal interview, December 28, 1993.

44. Tezuka Osamu, *Boku no manga jinsei* (My manga life), Iwanami shinsho series (Tokyo: Iwanami Shoten, 1997), 100, 105, 210.

45. Ōtsuka Eiji, "Disarming Atom: Tezuka Osamu's Manga at War and Peace," trans. Thomas Lamarre, *Mechademia 3: Limits of the Human,* ed. Frenchy Lunning, 111–25 (Minneapolis: University of Minnesota Press, 2008).

WENDY GOLDBERG

Transcending the Victim's History: Takahata Isao's *Grave of the Fireflies*

Grave of the Fireflies (*Hotaru no Haka*), a film directed by Takahata Isao in 1988 and based on the Naoki Award–winning short story by Nosaka Akiyuki (published 1967), was paired as a double feature with Miyazaki Hayao film, *My Neighbor Totoro* (*Tonari no Totoro*).[1] These two films, however, could not be more dissimilar. Miyazaki's work is a gentle fantasy of childhood imagination in the pastoral setting of 1950s Japan, a time seemingly untouched by war. *Grave,* on the other hand, set in Kobe 1945, in the waning days of World War II, is a realistic drama, focusing on the suffering and eventual starvation deaths of fourteen-year-old Seita and his four-year-old sister, Setsuko. The film opens with Seita's sore-ridden, emaciated body falling over in a train station. His voice, emanating from a spirit bathed in red light, tells us that on September 21, 1945, he has died. A worker looking through Seita's belongings finds a beat-up tin can, which he throws into the bushes. Pieces of bone roll out which turn into Setsuko's spirit, likewise cast in red light. She sees her brother's body and rushes to go to him, but she is restrained and then joyfully reunited with his spirit. The film then retraces how the two of them reached their moments of death.

Grave unflinchingly examines how these children suffer. The tragedy of this realistic depiction is compounded by the fact it is partly autobiographical. The author, Nosaka Akiyuki, was separated from his family during a bombing raid and was the only caretaker of his sixteen-month-old stepsister, who eventually perished from malnutrition under his care. Critic Igarashi Yoshikuni argues that "writing for Nosaka was a form of exorcism" and that by killing off his proxy, Seita, he attempts to assuage his guilt over his sister's death.[2] Likewise, Takahata Isao became drawn to this project not only for the critical acclaim of the original story (as well as by Miyazaki's urging and assured financial backing) but because he, too, with one of his siblings was separated from his family for two days during a firebombing. He calls it "the worst experience of his life."[3]

In addition to these autobiographical moments, with their painful examinations and unsuccessful exorcisms, is a biography of Japan's recent past—a defining era for generations of Japanese who lived through the time of the war and for those born after. In looking contextually at *Grave,* the film raises questions about how Japanese should talk about their history—one full of terrible suffering and yet also one of atrocities enacted against other Asian countries in the name of nationalism. How can discussions about the past both acknowledge the great suffering as well as come to terms with Japan's complicity in that suffering?

At first viewing, *Grave* is a terribly tragic film, which would lead one to label it simply as a historical document of suffering. Susan Napier states that, indeed, *Grave* is a "victim's history."[4] Does the film present a picture of victimhood, playing off the viewer's sentimental feelings toward the slow, starving death of an innocent girl, aestheticizing her suffering without addressing larger historical questions? Or is there something deeper at work in the film?

I argue that, while the film presents a realistic picture of suffering, it is also critical of a blind patriotism that masks selfish impulses during the war and, afterward, of Japan's inability to confront this past. Seita, who is not only the author's doppelganger of guilt, is also a figure who expresses selfishness masked by nationalistic fervor. When he, like others in the film, acts in the "name" of communal ideals, he is really performing for personal gain or pleasure. Throughout the film, Seita dreams of his father rescuing or revenging their wrongs (overtly, against Japan's enemies who are bombing their town, and, tacitly, against the alienating Japanese society) and pays the ultimate price for this choice. His fantasy world of righteousness and revenge is a mirror to the society in which he lives; visually and textually, Takahata links him to this national fantasy of war. Setsuko, on the other hand, is as much his victim as a victim of the war.

Is there a way out of Seita's self-delusion and Setsuko's suffering? Does the story, as critic Igarashi Yoshikuni suggests, "reject the time after the war," which leaves no place for the future to develop?[5] I argue that the film attempts to provide an alternate, natural history in order to reconcile this ideological split. To bridge this gap, both Nosaka and Takahata use the images of the fireflies, which are beautifully animated and are one of the only events that signify joy in the film. However, they also gesture to the fires that burned Japan and for the lives lost in the war. For the audience, the image of the fireflies is likewise contradictory: at once transcendent, unfixed from time, and yet at the same time nostalgic for a past that never was—or perhaps nostalgic for a future that never came to be. Since Japan has rebuilt and, especially in the 1980s, has thrived economically, the film asks the viewer to remember this wartime history paradoxically through the act of viewing the natural.

> IN LOOKING CONTEXTUALLY AT GRAVE, THE FILM RAISES QUESTIONS ABOUT HOW JAPANESE SHOULD TALK ABOUT THEIR HISTORY—ONE FULL OF TERRIBLE SUFFERING AND YET ALSO ONE OF ATROCITIES ENACTED AGAINST OTHER ASIAN COUNTRIES IN THE NAME OF NATIONALISM.

The dominant thread in the film, however, is that of Setsuko's suffering; her innocent death looms over the narrative and makes it difficult to discern a message in the film, let alone a hopeful one. In this section, I will explore how Takahata and Nosaka heighten the pathos in the texts, which leads viewers to ask, "Why does she have to die in such a terrible way?"

What makes Setsuko's suffering so terrible is that her portrayal of a little girl rings true with her play. In an early scene, she is taking a bath with her brother, and when he creates an air bubble with the washcloth, he splashes it into her surprised, then delighted, face. In another scene, Seita asks Setsuko to close her eyes and open her mouth. He gives her a candy. She calls out "fruit drop" and dances merrily around, until, in her excitement, she almost swallows it.

In tandem with these scenes of delight, the viewers see her utter dependence on her brother. She has constant needs that she cannot fulfill herself. At one point, early in the film, she whines that she is tired and asks Seita to carry her. Then, when they move to the cave by the side of the pond, she often complains that she is hungry. In another scene, in the middle of the road, Setsuko throws a fit. To placate her, Seita searches for a fruit drop from the tin can but it appears to be empty. Setsuko begins to cry and is only mollified when Seita finds a few stuck to the bottom. Setsuko's scenes of delight and of need heighten the viewer's sorrow over her suffering.

Setsuko's age was carefully chosen to produce this effect. While Nosaka's stepsister who died during the war was only sixteen months old, he raises her age to four years old in the fictional version. At this age, she is old enough to communicate wants and needs in a more direct way than a younger child. Film critic Roger Ebert offers a compelling reason for why Setsuko's suffering elicits such empathy in the audience. On the special edition of *Grave of the Fireflies*, rereleased by Central Park Media with a variety of commentaries and interviews, Ebert argues that when we see images of Setsuko starving and finally dying, because she is animated, she becomes the *idea* of a child starving and not the child herself. Should we watch a young actress play this role, we would be distracted, argues Ebert, by watching this individual girl perform. He says that the animated Setsuko is a "purer statement" about the horror of war.[6]

> WHILE WE MAY FOCUS ON SETSUKO'S GREAT SUFFERING THROUGHOUT THE FILM, WE ARE ALSO ASKED TO EXAMINE SEITA'S FAILURE TO PROTECT HER. HIS CHOICES REFLECT THE SOCIETY AT LARGE.

But there is a level of realism to her portrayal. Takahata eschewed older children to play the roles of the children. Instead, during voice casting he selected a four-year old girl to play the part of the four-year-old Setsuko.[7] While this caused some challenges in animating the film—for instance, they had to record her voice first and then animate, as opposed to the other way around, which is common in Japanese animation—by doing this, Takahata aims for a purer, more realistic image through the child's voice, yet still stylized by the animation.

At the end of the film, Setsuko's spirit seems comforted by her brother's spirit, but she is reunited with neither her mother nor her father, suggesting that she is eternally in her brother's care. Spirit Seita is now able to protect Setsuko, and it is a place where candy tins are always full. However, this is not a place of ease and respite—at least for him. Rather than rejoicing in their safe haven, his spirit restlessly runs after his living double, grieving over the choices he made while still alive.

At the beginning of the film, Seita's dying thought is "what day is it?" but his spirit knows, because he tells the viewer. The fact that he knows the date suggests that this is a day that he will not easily cast aside, ranking it even above more significant dates of the war, such as the atomic bombings at Nagasaki and Hiroshima and the Emperor's surrender. At the end of the film, Seita holds Setsuko's sleeping figure, his face stoically looking at the

FIGURE 1. The spirits of Seita and Setsuko from *Grave of the Fireflies (Hotaru no Haka)*, a film directed by Takahata Isao in 1988.

audience. The film begins and ends with Seita's death and the circularity suggests that this is a cycle that he cannot escape, even in death (Figure 1).

While we may focus on Setsuko's great suffering throughout the film, we are also asked to examine Seita's failure to protect her. His choices reflect the society at large. There are numerous subtle reminders throughout the film of Japan's nationalistic fervor at this time. During the first harrowing bombing scene, as the children run to safety through fire, a lone figure in a uniform, silhouetted in front of the burning town and behind cowering survivors, waves a mop and calls out "Long Live the Emperor!" The gesture, in light of so much devastation seems brazen as well as pointless—especially since the mop is part of the equipment of the fire brigade, tasked with putting out the flames from the bombs. We know this because as Seita runs out with his sister, we see him pause to look, in a sequence of stills, at the untouched bucket, mop, and water supply as the buildings catch on fire. The fire brigade have failed in their job to help the community, which makes this gesture of the lone figure, hoping for a miraculous resolution even as he fails at a practical solution, all the more hopeless.

However, Seita wears this same uniform of the fire brigade, and he is linked to the failure of this group. His pause is not only to implicate the others who have failed, but also his choice to spirit his sister out of the town without

> EVEN AS UNIFORMED INDIVIDUALS REPRESENT THE HOPES OF JAPAN AT THIS TIME, WE SEE OTHER VOICES IN THE FILM USING NATIONALISM TO MASK RESENTMENT FOR PERSONAL SACRIFICE.

doing his duty, thus emphasizing that, like many, he has chosen personal preservation over the community. He wears this uniform throughout the film, and we see it literally decay off his body, only to be replaced perfectly when he is a spirit (as if he cannot rid himself of these responsibilities). Brian McVeigh, in his study of Japanese school uniforms, states: "History was often invoked to account for why Japanese wore uniforms: 'the uniform system' (*seifuku seido*) we see today is connected to the wartime period. A sense of comradeship (*nakama ishiki*) and group consciousness (*minzoku ishiki*)" says one student.[8] The uniform in Japanese society, so often seen today in the sailor and military suits of schoolchildren, is a marker of group identity and solidarity. However, it is also a coded gesture in order to force these individual members to comply with that group's standards. The uniforms evoke the Japanese word, *seken*, or a "normalizing gaze."[9] McVeigh writes, "in order to ensure that everyone properly presents his or her part, the *seken*, a generalized audience, or, perhaps more ominously, a sort of omnipresent social spook, keeps an eye on everybody. Literally, the word means 'in the world,' but may be translated as public, the world, community, people, or society."[10] Uniforms represent the specified role of each individual, made visible to the Foucauldian panopticon. In Seita's case, as the normalizing gaze is also his spirit's gaze, his social role is as member of the fire brigade—a function we never see him fulfill. As *Grave* was marketed as an educational experience for Japanese schoolchildren, who likewise would be wearing school "military" uniforms, the message would be unmistakable. They are asked to see themselves in Seita.

Takahata explores these militaristic roots of the school uniform because Seita's appearance also links him to images of his father, whom we always see pictured wearing the uniform of a navy officer. When he imagines his father rescuing them, Seita decides to take on the role of rescuer of his sister. Despite the death and destruction around him, he is comforted by his unswerving belief that the war will be won and that his father will return to save them. After the bombing that destroys their house, Setsuko asks what they will do. Seita says, "Dad will make them pay."

Later, in the beautiful scene in the cave where he and Setsuko capture fireflies to light up the dark night, he refigures the glowing lights into images of battleships and cityscapes, recalling the naval review that he once witnessed. He tells Setsuko that she never saw this scene but he remembers it vividly. The viewer sees Seita's father again, saluting. In Seita's memory, fireworks shoot into the air, and then he sings about protecting the homeland, a song he most likely heard at that time. He shoots at imaginary enemy planes, as if he could be the soldier like his father who will protect his family and his nation. Ironically, Seita transforms the lovely image of the fireflies in the cave into propaganda. Fed by the ideologies that surround him—the grand spectacle of military might as well as a personal connection to them by his father, whom he emulates and admires—Seita's understanding of the war is not that deep. On some level, however, he is not certain what will happen in the future, even as the song promises victory. His face falls, and he says, "I wonder what dad is doing now?" In many ways, he is still a boy, feeling out a path to find his own way of being that hero.

That Japan will lose is made clear when, the next morning, Setsuko digs a grave for the fireflies that have died during the night. At this point, she says that mother must have such a grave too, revealing that she is aware that her mother has died. This grave of the fireflies is not only for her mother, and eventually for the children, but also signifies the destruction of the battleships that Seita had imagined the previous night.

Even as uniformed individuals represent the hopes of Japan at this time, we see other voices in the film using nationalism to mask resentment for personal sacrifice. As the aunt praises those who work for the good of the country, she singles Seita and his sister out for the special treatment they receive: "lucky your father is in the navy, he gets a truck and help to move their things." Again, when she admires the pickled plums he brings with them: She comments "soldiers get the best stuff." Upon their arrival, she tells Seita to write to his father, not only with news of his mother's death but also, it seems, to ask for more assistance for them and, by extension, her family.

In her quest for survival, the aunt demands further sacrifices from the children. She pulls out a box of their mother's kimonos and tells Seita that since his mother doesn't need them anymore, he should trade them for rice. Seita then remembers his mother's "uniform"—her kimonos that she wore on special occasions. Brian McVeigh writes: kimonos "tightly link Japanese femininity with national identity."[11] They are worn on important events (weddings, funerals, other festivals).[12] To sacrifice them is to let go of an identity connected to a happy past. Those sacrifices are made in the name of survival for the children but also for the survival of the nation, because, as the aunt tells Seita, "you can't be a soldier if you don't grow up strong," using the language of nationalism to cover her selfishness. Setsuko, who they did not realize was awake, however, tries to stop her from taking the kimonos. She

FIGURE 2. A family portrait in *Grave of the Fireflies*.

begins to cry loudly. The ghost Seita holds his ears, trying to keep her cries from his consciousness and the painful memories of his mother. Cherry blossoms, a common image in Japanese literature and film, representing both beauty and its transitory nature, float down.

Seita then remembers the day they took a family portrait, with his mother in her kimono and his father in his uniform. Seita stands next to him in his school uniform, linking himself visually to his father, the person he wishes to become (Figure 2). The cherry blossoms transform into falling rice and the viewer is transported to the present. After he has sold the kimonos, Seita is thrilled by the bounty. The aunt makes rice balls for her boarder and her daughter. Seita says to Setsuko that they will have rice balls for lunch, but the aunt says they will not because food is for those who work for their nation. She tells him, "Seita, you're old enough to know everybody has to cooperate." Even though the sacrifice of his mother, both by her physical death and the symbolic one through her kimonos, brings food, Setsuko's instinctual objections to the loss of her mother and the fleeting happiness that the rice brings, shows that the gesture is as insubstantial as the cherry blossoms. Seita, in reaction to his aunt's harsh statements, becomes increasingly unwilling to make these sacrifices for such little gain. The children will move out of the house and into the cave soon after.

Seita is on the cusp of adulthood, able to make decisions on his own, and is probing the boundaries of his own identity as a man and as a protector. When we look at the pair in this light, in the scenes where the aunt insults his ability to contribute to the war effort as a "soldier" (therefore, a man), his ego is wounded. He takes Setsuko away so he can protect her in the manner of his own choosing, without anyone's critique. By caring for her, he will show that he is a "man."

Nosaka Akiyuki states that when the children move into the fantasy world of the cave, "For Seita, it's like he can try to build a heaven for just the two of them . . . After all, it's a double-suicide story." Here, Nosaka refers to the plays of Monzaemon Chikamatsu (1653–1725), who composed more than a dozen highly successful plays on the theme of *shinjūmono* (love-suicide).[13] In the typical plot, reminiscent of Shakespeare's *Romeo and Juliet,* the male figure falls in love with a woman of a different social class. They run away together, refusing their prescribed social roles; their only solution is to die in a mutual pact.[14]

> THROUGHOUT THE FILM, PEOPLE'S CASUAL REACTIONS, EVEN INDIFFERENCE, TO THE DEVASTATION OF THE WAR REMINDS US THAT SEITA AND SETSUKO'S STORY IS ONLY ONE OF MANY TRAGEDIES.

Although it may be difficult to see erotic overtones between the brother and his much younger sister, we can see some elements of similarity between the film and the plays. The first is the rejection of society; in moving them to the cave and away from the social network of food and services, Seita tries to replicate a "world" for just the two of them. They play house by the pond and take on socially proscribed roles that mirror the outside world. Nosaka states that Setsuko "assumes the role of his mother at times."[15] Setsuko, in her eagerness to model her play on her mother, is happy to "play house" with him, in order to complete his fantasy of maturity and control. Even in the aunt's house, after they decide to cook and eat their meals separately from the rest of the family as a protest to their "second-class" treatment, Setsuko scolds Seita for lying back after the meal, an example of bad manners. He responds that they do not need to follow social conventions anymore. At the cave, they play house; Setsuko sets the table as Seita cooks the rice. Even in the moments before her death, she still "plays" at homemaking by offering her brother a "rice ball" she has made from mud (Figure 3).

It is rather easy to see the aunt and other members of society as antagonists to these children. However, Takahata complicates this simplistic vision. Throughout the film, people's casual reactions, even indifference, to the devastation of the war reminds us that Seita and Setsuko's story is only one of

FIGURE 3. Setsuko's dying act of offering a rice ball to Seita in *Grave of the Fireflies*.

many tragedies. The viewer sees subtle, but horrifying, pictures of the extent of the bombings' devastation that affected other people. Early in the film, as Seita and Setsuko walk through the wreckage, trying to get back to their mother, they see other survivors walking as well. They also see many burned bodies lying in the street and hear a woman crying out for her mother. One person comments in an almost casual way: "It's not like I'm the only who lost his house. We are all in the same boat." These words reflect a level of resignation to the horrors or war.

The danger of this resignation, however, is that it leads to a desire to "return to normal" and put the past behind, even if it means to forget the suffering. In the moment of Seita's death in the very first scene of the film, Seita is only one among a group of dying children. Some unseen people, walking through the station, comment how shameful it will be to have these figures around when the Americans come. Seita's body has become trash that someone has carelessly left behind. That this person becomes ashamed that the enemy will see this reflects a need to cast off the history of the war and return to "normal," a state of being, the film suggests, that will be impossible for the nation to experience, seeing as they are haunted by both Seita and Setsuko's spirits. The many dying and the dead bodies have numbed human compassion. Another boy has died at the same time as Seita; a worker pokes the body and says "another one."

This desire for survival and lack of compassion transform nationalism into weary resignation. Near the end of the film, when Seita stands in line at the bank, finally withdrawing his mother's money that he had been saving, he hears people talking about the looming typhoon, and they note ironically that they get the "divine wind" after the surrender. The shallow nationalism shown throughout the film is now exposed as the joke that it is. Now that the fighting is over, the people have resigned themselves to the reality of defeat. Seita, still living in this fantasy world, realizes that all his hopes were pinned on rescue by his father; his hope, with the death of his father, is destroyed. The fact that he was not aware of the Japanese surrender makes it clear that he has completely removed himself from society. Shortly after, Setsuko dies at the cave.

Seita, who has lost the one person who he has tried to save throughout the war, has nothing with which to build a future. When he prepares for Setsuko for cremation, he sees nicely dressed people return to their homes and hears a phonograph play "there's no place like home," a heartbreaking song that has no meaning. For others, however, homes can be rebuilt. Seita's presence on the fringes of these homecomings destabilizes the idea that life can return to "normal" even for those who may, on the surface, be less touched by the war.

The final image the viewer sees of Setsuko is not her death but a montage of Seita's vibrant memories of her play. These brief moments flicker like a firefly, causing joy at their illumination but also pain at their loss. At first, the viewer sees shots of the empty cave, discarded items, and bugs crawling on the watermelon. Then, a child's voice cries. We see Setsuko dance after butterflies then disappear. We see her on the swing, fall, and then disappear. We see her cleaning up the house with her doll on her back, like a mother doing housework with her baby. Now, she's fanning the stove, watching a butterfly go by and chasing it. Now, she has the umbrella, mud *odango* (little dumplings), and runs with a sheet flying out behind her; the image mirrored in the water of the pond (Figure 4). This montage is a farewell to her life and captures more fully not only what Seita remembers but also her childhood games and her joyful spirit. Takahata states that the image of the firefly also represents the "shortness of life—fireflies die in one day or so, and that links to the children."[16]

Since Japan has rebuilt and prospered after World War II, there are few direct daily reminders of the pain caused by the war. By using a natural image that many people in Japan could experience, Takahata and Nosaka use the image of the fireflies as a persistent natural reminder of this history in all its facets. The fireflies are a multivalent symbol, signifying the children's deaths and their spirits; the fires that burned the towns; Japanese soldiers and the

FIGURE 4. From Seita's memories of Setsuko after she has died: Setsuko runs back and forth in front of their cave with a sheet billowing out behind her. The image is mirrored in the water.

machinery of war; and the hopeful regeneration of life through nature—something pure and untouched by grief and war.

This natural history is also a nostalgic history, one that touches on happy memories of childhood (ironically portrayed in a film where childhood memories are not happy). Okpyo Moon, in her essay "Marketing Nature in Rural Japan," states that in the 1920s and 1930s, "fireflies were caught in abundance and it is said that hundreds were caught per person each night." However, their populations began to decline, and it was not until the 1960s and 1970s that people sought to recapture this "pure" past through "*hotaru* revival movements." Moon states "there are now eighty-five 'firefly villages' (*hotaru no sato*) or 'firefly towns' (*hotaru no machi*) in Japan, registered at the Ministry of the Environment under the programme of 'The living creature of our hometown' (*Furusato no ikimono*)."[17]

Though threatened by encroaching urbanization and pollution (although that has been disputed), the firefly, on one level, represents an alternative history that transcends the suffering of the war. They are regenerative and linger, if not in reality, then in memory. While fireflies were thought to be lost out of environmental mismanagement, which is not the theme of the film, the overlapping sense of loss in the film is manifested by the sense that "we have lost something within ourselves" as a result of war. To visit the fireflies is to reconnect with that which has been lost. It is a potent symbol for present-day Japanese audiences, because they may not be of the generation who lived through and survived the war. This idea of purity is one where the war never took place—no suffering and no nationalism. The marketing of rural spaces in Japan (as also seen in Takahata's film, *Omohide Poroporo* [1991]) becomes a place of remembrance of a cleaner, simpler past for these communities (but also, as Moon notes, a profitable, economic one). Takahata's film, coming as it did in the 1980s, while such festivals and towns prospered (even today, people attend firefly festivals in June and July throughout Japan) heightens the sense of loss in the film.

Ultimately, however, the fireflies upon which the film seems to pin all its hopes, is a not a simplistic answer. Fireflies are a constructed, artificial sign within present Japanese society of a compartmentalized purity—a perception of a time that can only be visited, not lived in, revealing the gap between pre- and postwar history. Their flickering essence in the flashing of their lights, as in the lives of these two children, suggests something that is paradoxically eternally transitory (like the two spirits living perpetually in the red-washed world).

Takahata and Nosaka further complicate the symbol. Visually and textually, fireflies are connected to something deadly beautiful (such as the firebombs and the planes that drop them from the sky). In one instance in the story, Setsuko says the kamikaze plane she sees looks like a firefly—an appropriate metaphor, although she does not know it, because of the swiftness at which this plane will destroy itself. Streaks of fire that rain down onto the towns are brief and bright like the fireflies, but horribly destructive. Further, Takahata does not use the normal *kanji* for "firefly" in the title and instead uses the character "fire,"[18] one that would clearly resonate with destruction, such as the widespread burning of the wooden houses in Kobe and other places in Japan. Critic Dennis Fukushima notes that Takahata's alteration to the title is "an appropriate image considering the parallels drawn in the film between fireflies, the M-69 incendiary bombs, the B-29 bomber planes, naval vessels, city lights, and human spirits, as well as eyewitness accounts of the bombings."[19] To draw parallels between both devastation and beauty is unsettling. Although what replaces historical text in the film is a nostalgic and transcendent fantasy of nature, Takahata destabilizes this "easy answer."

The power of the film is that the image of the fireflies attempts to transcend the suffering at the same time Takahata and Nosaka question the attempted transcendence. Their texts are about pain and suffering, but they are also critical of a nationalistic past. Japanese schoolchildren are asked to identify with both figures at the same time—not only to grieve over Setsuko's terrible death but also to connect with Seita whose poor choices led them down this path. But neither can we despise him; the film asks us to be critical of his refusal to be a part of this society at the same time we are asked to critique this society's patriotism and its attempt to revert to normal (i.e., life before the war). Society, Takahata argues, cannot return to a "normal" that never was, haunted as it is by the twin figures of suffering and of blind nationalism.

....

Notes

1. *Hotaru no Haka,* dir. Takahata Isao (1988); translated as *Grave of the Fireflies,* subtitled DVD (Central Park Media, 2002). *Tonari no Totoro,* dir. Miyazaki Hayao (1988); translated as *My Neighbor Totoro,* subtitled DVD (Walt Disney Home Entertainment, 2006). Nosaka Akiyuki, "A Grave of Fireflies," translated by James R. Abrams, *Japan Quarterly* 25, no. 4 (1978): 445–63.

2. Igarashi Yoshikuni, *Bodies of Memory: Narratives of War in Postwar Japanese Culture, 1945–1970* (Princeton, N.J.: Princeton University Press, 2000), 179.

3. Takahata Isao, "Isao Takahata on *Grave of the Fireflies,*" subtitled DVD commentary for *Grave of the Fireflies* (Central Park Media, 2002).

4. Susan Napier, *Anime: From "Akira" to "Princess Mononoke"* (New York: Palgrave, 2000), 165.

5. Igarashi, *Bodies of Memory,* 176.

6. Roger Ebert, "On *Grave of the Fireflies,*" DVD commentary, *Grave of the Fireflies* (Central Park Media, 2002).

7. Takahata, "Isao Takahata on *Grave of the Fireflies.*"

8. Brian McVeigh, *Wearing Ideology* (New York: Oxford, 2000), 86–87.

9. Ibid., 20.

10. Ibid.

11. Ibid., 105.

12. Ibid., 106.

13. "Interview with Nosaka Akiyuki and Isao Takahata" *Animage,* June 1987; translated in *Animerica Anime & Manga Monthly* 2, no. 11 (1995).

14. The central conflict in these plays is that of "*ninjo* ('passion') conflicted with complex *giri* ('duties' or 'obligations') to family." These plays were performed in *joruui* "puppet" plays. "*Shinjū* Introduction," http://etext.virginia.edu/japanese/chikamatsu/shinju/kennelly-shinju.html (accessed October 15, 2005).

15. "Interview with Nosaka Akiyuki."

16. Takahata Isao, interviewed by Eija Niskanen, Japan, June 2005.

17. Okpyo Moon, "Marking Nature in Rural Japan," in *Japanese Images of Nature*, ed. Pamela J. Asquith and Arne Kalland (Surrey, U.K.: Curzon Press, 1997), 224–25.

18. Takahata Isao interview, June 2005.

19. Dennis Fukushima, "The Lost Fireflies," http://www2.hawaii.edu/~dfukushi/Hotaru.html (accessed July 30, 2005).

Control Room

TOM LOOSER

Gothic Politics: Oshii, War, and Life without Death

Even before the recent Gulf wars brought on talk of a new kind of war without end, war has been a common, even ubiquitous theme in anime and manga. With this perhaps in mind, an interviewer asked an artist involved with the 2005 "Gundam: Generating Futures" exhibition at Tokyo's Mori Art Museum in Ueno Park how the "Gundam generation" could talk about war with "no actual experience of war." The reply was that, simply, "each of us has 'experienced' virtual war in a variety of ways."[1]

It could be interesting to pursue the importance of virtual war (as opposed to "actual" war) in social life, or perhaps of the experience of war within video games (a question, at least in part, of technology). Certainly Oshii Mamoru, the anime director, filmmaker, artist, and novelist, works with each of these themes at different points in his own, typically war-centered, oeuvre. This article, however, takes up a far more generalized statement on how to think about war. In Oshii's novel *Blood: The Last Vampire; Night of the Beasts* (2000, *Kemonotachi no yoru*), war as it now is configured is presented as part of a foundational logic of contemporary political and social life.[2]

This is not to say that "war" is merely figurative (or fictional) for Oshii. *Blood: The Last Vampire; Night of the Beasts* is centered in part on the Vietnam

War—a real war with real practical effects in Japan. But the earlier, anime version is less interested in war itself and more focused on the effects of digital technologies on social life and the structure of history; as elsewhere in Oshii's work, the anime version plays with a layering of style and narrative to indicate basic changes in conceptions of life. The novel, on the other hand, is almost tritely traditional in its narrative form; if Oshii continues to be interested in the transformation of social life, at least in this case it would seem that technology and narrative form are not the only ways to think through these changes. And it is a consideration of changing bases of social form that Oshii gives us. The novel can therefore be read as a kind of anthropology, or an anthropological sociology: it is a discursis on the forms and orderings of life now, in Japan but also in the post–Vietnam era world in general.

> ODDLY, THE RECENT CONTEXT FOR CONTEMPORARY GOTHIC CULTURE, AS WELL AS THE OSHII STORY, IS THE GENERAL REMOVAL OF DEATH FROM OUR LIVES.

In this case, Oshii tells the story in terms and relations that are gothic, or a breed of vampire goth. I will add some definition to this below, but some first points to draw from this are simply that it specifies a particular form of life (which includes a particular mode of reproduction); it involves a particular relation *to* life (and death), and a specific mode of articulating the lines of life and death; and in this very relation to life, there is a politics—the articulation of life and death is never neutral. In Oshii's novel, the stakes involve what might be called a gothic politics.

By 2005, gothic style (especially in its connection to "Lolita" fashion) in Japan had reached a level of mainstream culture generic enough to have spawned widely varying and dissimilar subgenres (gothloli, elegant gothic Lolita, aristocratic gothic Lolita, vampire Lolita, sweet Lolita, punk Lolita, black Lolita, Victorian Lolita, etc.). All of these have only vague association with the qualities typically attached to the European gothic era, but there are a few central characteristics of a more classic gothic attitude that I think are relevant to current gothic culture and especially to Oshii's story.

First, gothic style is organic. This organicism might be expressed in stone, or it can be a machinic organicism, or even technological—as in the view of life seen in the "gothic organic" style of Web design[3]—but in each case the emphasis is on (differing) images of organic life. The gothic is also a creative rather than imitative attitude, though it is not always thought of as such. It is therefore an open view of life. Stylistically, there is less in the way of simple symmetry, and more irregular, evolving, and potentially endless forms; in many ways, it is not really a style at all but a set of open traits that are played with differently in different locales (The emphasis on creativity has in literal ways continued to be part of goth culture in Japan. Goth culture is celebrated in art magazines, and popular magazines devoted to goth culture regularly include patterns to help fans create their own dresses. More generally, there is a general do-it-yourself attitude in goth culture, as celebrated in the definitive movie *Kamikaze Girls*.[4])

Not only creative and open, the gothic (as the name for a life form) is based on a particular relation to an origin: its origin is typically dark and perhaps dreamlike, and while the relation to this origin may be romantic, it is otherwise uncertain. As a relation to an origin, it is in effect also a mode of history. As a history (especially as it develops in the nineteenth century, and still true now), its origins are commonly located in part in religion and the church, but the popular history that traces back to this churchly origin is for the most part typically secular. So this is a secular relation to a religious, spiritual origin. The gothic world thus has a complex relation to its own past— this is not exactly a mimetic relation to its own origin, and for this reason, too, it implies an open and creative structure of identity and history.[5]

Its origin may also in fact be deathly, or death itself—death, in other words, might serve as the origin of this lifeworld. While creative and open, therefore, it is nonetheless also about real fear, terror, and death. It also includes practical politics (the supposedly first gothic novel, Horace Walpole's *The Castle of Otranto*, begins with a personal crisis that is also a political crisis[6]), and these politics often work more through affect and emotion than rational argument. But the most important point to emphasize here is that the gothic includes both open creativity and death; these are not opposed.

Oddly, the recent context for contemporary gothic culture, as well as the Oshii story, is the general removal of death from our lives. In the United States, governmental attempts to outlaw images of death from war are a well-known and obvious example of this (death has therefore even become criminalized), but the trend is not confined to the government or to the United States. Given this wish to deny death, it makes the efflorescence of gothic culture, and gothic culture's dependency on death, all the more interesting, if not problematic.

In fact for Oshii, in *Blood: The Last Vampire; Night of the Beasts*, death is itself a way of reading history: "human history is the history of the struggle to cope with the dead."[7] "Coping" with death here means getting rid of it. And death does not go away easily; we are given a nearly chapter-long chronicle of how corpses and body parts and bones can keep reappearing to confront those who would efface death, and the various methods devised by human society to first control and then get rid of this evidence of the dead. So, in Oshii's story, human history is defined by the progressive removal of death from the sphere of life and history. In the past, we are told, society had a place for death, including in terms of a logic of causality—death had a place in life, as a causal force. But we have removed death, first as a causal force (death being present only as an effect) and then removing death even as an effect; in Oshii's account, the desire seems to be to have all evidence of death expelled entirely.

The novel is still a detective story of sorts, and these themes enter at the level of plot, too. The possibility of death returning is part of the premise of Oshii's story. Death seems to have caused a situation. As a strange, vague, and random set of murders, and bodies that may or may not have been there, death is an anomalous event that erupts almost incomprehensibly into the protagonist's life; much of the book then has to do with figuring out what this was—not just who (or what) did it, but what if anything happened, and what precisely the real "crime" was. Ultimately, the implicit suggestion is that the mere existence of death itself, as an influential force on life, is the true "crime" to be dealt with (thus paralleling our own criminalizing of death during the Iraq war).[8]

But why go to all this trouble? Why get rid of even the sign of death? The story's detective, Gotouda, goes through a long list of obvious motives, from superstition to the practical concerns of hygiene, but none of these reasons seem to be sufficient on their own to explain this desperation to get death out of the picture.[9] To anticipate a fuller argument below, there are more complicated and more contemporary concerns of power and social order at stake. Reminiscent of Agamben's "bare life" though not quite the same thing, the trajectory is toward a politics and a social order based, at least as one possible starting point, on a specific relation to and control over the lines of life and death.

A quick review of some key points about the storyline will help. The book begins with practical politics—the organization of anti–Vietnam War demonstrations in 1969. These demonstrations are formed by small "cells" of protestors, and while there is already a hint of organic form in all of this, for the most part this is simply a context of practical politics. In the midst of this, the protagonist Rei, a student activist, suddenly encounters an unexplainable murder scene in which the criminal is a sword-bearing vampiric being. So there are two quite dissimilar contexts juxtaposed at the outset, and it is unclear what the story itself is about—a historical fiction of 1960s student protests, or a vampire story of death? There seems to be some possibility that these two worlds are brought into contact, insofar as the vampires may be attacking antiestablishment protestors in particular, but for the most part the two groups of incidents seem unrelated, and the reader is left wondering if they are part of the same story.

The novel is a detective story of sorts, and there is a real detective helping in the attempt to explain the murders. But the murders, even by themselves, are complicated events. The detective Gotouda, for example, is a fairly low-level member of the city police, investigating the murders as a local incident. But he is also, it turns out, an inquisitor for the Pope, and somehow there is something at stake in the incident for the Vatican. So here, too, is a blurring of a situation that appears to be at once small and quotidian (a murder) while also tied to a larger situation, and a larger order of social law (religious law, and the religious attempt at social control).

Further, in discussing the murders with the student activists, the detective for some reason feels compelled to give us not only a lengthy history of death but also full histories of the relation between human and animal, of evolution and theories of evolution, and of the globalization of capital. This is presented in the midst of a dinner scene of massive consumption and described within the context of international state politics (two principal characters may be members of the Israeli intelligence agency Mossad). Somehow, all this is meant to be relevant to the crime witnessed by Rei.

As for the vampires, as in all the versions of Oshii's *Blood* series, there are really two types. One, a pure vampire, is a more radically and simply destructive type, and the other is the girl Saya—she is a hybrid, but at the same time the "true original"; she is, in other words, a singular form, neither really human or vampire.

There is an overall plot to the story, and time proceeds—the last chapter takes place thirty years after the late-sixties protests—but it is unclear whether anything actually happens or whether anything truly changes. In a way, the book is just a history of the protagonist Rei, and in the end his life is not much changed by any of these events (either the political events or the vampire murders). By some accounts, it is therefore really just a boring book.

A few initial points can be drawn from this story. First, 1969 is presented as a moment of radically active politics, a moment that therefore is in stark contrast to our own era. This contrast is enhanced by the story's own final chapter, set roughly in our own time (around the year 2000), when the former activist Rei has fallen into the very pedestrian and routine life of a married, subway-riding worker with a slight middle-aged paunch. By this time, he thinks back to the sixties nostalgically, as a time of real vitality.[10] The vampiric death, too, works as a radical eruption of something violently different, even in relation to the 1960s demonstrations. The story thus holds out possibilities of real difference, within a generalized time of war, even if it is unclear what kind of difference the sixties could pose to our time, or really pose to a world largely defined by the everyday politics of war.

Whether or not one thinks of the desire for the sixties, or the gothic death of slashing vampires, as a malignant desire, the book presents these as *our* desires. We want not only the sixties, it seems, but the gothic death of vampires. Or we at least partly want this; it holds something, or some possibility, for us. At the same time, the story gives us a world that assumes a kind of globalization or universalization of life. It would therefore be logical to have some nostalgia or desire for difference, but insofar as it is a universal life, difference could only arise from within.

A universalized life and politics could be conceived in a variety of ways. Oshii's story mentions global war and global capital but focuses then on evolution and a somewhat idiosyncratic image of evolution in particular. Oshii sets up Darwinian evolutionary theory as a kind of straw man that could easily be criticized, but with the implication that this fits our current popular worldview. As described by the detective, human evolution has a clear teleology, a clear direction that all humans have followed and that forecloses human nature into a preordained and universal thing. According to the "hunting hypothesis," mankind may have its origins in brutality and animality, but because of a "major adaptive disparity"[11] between humans and even other anthropoids, humans were destined to be distinct from and superior to all other animals. Thus, "anthropologists acknowledged the universality and equality of all men, [but] they also had to acknowledge a clear separation between men and animals."[12]

So through evolution, in this view, humans gain control over animals and over nature. Our identity is therefore complete, and our opposition to nature and animals provides this completion. This is the *law* of evolution: we *must* be universal but distinct from other animal life, and it is that distinction in turn that gives us our universal identity. Furthermore, these natural laws come to be embodied in our lives as social beings. The laws of evolution also determined that we would become social creatures, developing a collective will that would come to be known as "society," which eventually becomes autonomous and reified so that *it* governs *us*—society becomes the cause, a priori to us, and we are controlled by society (the detective cites Hobbes's *Leviathan* as a step in this direction).

This does not yet tell us anything about the exclusion of death. But it does provide a view of universal life and how universal life for humans (as a species) is guaranteed by the laws of exclusion (from animality).[13] Not only does humanity evolve into a being that is uni-

> THIS IS THE *LAW* OF EVOLUTION: WE *MUST* BE UNIVERSAL BUT DISTINCT FROM OTHER ANIMAL LIFE, AND IT IS THAT DISTINCTION IN TURN THAT GIVES US OUR UNIVERSAL IDENTITY.

versally distinct from animals, but in effect we always were distinct—we were destined to be different from the start, and so were really already human, already different, from the start. Here, too, any hope for difference in human life would have to come from within.

To the extent that there actually is some desire still for difference and change in human life, Oshii's book gives us at least two alternative views of how this might happen. In one, the assumption is that life (both social life and life in general) is cellular—it is made up of smaller units, almost singularities, which can act up in the same way that antibodies do. The antiwar demonstrations occurring at the start of the book are an example of this. As Oshii portrays it, demonstrations and collective protest can only emerge through vastly differing political and sometimes apolitical "cells," which come together at only provisional moments. Out of this, things just happen. Organic collective sociopolitical movement may occur, but it does not start out as united by anything in particular; theoretically, though, this could open the possibility of large-scale change, both structural and symbolic. This would not be an example of evolutionary change, for the most part, but it could lead to even radical change in its own way.

But in conjunction with this cellular view of life and politics, Oshii constantly raises the specter of what might be called "security" (my term, drawing loosely on Foucault, and not Oshii). Rather than a simple overpowering system of control, as I am using the term, "security" implies an almost cellular kind of intervention and regulation of events and society. In the novel, very different representatives of "law"—from the detective/religious inquisitor Gotouda, to the state spies from Mossada, to the hybrid vampire Saya—for varied reasons come together to control the events in just this way. To the extent that they are successful, nothing seems to have happened, and the story can return to a world of unchanging universal human life. The cellular qualities of life therefore do not seem to offer much hope for the emergence of any real change or difference in human social life.

The second view of things focuses on a larger, even structural conception of subjectivity. In part, this is a matter of mimesis and the assumption that we gain our identity through reflection. This includes a mimetic relation to our own origins. We may have evolved and developed, but, as described by the detective, humans had an adaptive superiority to other animals from the very start, and so our superior origins only reflect and insure our position as distinct from the rest of nature. This originary separation of human superiority over and against animal nature also helps to underscore what we are not; animal nature, because it is excluded from human nature, helps reflect what we are by showing what we are not.

> DEATH SHOULD NOT RETURN TO LIFE—THAT WOULD EXERT AN UNCONTROLLABLE INFLUENCE OVER LIFE—SO DEATH IS EXCLUDED FROM SOCIAL LIFE.

This mimetic order is also, though, an order of power and of law, in a way that helps to explain all the attention given in Oshii's novel to the exclusion of death. Here, the model invoked is reminiscent of Giorgio Agamben (via Walter Benjamin's critique of Carl Schmitt) and the politics of "bare" life.[14] In Agambenian terms, "nature" and the natural life of animals as described by the detective—nature as distinct from humanity—is something like bare life. That is to say, nature might seem to be a relatively neutral kind of biological materiality and the stuff of which humanity might make something or use to make their own lives better (even simply as food). Nature, though, is consequently a distinct realm separated from the sociopolitical world of humanity and human control—it is excluded from that world. And yet that very image of nature, as excluded from the social and political world of humans, is precisely what constructs the position of humans as sovereign over nature (and of nature as merely the materiality that humans have control over). Further, that image of nature comes from the human world; it may appear to be neutral of any human social or political concerns, but it is defined from within humanity's laws of nature. The relation of natural life to humans is, therefore, an inclusive exclusion. Humanity has come to exclude nature, but in the form of bare life—a materiality of "life" excluded from the world of human sovereignty, even while it gained this position of excluded neutrality from within human sovereignty (one could also say that humanity thus partakes of natural life and the laws of nature but occupies an exceptional position over and above the laws of nature).

This gives humanity the image of sovereign control over life (the basis for the many commentaries on biopolitics). It also creates an image of nature on its own as free of politics, and humanity as the sole and autonomous realm of politics. Politics, therefore, is founded on that which is excluded from politics. This is key to Oshii's novel.

The same general principles apply to the historical exclusion of death from human social life, as given in Oshii's story. Death, in the detective's history, might still be visible as an effect, but the primary motivation in expelling death from human life was to expel death as an inexplicably causal force. Death should not return to life—that would exert an uncontrollable influence over life—so death is excluded from social life. Death might reflect back, in some general way, the boundaries of life as we know it, but it should not and cannot come back to actually influence and trouble our conceptions of life itself, or change them (that would be showing the *real* limits of our image of life, and productively pointing to other potential conceptions). Death, as the excluded other to life, therefore only helps to firm up the image of life as we know it. In a sense, death abandons any claim to effective meaningful causation in life—to making us see different possibilities in life—and in doing so, abandons itself to the sovereignty of a sort of pure life (life that fully controls the image of death and therefore the limits of life). And lastly, paralleling the relationship between humanity and nature, death is placed in a position ostensibly free of politics, while politics is confined to the realm of life alone. In the story, for example, one could think of the opening juxtaposition of the vampiric murders to the obviously political conflicts of the antiwar demonstration; though concurrent, they apparently had no relation (and if there were politics behind the vampire murders, it is precisely that connection that the various characters want to keep hidden). In our own world, one could think again of the policy of criminalizing images of deceased soldiers, as if those very images of death might come back, as political, and influence daily life. In these ways too, death is the excluded exception to life, apparently free of politics and power, even while this excluded position itself is given by political law and helps to firm up the sovereign control of political law over death (and therefore over the lines of life and death).

This helps explain the complicated significance of the murders that appear in the midst of the antiwar demonstrations, and the apparent disjuncture between the two sets of events (random vampiric murder versus student demonstrations). Insofar as the initial murder seems to be random and quotidian, having nothing to do with the demonstrations, it reinforces the opposition of war (as political) and death (as quotidian and apolitical); an everyday death has no relevance to the larger political situation, and the lines between everyday life and war are kept neat and clear.[15] One could even say the same about the two sets of events as genres or story types that seem to be incompatible (a vampire fantasy versus a historical fiction of the 1960s student demonstrations in Japan): a vampire story, as only a fantasy, should not have any real influence over a real historical fiction, or beyond that, over real historical political conditions. There is nothing political about a vampire story by these terms. And yet it is this very exclusion of vampire-as-fantasy as defined by our vision of the "real" politics of history that helps affirm that there can be only one real approach to understanding of the politics of the Vietnam War, or of war in general—a practical politics, unconcerned with larger abstract notions of life, or the relation between conceptions of life and social structures of power.

The first and more obvious effect of this is that it hence brings life itself, and the dividing lines of life versus death and humanity versus nature, into play as an element of politics and power. It makes human life seem naturally distinct from nature, and the lines between politics and death clear and permanent. Death is now subsumed under the sovereignty of life and politics, and it affirms the sovereignty of life and politics. But more importantly, it makes politics into a separate realm. Why should a murder, or a vampire story, have anything to do with the Vietnam War? Why should those opposed to the Vietnam War care in any way about vampires, or the history of death, or evolution? Politics, therefore, has nothing to do with mediation, and in particular it has nothing to do with the mediations upon which social order is apparently built. Politics, then, is divorced from the more general mediations and logics that underpin the social order as it is.

There is, in other words, a lot riding on that separation of politics from murder and death that the book gives us at the outset. That would seem to be where the laws of evolution have led us: a world in which humans have power not only over animals but over natural life, and death and politics have nothing to do with that division. In effect, this implies that the very laws of evolution are potentially at stake in the process of keeping the vampire murders from intruding into the political scene of the antiwar protests. It is a matter of police law, of course, but also the laws of life. Nor is that the only thing at stake in the strange events of the vampire murders, although Oshii's characters are much less clear on this.

As the principal characters continue to discuss the murders and who committed them, the conversation shifts from the history of life and death to a history of the Rothschild family, portrayed as a unique and uniquely powerful economic power ("Apparently, the conversation was shifting from anthropology to economics").[16] This family too, somehow, was part of the criminal context of the murders and tied in with the vampirism—they are connected to the vampire Saya in particular (I return to this connection below). There are several distinguishing features of the family. For one, they were founders of a multinational corporation, but they were in fact deeply involved in manipulating the internal politics of nation-states. For this reason, parallel to the risk of death intruding into the realm of politics, there is the risk of politics intruding into the ostensibly sovereign realm of corporate finance. Also, because this was not only a multinational corporation but a truly transnational family, there was the apparent risk of unbounded family and finance ties intruding into the sovereign political power of nations. This would explain why the two men from the Israeli secret police, Mossad, were hunting the vampires. Further, although the Rothschilds were Catholics, they worked with Jews; the risk here is that the sovereignty of Catholic law would be breached if the exclusion of Jews were not maintained. This would explain the interest of the detective Gotouda—who is really a Vatican inquisitor—in hunting the vampires (and ultimately it is the sovereignty of religious law in general that he is there to protect; the inquisitors, we are told, embarked on a violent campaign precisely to protect religious truth over freedom and to maintain the exclusion even of the state from religion in order to protect the sovereignty of religious law as truth).

What is really at stake in the vampire murders, in other words, is not only sovereignty but a whole set of realms of sociopolitical sovereignty and the connections between these: the sovereign political power over life and the limits of life, given to society by evolutionary law (which also, as science, provides for the sovereign identity of humans over animal nature); the sovereignty of truth over freedom, as given by religion; the sovereignty of politics over and against corporate finance, as given by history; the sovereignty of nations over transnational formations, as also given by history; and the sovereignty of each of these realms (life, science, religion, finance, and nationalism) not only from each other but in particular from any real politics of death. Somehow, all of these interests are condensed in the murders and in the vampires. It is that condensation, or bringing together of things— and the revelation that they *are* connected—that may be the biggest or most monstrous threat of all. Thus, although none of the characters involved with the murders have any other interest in common, and although each remains independent, all of them conspire together, as "law," to fight the vampires.

These workings might be made clearer by looking at the vampires themselves. Vampires are, first of all, very much like humans in this story. They have common evolutionary origins with humans, and they look just like us. They thus do have a mimetic relationship with us and could reflect precisely what we are (Rei, therefore, is initially horrified that the vampires are all "pursuing and destroying man's mirror image").[17] But they are also unlike us—they branched off into a parallel evolutionary branch; they are animal-istic and are out to destroy us. They are therefore figures of death, and can and should be destroyed as such. If there is a mimetic relation, it is really one of inversion or opposition: they are more like basic natural animals, who in turn reflect the "humanity" in us; they are uncertain in their boundaries (they are human in form but can morph their bodies into beings with wings) in ways that reflect the certainty of our own species; and they are therefore a threat to the clarity of life itself in ways that we supposedly are not. They are accordingly that element of humankind that is excluded from humanity, and through this exclusion they confirm the identity of the human species (as above mere animalism and so on) and the sovereignty of humans and of human law in all the forms just described. Like Agamben's reading of the Ro-man *homo sacer*, they are the portion of humanity that law stipulates must be expelled as criminal and that can be killed but not sacrificed—that is, they can be killed, but not in ways that might be significant to the given form of human society. They only confirm the given law of society, which governs their own exclusion.[18]

To the extent that this explains Oshii's vampires, then vampires (and vampiric death) function for the secure law of power and sovereignty. They reflexively secure the boundaries between life and death, human and animal, and so on, and, as figures of the controlled criminalization of death, they embody the giving over of their own substance (natural life and so on) to the sovereignty of society. More simply put, the relation between humans and vampires creates an image of life that is controlled and fixed. Life and exis-tence as potentiality is foreclosed. Consequently, there is not much possibil-ity for anything other than the status quo—no alternative visions or opening of life, truth, or politics. The exclusion of death from daily life that one sees in our times would seem to be an ultimate carry-through of this logic: because the normalcy and stability of the status quo, and of the current organiza-tion of power, is still somehow dependent on that excluded element (death or vampires), that element of exclusion remains somewhat threatening. The (impossible) ideal would therefore be to somehow truly excise it altogether, leaving an order that is naturalized, and so unquestionably correct. The de-sire to excise the image of death thus is an outcome of a tendency toward a kind of totalitarianism.

This in many ways sounds like the pessimistic readings one sees of Fou-cault and Agamben, in which subjectivity is described as only an effect of power, and not much place is given for agency or critique. But within the mimetic relations of vampire and human, there is perhaps some possibility yet. This includes a possibility within mimesis that does not figure in Agamben's analyses.

As Oshii's novel shows, vampires may be excluded from the realm of humanity, but the mimetic relationship does not entirely go away. They may have branched off from the genealogical line of humanity, but they retain a "parallel" genealogy to us. Thus, their origins are our origins, and they continue to parallel us—they continue, in part, to look like us, so the mimetic relationship holds. At the same time, they are not like us, as we have seen. They are animal-like, they can push their bodies into other forms, and they do not die in the same way (they live in a different time frame, for example) that humans do. Therefore, as one character puts it, "the mirror-image of man is a hideous monster."[19] To the extent that vampires are like us, in other words, they destabilize the mimetic relations of sameness and opposition. They reflect us, but in doing so they might also reflect an instability within us. It is a complicated mimesis.

> **THE RELATION BETWEEN HUMANS AND VAMPIRES CREATES AN IMAGE OF LIFE THAT IS CONTROLLED AND FIXED. LIFE AND EXISTENCE AS POTENTIALITY IS FORECLOSED.**

This double agency is evident in the vampires themselves. On the one hand, although they are like us, regular vampires are also of a clearly separate species (and can be killed), and so even if they somehow present a threat to the stable laws of humankind, they can be both excluded and dispensed with in untroubling ways. They therefore are the perfect "criminal" to the laws of humanity. But, on the other hand, the most important vampire, Saya, is less easily placed. She is a hybrid of sorts, with mixed vampire and human blood. She is very unlike humans in some ways (she never seems to change or age, for example, and she too can sprout vampire wings), and yet she looks just like humans. She is also, as noted earlier, the "original" vampire. She therefore embodies mixture and uncertainty, and so, as the true original, this uncertainty and this singularity would appear to be the true essence of vampirism. Further, she is a product of the Rothschild family described above (a criminal family that, like the vampires in general, is described as "parallel" to normal human society), and it is the Rothschild family that is involved in all the overlapping interests described above (of cross-religious powers, transnational business, corporate meddling in politics, and so on). Saya may be a vampire, but her appearance will thus start to complicate all the lines of division and exclusion that sovereignty is based on, including the separation of animal from human, and of nature and death from politics. A murder scene in which Saya is involved thus raises all kinds of complicated questions and cannot be dismissed as "just" a death, unrelated to antiwar demonstrations or other sociopolitical concerns.

Saya is, therefore, a far greater threat to society than other vampires. She threatens to reflect back an uncertainty in all the boundaries that sovereign social law depends on, as well as the codependency and conspiratorial character of all these laws (evolutionary, political, etc.). It is in her being that one can see how death might have political consequences, how humans might be also animalistic (a kind of ongoing openness), how international business might be working for or against national political sovereignty, how religious truth could be tied up with political suppression, and how all of these lines and laws of society are co-implicated with each other. Saya is hence the greatest threat of all—not a threat that is controllable but a threat to the larger bases of sovereign power. To the extent that her appearance in the murder scenes threatens to reveal all these connections, the murder events *are* far more than simple crime scenes. It is perhaps for this reason that one of the principal characters involved with chasing the vampires says that the goal is not just to kill vampires but, more importantly, to conceal their very existence, and not just to get rid of the bodies but to get rid of all evidence that any such event (or any such being) ever existed.[20] The mere existence of vampires and death, even as elements that appear as that which is excluded from humanity and politics, is just too dangerous. Mimesis itself thus can be dangerous, and can provide the opening to potentiality and difference.[21]

The ultimate trajectory of all this is consequently a desire for a world free of the threats of mimesis, and therefore a world free of the threats of death—a desire, that is, for an impossible world of pure or universal life. Although Oshii's story attempts to hint at the varieties of social law that are co-implicated in this logic of power, it is therefore death and its separation from politics that gets the most focus. Death is also the primary basis for Saya's own uncertainty of being. As a hybrid, she brings death, but she also saves life. She can be killed, but she seems to live forever. She even looks deathly, and yet she is erotically beautiful; she is a true goth. Rei, the story's male protagonist and human parallel of Saya, is at times clearly in love (or lust) with her.

The necrophilia of Saya, then, is equivalent to the possibility that death itself might return to show the limits of a supposedly universal life, of pure life and empty politics. Death and vampires might reflect back to us the violence of a system that continues—like a world with war that continues—supposedly without meaningful death, and in which politics is supposedly without ties to death, science, religion, or transnational corporate finance. A world that logically can and would continue as is, indefinitely, precisely because it is the basis of pure universal life.

In thinking through the practical implications of this, Oshii would seem to be coming dangerously close to calling for the kind of actual terrorism of suicide bombers that we now see in the midst of war—a real death that we cannot easily answer and that therefore is potent. And within the story, Oshii does have Rei say, early on, that he must accept the idea of being violent and of doing violence to another person. That, says Rei, is the only way to do something that is truly irrevocable, creating an irrevocable change.

But it is also more than just Rei's relationship to Saya that seems to hold a similar possibility. For Rei, Saya is the only figure of real change, and real desire, and therefore real life. He is in effect possessed by her, in what is a kind of gothic possession, perhaps with death. This is evident already in their first meeting, when he is "pulled in and held captive" by her eyes, even while these eyes are "piercing him with an acutely homicidal glare."[22] There is something potentially productive or open about this. Possession, after all, entails a willingness to give oneself over to another, and so to otherness, as Saya surely is for Rei. Rei's commitment to irrevocable change emphasizes this: a desire for irrevocable change, after all, implies not just a tolerance of change and difference but a wish for and a responsibility *to* it.

Is this, then, where the *Blood: The Last Vampire* novel leaves us? With a new, more critically and creatively open vision of life and politics? Not necessarily. It is not that easy or that simple. The story certainly does not lead to much that is new and different for Rei. In the final chapter of the book, Rei has simply ended up caught in the same routine structures of everyday life that have characterized much of postwar Japan. The sixties protests, and the vampires too, have accordingly become nothing more than the originary past of the same old world. Each of Rei's compatriots, also, end up in that same everyday world with its hackneyed, trite problems.

Saya herself, having returned after thirty years, is "completely unchanged." We are told that "the only thing . . . different was the image of Rei that must have been reflected in her eyes," and although he has been "completely altered," what is different about him is simply that he has given up on all the rage and indignation he had as a student activist, and given in to the harsh realities of life.[23] He has given in to the law of life as unchangeable.[24]

Both the vampires and the sixties politics, therefore, reflect back nothing but the everyday *as* banal, and as unchanging—a pure life, perhaps. War may have continued through much of this time, but as one sees with television,

> IN HIS ONGOING DESIRE TO SEE HIMSELF REFLECTED IN HER EYES, THOSE "MONSTER" EYES CONTINUE TO RETURN TO HIM ALL THE OPENNESS AND MEDIATING CONNECTIONS TO POLITICS THAT HE SEEMED TO HAVE LOST.

antiwar protest and vampires and the gothic in general end up merely as spectacles of death and change. By these terms, it may be that a true gothic politics is not possible.

This is not therefore a cheerfully optimistic story; it is at best cautionary, and perhaps not even that. But still, Saya does not just go away. And although she is described as unchanged, what is unchanging about her is precisely her status as a singularity, as open and uncertain, and as an embodiment of all the mediations between death and politics and everyday life that seem to have been overcome. Furthermore, at the end of the story Rei is still possessed by Saya—he is still bewitched by her eyes.[25] He sees, reflected in Saya's eyes, what he has lost, and the politics and possibilities that have not been realized. But those "precious days [*do*] come rushing back to Rei" when he looks at her; that mimesis is still alive. In his ongoing desire to see himself reflected in her eyes, those "monster" eyes continue to return to him all the openness and mediating connections to politics that he seemed to have lost. She is a return to mediation between all those links that appear to have been severed, including between life and death, human and animal, identity and possibility. As a return to mediation, she is a return to politics.

Life can never be completely subsumed by law. Life will never be entirely a self-same proposition (Oshii tells us that over and over in his various works), and so the idea of a pure or universal life is an impossibility. Death can never be made to go away from society or be wholly separated from obvious social and political concerns and implications. Sovereignty over life, therefore, can never be complete. Reflecting on life itself seems to reveal this, in the same way that a fictional story of a vampiric murder can serve as a critical reflection on contemporary politics.

Notes

1. *Art It* 3, no. 3 (Summer/Fall 2005): 62. The artist referred to is Odani Motohiko. For more on the "Gundam: Generating Futures" exhibition, see Takayuki Tatsumi, "*Gundam* and the Future of Japanoid Art," and Christopher Bolton's response, *Mechademia* 3 (2008): 191–98.

2. Oshii Mamoru, *Blood: The Last Vampire; Night of the Beasts,* trans. Camellia Nieh (Milwaukie, Ore.: Dark Horse Press, 2000). For a more direct and clearer discussion of the story itself, see Timothy Perper and Martha Cornog's review in *Mechademia 2: Networks of*

Desire (2007): 295–98. I would like to have taken that (and related articles in *Mechademia*) up more fully, but this paper remains primarily as first formulated for the Bloodlines conference at McGill University in winter 2007.

3. This is a style developed by Aurelia Harvey, among others. As a technique and an image of life, it would seem to involve characteristics now typically associated with new digital media: it uses analog imagery of life, but only as "building blocks" that can be digitally combined in various ways. In this view, life is irregular, multilayered, imperfect, and open (and therefore at times mysterious) but also decadent and deathly.

4. *Shimotsuma monogatari*, dir. Nakashima Tetsuya; translated as *Kamikaze Girls*, subtitled DVD (VIZ Media, 2004). The film is based on the novel by the same name; for an English language translation (by Akemi Wegmuller), see Takemoto Novala, *Kamikaze Girls* (San Francisco: VIZ Media, 2008).

5. In practical history, there are in fact at least three relatively distinct, even unrelated sets of origins to the gothic. These include reference to the Visigoths and Ostrogoths, Germanic peoples who harried and eventually overthrew portions of the Roman Empire in the third through sixth centuries. A second reference is the style of architecture, largely religious (cathedrals, churches, and abbeys) but including some universities, in the European Middle Ages. And a third would be the romantic literature begun in the Victorian and Edwardian eras, and still referred to today. Not only are gothic culture's origins complicated, therefore, they are also multiple and open in that sense. Furthermore, one of the characteristics of the term "gothic" that does seem to carry through these different eras is the idea of the gothic as barbarian and, at least initially, violent. That is, there is a common idea of the "gothic" as an attitude that opposes the status quo, perhaps violently, but especially in more recent times, more creatively (even medieval churches were considered barbarically creative in their wildly ornate forms) and openly.

6. In this sense, as genres, the gothic might be thought of as opposed to melodrama. See Horace Walpole, *The Castle of Otranto* (London: Penguin, 2001), originally written in 1764.

7. Oshii, *Blood,* 115.

8. Going over the possible ways of dealing with dead bodies, the detective Gotouda explains that, while bodies might be dispensed with either to hide just the body itself as evidence or to use the body so that it might be discovered in a controlled way, the truest motive for hiding a body is to "conceal the incidents themselves"—to make it seem as if none exists (144). That is the case with the incidents in this story. There is no certainty that they actually did exist and that there was therefore any death at all.

9. The detective's name would be "Gotōda" in the romanization system used elsewhere in this volume, but here I have kept the alternate spelling "Gotouda" used in Nieh's translation.

10. At the story's end, as Rei thinks he has caught a glimpse of someone who could have been Saya, "the memory of those long-gone, ridiculously precious days came rushing back to Rei, accompanied by a deep ache of regret" (298).

11. Ibid., 277.

12. Ibid., 246.

13. In the detective's vision, animality displaces race. As he describes it, prior to World War II science attempted to explain human identity as hierarchical, using race as the

basis of that hierarchy. This became impossible after the Nazis, and this political impossibility was itself a step toward the postwar universalizing of "human" equality, and the discursive opposition of humanity and animality. See 232 and 245–47.

14. I will not try to fully summarize Agamben's writings on bare life here—this article is not meant to be wholly in dialog with Agamben's framework—but there are a few salient points that are key to the argument I am trying to make and that may be worth some detail. Agamben is perhaps less interested in social form and more interested in an analysis of the general nature of sovereign power. Sovereignty, as Agamben describes it, is first of all dependent on a relation to law, but in such a way that law is in part excluded from sovereignty. At one end of social life, Agamben points to the early Roman role of the *homo sacer,* a person legally defined as a criminal who can be ostracized from everyday life. He is therefore placed outside of the law, and though placed in that position by law, he is no longer protected by social law; others can therefore kill him. The *homo sacer* is accordingly beyond the juridical order, and yet his position of exclusion also reaffirms the legitimacy of the juridical order; and although he is not protected by law, he is therefore also considered somehow "sacred." At the opposite end of the social order, the ruler is in an inverse but similar position. The ruler's place as legitimate ruler comes from the legal order, and yet the ruler's ultimate expression of power is the power *over* the law, the power to suspend the law and create exceptions to the law. The law gives the ruler the right to do this (to stand above the law); sovereignty, therefore, depends on the law, and yet in its ultimate form it is beyond the law. Sovereignty thus is premised on the presence of a legal order and the appearance of legal order, but it is in fact also outside of this order and based on a state of extralegal exception and exclusion.

Second, life and the definition of life are incorporated as part of this connection between law and sovereignty. In some ways, life is encompassed as the most important aspect of this juridical relation. Although biological life at its most basic and generic level might seem to be prior to any legal definition and therefore neutral, Agamben shows this basic level of life to be defined and circumscribed by law, and so derived from law. This is "bare" life—life that social law defines as prior to or outside social law. It is life that can and should be made into good social and political form, but that is nonetheless excluded from society and politics. The implication is that social and political form, and therefore social and political sovereignty, depend on the ability to control and define life, including the very distinction between "bare" life and the well-formed life given by the social and political order. Sovereignty for Agamben thus has always involved not only the state of exception but also the control over life at its most basic levels; these are part of the essential nature of sovereignty rather than a new social and historical development. My own view is closer to Foucault's emphasis on a historical shift toward an increasing control over life, and my reading of Oshii's novel assumes a historically specific set of convergences.

Lastly (but most relevant to this article), because "bare" life is defined within a framework that excludes it from the everyday sociopolitical order of things, life appears to be naturally excluded from politics—even though life is a critical grounds for politics and sovereignty.

See in particular Giorgio Agamben, *Homo Sacer: Sovereign Power and Bare Life* (Stanford, Calif.: Stanford University Press, 1998), and *State of Exception* (Chicago: University of Chicago Press, 2005).

15. But if one pushes this logic just a little bit, there is one crucial shift that this reveals: while war might be the exception to everyday life, it is here put in the realm of politics and sovereignty, while everyday life would seem to be excluded from real politics and action. War, in other words, is shown to rule over everyday life rather than the other way around.

16. Oshii, *Blood*, 258.

17. Ibid., 252.

18. The obvious example in contemporary life would again be the American soldiers in the Iraq war. They are allowed to be killed, but their deaths are not thought of as "sacrifices"—their deaths should not come back to meaningfully intrude on, or haunt, society's perception of the war or society's perception of current life during war. (In fact, as has been frequently noted in the U.S. media, sacrifice seems to be a concept that is part of this war's exclusion.)

19. Oshii, *Blood*, 252.

20. Ibid.

21. It may be for this reason that the detective Gotouda says of vampires, "their only real threat is the ethical crisis they present to human beings" (ibid., 254). Rather than some strange animal that just wants to kill or eat us, they are challenges to our basic laws of society and the ways in which these laws ground the appearance of certainty, clarity, and sovereign control over identity.

22. Ibid., 26.

23. Ibid., 297.

24. The implication is that not only life but change and the possibility of change have come under the sovereign control of society as it is constituted.

25. Saya, dressed like a high school girl, is at this endpoint of the story placed in opposition to normal high school girls. Rei has come to hate normal high schools—their heavily made-up faces make them look "like ageless monsters." In other words, they have come to mirror the kind of unchanging life that is so meaningless to Rei. Saya, on the other hand, still holds real interest for real life and real change, even while she is still so deathly. Oshii, *Blood*, 296–97.

MARK ANDERSON

Oshii Mamoru's *Patlabor 2*: Terror, Theatricality, and Exceptions That Prove the Rule

In foregrounding controversy surrounding the Japanese use of military force, *Patlabor 2* (1993, *Kidō keisatsu Patoreibaa 2 the Movie*) is a work that participated in the widespread early 1990s Japanese questioning of Japan's postwar settlement with the United States. It specifically raises questions about the qualification of Japanese national sovereignty that flowed from Article 9 and the U.S.–Japan Security Treaty.[1] It thus questions Japanese complicity in postwar U.S. "global police" violence (the most immediate context was the Gulf War conducted two years before the film's release), dramatizing what critics began to suggest was a mistaken conflation of Japanese and U.S. security as institutionalized in the very one-sided U.S.–Japan security relationship. In *Patlabor 2*, the boundaries of Japanese identity and security strategy appear riven and contested, with a range of conflicting approaches to controlling and resolving these claims depicted. In addition, the film connects analog and digital media to competing perspectives on the status of 1990s Japan as a nation and Tokyo as a globalized city. In sum, *Patlabor 2* offers an exploration of the shifting status of media, sovereignty, and warfare in the Pacific in the post–Gulf War era.

Patlabor 2 stages a series of attacks— it is initially unclear if the attacks are the military acts of governments or terrorist acts—that are depicted as too singular to be framed within the established rules and procedures of the Japanese security bureaucracy, the security police, and the Self-Defense Forces. The film depicts opportunism and moral abjection in the civilian leadership of Japanese security. It argues that Japanese security has reached a state of emergency that its legally responsible leadership fails to recognize as such. It dramatizes the efforts of competing factions of the Japanese security state to determine the exception to the rule of Japanese law. In this respect, to use Carl Schmitt's terms, the film shows how factions within Japan struggle to determine the location of sovereignty with respect to Japanese security.[2]

The media and technologies of perception that *Patlabor* 2 relentlessly foregrounds are implicated in the theatricality of such attempts to both challenge and unify the space of Japanese national and personal identity, strategic theaters of conflict, and national law and order. The first domestic attack depicted is on the Yokohama Bay Bridge (Figure 1). Visually, as Ueno and Fisch have noted, the attack scene is reminiscent of video footage from "smart" munitions deployed by the United States during the Gulf War.[3] As if to confirm the associations with the Gulf War, the accompanying news report uses language that nearly elides the term for the bridge attack with that for the Gulf War (*Wangansen/Wangan sensō*). Thus the film indirectly but provocatively invites the viewer to associate what is at one point feared to have been a U.S. fighter jet's unprovoked peacetime attack on a Japanese bridge with U.S. conduct of the first Gulf War.

During the Gulf War, many critics decried the dearth of images and the manipulation of images from the war zone, which contributed to a sense that the war reporting conflated spectacle and war, and in a manner that implicated viewers in its mendacity and manipulation. It was widely seen as a spectacle in which obvious strategic interests were routinely disavowed and misrepresented: namely, it was reported that the United States fought for Kuwaiti freedom, not for control over and access to Kuwaiti oil; that the war was for democracy, not to restore the Kuwaiti aristocracy to power or further the subjugation of Islam within the capitalist world order; that Saddam was Hitler reincarnated, not a former client of the U.S. intelligence

FIGURE 1. This video from a Hellfire missile closing in on the Yokohama Bay Bridge closely resembles video from the "smart bombs" that memorably defined the Pentagon's carefully orchestrated presentation of the first Gulf War.

state whose interests began to diverge from those of the United States. Some commentators stressed that the media staging of the war barred communication between those on opposite sides of the TV screen on which the war was depicted.[4] In general, the spectacle of war was construed as a degradation of war, in which war had become a "war-like event" made to fit into the media programming and advertising requirements of a consumerist society. Information seemed to generate the event, where one might have expected or hoped the event would guide the information.[5]

Many called for an interrogation into the status of the war as an event, describing it as a simulation, a fraud, and a farce.[6] For some critics, the real warmongers were those who were willing to pretend that the Gulf War was a traditional or conventional war rather than acknowledging it to be a new variety of promotional campaign on behalf of weapons sales, U.S. international authority, and militarized globalization. For others still, it reflected a new co-implication of media, the military, and the state, which had restructured the very concept of a theater of war, making it subject to real-time media coverage that reduced the significance of territorial spatiality.[7] The Gulf War was also identified with a deference of military will to an international legal order divorced from justice on the part of the U.S.- and UN-aligned forces, given that they effectively permitted and oversaw Saddam Hussein's slaughter of Kurdish and Shiite Iraqi resistance subsequent to the end of formal hostilities between Iraq and UN forces in the name of respecting the principle of national sovereignty.

Patlabor 2 opens with scenes three years prior to the present of the film. After mechanical failure debilitates a Japanese mecha, several other Japanese mecha from the same unit stationed in Southeast Asia with UN markings come under fire from tanks and rocket-propelled grenades presumably controlled by local forces. The Japanese pilots request permission from UN officials to return fire, but permission is twice denied. The pilots are instructed to wait until armed Canadian assistance arrives. The unit leader, Tsuge Yukihito, ultimately defies these orders, killing the most immediately threatening enemy target, a tank. But he is too late to save his men. As a direct result of dysfunctional rules of engagement that prohibit Japanese peacekeepers from exercising their right of self-defense, all members of the Japanese unit appear to lose their lives, with the exception of Tsuge.[8]

Contemporary action in the film begins with the destruction of the Yokohama Bay Bridge by air-to-surface missile from an F-16 fighter.[9] News reports announce that the fighter appears to have been a plane from the Japan Self-Defense Force, but the JSDF directly denies this. The two protagonists, Gotō and Nagumo (captains of the second section of the security police whose units are responsible for the mecha referred to in the title as "patlabors"), meet with a JSDF intelligence officer, Arakawa. Arakawa informs them that the plane in question was stolen from a U.S. base in Japan, and the prime suspect is Tsuge Yukihito and the group associated with him. Arakawa delivers an extended disquisition on the hypocrisy of Japan's current pretense to be at peace and to represent an alternative to the rule of force in international affairs. His point is that this makes accepted understandings of Article 9 and the U.S.–Japan security alliance illegitimate, even anti-Japanese. Shortly afterward Tokyo comes under threat of attack from three Japanese F-16s (detected on JSDF headquarters radar), but the attack proves to be a phantom attack produced by hackers who compromised the JSDF network.[10]

As Gotō and Nagumo begin their search for Tsuge, their work is interrupted by an order from their superiors to mobilize the police around a JSDF base at Nerima. Gotō and Nagumo deploy their personnel, but in a manner that their bosses interpret as defiant. While civilian leadership initially creates difficulties by falsely impugning the JSDF, it proceeds to compound the error by blaming the police for the standoff created by its own actions.

It then declares martial law, mobilizing select units of the SDF throughout the Tokyo area.[11]

Under interrogation by their civilian superiors, Nagumo and Gotō express their contempt for the behavior of civilian government officials who have sacrificed the reputation of the Japanese military and police, and whose desire for personal political gain has obfuscated responsibility and thus endangered the people. Both officers are then relieved of duty and taken into custody. At the same time, the Tsuge group has mounted an attack on Tokyo with three helicopter gunships. Several bridges are destroyed, and JSDF command and control connections are taken out. Gotō and Nagumo physically attack the officers who detain them, escaping in a patrol car while Tsuge's attack copters strafe the police building.

While suspended from duty, Gotō and Nagumo organize a paramilitary, extralegal response to Tsuge, using the manpower and resources of their security police section to capture Tsuge by force. They eventually succeed in placing him under arrest. In the meantime, Tokyo is held hostage by three airships circling over the city and carrying poison gas. In defiance of direct orders, Gotō and Nagumo ultimately prevail over Tsuge by force of arms in a paramilitary action, which all concerned know to be illegal and unapproved. The JSDF intelligence officer, Arakawa, is arrested while the vigilante action is in progress, but the arresting officers never question the legality of Gotō and Nagumo's ongoing activities. The film ends with Tsuge in detention and no hint of legal sanctions or consequences for the actions of Captains Gotō and Nagumo.[12]

THEATRICALITY AND *PATLABOR 2*

Sam Weber writes that, insofar as a medium may not be construed as self-contained or self-regulating, an element of theatricality accompanies the spread of the contemporary electronic media. The electronic media are relational and situational; they constitutively depend on extraneous elements such as spectators or audiences. The media involve not only a delocalization of physical settings but also a change in the structure and function of such settings in their relation to the physical; including physical bodies. Consequently, there can be no delocalization of media or of modes of perception without a corresponding relocalization.[13]

Weber suggests that the military sense of the term "theater" speaks to a salient trait of media: it is a medium in which conflicting forces strive to secure the perimeter of a place in dispute. Theater implies the imposition of a border rather than a representational-aesthetic genre. That means theatricality is a problematic process of placing, framing, and situating rather than a process of representation.[14]

The opening sequence of *Patlabor 2* presents a highly mediated experience of combat, which is depicted largely via digital control screens in conjunction with overwrought, near hysterical radio communication between the participants. This is followed by a sequence of what appears to be a less mediated and more spontaneous depiction of testing a "labor," that is, a labor mecha. But we later discover that it is simulated operation of a labor for the purpose of pilot training. Early in the film, then, we confront the paradox whereby *simulated* civilian experience appears less mediated and more "real" than the highly mediated *real-life* experience of contemporary warfare. For viewers of the film, the boundary between simulated experience and real experience (albeit highly mediated) of characters becomes extremely difficult to distinguish.

The film also systematically stages the delocalization and relocalization of visual experience that occurs with analog broadcast television: the screen before the viewer depicts television monitors carrying news broadcasts.[15] The film shows the news broadcast announcing military mobilization and a state of emergency by following it across TV monitors of various sizes over a range of private and public settings, from homes to offices to shop windows to enormous outdoor displays in public squares. At other points, the viewer is presented with videotape produced for a karaoke video being replayed and digitally manipulated as evidence for the purpose of surveillance. The tape directly contradicts visual evidence on a public news broadcast.

In other words, there is visual evidence that suggests the official broadcast presentation of national reality is at best dubious or unknowable, at worst simply false.[16] *Patlabor 2* thus shows corporate TV news broadcasts as a powerful site for the manipulation of public opinion by forces as yet unknown. Broadcasts effectively function as weaponry within a public sphere that is somehow broken and no longer rational or coherent. The visual evidence casts doubt on the veracity of both the Japanese state and news authorities, hinting that they routinely lie.

On the more typically cybernetic side of things, the film vividly depicts smaller military theaters entailing individual weapon-targeting systems, and larger-scale theaters of national and regional military conflict. Much of the screen time is taken up with emulation of weapons and reconnaissance monitoring systems little distinct from the computer graphics technology used to produce segments of the film itself. The film sutures viewers into the virtual reality of a broad range of perceptual machinery: labor sensors operating in the jungles of Southeast Asia and on the streets of Tokyo; the calibra-

> EARLY IN THE FILM, WE CONFRONT THE PARADOX WHEREBY *SIMULATED* CIVILIAN EXPERIENCE APPEARS LESS MEDIATED AND MORE "REAL" THAN THE HIGHLY MEDIATED *REAL-LIFE* EXPERIENCE OF CONTEMPORARY WARFARE.

tion of sensors and cybernetic feedback systems; the camera's-eye view of a camera-guided air-to-surface missile as it closes in on its target in Yokohama Bay; night-vision goggles; binoculars; jet fighter and attack helicopter targeting systems; an unmanned airship cockpit; computerized architectural blueprints utilized in the course of tactical planning; and, the most spectacular, a JSDF radar system on which the viewer observes a phantom attack on Tokyo led by three JSDF fighter jets, organized by hackers.

Patlabor 2's persistent focus on the mediation of experience has understandably led critics such as Ueno Toshiya to read it in terms of a Baudrillardean hermeneutic that foregrounds a purported blurring of the boundary between the simulated and the real, between image and fact. Ueno submits that in *Patlabor 2* the simulated and the real are mutually implicated. He seemingly follows Baudrillard in suggesting that the simulated and the real remain so inextricably intertwined that it is no longer meaningful to attempt to distinguish the two. He reads *Patlabor 2* as making the implicitly Baudrillardean point that all contemporary experience is mediated to such an extent that, while we need to reflect on how this is changing our life/world, there is no meaningful "outside" to the media and simulation to which we might turn in order to draw the distinction. He describes Tsuge and Gotō's projects as efforts to alter the balance between the two, concluding that both characters are quixotically trying to influence forces far beyond their control by attempting to discriminate orders of reality that cannot be effectively distinguished from the vantage point of contemporary human experience.[17]

In an effort to outflank the Baudrillardean problematic, Christopher Bolton turns to the phenomenological approach to film analysis developed by Vivian Sobchack.[18] He follows Sobchack in positing two regimes of visuality, a traditional experience of film viewing that inscribes a conventional sense of embodied, human corporeality, and a disruptive digital experience of digital media that inscribes a flattened, disembodied loss of human corporeality. While he finds both modes operative in *Patlabor 2*, he shows a preference for the filmic regime he evokes in criticism of an allegedly disembodied regime of digital media.[19]

For all my appreciation of Bolton's analysis of *Patlabor 2,* and as a sign of that appreciation, I would like to insist on some of the key differences with my analysis. Methodologically, when Sobchack incorporates Guy Debord and Fredric Jameson's notion of a pervasive and inescapable mediation of spatial experience into her phenomenological reading of cinematic embodiment, she imports with it their take on digital experience, which follows from Baudrillard's reduction of the real to simulacral virtuality.[20] In their analysis, however, the category of digital media runs counter to the phenomenological frame of reference, which Sobchak evokes to characterize her analysis. As a result, the experience of the digital falls outside Sobchak's analysis, and she ends up capitulating to Baudrillard, insisting that, in the case of digital media, any notion of a bodily schema is effectively evacuated.[21]

> AN ANALYSIS OF WAR AND MEDIA CENTERED ON REPRESENTATION WILL INEVITABLY IGNORE THE PROBLEMATIC THAT ORGANIZES THE FILM AS A WHOLE, THE BLURRING LINE BETWEEN TERROR AND WARFARE AND THUS BETWEEN WAR AND PEACE.

Because Bolton adopts Sobchak's take, his reading of *Patlabor 2* remains within the interpretive horizon of Baudrillard's simulacrum. His manner of thinking the digital is ultimately very similar to that of Ueno Toshiya, with which he takes issue.

In contrast with Sobchak, Weber's approach has the advantage of insisting that both analog and digital media involve a delocalization and relocalization of the corporal position of the viewer. Weber persuasively argues that the status of theatrical spectatorship is more effectively approached through an analysis of framing and the imposition of contested boundaries, rather than through an analysis of aesthetic representation in the manner of Sobchak and Bolton.[22] If we refuse to grapple with the role of media and spectacle in contemporary terrorism/warfare, we fail to recognize the challenge that *Patlabor 2* extends to us in presenting an event that blurs the line between a military and a terrorist event. I would argue that the film makes a strong case that it is no longer possible to distinguish the spectacle of contemporary interstate warfare from the mediated spectacle that constitutes the regime of contemporary terrorism and, analogously, that it is no longer possible to distinguish war from peace. An analysis of war and media centered on representation will inevitably ignore the problematic that organizes the film as a whole, the blurring line between terror and warfare and thus between war and peace.

Patlabor 2 comprises two basic visual modes, the emulation of conventional camera movement and the emulation of weapons and reconnaissance systems. The film is a visual *tour de force* that insistently foregrounds the challenge that emulation presents for human perception. *Patlabor 2* features animated emulation of conventional camera movement such as tracking, crane, and helicopter shots. The extraordinarily sophisticated emulation of lighting effects includes dazzling, dynamic reflections of light on polished animated surfaces and the impression of multisource "natural" lighting in urban settings. The natural lighting effects include the blinding flash of a train passing at night and the stroboscopic effect of highway lights from within a darkened, moving car. The effect of this vast array of visual modes on the viewer ranges from a sense of hyperreality in the attention to the detail and dynamism of virtual reflections to the sheer physical challenge of processing nearly blinding flashes of light and stroboscopic set pieces in the midst of ongoing action and dialogue. The film is literally stunning in that it consistently strains or overloads the optical capacity of the viewer.

Visual technology figures prominently in the efforts of various characters to distinguish truth and falsehood. Characters frequently call on visuals to challenge what they perceive to be falsehoods concerning the status of contemporary Japan. For instance, the JSDF intelligence officer Arakawa uses videotape in his attempt to persuade security police officers Gotō and Nagumo that the official news media account of the bridge attack is misleading and distorted. The implication is that the public media is a site for manipulating perception rather than solving problems or sharing information. News reports of SDF responsibility for the Bay Bridge attack explicitly set the stage for the later decision of civilian security bureaucrats to unfairly scapegoat the air branch of the SDF. But these reports may well be false. Subsequently, the broadcast media provide cover when the bureaucracy chooses to shift blame to the security police. This is part of the public declaration of emergency by which the SDF is mobilized in the name of militarizing a purportedly ineffective police operation.

The public sphere of the broadcast media is implicitly depicted as a site of public manipulation. We see how news broadcasts act on behalf of forces that are never overtly acknowledged. Arakawa, Gotō, and Nagumo consistently reiterate that politics and civilian control is *the problem with* rather than *the solution to* Japan's paralysis regarding security issues. They imply that, contrary to the received wisdom in postwar Japan that holds civilian control over security to be intrinsically democratic, civilian control is seen to open the public sphere to bureaucratic manipulation. Civilian control does not brake the abuse of state powers.[23] *Patlabor 2* implies that broadcast news and the public sphere are an emergency broadcast system in waiting. This system purports to do other things while in fact serving its only effective purpose, that of emergency mobilization of the population in accordance with bureaucratic intentions. Bureaucratic intentions are directly realized through the declaration of emergency by way of the broadcast media and the deployment of SDF forces in the streets of Tokyo.

The JSDF air defense system serves as yet another stage upon which Tsuge and Arakawa's demands for Japanese strategic sovereignty clearly founder. The virtual air attack on Tokyo by three phantom JSDF F-16s purportedly stationed in Misawa allows Tsuge to reveal that the JSDF security network is compromised by its alliance with the United States, and thus Japanese security and sovereignty are undermined. Ties to the United States are consistently shown to sabotage or fatally expose Japanese strategic control over its territorial borders and airspace. In both the dramatic and military sense, Tsuge directs a series of virtual and physical attacks on Tokyo. His attacks constitute *an attack on media spectacle per se* intended to produce an effect on its audience, the Japanese people, *by removing them from their status as spectators, as an audience.* To the degree that we may discern any logic at the heart of Tsuge's project, his goal appears to be an attack on spectacle, rather than achievement of a conventional strategic objective such as capture of government ministries or state power.[24]

THE COMPETING POSITIONS IN *PATLABOR 2*

Patlabor 2 presents an unusual combination of plot-driven action with lengthy discussions of abjection, national sovereignty, and social authority. Director Oshii Mamoru and writer Itō Kazunori have characters hold forth to a degree rarely seen outside nonfiction documentary or academic lecture. How do the competing rhetorical positions articulated within *Patlabor 2* variously seek to contest, unify, delimit, or control competing projections of national and metropolitan space?

On one hand, the film does not have its characters denounce the attacks on legal grounds, which would entail a simple reiteration of the prewar responses to attempts at military coup that typified the 1930s, such as the 2-2-6 Incident (a coup attempt in Tokyo undertaken on February 26, 1936) that was linked to the Japanese takeover of Manchuria. The character Ōta, for instance, unambiguously embodies a spiritual devotion to martial values often associated with wartime militarism. The film develops a contrast between Ōta and other characters, to assure that we do not mistake Ōta's perspective (or theirs) for that of the film. Ōta appears as a danger to Japanese security, due in part to his indifference to economic concerns, but above all due to his irrational and willful lack of interest in the military technology that is otherwise fetishized throughout the film. Gotō explicitly asks his boss to speak to Ōta about his misguided and irrational understanding of both police work and training.

On the other hand, the police recruit Ōta for the unit that attacks Tsuge's heavily fortified position on Lot 18 when Gotō and Nagumo's police unit prepares for its final and illegal paramilitary action at the end of the film—even after Ota has been arrested and detained by military officials for attempting to organize a military rebellion against offending civilian officials. The implication is that the security police have replaced the military as the site of lawless and potentially authoritarian action in contemporary Japan.

At the same time, the film presents a series of uniformed military and police figures—Tsuge, Nagumo, Gotō—as martyrs and victims of spineless, abject, out-of-control civilian bureaucrats and politicians. In sum, rather than contest special police operations on legal grounds, the film takes seriously the stance associated with rebellious military figures of 1930s Japan. One of the premises of the film is that claims on the part of the civilian leadership to defend the public from the nonexistent threat of a 1930s-style military rebellion are malicious and self-serving. Ultimately, however, the film sends a very mixed message on this score. Events in the film are apparently supposed to give the lie to the suggestion that civilian seizure of authoritarian power serves any cause beyond delaying and obstructing public understanding of the incompetence of the civilian leadership as well as its danger to the public itself. Yet civilian control and postwar democracy per se are relentlessly depicted as absolute shams that effectively invite authoritarian action through a failure of will and principled concern for the Japanese common good, views that actually were important to 1930s-era military terrorism at home and adventurism abroad.

NEW-FASHIONED MILITARY AUTONOMY

The evocation of Angkor-Thom in the initial action scenes clearly situates the events in Cambodia (Figure 2). Japan's first UN peacekeeping mission in the early nineties was to Cambodia, and on that mission, two Japanese lives were lost.[25] The opening sequence, culminating in the decimation of Tsuge's unit, thus alludes to the loss of Japanese lives in this early 1990s UNTAC mission to Cambodia, in which the rules of engagement were widely held responsible for their demise. The same legislation concerning rules of engagement was still in effect at the time of *Patlabor 2*'s release. This explains why Tsuge presumably feels the loss of Japanese life in Cambodia reveals the danger to which civilian rule exposes Japanese security.

Tsuge's airships hovering over Tokyo carry the phrase *ultima ratio* in enormous black letters. *Ultima ratio* means "the last argument," which is associated with the phrase *ultima ratio regum* ("the last argument of kings") that the French King Louis XIV famously engraved upon his cannon. The implication is that Tsuge thinks that laws mean no more and no less than the force available at any given moment to enforce those laws.[26] Tsuge thus implies that, without the threat of force, adherence to the rule of law is a dangerous and false pretense, which situation he intends to correct. For Tsuge, the 1990s legal status quo under which Japanese security personnel lacked the right of self-defense at home or abroad is a dangerous illusion that must

FIGURE 2. This statuary evokes Angkor-Thom in Cambodia. It is a sculpture of the Buddhist bodhisattva Avalokitesvara (in Japanese, *Kannon*), who was identified with compassion and attending to the cries of the suffering. He refused to leave this world until all sentient beings had been freed from the illusion of *samsara*.

be forcibly shaken in order to cease risking Japanese security personnel and the safety of Japanese citizens for the sake of legal fictions. This motto thus implicitly serves as an indirect criticism of UN and Japanese doctrines of international law that purport to apply it without ac-

> THE FILM ESTABLISHES AN ANALOGY BETWEEN THE BUDDHIST CONCERN WITH FREEING ONESELF FROM THIS WORLD OF ILLUSION AND TSUGE'S QUEST TO FREE JAPAN FROM MODERN, TECHNOLOGICALLY DRIVEN FORMS OF ILLUSION.

knowledging the strategic requirements that would be realistically required to make Japan's UN-associated, wishful half-measures a reality.

Arakawa identifies Tsuge as a member of the "national defense tribe" (kokubōzoku, also bōeizoku), with which Arakawa himself is identified later in the film. This term refers to an actual group of individuals who constitute an important political link between state and society on defense matters. Such individuals have exhibited an ongoing interest in Japanese defense policy and a general support for increased defense spending. They include bureaucrats who have served in the Japan Defense Agency, former civilian or uniformed officials in the Japan Defense Agency, and Diet members whose electoral districts include military bases.[27] Evidently, Tsuge's actions constitute an attempt to communicate an essential truth to other Japanese: that the contemporary Japanese state mistakenly continues to act as if domestic security and international security remain clearly distinguishable. Tsuge argues, in effect, that the institutional demarcation between law and force is a false and unreal boundary, and that reality has bypassed these statutes and policies. Given that the legislation governing the status of Japanese forces under UN command follows legally from Article 9, Tsuge's position ultimately requires the abolition of Article 9 or its legal reinterpretation, which would amount to the same thing. Tsuge's actions strive to show that these issues intersect at both ends, and that the official Japanese position will necessarily lead to failure in both international and domestic security contexts.

Quasi-religious associations accompany Tsuge's actions. The opening scene, for instance, lingers on Buddhist imagery, the statue of a bodhisattva, Avalokitesvara, who attained enlightenment yet refused departure from this world until all sentient beings had also been freed from the delusion of samsara.[28] This bodhisattva was particularly concerned with the cries of the suffering. Thus the film establishes an analogy between the Buddhist concern with freeing oneself from this world of illusion and Tsuge's quest to free Japan from modern, technologically driven forms of illusion, as if to allow Japan at last to hear foreign cries of suffering.

Presumably, Tsuge's terrorist act is calculated to make visible the loss of Japanese life in Cambodia for civilian Japanese on Japanese soil, and thus to allow his men's actions to take on a significance greater than that of this particular conflict or moment. Tsuge's response holds out the hope of a future Japan in which the frailty and finitude of his mission's abjection and failure will be sublimated and overcome by greater Japanese force of will. He seeks to awaken contemporary Japan from its delusion so that in the future perhaps Japan may survive and ultimately triumph over the death by which it currently continues to be threatened.

> FOR ARAKAWA, CLAIMS TO DEFEND JAPANESE PEACE ARE SIMPLE-MINDED, FALSE, AND SELF-SERVING BECAUSE THEY ENTAIL A DISAVOWAL OF JAPANESE COMPLICITY IN GLOBAL POLICE VIOLENCE.

Tsuge's personal refusal to die for his cause may also be read in Buddhist terms as the ethic of a bodhisattva who refuses to move on to the next life until he has done his part to save others in this one.

In addition, Tsuge's letter to Nagumo expresses in Biblical terms a concern with restoring unity to Japanese relations.[29] It is important to note, however, that this passage's discussion of familial/national dissension also implicitly evokes a falling away from the ideals of a founding document of the Japanese family-state in the Meiji era, the Imperial Rescript on Education. Similarly, Arakawa states that men will act where gods do not and that, with contemporary technology, any man can be a god. Tsuge also uses Biblical text as computer code. In sum, Tsuge's disruption of modern communications technologies and weapons systems takes on distinctly religious connotations, related to the Japanese imperial cult, to Buddhism, and to Christianity.

Significantly, the passage from the Bible functions both as computer code *and* as a commentary on lost Japanese national unity. Tsuge's actions thus recall Baudrillard's ideas about symbolic protest in *Symbolic Exchange and Death*. Tsuge's actions operate as a symbolic protest against the contemporary and secular codes of Japanese modernity, in which the translation of the Bible into computer code functions as an anagram, with Tsuge's terrorist acts working to bring the contemporary system crashing down around its own contradictions. But I lack the space to fully explore such a possibility in this essay.[30]

Lastly, Tsuge designates as illusory (*maboroshi*) those conceptions that resist the sense of immersion and empathic mutual existence he would purport to restore to Japanese modes of life in Japanese space. His actions imply that the notion of a meaningful boundary between post–Second World War Japanese peace and the globalized violence undertaken by its U.S. ally during the same period, and from which Japan profited, is illusory and false; they imply that the international legal order sustaining such a boundary is illegitimate.[31] In this respect, Tsuge's critique deeply resonates with Carl Schmitt's mid-twentieth-century challenge to the legitimacy of Anglo-American centered "peace" whose maintenance demanded colonial and imperial violence. Significantly, when we finally hear Tsuge's own words, he expresses his concern for the future of Tokyo, rather than a concern for the nation of Japan. While his Biblical quote implies a concern with national unity, his own words almost immediately link him with metropolitan media networks rather the nationalist project.

Arakawa has the longest extended monolog in the film. Along with the sequences of military mobilization in Tokyo, Arakawa's speech on peace, war, and the use of force is accompanied by the most emotionally haunting soundtrack music in the film.[32] Arakawa observes that the responsibility of the SDF and the security police is to maintain peace, but he challenges conventional understandings of peace as superficial and hypocritical. He asserts that conventional understandings assume an illusory integrity of Japanese space that disavows Japanese implication in international, strategic, and economic relations. For Arakawa, claims to defend Japanese peace are simple-minded, false, and self-serving because they entail a disavowal of Japanese complicity in global police violence.

Arakawa argues that Japan is today implicated in postwar U.S. militarism, much as it was in prewar militarism. Globalization implicates Japan in the violence used to sustain the global order from which Japan profits. *For Arakawa, Japanese protestations of pacifism entail faith in a fiction of Japanese control and unity.* He argues that Japanese must come to understand peace as something more complex than "not war." He argues that, given the brutality that defines the international status quo, the defense of "peace" constitutes a particularly dangerous illusion.

Arakawa broadens the discussion of peace and war to questions about international order and legitimacy. There does not exist, in his opinion, an international order that does not ultimately ground itself in force. He insists that any peace grounded in observation of the law requires enforcement. To counter how the Japanese state has made a fetish of peace, Arakawa offers a larger view that reveals Japan's implication in regimes of force; Japan relies on such regimes but continues to disavow them through its professed adherence to Article 9 and its refusal to fully participate in UN peacekeeping missions.

Arakawa builds on the widespread sense that the Gulf War was a war that featured a failure of communication across the televisual media to portray the

Japanese television viewer's relation to military conflict and international relations as a mode that includes foreign affairs within broadcast television news coverage, but by way of exclusion, that is, through a logic of relation as nonrelation:

> While we steadfastly reap the benefits of these conflicts, we banish war to a realm beyond the [TV] screen, forgetting that—no, pretending to forget—that we are on the rear lines of that struggle. If we continue to deny our responsibility, in the end we'll receive a great punishment.[33]

Arakawa thus lays out a critique of Japanese media and war suited to the global televisual theater of war. His insistence that foreign war is included within media by way of exclusion recalls Giorgio Agamben's reading of the state of exception in domestic and international law (Figure 3). Agamben argues that a state of exception emerged in the domestic and international law of developed nations since the First World War, which constitutively incorporates individuals and groups within the law and sovereignty by way of their exclusion. This "exclusive inclusion" builds on the logic of relation as nonrelation, which is manifest in the logic of the ban.[34]

Arakawa's speech requires us to account for the state of exception to international law as instituted by U.S.–Japan security policy in the immediate postwar years.[35] Because of Japan's formal lack of military forces, the 1951 Japan–U.S. Security Treaty was a completely unilateral affair. The treaty did not proceed from the United Nations, which meant that the terms for the deployment of U.S. forces were subject only to the unilateral discretion of the United States; it did not require consultation with the government of Japan and thus did not even rise to the status of a mutual security treaty.[36] It entailed, in effect, the institutionalization of a state of exception in international law, wherein unilateral U.S. security interest took the place of UN auspices. The 1960 revision of the treaty made reference to the UN and allowed for a very loose, formal process of U.S.–Japanese consultation, but the treaty remains one-sided and toothless.[37] To make matters worse, it is primarily the United States that has exerted extreme and unrelenting pressure on Japan to field a military force, tirelessly demanding that Japan violate the very peace constitution imposed on it under U.S. military occupation. Both Oshii and Agamben show an awareness of this problem, which opens the possibility for a substantial critique of unilateral U.S. power. Ultimately, however, both Oshii and Agamben also share a narrowness of focus that prevents them from directly connecting their criticisms of media and sovereignty to a broader critique of

FIGURE 3. The visual logic of this shot parallels Arakawa's claim of foreign affairs being included in Japanese media by way of exclusion, the relation of nonrelation. The billboard depicts a foreign land stereotyped and commodified for the purpose of promoting long-distance telephone service, yet any connection of the territory in question to contemporary power politics is entirely elided.

the biopolitical aspects of capitalist exploitation, either in Japan specifically or in East Asia generally.[38] Even as the very idea of the relation as nonrelation Oshii deploys opens out onto a broader, less nation-centered problematic, the film's main characters nevertheless remain centrally concerned to reinstitute effective Japanese national boundaries and sovereignty.

To some extent, Arakawa's criticisms of the U.S.–Japan security alliance reflect a general Japanese questioning of the U.S.–Japan relationship in the early 1990s. With the end of the Cold War, a Japanese public opinion poll conducted in July 1991 reported that more Japanese saw the United States as the primary threat to Japanese security for the first time since 1945.[39] Similarly, Arakawa stresses that the U.S.–Japanese security relationship undermines Japanese sovereignty and the integrity of the Japanese security apparatus. For Arakawa, Japanese security is compromised by U.S.–Japan politics: agreements made with the United States sabotage Japanese strategic agency and autonomy. Arakawa's emphasis reflects the consensus view of security professionals in Japan during the 1990s. SDF policy is set by civilian ministries such as the Ministry of Foreign Affairs, which places high priority on meeting the demands of the U.S.–Japan relationship, sacrificing the desires of SDF commanders for the sake of maintaining that relationship.[40]

Arakawa repeatedly submits that integration of the Japanese security apparatus within U.S. networks debases Japanese sovereignty and fundamentally compromises any effort to defend Japan from any given enemy, even if that enemy is not necessarily an agent of the U.S. per se. He argues that Japanese policy dangerously conflates U.S. and Japanese interests, even in contexts in which they demonstrably do not correspond. For Arakawa, Japan's only option is either to rely on the military force of the U.S., whose security interests already diverge from those of Japan, or to take responsibility for the use of military force on its own terms. The effective premise of nearly every word of Arakawa's speech is that genuine concern for Japanese security requires the abandonment of Article 9 and a restoration of Japanese military sovereignty, which would require a serious Japanese challenge to the U.S.-imposed state of exception in the international law of the Pacific.

POLICE POWER IN THE JAPANESE POLICE STATE

Arakawa intimates that he chose to confide in Gotō because the Kanagawa police have a reputation for indulging in extralegal domestic security activity. He consequently sees them as useful allies in a common effort to expose how the exception operates in the application of Japanese security law. Gotō dismisses Arakawa's analysis as a misunderstanding, but their exchange alludes to an actual incident.

In November 1986, Kanagawa security police wiretapped the executive leader of the Japanese Communist Party, illegally, in defiance of Japanese law. Despite two separate recommendations for prosecution, the Tokyo Prosecutors' Office decided not to prosecute due to sympathy for the guilty policemen and fear of bureaucratic retribution.[41] The incident highlights how, in stark contrast to contemporary Japanese military forces, the Japanese security police are almost entirely shielded from political supervision of any kind.[42] Indeed, former Prime Minister Nakasone Yasuhiro, a former police inspector, was part of a new trend in Japanese politics in which former police officials reached high political position and began to comprise a very powerful faction within the government, connecting the cabinet to the bureaucracy.[43] This trend became pronounced from the 1980s.

Gotō describes the civilian security leadership's response to Tsuge as a theatrical farce played by characters who are miscast, who would not normally choose to play their assigned parts. Gotō claims that the civilian leadership has effectively militarized state functions under the aegis of defending the state from the (phantom) threat of military subversion. Gotō's points echo the polemics of General Kurisu, who was the head of the Joint Staff Council during the 1970s. Kurisu insisted that Japanese law, as regards the civilian chain of command and response to surprise attacks, was inadequate, requiring carefully tailored legislation that allows uniformed military officers to respond in real time. Without such legal reform, Kurisu insisted, a real-world security emergency or surprise attack would surely require extralegal military response. Kurisu was made a scapegoat and forced to resign, for his remarks were seen as evocative of 1930s-era military rejection of civilian control. Yet the policy remedies that Kurisu advocated essentially called for restructuring the Japanese Defense Agency chain of command along the lines of the U.S. Department of Defense.[44]

In response to Arakawa's long speech on the increasingly blurred distinction between peace and war at the center of the film, Gotō recites a long excerpt from James Dunnigan's *How to Make War*: the farther a decision maker is from the theater of battle, the greater the degree to which decisions on strategic questions become detached from reality; such a tendency is even further exacerbated when a nation is on the losing side of an ongoing war.[45] Dunnigan, a war game designer and historian, has served as a military consultant to the CIA and the U.S. War College. Elsewhere in the book, Dunnigan presents historical research concluding that military rebellions have more frequently been instigated by civilian rather than military authorities. The Gotō–Dunnigan connection demonstrates the degree to which the screenwriter Itō and the director Oshii impart to Gotō a transnational and avowedly apolitical perspective that is characteristic of the contemporary military professional.

While Gotō comes to agree with Arakawa that war is already underway and that the peace the civilian authorities imagine they are defending is now illusory, he also criticizes Tsuge's event—his "little war"—as even more false or illusory than the falsehood of the postwar peace that Tsuge and Arakawa lament. Gotō states that destruction is the goal of Tsuge's actions, not a byproduct. Gotō's remark resonates with Naomi Klein's recent argument that postwar neoliberalism is ultimately a political project grounded in destruction.[46] By suggesting that American seizure of power would mean Japan has to start all over, Arakawa frames the U.S. occupation of Japan as one more byway on the path of destruction charted by postwar capitalism centered in the United States.

Gotō and Nagumo's contempt for the fecklessness in civilian response to emergency is yet another point at which the film alludes to public Japanese debates. Fear of military takeover along the line of the various coup attempts of the 1930s had made emergency legislation so politically charged in the postwar that the Diet did not even consider emergency legislation: "One observer pointed out in 1975 that Japan's military defense lacked a mobilization plan, a military court system, emergency legislation, and a civil defense system."[47] As of the early 1990s, it still lacked all of those things. News reports featured in the film relate this information in passing.

Gotō consistently regards Tsuge as a target for coercive paramilitary action where necessary, and for arrest where possible. In violating the social order, Tsuge becomes a criminal who must be stopped before he endangers more people. For Gotō, targeting, arresting, and preempting Tsuge's further action resolves the challenge that he poses to Japanese social space for the time being. In other words, Gotō aims to reintegrate Tsuge into the Japanese social order.

Gotō's speech on the two kinds of government figures who violate the law could have come out of a silent-era *jidaigeki*: "There are those who are forces for justice (*seigi*) and those who are forces for evil." Yet the speech also resonates with Walter Benjamin's discussion of law and force in "Critique of Violence." Gotō advocates what Benjamin describes as law-preserving violence, the suspension of the law and the use of force for the sake of restoring the rule of law.[48] Gotō purports to violate the law for the sake of restoring normality and the rule of law, the rule of the state, and the public interest. In effect, Gotō arbitrarily delimits the apparently unmanageable network that Arakawa and Tsuge have spun between law, force, and legitimacy. Gotō makes it thinkable in simple terms, in the terms of criminal justice and the restoration of law and order.

In effect, however, Gotō's actions constitute an exception even to the state of exception—they violate the very terms of the state of exception laid out by his superiors in the security hierarchy of the Japanese state. Gotō and Nagumo's actions can be seen as a coup within a coup. They present a decision that effectively decides the exception in the context of the nonstate threat with which the film presents us. Their decision determines that the sovereignty of the Japanese state vis-à-vis security resides with Gotō and Nagumo's unit, the SV2. The implication is that civilian bureaucrats are not capable of defending Japan; therefore security professionals must step into the breach even when their civilian superiors have expressly prohibited such action. While Gotō and Nagumo thus shut down many of the larger questions raised by Tsuge's action, they are ultimately in agreement with Arakawa that Japanese civilian leadership is incompetent and untrustworthy. One of the primary targets of the film is the Japanese bureaucrat. Where postwar Japanese popular opinion has sometimes deprecated Japanese politicians and idealized bureaucrats as unselfish civil servants, *Patlabor 2* aims to smear bureaucrats and politicians interchangeably as "civilians" who are unworthy of authority in situations where Japanese security comes under serious threat.

Nagumo, like Gotō, directly challenges civilian Japanese security leadership as opportunistic, incompetent, and dangerous. She also takes issue with Tsuge, advocating that the citizens of Tokyo possess existential value as concrete living creatures. She implies that his insistence that Tokyoites live in an illusion seems to discount or abstract the value of their lives as such. She implies that Tsuge reduces the citizens of Tokyo to pawns in a contest over the parameters and unity of contemporary Japanese space. Tsuge's actions suggest that he believes an increased militarization of Japanese security is necessary at home and abroad and can only be undertaken by Japanese security professionals, not civilians who will surely botch the job and endanger everyone else in the process. In Nagumo's opinion, however, Tsuge's approach cheapens or even erases the value of human lives as such.

THE MENAGERIE

The recurrent depiction of nonhuman agents such as fish, dogs, and birds may serve to reinforce Nagumo's explicit challenge to Tsuge's terror plot: war is of flesh and blood as well as of images and symbols. Birds, for instance, interfere with security police targeting of Tsuge's remote-controlled airship. Security forces aligned with the state thus express an explicit disregard for the fate of nonhuman life.

The overwhelming visual domination of thousands of seagulls over Lot 18 both on the ground and in the air in the final sequence of the film—over land reclaimed by humans from the ocean—vividly raises the issue of the unintended consequences of human action on nonhuman life as well as human life, on life as such (Figure 4). On the one hand, the seagulls' status as a form of life on Lot 18, seemingly disconnected from direct human control, stands as a trace of life that at least momentarily falls outside the relentless economic imperative to organize all forms of matter and life for the purpose of the reproduction of capital. On the other hand, the process of land "reclamation" that produced Lot 18 from what was previously part of Tokyo Bay is a form of technological destruction of natural habitat pervasive in modern Japan, frequently catastrophic for both human and nonhuman life from an ecological perspective. It is tempting to draw a connection between the assault on nature that creates Lot 18, where Tsuge takes his stand, and the smashup between nature and technology staged in the first *Patlabor* film, where the Ark project turns ocean into land and raises towers (monuments to modern construction technology) that create unintended effects—under tidal wave conditions, resonance created by wind interacting with the buildings is designed to trigger a rampage of Patlabor mecha with the HOS operating system. In both cases, technological human assault on the environment leads to a sort of revenge. In *Patlabor 1,* Hoba's cyber-terrorism utilizes a natural environmental trigger that requires destruction of the Ark built on Tokyo Bay. In *Patlabor 2,* Tsuge's actions also appear to be somewhat inspired by a concern for nature. He seemingly calls for a less technologized and more empathic relation to the environment and other creatures both human and nonhuman, and he directs his plot from the newly installed landfill that is Lot 18. The very name of the location communicates the transformation of an ocean habitat into a unit of land that produces economic property at the expense of the environment and that is now ripe for manipulation and exploitation.[49]

FIGURE 4. Seagulls visually dominate the scene at Lot 18 where Tsuge made his headquarters and where he is captured by Nagumo's band of vigilantes.

For all its consistent association with the character of Tsuge, animal life thus seems to represent a surviving form of organization and perception not yet drawn into the fierce demands of social reproduction largely enforced by the forms of technology and altered perception more predominantly featured in the film. Baudrillard offers a seagull soaked in oil as an emblem of the television viewer's implication in the media manipulation of the Gulf War.[50] Oshii seems to offer the seagull, the fish, and the dog as animals that have avoided abjection by what Tsuge at least appears to consider the pathological mediation of contemporary Japanese experience (Figure 5). Oshii's work thus raises the issue of speciesism, the role of the animal in sustaining or challenging humanism, and the possibility of challenges to this mode of thought from the subject position of nonhuman animals.[51] The film thus in part seems to actively champion a mode of mutual empathy and cobelonging it depicts as characterizing the behavior of nonhuman animals as an ideal to be aspired to by human animals, and that would have positive consequences for all life forms, including other humans. Rather than arguing that animals are much more human than previously realized as more liberal animal-rights activists would have it, the film on the contrary uses the behavior of animals as a criterion by which to judge human behavior and find humans seriously wanting.[52]

FIGURE 5. Along with various birds and fish, this basset hound is one of several dogs Oshii depicts in the film as possessed of a gaze and a power of vision that is seemingly uncontaminated by the mendacity of the mass media that corrupts human perception.

Patlabor 2 screens Arakawa and Gotō acknowledging, with Tsuge, a blurred boundary between war and peace. The film depicts a world that reinforces Arakawa's thesis that the Japanese media relate to foreign affairs by way of a strategy of inclusion by exclusion. The former is foundational for claims of a state of emergency that has become the norm. The latter mirrors the logic of Giorgo Agamben's reading of the state of exception as informed by a logic of relation as nonrelation.

On one hand, the film conveys an important and useful warning to Japanese regarding their own implication in the catastrophic international destruction of postwar U.S. imperial practice. Nevertheless, the film's insistence on the collapsed boundary between war and peace and the rise of a permanent state of exception is also quite congenial to the contemporary neoconservative Japanese national defense tribe's own variant of the "war on terror" grounded on just this premise. In effect, *Patlabor 2* ultimately appears to advocate militarizing Japanese foreign and domestic policy and saving it from what the film depicts as ultimately the greatest threat of all—*civilian rule that refuses to recognize an ongoing and potentially permanent state of emergency.*

> JAPAN'S "DEFENSE" POSTURE HAS BEEN MILITARIZED IN THE MEANTIME, BUT BY WAY OF FURTHER DEEPENING U.S.-JAPAN COOPERATION RATHER THAN BY MOVING AWAY FROM IT AS *PATLABOR 2* STRONGLY ADVOCATES.

Given the general identification of so much of *Patlabor 2* with the perspective of the Japanese military professional, much of the argument seems to be driven by a variety of technological determinism. The technology of the weapons Japan deployed in the 1990s seamlessly pulled the JSDF from a posture of defending Japanese territory to a posture of projecting power as far as Korea and the Taiwan Straits for the purpose of a greatly enlarged notion of self-defense.[53] In this sense, it is the technology fetishized by most of the film that sustains a theater of security operations that reaches far beyond the geographical boundaries of Japan and thus presents a theater of Japanese security interests that causes Article 9 and the Japanese constitution to appear obsolete in the manner suggested by Tsuge, Arakawa, and, to a lesser degree, Gotō.

With the advent of the Koizumi administration, the Heisei militarization foreshadowed in *Patlabor 2* intersected with Japanese reception of the Bush Doctrine. In the event, Japanese neoconservatives have gleefully retrofitted outstanding demands of the Japanese national defense tribe as the only natural and appropriate response to a global war on terror. Japanese neoconservatives have used the spectacle of a missile threat from North Korea and media-fueled hysteria over decades-old kidnappings of Japanese by North Korean intelligence as a screen memory to generate Japanese self-righteousness, erase all memory of Japanese colonial oppression of millions on the continent, and to clear the Japanese public conscience regarding re-militarization.

Just since the turn of this century, Japan has joined the international coalition to cooperate with international police and intelligence efforts to track terrorist groups. It has proclaimed a right to preemptively attack North Korea. An Anti-Terrorism Special Measures Law was passed that led to deployment of Japanese air and maritime SDF troops in the Indian Ocean in support of U.S. operations outside a United Nations peacekeeping force structure. The Koizumi cabinet announced its intention to deploy U.S.-built missile defense systems.[54]

In other words, Japan's "defense" posture has been militarized in the meantime, but by way of further deepening U.S.–Japan cooperation rather than by moving away from it as *Patlabor 2* strongly advocates. From the perspective of Arakawa, this would mean that Japanese security has been further endangered and abjected. During televised debate over deployment of Japanese troops to Iraq on the Fujisankei network, the Liberal Democratic Party (LDP) representative wholeheartedly supported Bush administration objectives of Japanese deployment while the Democratic Party of Japan (DPJ) opposed deployment as a violation of Article 9 and Japanese legislation requiring the troops to be stationed in a pacified area. Only the nationalist manga writer Kobayashi Yoshinori consistently advocated the longer-term project of articulating Japanese security objectives distinct from those of the United States. He was repeatedly derided by the moderator for being hopelessly naïve as regards the reality of U.S. power.[55] The Japanese public sphere thus currently presents a competition between a neoconservative Japanese nationalism that identifies Japanese and U.S. security interests for the purpose of advancing Japanese militarism, a legalistic pacifism that fails to address neoconservative claims of an unrecognizably transformed security environment, and competing varieties of Japanese nationalism that insist on distinguishing between the U.S. and Japanese interests such as advocated by Ishihara and Kobayashi. To date, Japanese leaders have managed to institute and expand militarizing policies despite consistent and widespread popular opposition to them among the Japanese voting public.

In sum, *Patlabor 2* stages an intersection of the theatricality of cybernetics with the theater of military operations as a contest for control over national and metropolitan space. It concludes that the overarching and decisive outcome of this development is an abolition of the boundary between war and peace, that Japan now lives under a permanent state of emergency. It further suggests that, in the wake of the first Gulf War, it is now virtually impossible to distinguish between interstate warfare and nonstate terrorism as modes of terrorist spectacle. While the film distances itself from the revival of 1930s wartime militarism in some respects, it depicts an alternative threat of authoritarianism in the security police, and an abject irresponsibility and failure of civilian democratic leadership. It follows hegemonic professional military understandings of the technology it so consistently features in effectively demanding increasingly militarized Japanese foreign relations, though it also challenges certain premises of Japanese neoconservatism and speciesist humanism.

··

Notes

1. To my knowledge, Michael Fisch was the first to seriously explore *Patlabor 2* as a commentary on Japan's international position. Fisch argues that what emerges is ultimately a voice of anti-American Japanese nationalism. While I find Fisch's reading a bit U.S.-centered, I think most of what he has to say on the subject is insightful and important. I would distinguish the project of this article from Fisch's reading in two respects: (1) Where Fisch is primarily concerned with the vicissitudes of Japanese nationalism, my own analysis is grounded in the assumption that postwar and contemporary Japan has not been a sovereign nation in many respects, and thus I also attempt to address the question of Japan's domestic and international status in terms that escape or fail the national project. (2) My analysis is grounded in a methodological approach that assumes the media are as implicated in contemporary warfare and international affairs as they are in film study. I would say that this essay attempts to conceive film study and international affairs as more intrinsically interrelated than Fisch's approach would seem to suppose. See Michael Fisch, "Nation, War, and Japan's Future in the Science Fiction Anime Film *Patlabor II*," *Science Fiction Studies* 27, no. 1 (March 2000): 49–68.

2. This sentence alludes to a passage in Carl Schmitt: "Sovereign is: He who decides on the state of exception" From *Politische Theologie* (Berlin, 1990), translated in David Dyzenhaus, *Legality and Legitimacy: Karl Schmitt, Hans Kelsen, and Hermann Heller in Weimar* (Oxford: Oxford University Press, 1999).

3. Fisch, "Nation, War, and Japan's Future," 12; Ueno Toshiya, *Kurenai no metaru sūtsu: Anime to iu senjō* (Metalsuits the red: Wars in animation) (Tokyo: Kinokuniya Shoten, 1998), 41.

4. "Fine illustration of the communication schema in which emitter and receiver on opposite sides of the screen, never connect with each other." Jean Baudrillard, *The Gulf*

War Did Not Take Place, trans. Paul Patton (Bloomington: Indiana University Press, 1995), 44, 48.

5. Noam Chomsky, for example, concluded that the Gulf War was not a conventional war involving fighting between opposed sides, but came closer to a combination of mutual state terrorism and mass slaughter. Noam Chomsky, "The Media and the War: What War?" in *Triumph of the Image: The Media's War in the Persian Gulf—A Global Perspective* (Boulder, Colo.: Westview Press, 1992), 51.

6. Ibid., 58, 59, 63.

7. "Detection and deception forming henceforth the foundational couplings of the American *Air Land Battle* strategy . . . the question of remote detection becomes crucial . . . From this revolutionary pursuit comes . . . a physical form of the materiel of war . . . which depends nearly exclusively on its remote image, its 'radar echo' or 'thermal signature'" (Paul Virilio, *The Virilio Reader* [Malden, Mass.: Blackwell Publishing, 1998], 167). "It is somewhat as if the image in the mirror were suddenly modifying our face: the electronic representation on the screen, the radar console, modifies the aerodynamic silhouette of the weapon, the virtual image dominating in fact 'the thing' of which it was, until now, only the 'image'" (ibid., 168). "The strategic and political importance of the control of public and private televisions in the war of *real time,* even beyond that of the *Gulf,* is now more evident than ever" (ibid., 169). "Arms of communication prevail for the first time in the history of combat over the traditional supremacy of arms of destruction . . . We will attempt therefore to identify and analyze this new 'site,' this so-called 'milieu,' to the degree the technologies which compose and organize it are those which tomorrow will structure the city, the global village" (ibid., 170).

8. Christopher Bolton has argued intriguingly that this scene depicts an alienation of the mecha pilots from a visceral sense of threat and the necessity of their own self-defense as a result of the mediation of their experience by the digital control displays through which they control their mechas. He suggests that this also instances a fear of dehumanization that pervades a significant segment of science fiction more broadly.

While Bolton has a quote from Oshii himself in support of this reading, my own repeated viewings of the scene in question find the experience depicted fairly terrifying and the depicted response of the characters in the scene as closer to hysterical than distanced or delayed (including heavy breathing and frantic shouting on their radios), a sense that forces me to question the degree to which one can argue that this particular scene depicts digital mediation as a cause of distancing from the immediacy of danger. On the contrary, I receive a palpable sense of the alienation of justice and force from the law in this scene, but experience the depicted digital control displays during the scene as anticipating, marking, and if anything magnifying the imminent threat rather than diminishing it.

Rather, what I think Bolton's intuition here points toward is an alienation and distancing from the possibility of being immersed in a mutual relation with one's surroundings associated with aural and audio experience. This alternative mode of experience is screened when Tsuge emerges from his mecha, removes his helmet, and hears the sound of a bird's cry and feels the wetness of falling rain, sounds and bodily stimuli that draw him into a mutual relation with his surroundings in a manner precluded by the visually oriented digital display and isolation that characterized the previous scene in the mecha. The Angkor Thom–type statuary toward which our attention is then turned depicts

Avalitokesvara, a Mahayana Buddhist bodhisattva known for being open to hearing the cries of the suffering who have not yet found Buddhist enlightenment. The bird's cry on the soundtrack just as Tsuge removes his helmet surely pushes Tsuge and the audience toward an aural position enveloped by the surroundings that is starkly different from the narrow instrumental relationship with the environment staged in the immediately preceding fighting sequence. I would argue that the Buddhist symbolism of the statuary (which also poses a nostalgic aspect of the romantic ruin) fairly directly associates these distinct types of experience with one's ability to maintain concern for the suffering of others and more particularly, with one's ability to listen empathetically rather than to act based on technologized and emotionally distancing visual cues.

Like Fisch, I would argue that the mechas at least in part signify a Japanese technological superiority over the threat so profound that the scene requires the viewer to conclude that only a self-inflicted lack of will or effort at self-defense could have resulted in the meaningless sacrifice of Japanese lives we witness. This is pretty clearly meant to be a commentary on the failure of will codified in Japanese arrangements with the United Nations. I do find Bolton's suggestion that the film presents a reversal of the picture of Gulf War–style war as war game to be very insightful as regards later sections of the film but don't find the argument persuasive as regards the opening scene. See Christopher Bolton, "The Mecha's Blind Spot: *Patlabor 2* and the Phenomenology of Anime," *Science Fiction Studies* 29, no. 3 (November 2002): 453–74.

9. Bolton curiously refers to this weapon as a "cruise missile." In American English, the term "cruise missile" typically refers to a Tomahawk missile, an enormous long-range strategic missile that can only be deployed from a ship or, in the case of other cruise missile types, from the largest bombers. Perhaps this is a question of dialect. The missile attack in *Patlabor 2* gives every appearance of being a Hellfire air-to-ground missile launched from an F-16. Hellfire missiles are most commonly launched from attack helicopters such as the Apache, but they may also be fired from an F-16 fighter jet. Hellfire missiles have more recently become the weapon typically launched from the Predator drone that has become such a central aspect of the Obama administration's military strategy in Afghanistan and Pakistan.

10. Not only are the planes in question explicitly identified as JSDF fighters from Misawa Air Force Base, but the film previews this issue by earlier informing us in a newscast that F-16s were adopted by the JSDF in the fictional past of the film, 1998, and that 190 are stationed at Misawa. At present, Misawa Air Force Base houses both Japanese and U.S. air units, but only the JSDF units currently deploy F-16s. Interestingly, the fighters mustered to intercept the three phantom jets are F-15s, a distinct type of fighter jet that is actually deployed at the JSDF air bases referred to in the film.

11. Fisch suggests that the occupation of Tokyo by the SDF somehow evokes Japanese occupation by the U.S. army. I'm not persuaded. Given the weather depicted, surely the most immediate association would be with mobilization of the Japanese army in Tokyo on Feb. 2, 1931 in response to the most famous of a series of attempted *coups d-etat* in the 1930s, the 2-2-6 Incident. It strikes me that a difference in the identity of the occupying army of such stark proportions as domestic vs. foreign troops must surely be decisive in shaping any historical associations evoked by the sequence.

12. Their accomplices from the SV2 security police unit do, however, discuss how

participating in the final paramilitary action against Tsuge in violation of direct orders from their superiors *is* destined to end their professional careers, so it is possible that untoward consequences not depicted on screen are in store for Gotō and Nagumo.

13. Samuel Weber, *Theatricality as Medium* (New York: Fordham University Press, 2004), 42.

14. Ibid., 314–15.

15. Christopher Bolton curiously tries to subsume centralized analog TV network broadcasts transmitting government propaganda within the category of distributed digital media that hold uniquely digital, disembodied properties for the viewer. This strikes me as a category mistake.

16. This is somewhat reminiscent of the first George Bush administration's production of satellite intelligence showing Iraqi troops massed on the border of Saudi Arabia that later investigation by the *Miami Herald* based on satellite evidence from private services demonstrated to have been entirely fabricated.

17. Ueno, *Kurenai no metaru sūtsu,* 40–45, 50–64.

18. "My reading of the film declines Ueno's 'invisibility' and its associations with the epistemologically undecidable or unknowable, opting instead for the metaphor of an obstacle to vision that insulates us from an outside reality without rendering that reality irrelevant, an obstacle that can be partially if never totally overcome" (Bolton, "The Mecha's Blind Spot," 461). "Sobchack's work offers a considered framework for looking at explorations of mediated experience in contexts (like film) that are already more or less mediated themselves . . . These two ideas come together in Sobchack's larger phenomenology of film experience, a theory that speaks directly to the differences between electronic and cinematic presence, and by extension to the differences between the experience of animation versus live-action cinema" (ibid., 466).

19. Ibid., 469.

20. "In 'Postmodernism, or The Cultural Logic of Late Capitalism'" (the essay that critically informs both the structure and emphasis of this present chapter), Fredric Jameson tells us that we are in the midst of 'a prodigious expansion of culture throughout the social realism' . . . Immersed in media experience, conscious of mediated experience, we no longer experience any realm of human existence as unmediated, immediate, 'natural.' We can only imagine such an experience . . . Through the last decade, even our bodies have become pervasively re-cognized as cultural, commodified, and technologized objects." Vivian Sobchack, *Screening Space* (New Brunswick, N.J.: Rutgers University Press, 1980), 236–37.

"Digital and schematic, abstracted from *reproducing* the empirical objectivity of 'nature' that informs the photographic and from *presenting a representation* of individual embodied subjectivity that informs the cinematic, the electronic constructs and refers to a 'virtual reality'—a meta-world in which ethical investment and value are located neither in concrete things nor in human lived bodies but in *representation-in-itself*. As Guy Debord has eloquently and succinctly put it, our electronic culture experiences its historical moment as if 'everything that was lived directly has moved away into a representation.'

"The materiality of the electronic digitizes existential *durée* and situation so that a centered and coherent investment in the lived-body is atomized and dispersed across various systems and networks that constitute temporality not as an *intentional flow of conscious experience* but as an *unselective transmission of random information*. The existential, bodily situation of 'being-in-the-world' becomes itself digitized, becomes a conceptual and schematic space that is both compelling and inhospitable. That is, the lived-body cannot intelligibly inhabit it . . . In an important sense, *electronic space dis-embodies*." Vivian Sobchack, *The Address of the Eye* (Princeton, N.J.: Princeton University Press, 1992), 301.

21. "But with the advent of electronic technology, from video tape on, cinema's ordering of space and time gives way to dispersal and discontinuity, an alternative and absolute world that uniquely incorporates the spectator/user in a spatially decentered, weakly temporalized, and quasi-disembodied state" (Bolton, "The Mecha's Blind Spot," 466). "The film imitates or simulates both the unified cinematic body and its electronic dissolution, resulting in an oscillation between cinematic and electronic vision" (469).

22. Bolton's analysis certainly fits with Gotō's stance, insofar as Gotō also seeks to distinguish between a shooting war and a war designed to recreate a wartime state of emergency in Tokyo. Several problems appear in Bolton's analysis, which follow directly from the Sobchak-inspired incorporation of Baudrillard in conjunction with an emphasis on representation. First, Sobchack's dichotomy of filmic and digital experience encourages Bolton to see a (false) parallel between the very *present danger* of the enemy depicted on digital screens in the opening scene of the film and *the absence* of any clear depiction of war and its violence on the TV screens of Japanese living in Tokyo alluded to in Arakawa's extended disquisition on postwar Japanese affairs. Second, by centering his analysis on modes of representation, Bolton ends up sustaining a modernist dichotomy between reality (international power politics) and representation (media) at the very moment when *Patlabor 2*, like the Gulf War, demands some reckoning with the *co-implication* of media, violence, and power. Third, Bolton strives to distinguish Tsuge's attack on Tokyo from a conventional shooting war, concluding that Tsuge's attack was not a war. Yet the strategic and tactical lesson of the Gulf War was that modern warfare incorporates deception, and that media strategy and attacks on command and control comprise its very essence. While we overhear Tsuge's forces repeating orders to kill as few people as possible, their scruples do not necessarily distinguish their project from newer, more contemporary command and control–oriented modes of warfare. While allowing for the possibility of a continuum between a deliberate shooting war and a war on mediated spectacle, I think it is also important to think through the global shift in contemporary military tactics. There has been a move from an older tactics organized around a territorial conception of the theater of war to a newer military tactics that assume a more virtual and global understanding of the theater of war that effectively incorporates attacks on command, control, and media as central aspects of state-of-the-art tactics. In other words, there is something of an uncanny convergence between Tsuge's avowed war on mediated spectacle and run-of-the-mill contemporary strategic doctrines that self-consciously focus on command-and-control systems (often including mass media) as high-value targets in what now passes for a conventional military attack. The primary difference would appear to be that, whereas the latter are typically directed at a foreign power, the former is directed at Tsuge's own country of origin. In this restricted sense, it can be seen as running counter to the conscious development of home-front media spectacle so prominent in contemporary visions of military strategy.

In his insistence that Tsuge's attack is entirely on the media, Bolton runs the risk of making claims like those of the Pentagon during the Gulf War, which insisted that the Gulf War was a clean war involving surgical attacks aimed exclusively at targets of strategic value and producing minimal casualties. The number of casualties depicted on the screen can hardly be presumed to be decisive in the context of this film. After all, the film explicitly criticizes the apathy of a Japanese public that does not understand that war produces casualties whether those casualties actually make it to the TV screen or not. A character in the last scene of the film makes the point perfectly explicit: he states that the number of casualties and the extent of the property damage caused by Tsuge's actions remain incalculable. It is precisely such evidence of the co-implication of war and media that Bolton overlooks due to his emphasis on representation.

In sum, by drawing a line, however tentatively, between a "clean" media war and a conventional shooting war, Bolton ignores the film's presentation of a war–media event that overtly blurs the boundary between an act of war and an act of terrorism, which also serves to blur the boundary between war and peace.

23. Fisch suggests that the film criticizes particular leaders rather than the system as a whole, but my viewings suggest that the delegitimation of civilian control is pervasive and done with a very broad brush.

24. It is difficult not to see a significant aspect of George W. Bush's invasion of Iraq as having involved similar psy-ops aimed at the American people and as having been conducted at the expense of claims to democratic political process in the United States and the achievement of more genuine strategic objectives that were long ignored for the sake of sustaining the spectacle of the neoconservative fantasy of the administration's choice.

25. "An example of the rules Japan has placed on its SDF forces is that, until recently under Japanese law, officers and noncommissioned officers (NCOs) were not permitted to order their troops to fire or withhold fire. This rule effectively prevented the SDF troops from acting as a unit in any combat situation, thus destroying their effectiveness. The reality of the situation was that the commanders in the field ordered their troops to fire only when ordered to do so. If an incident occurred, the field commanders took full responsibility for violating Japanese law. The field commanders were told by their superiors that they would be protected as much as possible but that they might have to take the fall if the incident caused a backlash. No incident ever took place, and in spring 1999 the Japanese Diet amended the law to permit its troops to act as a normal military unit for self-defense." Kevin Cooney, *Japan's Foreign Policy since 1945* (Armonk, N.Y.: M.E. Sharpe, 2007), 47–48.

26. In this regard, Tsuge's position resembles that of Alfred Mahan and Theodore Roosevelt, avowed models for the unilateral exceptionalism of the Bush Doctrine: "The trouble with law is that, being artificial and often of long date, it frequently is inapplicable to a present dispute . . . The settlement, therefore, is insecure, its foundations are not solid; whereas in the long run the play of natural forces reaches an adjustment corresponding to the fundamental facts of the case . . . There can be little doubt that these matters will be settled in a manner far more advantageous to the world by leaving them to the play of natural forces. It will be better to depend upon the great armaments, as institutions maintaining peace, which they have done effectually for forty years in Europe itself." Alfred Mahan, *Arbitration and Armaments, or The Place of Force in the International Relations of States* (New York: Harper and Brothers, 1912), 13.

27. Peter Katzenstein and Nobuo Okawara, *Japan's National Security* (Ithaca, N.Y.: East Asia Program, Cornell University, 1993), 44–45, 62.

28. The figure depicted in the film resembles statuary at the Angkor Thom complex in

Cambodia. Such figures are generally believed to depict a Mahayana Buddhist bodhisattva, Avalokitesvara. Dawn Rooney, *Angkor* (London: Odyssey Publications, 1999), 59 and 170. *Avalokitesvara* is translated as "sound perceiver," an apparent reference to his mission to listen and respond to the cries of unenlightened beings in distress. Alexander Studholme, *The Origins of "Om Manipadme Hum"* (Albany: State University of New York Press, 2002), 55.

29. I find Fisch's reading of the passage quite persuasive. He suggests that Jesus argues against the Pharisees' collaboration with Rome just as Tsuge's actions implicitly argue against Japanese collaboration with the United States. Fisch, "Nation, War, and Japan's Future," 10–11.

30. "We will never defeat the system on the plan of the real . . . We must therefore displace everything into the sphere of the symbolic, where challenge, reversal and overbidding are the law, so that we can respond to death only by an equal or superior death. There is no question here of real violence or force, the only question concerns the challenge and the logic of the symbolic . . . to turn the principle of its power back against the system itself . . . To defy the system with a gift to which it cannot respond save by its own collapse and death . . . the terrorists' demands amounted to a radical denial of negotiation. It is precisely here that everything is played out, for with the impossibility of all negotiation we pass into the symbolic order, which is ignorant of this type of calculation and exchange . . . The police and the army, all the institutions and mobilized violence of power whether individually or massed together, can do nothing against this lowly but symbolic death." Jean Baudrillard, *Symbolic Exchange and Death,* trans. Iain Hamilton Grant (London: Sage Publications, 1993), 36–38.

31. Michael Fisch also touches on this very important point.

32. It should be noted that the soundtrack music has been significantly rewritten and reedited for the second DVD release in terms of atmosphere and pacing.

33. This is my own translation of Arakawa's monologue. Both Fisch and Bolton discuss this monolog at some length.

34. "What is the relation between politics and life, if life presents itself as what is included by means of an exclusion? . . . In Western politics, bare life has the peculiar privilege of being that whose exclusion founds the city of men . . . The fundamental categorical pair of Western politics is not that of friend/enemy but that of bare life/political existence, *zoe/bios,* exclusion/inclusions. There is politics because man is the living being who, in language, separates and opposes himself to his own bare life and, at the same time, maintains himself in relation to that bare life in an inclusive exclusion." Giorgio Agamben, *Homo Sacer: Sovereign Power and Bare Life,* trans. Daniel Heller-Roazen (Stanford, Calif.: Stanford University Press, 1998), 7–8.

35. I would like to acknowledge that Jon Solomon's article "Taiwan Incorporated" was important for arriving at this reading of sovereignty in the Pacific as a unilateral, U.S.-centered state of exception. See Jon Solomon, "Taiwan Incorporated: A Survey of Biopolitics in the Sovereign Police's Pacific Theater of Operations," in *Impacts of Modernities,* Traces 3, ed. Thomas Lamarre and Kang Nae-hui, 229–54 (Hong Kong: Hong Kong University Press, 2004).

36. Katzenstein and Okawara, *Japan's National Security,* 132–33.

37. Ibid., 133–34.

38. I consider Aiwha Ong's *Flexible Citizenship* (Durham, N.C.: Duke University Press,

1999) and *Neoliberalism as Exception* (Durham, N.C.: Duke University Press, 2006) to be outstanding examples of scholarship that connects the issue of biopower to transnational institutions in a more far-reaching way than do Oshii or Agamben. "There are two conceptual problems with this exclusive focus on the legal and the simple bifurcation of the population into two halves: political beings and bare life. First, this axis discounts the validity of other universalizing moral discourses—the great religions, in particular—that pose alternative ethical norms of humanity . . . Agamben's fundamental reference of bare life in a state of permanent exception thus ignores the possibility of complex negotiations of claims for those without territorialized citizenship . . . But in this rigid binary opposition, Agamben seems to preclude the possibility of non-rights mediation or complex distinctions that can buttress claims for moral protection and legitimacy. It is politically and ethnographically incorrect and even dangerous to present the concentration camp as the norm of modern sovereignty. The shifting legal and moral terrain of humanity has become infinitely more complex.

Economic globalization is associated with staggering numbers of the globally excluded . . . *legal citizenship is merely one form of human protection* . . . The nonstate administration of excluded humanity is an emergent transnational phenomenon . . . Indeed, bare life itself has its own moral legitimacy, and its relationship to ethics and to labor is always open to neoliberalism as exception" [italics added]. Ong, *Neoliberalism*, 22–24.

Agamben's tendency to reduce the state of exception to a quasi-universalized and relatively ahistorical opposition between Carl Schmitt and Walter Benjamin strongly tends to obscure the competing matrices of power and agency with which Schmitt and Benjamin were often in dialogue. In my own research, this binary tends to obscure the degree to which Schmitt's own theorization of the state of exception responded to various Japanese intellectuals' earlier identification of a state of exception in international law (frequently involving the Monroe Doctrine and Japan's Monroe Doctrine for Asia) in the Pacific and was itself later widely discussed in the context of Japanese efforts to legally theorize the Greater East Asian Co-Prosperity Sphere. In addition, Agamben's binary tends to obscure the degree to which Schmitt's own position was a polemic response to the United States' positivist insistence that there was no significant conflict between a League of Nations charter that proscribed wars of aggression and the clause in the charter that specifically excepted the Monroe Doctrine from the charter such that it effectively did not apply to U.S. action in the Western Hemisphere or, indeed, anywhere the United States chose to claim their action was inspired by the Monroe Doctrine as foreign policy that did not rise to the level of codified international law.

39. *Wall Street Journal*, 1991, cited in Katzenstein and Okawara, *Japan's National Security*, 1.

40. Japan's security policy is formulated within institutional structures that bias policy strongly against a forceful articulation of military security objectives and accord pride of place instead to a comprehensive definition of security that centers on economics and political dimensions of national security. To the extent that it is purely domestic, this institutional structure subordinates military to economic and political security concerns . . . The key unity of MOFA dealing with security policy is thus placed in an organization that happens to have considerable autonomy in policy-making and accords great importance to good relations with the United States." Katzenstein and Okawara, *Japan's National Security*, 21, 29.

41. Peter Katzenstein and Yutaka Tsujinaka, *Defending the Japanese State: Structures, Norms, and the Political Responses to Terrorism and Violent Social Protest in the 1970s and 1980s* (Ithaca, N.Y.: Cornell East Asia Series, 1991), 71.

42. "Political supervision of the MPD and the other prefectural police forces by the Tokyo Metropolitan Government and other prefectural governments is almost non-existent." Ibid., 64.

43. "Under Prime Minister Nakasone, himself originally an Inspector in the MPD, many former police bureaucrats who entered politics have been given important offices . . . Over time it has been the police rather than a revived MOHA that has created a link between the cabinet and politics. This key role of the police is evidence for a qualitative increase in police power." Ibid., 80.

44. Katzenstein and Okawara, *Japan's National Security*, 54.

45. "Secrecy is a goal that governments pursue at all times. During a war, secrecy is a veritable article of faith. The temptation to manipulate the news during a war is frequently overwhelming. The farther away from the slaughter, the more optimism replaces reality. Reality is often nonexistent at the highest decision-making levels. This is especially true when you are losing a war." James Dunnigan, *How to Make War: A Comprehensive Guide to Modern Warfare* (New York: Quill, 1988), 344. I would like to thank the subtitle translator of the Bandai Visual USA DVD release of *Patlabor 2,* Dan Kanemitsu, for identifying this quotation.

46. Naomi Klein, *The Shock Doctrine: The Rise of Disaster Capitalism* (New York: First Edition Books, 2007). Tom Lamarre has recently connected Klein's point to a reading of Japanese atomic *anime* as a genre. This thesis also strongly resonates with Walter Bello's thesis that much global economic development since the Second World War in significant respects has been a function of capitalist overcapacity. In recent human history, wars and depressions have been the only effective means of countering the fundamental irrationality of this aspect of global capitalist development short of state-administered production controls.

47. Katzenstein and Okawara, *Japan's National Security*, 56.

48. "All violence as a means is either lawmaking or law-preserving. If it lays claim to neither of these predicates, it forfeits all validity. It follows, however, that all violence as a means, even in the most favorable case, is implicated in the problematic nature of law itself." Walter Benjamin, "Critique of Violence," in *Walter Benjamin: Selected Writings, Volume 1: 1913–1926* (Cambridge, Mass.: The Bellknap Press of Harvard University Press, 1996), 243.

49. Ueno touches on the issue of "constructed nature" in *Kurenai no metaru sūtsu,* 39.

50. "The war . . . watches itself in a mirror . . . And this uncertainty invades our screens like a real oil slick, in the image of that blind sea bird stranded on a beach in the Gulf, which will remain the symbol image of what we all are in front of our screens, in front of that sticky and unintelligible event." Baudrillard, *Gulf War,* 32.

51. "Now my point here is not to harangue you about animal rights, but rather to point up that current critical practice, for all its innovation and progressive ethical and political agenda, takes for granted and reproduces a rather traditional version of what I will call the discourse of speciesism . . . As Cavell's early work suggests, the traditional humanist subject finds this prospect of the animal other's knowing us in ways we cannot know and master *simply unnerving.* And in response to that 'skeptical terror,' we have mobilized

a whole array of prophylactics." Cary Wolfe, *Animal Rites: American Culture, the Discourse of Species, and Posthumanist Theory* (Chicago: University of Chicago Press, 2003), 2, 4. *Patlabor 2* is shot through with examples of the animal gaze, occasionally even involving shot/countershot structure. My research on the wartime films *Miyamoto Musashi* (1942) and *Sugata Sanshirō* (1943) suggests that wartime conceptions of a uniquely Japanese *bildung* confront the specter of coloniality and varieties of hierarchical and transnational sovereignty in the guise of conceptions of the savage, the human/animal boundary, and religious enlightenment. Unpublished research by Tom Lamarre has revealed that the deployment of animals in Japanese anime must also confront these issues of coloniality and qualified sovereignty on much the same ground.

52. Glen Mazis's *Humans Animals Machines* (Albany: State University of New York Press, 2008) sketches a notion of emotionally driven perception that seems to capture the qualities Oshii appears to associate with nonhuman animal perception generally: "We have spoken, however, as if there is a human subject—a perceiver or thinker. If we are embodied beings who first through perception and its emotional depths are connected to and oriented within a surround that becomes an extension of our body, then the dimension we have not articulated yet is that this emotional sense is a shared sense with others with whom we are emotionally interwoven" (109).

"If approached from this perspective, then instinct could be seen as part of the rhythm in which immediate flows of affect, sensation, projection, and kinesthesis are drawn toward a vaguely unattainable but highly charged and meaningful direction that pulls animals beyond themselves into an encounter with the embrace of the world. I use the word 'embrace' to indicate a kind of dance between animals and the world, a moving out of themselves in recognition toward a partnership with the other that may be fevered, and on the part of the animals might be a throwing of themselves toward the irresistibility of the other (191).

53. "The GSDF is no longer a paramilitary force with a primary mission of containing internal subversion. It has become instead a military force that, in the pursuit of "self-defense," is driven by technology and geography to project its power offshore . . . it broadens this meaning and practice of the notion of "self-defense." Katzenstein and Okawara, *Japan's National Security,* 176.

54. Richard Tanter, "With Eyes Wide Shut: Japan, Heisei Militarization, and the Bush Doctrine," in *Confronting the Bush Doctrine,* ed. Mel Gurtov and Peter Van Ness (London: RoutledgeCurzon, 2005), 157–58.

55. This observation comes from a policy debate on Fujisankei I taped during live network broadcast on the evening of December 31, 2003, and the morning of January 1, 2004.

CHRISTOPHE THOUNY

Waiting for the Messiah: The Becoming-Myth of *Evangelion* and *Densha otoko*

Wednesday, October 4, 1995, 6:30 PM, on Tokyo Channel 12, a new robot ani-mation begins, *Neon Genesis Evangelion* (otherwise known as *EVA*).[1] The TV series will consist of twenty-six episodes (1995–96), several movies remaking the ending of the TV series (1997, 2008), and an undiminished flow of manga and videogame adaptations. Originally aiming at a public of hardcore local otaku, the series soon becomes a social phenomenon capturing the attention of cultural theorists inside and outside of Japan.

Almost ten years later, *EVA* returns as a parody in the "coming of age" story of a nerdy boy, "Densha otoko" (literally "Train Man"). The story of Densha, born in the online message board 2channel, is another unexpected social boom and commercial success. Published in book form in October 2004, it had sold 1,015,000 copies by June 2005, finding exceptional popular-ity among young office ladies as a "Pure Love" (*jun'ai*) story.[2] Following the book, Densha moves across media forms to become a movie (June 2005), a TV series (July–October, 2005), several manga (the first in March 2005), and a theatrical play (August–September, 2005).

EVA and *Densha otoko* are unexpected successes, both inside and outside of Japan. They are literally translocal and transmedia events that cannot be understood simply in terms of a modern capitalist form of social collectivity grounded in a single national territory. Despite their differences in media form and content, I think that both texts explore in similar ways other forms of social collectivity at a historical moment when the everyday and war are no longer opposed and literally coexist in a singular temporality of *waiting*. This new situation forces us to rethink the definition of a social collectivity when it cannot be defined by the rhythmic alternation of war and peace. *EVA* and *Densha otoko* allow us to imagine another form of collectivity in what I call a Waiting-Room, a space of transit in which a collective subjectivity can recover a form of agency in a narrative becoming.

THE QUOTIDIANIZATION OF THE APOCALYPSE: *EVA*

On the 13 September 2000, a meteorite crashes on Mount Markham in Antarctica, melting the icecap. But in the narrative of *EVA*, this is only the official version. In reality, the "Second Impact" was provoked by Ikari Gendō and a secret organization named the SEELE[3] after their attempt to return Adam, the First Angel, to the state of an embryo. The melting of the icecap causes a rising of the water level, a change in the orbital axis of the Earth, numerous volcanic eruptions, and radical climate changes. In the disaster and civil disorder that ensue, half of the human population disappears. In a new post-apocalyptic world, the defense of peace has become the responsibility of the United Nations, which now controls both the East and the West military blocks. This state of peace is a constant negotiation of war and peace, Total Peace being another name for Total War. The new geopolitical order marks the end of a modern capitalist society, until then regulated by the alternation of war and peace, and reopens the question of the production of social collectivities.

A social collectivity in capitalist modernity can be understood as a social structure defined by a state of peace opposed to a state of war. The project of constructing a civil society would then aim at the disappearance of war. In this regard, it is not surprising that one of the most famous and controversial theories of civil society was elaborated in postwar Germany. I refer of course to Jürgen Habermas's concept of the public sphere, an artificial space of communication that through a variety of procedures aims at canceling out the possibility of conflict and war. What happens, then, when civil society can no longer be defined in opposition to war? How can it even exist as such? Or, put another way, is it even possible to conceive of a social collectivity as a social project? And if the social collectivity is not defined as a social project, what form of agency can it allow its members? If there is no more alternation between war and peace, what can be posed against civil society to allow for any kind of critical distance? Or does the coexistence of the time of war and peace in the everyday call for another imagining of the social, where a different form of collectivity can recover some form of agency?

In *EVA*, the blurring of the boundary between the time of war and the time of peace is first expressed by the end of the cycle of seasons. The Second Impact has plunged humanity into an endless summer. Time has been arrested or, rather, suspended. It has been detached from the natural cycle of seasons to become the artificial creation of an integrated social structure that would have realized its dream of completeness and wholeness. The world of *EVA*, then, is truly a second nature, defined not by natural cyclic time or by the linear time of progress but by a state of suspension, an endless summer. What is interesting here is that it is never made clear whether this human creation is voluntary or the result of an accident (a failed experiment). Indeed *EVA* constantly oscillates between the idea of absolute control in the form of a totalizing structure, through Ikari Gendō's Instrumentality Project designed to bring about the completion of the human, and the idea of the accident as absolute contingency. And interestingly enough, both ideas are problematized in relation to the question of an oncoming apocalypse. The question then becomes one of the attitude adopted toward that apocalypse, a nihilist resignation or a willful embracing. And *EVA* suggests the possibility of a third attitude, a *pathic* waiting,[4] where the apocalypse is suspended and denied. This is a different form of temporality (yet still an apocalyptic one) that, as I will argue, allows for the constitution of a collective subjectivity that does not rely on the modern individual subject of action.

> IN *EVA*, THE BLURRING OF THE BOUNDARY BETWEEN THE TIME OF WAR AND THE TIME OF PEACE IS FIRST EXPRESSED BY THE END OF THE CYCLE OF SEASONS.

What is at stake here is the question of the apocalypse as a real event opening social reality to another horizon of experience. The world of *EVA* is caught between two apocalypses, suspended in an intermediary state. It is born out of the Second Impact, already removed from an originary First Impact about which nothing is ever told. And it is awaiting a third one. In this regard, *EVA* occupies a middle position between the two forms of apocalypse defined by sociologist Miyadai Shinji, the post-apocalyptic community and the endless repetition of the everyday.[5] It is a post-apocalyptic world, but the Second Impact never becomes the originary moment that can provide

> BY REINTRODUCING WAR IN THE FORM OF A DESIRE FOR TRANSCENDENCE, EVA OPENS THE POSSIBILITY FOR ANOTHER FORM OF SOCIAL COLLECTIVITY IN WHAT I CALL THE WAITING-ROOM.

a sense of unity and consistency necessary to the reproduction of a social collectivity. On the contrary, it realizes the abstraction of society from any origin, either natural or human. Time is no longer marked by the passage of seasons, nor even by the controlled alternation of war and peace. Natural time and social time (if we define the alternation of war and peace as the classical temporal regime of civil society) have been replaced by a continuous moment of waiting.

This continuous waiting is in a way close to Miyadai Shinji's notion of a *never-ending everyday*. In the never-ending everyday, the apocalypse does not open any new horizon of experience. It has become entirely immanent to the social collectivity and actually means the impossibility of a social project of any kind, because it has no exterior. The apocalypse has become the imperative to reproduce the social structure, at the very level of everyday life. The everyday is now the critical moment, "the minimal temporal unit of experience,"[6] at which the social structure faces its desire for eternity, and potentially the impossibility of its reproduction.

As Félix Guattari argues, "Structure implies feedback loops, it puts into play a concept of totalization that it itself masters. It is occupied by inputs and outputs whose purpose is to make the structure function according to a principle of eternal return. It is haunted by a desire for eternity."[7] The aim of the social structure is therefore the abolition of linear time and of any difference between an inside and an outside, and in fact between war and peace. In Miyadai's never-ending everyday, the social structure is no longer oriented by a social project such as the abolition of war. Linear time has turned on itself to become a continuous moment, and individual subjectivity is now caught between the structure and the dream of the structure, between the collectivity of individual subjects and their integration and fusion into a mythic community.

Those two faces of the social structure as never-ending everyday are the two fantasies of modern social collectivity: civil society composed of rational individuals bound by a contract, and the mythic community of the village based on empathic ties that subsume individual differences in a homogeneous social space. Both define the two sides of a modern social structure that relies on the production of individual subjects forced to occupy an agonistic position: that of having to navigate between the two dangers of a complete isolation of the self from the social collectivity in a movement of infinite fragmentation and of both the fusion and dissolution of the self. In the end, the self is nothing but a fiction, an effect of the structure, and its agency is limited to an incessant oscillation between the two polarities of immanence and transcendence, two relative deaths that never really open onto another horizon of experience.

In *EVA* the social collectivity is still polarized by those two deaths, one in the form of the absent father (the dream of absolute control in a structure, a scenario) and the other in the form of the lost mother (the dream of a state of completion and wholeness). Yet the social collectivity never really functions as an integrated structure. This is not a question of realizing the dream of the structure: that is in fact impossible. What allows for the reproduction of the structure is precisely this oscillation between absolute fragmentation and plenitude, Big Brother and Mother Nature. And this is only possible by opening the social structure to the exterior as war. The social structure can only actualize itself against the irruption of war, but only one step removed from it, to preserve the imperative of social reproduction without falling into utter madness and destruction. In this regard, the never-ending everyday is only a social fantasy, the dream of a structure whose members have forgotten that their world can only exist against the possibility of war and destruction, that its survival relies on its opening to what Félix Guattari calls "domains of alterification."[8]

The interesting move of *EVA* is that it manages to reopen the question of the relation between war and the everyday in the formation of a social collectivity without falling back onto the model of modern civil society. By reintroducing war in the form of a desire for transcendence, *EVA* opens the possibility for another form of social collectivity in what I call the Waiting-Room.

ENTERING THE WAITING-ROOM

The opening of the structure to the world as exterior, to the possibility of "breakdown and catastrophe," allows for the emergence of an abstract machine, a Waiting-Room, as the incubator for a distinct form of social collectivity and a singular collective subjectivity. On the one hand, *EVA*'s everyday is fragmented into a multiplicity of segments that cannot constitute anymore a coherent and integrated whole. The sphere of power is as well exploded into a multiplicity of competing agencies (the United Nations, the Japanese government, NERV, SEELE, and so on). Civil society itself is completely dysfunctional, composed of autistic individuals that literally cannot hold themselves together. What happened? No real explanation is given to explain this state of things, and it might well be because the origin of the problem is not exterior but internal to the social structure itself, the effect of a movement immanent to a social structure that can only be lived as a dream, endlessly repeating itself. It is indeed a question of repetition that is at the heart of the problem here, a return of the apocalypse in a movement of transcendence.

What opens the structure to its abstract machine is a movement of repetition, a repetition composed of two moments, suspension and denial.[9] Again, this is a question of time, and the first moment of the repetition is a suspension of time, as time becomes a continuous present. This continuous present is oriented. It is a present of arrival. There is no departure, no aim to reach or home to return to. There is no social project possible here, no individual agency, only a passive or rather pathic waiting. But waiting already implies an object of waiting. It already introduces a gap into the dream of the structure, and a temporal movement that is both linear, if reversed (there is no aim as such, but only arrivals), and cyclic (but it is a repetition in difference this time, not a repetition of the same). Waiting opens the everyday to the world as open, pure exteriority, and here, war.

Fifteen years after the Second Impact, the Angels (*shito*) start randomly attacking Shin-Tokyo3. We do not know who they are, where they come from, or the reason for their attacks. The Angels are polymorphous figures of destruction that mark the irruption of the world into the everyday, the opening of the social structure to alterity and death. This is the initial setting of *EVA* and it seems in the first episodes that this external menace, these incessant and random attacks of the Angels, would allow for a mobilization of a community of fighters, a team of children using giant robots to fight for the survival of humanity. This is the grand narrative of *EVA*, and Shinji is to be the Messiah, the savior and the redeemer of humanity. But *EVA* is not a spin-off of *Gundam*.[10] This continuous exposure of the everyday to the world does not end in a commitment to war and a subjection of the individual to the social collectivity— the sacrifice of the self for the survival of the community (Figure 1).

In *EVA*, there is no return home. There is no nature to come back to, no god to appeal to, no origin—as everything is a secondary product. War cannot be avoided; it does not become a temporary space of exception before the return to a peaceful community. There is no mediation possible between the everyday and the world as war, at least not in the modern understanding of technological mediation as "means to an end," which is really what the idea of the Public Sphere is about. "To ride or not to ride" is the existential question for Shinji, who never really questions the "why" of the war itself, nor the

FIGURE 1. Shinji in transit from *Neon Genesis Evangelion*.

motivations of other individuals. Shinji does not reject his situation, his role, his identity; he denies it. Riding the EVA is what defines his very identity as an individual subject of action, the very subject produced by the structure, and this is why he constantly defers his commitment to the grand narrative. The EVA-robot symbolizes this denial of individual subjectivity and instrumental technology as a temporal movement of delaying.

In contrast to *Gundam, EVA* completely blurs the distinction between the mechanical and the organic, the EVA-robot and the child-pilot. We learn at the end of the series that the soul of each pilot's mother has been transplanted in their respective EVAs, while the EVA units themselves have been made out of Adam, the first Angel (and Lilith in the case of EVA 01, piloted by Ikari Shinji). Humanity is the last generation of Angels, the end product of a long line of genetic experiments starting with Adam and Lilith. The line is definitively blurred between the pilot and the robot; they are cousins, different and not so different. The pilot and the EVA-robot are two distinct entities that must enter into a relation of co-penetration, as suggested by the imagery of the entry plug and the amniotic-like liquid (LCL) in which the pilot is immersed. The nature of the relation between the pilot and the EVA-robot forces the externalization and relocation of subjectivity into the interface itself, thus opening the social structure to its abstract machine. Subjectivity is externalized as mediation between the heterogeneous segments of a machinic assemblage. The pilot and the robot are partial subjects, positions allowed by the interface of a social machine.

The relation between the pilot and the robot is analogical to the one between the subjects of *EVA*'s community of fighters. They only exist as partial subjects, segments of a social machine that exist in their own terms as autopoietic segments.[11] Each segment of the machine is a partial subject, a partial enunciation, with its own consistency, its own temporality of movement. How then is "machinic synchrony" possible without dissolving all its elements into a homogeneous whole? What holds the collectivity together if it cannot be a commitment to a common social project through the instrumental mediation of war?

WEAVING A STORY

EVA offers an interesting case for considering the formation of a social collectivity at a historical moment defined by the quotidianization of the apocalypse. This is first a question of technological mediation, but also very clearly one of temporality. When there is no more alternation between war and peace but literally an overexposure of the everyday to the world *as* war, when the quotidianization of the apocalypse has become the new social reality, how can a social collectivity find a form of consistency without falling back onto the modern social structure? What can allow for a synchronous movement of its members as heterogeneous segments of a machinic assemblage defined by a temporality of waiting? How can the Waiting-Room become a social machine that allows for such a community to emerge and hold?

This is where *EVA*, as well as the more recent *Densha otoko*, propose an interesting alternative to Azuma Hiroki's database theory.[12] What allows for the subversion of a totalizing social structure, of which the database would constitute the extreme incarnation, is here the collective production of a narrative. But the movement of the narrative in both *EVA* and *Densha otoko* is not based on a classical developmental model of narrativity (maturation, quest for origins, or simply realization of an objective) but rather follows a logic of repetition akin to the one analyzed by Gilles Deleuze in the case of masochism, a repetition that combines denial and suspension.[13] Denial is not a negation of the given (the world, society, the self). It is the opening of a critical space (what I call the Waiting-Room) through a movement of suspension and delaying, where the given can be contested (but not rejected or destroyed). It is the space where the given social structure can be suspended and neutralized as a fact, so that a new horizon can be opened in the form of an ideal figure suspended in a fantasy. What is critical here is this continuous hovering at the limit that allows for a pathic relation with the world, in the everyday opening to the apocalypse. By a double process of abstraction and idealization, the Waiting-Room allows for a critical distance with the world that is not a separation from (this is not a question of alienation) nor a fusion with but rather an opening to the world as alterity in the liberation of a desire for transcendence that fuels the movement of the narrative.[14]

> THE MOVEMENT OF THE NARRATIVE IN BOTH *EVA* AND *DENSHA OTOKO* IS NOT BASED ON A CLASSICAL DEVELOPMENTAL MODEL OF NARRATIVITY, BUT RATHER FOLLOWS A LOGIC OF REPETITION AKIN TO THE ONE ANALYZED BY GILLES DELEUZE IN THE CASE OF MASOCHISM, A REPETITION THAT COMBINES DENIAL AND SUSPENSION.

In *EVA* the narrative structure should be considered at two distinct but parallel levels. On the one hand there is the belief in a grand narrative of salvation sustained by a singular external worldview. On the other hand, there is a multiplicity of serial narratives based on character figures. The narrative movement of *EVA* consists then in the mediation from one level to the other, and it is here that *EVA* becomes truly innovative. In the second part of the TV series, from episode 16, the grand narrative structure is literally destroyed in favor of a proliferation of character-based small narratives. And that is deployed through a liberation of a logic of quotation that gradually undermines the overarching narrative of salvation by producing a multitude of enigmas and an excess of information. The logic of quotation, no longer subjected to the narrative of salvation, takes on a life of its own and produces a saturated field of references, a sea of information (rather than Azuma's structured database of information), the LCL or "primordial soup of life" from which emerges a multiplicity of partial subjects.

What happens here is actually the exacerbation of the commercial logic of narrative marketing analyzed by Ōtsuka Eiji in his *Teibon monogatari shōhiron* (Standard theory of narrative consumption).[15] This marketing strategy, akin to detective fiction's structure of play, consists in producing the desire for an overarching grand narrative by randomly giving bits and pieces of information to the consumers (following a logic of quotation), so that they will attempt to rebuild the grand narrative by themselves through the purchase of commercial goods. The goods here are the episodes of the TV series, and the grand narrative, the mecha genre's narrative of salvation. This particular form of narrative crystallizes the double bind of the structure, a narrative movement of progress and maturation and a totalizing and homogeneous social structure. In *EVA* the logic of quotation does not work anymore as a mediating technology giving access to the dream of the structure, the figure of completeness and wholeness, nor does it end up in a free-floating space of polymorphous subjectivity. However, the grand narrative is not exactly rejected; it is denied, by being abstracted from the movement of the narrative, the narratable,[16] and suspended in the form of an ideal figure, the mythical mother Rei of *The End of Evangelion*.

The case of Ayanami Rei is interesting to examine here as she becomes in *EVA* the central figure for this subversion of the narrative structure (Figure 2). She is an enigmatic character, embodying the two polarities of the modern social subject: the isolated, fragmented, and artificial self (Rei appears to have been created by Ikari Gendō, and there exists a multiplicity of dummies of her), and the all-encompassing, whole and natural self. Rei is an artificial double of Yui, Shinji's mother, and she becomes in *The End of Evangelion*, the ideal, primitive mother that absorbs all individual beings into

FIGURE 2. The three incarnations of Rei from *Neon Genesis Evangelion*.

a homogeneous undifferentiated whole.[17] Ayanami Rei only exists as a figure continuously moving along a line of becoming: from partial subject to partial subject.[18] She actualizes an image of life as narrative becoming in a continuous mediating movement allowed by the opening to death. This mediating movement is a repetition as suspension and denial of the apocalyptic arrival of the primitive mother, and it is realized through the figure of the Messiah, Ikari Shinji as EVA pilot. As I will argue in the last part of this paper, Densha plays a similar role in *Densha otoko* in relation to Hermes.

EVA thus actualizes a real movement of subversion of the structure. Mobilizing the expectations of its spectators-consumers, it elevates the mythical mother into the figure of an ideal, and thus liberates a collective process of narrative production. The adventure (the narratable) is no longer a detour on the way back home. It has become identified with the everyday itself, in its endless opening to the ideal figure of the primitive mother. The desire for the grand narrative produced by the marketing strategy has been displaced onto a desire for transcendence, incarnated in the figure of the Messiah. The suspension and delaying of the final arrival of the apocalypse is what opens the Waiting-Room as a space of collective narrative production. It allows a form of synchrony to emerge between the everyday and the world, through the mediation of the Messianic figure, by the opening of a gap, a critical space, in which a social collectivity can recreate itself in a collective narrative becoming.

BECOMING-MYTH

EVA thus stages the birth of the Waiting-Room as a spatial form that unifies the disparate fragments of the everyday into a collective narrative oriented by a desire for transcendence. This is neither a return to the dream of the structure nor really a departure from it. The Waiting-Room emerges through a repetition that combines a moment of suspension with a moment of delay—the denial of the end of the coming apocalypse and of the ideal of the primitive mother. The messiah becomes the figure that mediates between the everyday and the world, not to neutralize and incorporate the exterior (the world) into an everyday totalizing social structure but rather to allow for the emergence of the Waiting-Room through the manipulation of the axis of time, a liberation of the narrative as a movement of narrative becoming from which can emerge a collective subjectivity. This is not then, a question of proclaiming an absolute rupture and departure from a modern social collectivity (and the narrative form through which it reproduces itself) but rather of creating a

> DENSHA OTOKO IS FIRST ABOUT AN ONLINE COMMUNITY, A COMMUNITY OF 2CHANNELERS THAT REPRODUCES ITSELF THROUGH THE COLLECTIVE PRODUCTION OF A HETEROGENEOUS NARRATIVE AND A SINGULAR CHARACTER, "DENSHA."

productive tension between an ideal figure actualizing the utopia of modernity and a never-ending everyday.

In *Densha otoko*, the emergence of the Waiting-Room and of a collective subjectivity is again realized through a singular process of narrativization. *Densha otoko* is a standard romantic fantasy, the dream of a heteronormative capitalist structure functioning as an imaginary law elevated to the status of a transcendental ideal. A young otaku, our typical introverted nerdy young man, takes up the defense of a young (but older) office lady in her twenties when she is harassed by a drunken old man in a Tokyo commuter train. The story then centers on the building relationship between the two over the conventional course of their dating (restaurant—first kiss—confession of love). There is no surprise in the story line. There might be accidental episodes, but the outcome is defined by a simple question: "Will Densha succeed in conquering the young woman, Hermes?" Here the question is not about "riding or not riding," as in *EVA*, but rather becomes one of committing to the community of 2channelers, "leaving or not leaving."[19] The grand narrative of *Densha otoko* is a parodic repetition of *EVA* in another media form. If it starts from the staging of a desire to escape from the closed world of the otaku to become part of a heteronormative consumerist social structure, the initial question remains the same, "should I stay or should I go?" Again the "why" is not an issue as such. Nobody questions the ideal fantasy figure in its multiple arrivals. *Densha otoko* is more directly concerned with the narratable, the process of narrativization itself, than with reaching the end and bringing the narrative to closure. The story starts in the space of transit par excellence, the commuter train that gives its name to Densha and brings the goddess Hermes, the messenger of the gods.[20]

However *Densha otoko* is first about an online community, a community of 2channelers that reproduces itself through the collective production of a heterogeneous narrative and a singular character, "Densha." In this regard, it is a parodic repetition of *EVA*, but one that further embraces the liberatory potential of Ōtsuka's narrative logic by staging the collective production of the narrative itself. This is why the denial of the final apocalypse is even more clearly associated here with a question of authorship, as it is impossible to really identify the "author" of the online story or even of the book on which I base my analysis. The book actually further intensifies the tension between the individual subjectivity of the modern social structure and the collective subjectivity of the social machine by opening itself to a proliferation of character-based narratives across various media.

The narrative movement of *Densha otoko* can be defined by three vectors subscribing to the social machine's demand for self-referentiality and heteropoiesis:[21] a seriality of ordinal segments, ontological intensity (acceleration and condensation), and externalization of subjective memories. *Densha otoko* is a compilation of threads posted on 2channel, an anonymous online message board started in 1999, where each posting is minimally defined by the time of the posting and an ordinal number (Figure 3) but not necessarily a proper name pointing to a single individual (the title of each posting is by definition set as "Nanashi-san," or "Mr. No-name"). This makes for a sequential reading from posting to posting, from one voice to another, the only shifters appearing in the form of pointers to previous postings (">> 296"). Two series already run parallel here, an ordinal series and a temporal one (relative timing), the conjunction of both giving to the thread[22] a singular quality of duration. This duration is itself double, pointing simultaneously in two directions. On the one hand, it tends toward a maximum of immediacy that dissolves the mechanical succession of past, present, and future postings into a continuous moment of posting-arrivals, marked by an overflow of postings for the same moment t. On the other hand, a posting is itself already an archived trace of a past arrival on the board, and the totality of postings of a given thread from $t1$ to tx is always accessible for a retrospective

```
613 ：Mr.名無しさん ：04/05/09 04:44
    キターヾ(    )ノ゛ ヾ( ゜д)ノ゛ ヾ(゜д゜)ノ゛ ヾ(д゜ )ノ゛ ヾ(    )ノ゛ ――!!
    キタY⌒Y⌒ ( ∀゛)⌒Y⌒ (。A。)⌒Y⌒ ( ∀゛)⌒Y⌒Y  !!!
    キターヾ(    )ノ゛ ヾ( ゜д)ノ゛ ヾ(゜д゜)ノ゛ ヾ(д゜ )ノ゛ ヾ(    )ノ゛ ――!!
    キタ――――――( ∀゛)――――――― !!!!
    キタ― 〔｀∈´/) ―∈ ('/ ) ― 〔    〕 ― 〔 ､｀〕 ∋― 〔｀∈´/) ――!!!!
    キタキタキタキタ――――( ∀゛≡( ∀゛≡゛∀゛)≡゛∀゛)――――――!!!!!!!!!!
    キタ――( ∀゛)―(゛∀)―(゛ ゛)―(    )―(    )―(。  )―(A 。)―(。A。 )―――!!!
    キ…(-_-)キ(_- )キ!(- )キッ!( )キタ(.゛∀)キタ!!(゛∀)キタ!!(゛∀゛ )キタ―――!!!!
    曲・げ・て・キタ――――――( ∀゛)―――――――!!!!
    キタワァ.*゛゛ ・*:..。..。:*・゛(n ゛∀ ゛) η ・*:..。 ..。:*・゛゛ ・*!!!!☆
    キタ―(´_ゝ｀)´_>｀) ・―・)゛∀゛ミ;;;;)´A｀)´―゛)・ω・｀)゛д´)OⅢO)´∀｀)・(Ⅰ)・) ―!!!

    持ってるキタ-を全部張ってみますた
```

FIGURE 3. ASCII art from the "raw archive" of Densha Otoko's story on 2channel. http://f41.aaa.livedoor.jp/~outerdat/ (accessed July 4, 2008).

reading of the whole thread. Those two temporal series then allow for the emergence of a third one, constituted by the movements between individual postings, as direct answers, commentaries, or side musings, from posting to posting or groups of postings. Each posting is itself identified either by a proper name ("Densha otoko" being the only one here), a singular form of expression (writing and/or ASCII art) or content (pointing to an external individual state of things—a person). The text of *Densha otoko* is structured by a multiplicity of voices, a heterogeneous series of characters from which can emerge a collective enunciation.

Densha is a transcendental figure that comes from the exterior, from the world. Its appearance in 2channel is what brings about the constitution of the community of 2channelers. This community of anonymous but singular voices is always acting in reaction to Densha's postings, always waiting for the next posting, the next report. And the longer the waiting, the more intense the production of collective fantasies exploring the possible outcomes of Densha's adventures in the world, a proliferation of possible worlds brought to a momentary end by the arrival of the next report.[23]

"Transcendental" here does not refer to an a priori essence or form, pre-existing the constitution of the social collectivity. Following Bruno Latour, I suggest then that we understand transcendence as "the utterance, or the delegation, or the sending of a message or a messenger, [that] makes it possible to remain in presence—that is to exist."[24] Each report is a presenting of an ideal fantasy, a message from the world brought by the Messianic figure. The transcendental figure of the Messiah, Shinji in *EVA* and Densha in *Densha otoko,* mediates the catastrophic irruption of the world into the everyday, opening the Waiting-Room to a new horizon of experience. Densha's arrival is desired, and it is at the same time always a small death, a little apocalypse, but one that restarts the movement of the narrative. Densha's postings are described as a continuous series of attacks, successive bombings that expose the entrenched community of 2channelers (Figure 4). The quotidianization of the apocalypse has been internalized as a social condition of everyday life, a singular temporality and a form of expression not attached anymore to a theme of war.

Densha as Messiah, the ideal figure that activates the community of 2channelers, is thus actualized through the collective making of a narrative. And more importantly, it is a complete fabrication of a community that acts as a collective puppet master, devising the strategy of action for Densha (through advice, encouragement, critiques, and so on) and managing the flow of arrivals (Densha's reports) through the making of a narrative.

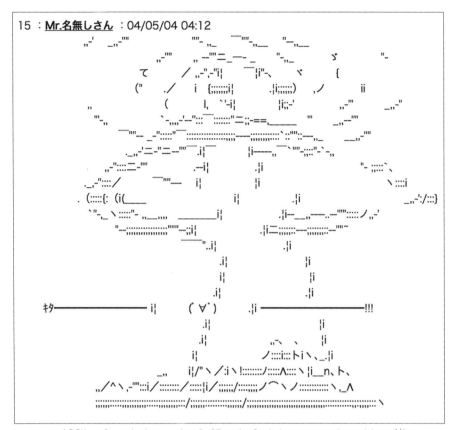

15 ：**Mr.名無しさん** ：04/05/04 04:12

FIGURE 4. ASCII art from the "raw archive" of Densha Otoko's story on 2channel. http://f41.aaa.livedoor.jp/~outerdat/ (accessed July 4, 2008).

This narrative is not so much based on a plot as on a politics of speed, one that through the operation of delaying, allows for the machinic synchrony of a collective subjectivity. As the narrative gets closer to the realization of Densha's desire (dating Hermes) the community intensifies the movement of denial and suspension by both marking its distance from Densha ("Who would have thought it would grow into such a monster?" "This is Densha and Hermes' story. Nobody can disturb them")[25] and delaying the final resolution. The multiplication of postings brings the emergence of a continuous present of arrivals, best expressed in the multiplication of "Kita"-based ASCII art (Figures 3 and 4).[26]

In the end, Densha returns to the Waiting-Room with Hermes, in preparation for the dissemination of their offspring in a transmedia world. Those successive versions of *Densha otoko* can look like degraded versions of the original online story that reground the narrative on individual life stories.

The movie is indeed nothing else but a tasteless Hollywood-style melodrama, which can make us wonder about the real potential of transmedia proliferation.[27] However, rather than a return to the individual subject, what we can see here is the proliferation across media of multiple series of character-based narratives that allow for the continuous emergence of collective subjectivities. This is what realizes the quotidianization of the apocalypse, as it prepares the Waiting-Room for the arrival of the new human, the Messiah. But the Messiah never comes as such in person, nor does it mark an objective to be reached. It can only be a suspended ideal, a becoming-myth.

IN TRANSIT

EVA and *Densha otoko* both can be read as possible answers to what I have called the quotidianization of the apocalypse, a singular temporality where the alternation between war and peace can no longer be the ground for defining a social collectivity. The overexposure of the everyday to the world calls for another form of community distinct from the model of the Public Sphere and closer to Guattari's concept of the machine. A new form of mediation is necessary, which implies a distinct narrative movement.

The Waiting-Room becomes this nonplace where a social collectivity can recreate itself through the mediation of the figure of the Messiah. A desire for transcendence emerges again, but this time associated with a singular temporality of waiting. This singular duration defined by an opening to a transcendental exterior, and the interruption of its passage by a double movement of suspension and denial allows for a synchronization of the everyday with the world, and of the multiple segments of the social collectivity with each other, in a continuous movement of passage. This is a real subversion of the social structure, and while the danger of falling back into fascism always exists, I think what keeps it at bay in these two texts is both the denial of a total departure from the modern structure and the resingularization of subjectivities in a collective narrative becoming. This allows for the emergence of a collectivity in transit, in the waiting for an apocalypse that never ceases to come, and pass.

Notes

I would like to thank Phil Kaffen, Thomas Lamarre, Thomas Looser, Keith Vincent and *Mechademia*'s editorial board for their support and stimulating comments during the writing of this article.

1. *Shinseiki evangerion,* dir. Anno Hideaki, TV series, twenty-six episodes (1995–96); translated as *Neon Genesis Evangelion: Perfect Collection,* six-DVD box set (ADV Films, 2005); *End of Evangelion,* dir. Anno Hideaki (1997), DVD (Manga Entertainment, 2002). From now on, I will use "*EVA*" to refer to the original Japanese TV series and the movies, but always as part of a larger paratext including the multiple endings, movies, manga, and parodies.

2. I will refer only to the book version, but as in the case of *EVA,* this is part of a larger paratext moving from the online forum 2channel to the multiple manga versions, TV series, theatrical play, and movie. In the novel, we never learn the "real" name of the hero who is called "Densha otoko," or simply "Densha." I will use "Densha" to designate the hero of the narrative. The author of the book version is given as Nakano Hitori, a made-up name for "individual people gathering on an internet message board," in other words 2channelers. Nakano Hitori, *Densha otoko* (Tokyo: Shinchōsha, 2004); translated by Bonnie Elliot as *Train Man: The Novel* (New York: Del Rey/Ballantine Books, 2007). I have relied on the Japanese version for this article.

3. NERV is the United Nations' special agency directed by Ikari Gendō and in charge of the fight against the Angels. But it is in fact following the orders of a secret agency, SEELE.

4. The term "pathic" is central to a genealogy of thought on affectivity that goes back to Henri Maldiney and Erwin Strauss. Strauss distinguishes two modes of connecting with the world, the pathic mode and the gnostic mode, each respectively associated with sensing and perception, the *how* and the *what* of experience: "The gnostic moment merely develops the *what* of the given in its object character, the pathic the *how* of its being as given." Erwin Strauss, *Phenomenological Psychology: The Selected Papers of Erwin W. Strauss* (New York: Basic Books, 1966) 12, quoted in Renaud Barbaras, "Affectivity and Movement: The Sense of Sensing in Erwin Strauss," *Phenomenology and the Cognitive Sciences* 3 (2004): 215–28 at 219. The pathic thus refers to a form of subjectivity grounded in sensation that does not rely on the distinction between the subject and the object (as in gnostic perception); it emerges in an active encounter with the world. In *EVA,* this encounter is best defined by a temporal form, a waiting that, as a pathic experience, suggests the possibility for another form of collective agency not based on the individual subject of action.

5. Miyadai Shinji, *Owarinaki nichijō o ikiro! Oum kanzen kokufuku manyuaru* (Live an endless everyday: A manual for completely overcoming Aum) (Tokyo: Tsikuma Shobō), 111.

6. Harry Harootunian, *History's Disquiet: Modernity, Cultural Practice, and the Question of Everyday Life* (New York: Columbia University Press, 2000), 4.

7. Félix Guattari, *Chaosmosis: An Ethico-Aesthetic Paradigm,* trans. Paul Bains and Julian Pefanis (Bloomington: Indiana University Press, 1995), 37.

8. Ibid, 45.

9. Those two moments of suspension and denial are not related in terms of prior/anterior or cause/effect. They are two logical moments of a single movement taking place simultaneously.

10. *Gundam* is a Japanese animation series created by Tomino Yoshiyuki and composed of TV series, movies, and OVAs (original video animations). The first TV series *Kidōsenshi Gandamu* aired in Tokyo from 1979 to 1980. Tomino Yoshiyuki has continued to produce *Gundam* series that take place either before or after the original series, or in

alternate universes. *Kidōsenshi Gandamu,* dir. Tomino Yoshiyuki, TV series, forty-three episodes (1979–1980); translated as *Mobile Suit Gundam,* ten DVDs (Bandai, 2001–2002).

11. The term "autopoietic" comes from cybernetics and neurology and is being used by Humberto Maturana and Francisco Varela to characterize the nature of living cells. Autopoietic machines are opposed to "allopoietic machines," which produce something other than themselves. In Félix Guattari's reappropriation of these terms, they are "auto-produced" autonomous entitites that maintain an internal level of consistency in their opening to external perturbations. Each segment of the machine is autopoietic because it manages to preserve a level of internal consistency while opening itself to and combining with other segments in the making of a machinic assemblage. In this sense, the social machine is actually a heteropoiesis. And each segment of the machine is in fact essentially a machinic heteropoiesis. Heteropoiesis thus means the necessary opening to an internal and external exteriority, to an absolute alterity, for the production of collective singularities. Humberto Marutana and Francisco Varela, *Autopoiesis and Cognition: The Realization of the Living* (Boston: D. Reidel, 1980).

12. Azuma Hiroki, *Dōbutsuka suru posutomodan: Otaku kara mita nihon shakai* (Tokyo: Kōdansha Gendai Shinsho, 2001); translated as *Otaku: Japan's Database Animals,* trans. Jonathan E. Abel and Shion Kono (Minneapolis: University of Minnesota Press, 2009). Azuma claims that contemporary societies, and in particular Japanese society, have entered "The Age of Animals." This is the full realization of the postmodern, when the grand narrative as a system of social formation and control has been replaced by a database structure. For Azuma, the database becomes the imperative basis for the constitution of subjectivity through the consumption of images at the level of affects. Questions of subjectivity appear as "effects, not causes, of the movement of images" and subjectivity is thus opened to "the implementation of social control." And it is thus at the level of affect (hence his interest in otaku sexuality) that a possibility of critique and resistance to the database would be possible. See Thomas Lamarre's introduction to Azuma Hiroki, "The Animalization of Otaku Culture" *Mechademia* 2 (2007): 177.

13. Gilles Deleuze, *Présentation de Sacher Masoch* (Paris: Minuit, 2007), 28–30; translated by Jean McNeil as *Sacher-Masoch: An Interpretation* (London: Faber, 1971), 30. This essay was first published by Minuit in 1967 in the collection *Arguments.*

14. The pathic subjectivity I evoked above is thus defined by a pathic relation with the world as exterior, allowing for a possibility of agency to emerge in the Waiting-Room, in the production of a collective narrative. Critical here should then be understood in its two senses of critical distance and critical moment in the delaying of the apocalypse.

15. Ōtsuka Eiji, *Teibon monogatari shōhiron* (Standard theory of narrative consumption) (Tokyo: Kadokawa Shoten, 1989).

16. The narrative movement I analyze in *EVA* and *Densha otoko* is akin to what Henry Miller calls "the narratable": "the instance of disequilibrium, suspense, and general insufficiency from which a given narrative appears to arise." While longing for completeness and wholeness, "the narratable inherently lacks finality." Henry Miller, *Narrative and its Discontents: Problems of Closure in the Traditional Novel* (Princeton, N.J.: Princeton University Press, 1981), ix, xi.

17. For a provocative reading of the function of Rei in *The End of Evangelion,* see the article from Mariana Ortega in the second volume of *Mechademia.* Mariana Ortega, "My

Father, He Killed Me; My Mother, She Ate Me: Self, Desire, Engendering, and the Mother in *Neon Genesis Evangelion*," *Mechademia* 2 (2007): 216–32.

18. EVA01 (in which the soul of Shinji's mother has been transplanted)—Ikari Yui (died in 2004)—Ayanami Rei (killed in 2010 by Akagi Naoko)—Ayanami Rei #2 (self-destruction in 2015, episode 23)—Ayanami Rei #3—the multiple clones of Rei immersed in the LCL (destroyed by Akagi Ritsuko)—The primitive mother. Rei is then a double of Shinji both in her connection to the ideal, transcendental mother and the mediating figure of the EVA-robot.

19. Azuma Hiroki and Kitada Akihiro have discussed the question of freedom in the Age of Animals as the one of *"oriru jiyū."* *Oriru* means to get off something like a train and, by extension, refusing to commit to a social imperative, as well as going offline. *Oriru jiyū* points at the possibility of choosing to unplug, of not committing, which can only be a form of social, if not physical, suicide. My problem with their discussion of freedom is that it remains a question of agency based on an individual subjectivity. If we are to address the question of freedom here, I would rather discuss it in terms of a strategy of denial, as there is no departure as such but only arrivals. Azuma Hiroki, ed., *Hajō genron S kai* (Net-shaped discourse S) (Tokyo: Seidosha, 2005), 227–37.

20. Interestingly, here Hermes has been feminized and turned into a goddess.

21. Heteropoiesis is literally a process of creation defined by the combination of heterogeneous elements. See note 11.

22. "Thread" (*sureddo*) is the term used in 2channel and other online forums to designate a series of postings on a given topic. After having reached the maximum number of postings for one single thread (1,000), a new one has to be created.

23. The most common forms taken by these fantasies are imaginary dialogues between Densha and Hermes, exploring all the possibilities of erotic interaction.

24. Bruno Latour, *Nous n'avons jamais été modernes* (Paris: La Découverte, 1991); translated by Catherine Porter as *We Have Never Been Modern* (Cambridge, Mass.: Harvard University Press, 1993), 129.

25. Nakano Hitori, *Densha otoko,* 145, 329. These are my translations.

26. In Japanese *kita* can mean "it has arrived," "it is here," "it is coming." It becomes in *Densha otoko* a visual onomatopoeia, integrated into ASCII art as a pure visual explosion akin to a time-image. *Kita* is thus particularly representative of this continuous presence of arrival as it blurs the distinction between past, present, and future. The end never comes but never ceases to arrive.

27. But then there is no original even to *Densha otoko,* since the publication of Densha's story in book form, as well as its successive adaptations in other media, always feed back onto 2channel through the creation of new threads and the constitution of ever-expansive online archives. In that sense, I would argue that it is not so much 2channel as the translation of Densha's story in a book form that allows for the becoming-myth of Densha as a transmedia and translocal proliferation.

MICHAEL FISCH

• • •

War by Metaphor
in *Densha otoko*

From the autumn of 2004 through the winter of 2005, the story of *Densha otoko* (*Train Man*) was nothing less than a national sensation in Japan. Emerging from a discussion forum on Japan's reputed 2channel (*ni channeru*) subculture otaku Web site, *Densha otoko* concerns a virtual otaku community that coalesces around a supposedly true romance involving a young woman and an otaku sparked by an incident on a train.[1] As an event and topic of discussion, *Densha otoko* drew its currency from a popular discourse on otaku practices with origins in the media and academia.[2] Marketed as a "pure love story" (*jun'ai monogatari*)—a genre that was extremely popular at the time—the story derived its particular novelty from the assumption that an otaku is incapable of developing normal relations with a woman, let alone an attractive one.[3]

Part of what contributed to the identification of *Densha otoko* as an otaku expression is the appearance in the story of numerous military metaphors. The metaphors escalate as the story progresses, threatening at times to overwhelm the central romantic narrative. In the following discussion I look at these metaphors not only as instantiations of an otaku culture but, moreover, in terms of their effect in creating the sense of a shared and embodied scene. The latter, I suggest, emerges via the capacity of metaphor to produce equivalence by vanishing interval, or medium, which is an impulse that I identify as relevant to narratives of technological progress and modern war. I then posit that in contrast to the military metaphors, other textual attributes in *Densha otoko* emphasize medium, relaying an extravagance that is commensurate with computer-generated representations of war. What we can discover through *Densha otoko*, I think, is a transformation of some of the central phenomena of modern technological progress, from the interval in the commuter train to the meaning of the spectacle of war.

AN UNLIKELY ENCOUNTER

Densha otoko was initially an online 2channel dialogue that lasted just over two months. In the course of the event, one of the participants compiled and archived on the server an edited version of the discussion thread, which remains accessible.[4] The final product is six chapterlike sections, labeled as "Missions," and an epilogue devoted to congratulations.

The story begins with a posting on an evening in March 2004, by an anonymous individual who describes himself only as a twenty-two-year-old *Akiba-kei* otaku with no experience with women.[5] He reports that he has just returned from browsing stores in Akihabara and intervened when a drunk began harassing a young woman on the train home. A struggle ensued, he writes, but was brought to a quick conclusion when a young salaryman and then train attendants came to his aid. With the drunk subdued, he and some other passengers were asked to file a police report at the next station, following which the young woman asked him for his address, saying that she wanted to send a gift of thanks for his courage. Bewildered to find himself being thanked by (an attractive) young woman for the first time in his life, he explains that he complied but rushed away, thus missing perhaps the chance of a lifetime.

When a thank-you gift of a Hermès teacup set arrives from the young woman two days later, the otaku again appears on the 2channel forum to report the exciting development and seek advice. Inspired by the event, the 2channel members rise to the occasion. They designate the otaku "Densha otoko" (the "Train Man")—or just "Densha" ("Train")—and the young woman "Hermès," on account of her gift, which they interpret as a sign of her refined character and tastes, and they coach Densha in his courtship of Hermès. They hold council on how Densha should ask Hermès on a date when he calls to thank her for the gift, and they prepare him for the date with a list of conversation topics, links to clothing stores, hairstylists, and restaurants, ultimately transforming him from an otaku into an apparently regular adult male. In return, Densha relays to the forum members the events of the date and each subsequent date thereafter for just over two months, drawing their envy as well as their continuous encouragement as he works up the courage to confess his love to Hermès.

A few months later, Shinchōsha, one of Japan's major publishers, picked up the story and published it with only minor revisions and maintaining the Web page format.[6] Emphasizing the challenge to authorial conventions presented by the story's Internet bulletin board origin, the author of the publication is listed as "Nakano Hitori," which works phonetically as a play on words to mean "one among the group" and is meant to refer to Densha as well as all of the anonymous 2channel contributors.[7] Over the course of the next year *Densha otoko* became an unprecedented success and was serialized in anime, manga, and a minidrama before appearing as a feature-length film. The phenomenon spurred spin-off events and discussions on the Internet and television shows and was the topic of numerous feature articles in weekly and monthly magazines, many of which suggested a need to reevaluate the negative view of otaku practices.[8]

THE MODERN INTERVAL

By virtue of its depiction of a virtual community harmoniously integrating multiplicity, and by the manner in which it foregrounds computer-mediated communication as both the subject and medium of its story, *Densha otoko* is what Richard Coyne calls a "digital narrative."[9] The pretext in *Densha otoko* for this new social form engendered through the possibilities of digital communication, however, is the modern commuter-train network and the romantic train-encounter trope.

Train cars have provided a *mise-en-scène* for romantic encounter since the advent of the railroad. First in literature and then in cinema, the train encounter is a classic motif that draws on the promises and risks inherent to mass transportation as a paradigmatic space and time of urban life. It foregrounds the train car as an intensified site of the urban crowd in which strangers are brought together, united only by their common subjection to the imperatives of mass production and consumption.[10] The train-encounter trope, moreover, manifests a certain investment of desire, hope, and anxiety in the intervals that characterize modern technological systems. It presents the interval as an overdetermined space and time that is nevertheless troubled by the conflicting impulse to maintain it as a site of creative potential and eliminate it under the rationalizing principles of a capitalist ethos.

The train encounter in *Densha otoko,* however, is merely a vehicle for Internet encounter, and it is the story of the spontaneous emergence of a virtual community that turns an otherwise unremarkable romance into an unusual event.[11] Consequently, the urban train network becomes ancillary to the Internet, rendering themes of transportation supplemental to motifs of communication, and reorganizing the space and time of the urban train under a different set of relations in a manner that reflects the fusion of train and Internet in contemporary Japan. The train car is transformed from a spatiotemporal construct dominated by visual practices (specifically reading and image viewing) into a space and time marked equally by communication. Nothing reflects this better then the trailer for the *Densha otoko* film in which Densha and Hermès share an otherwise empty train, communicating with one another first by *keitai* before coming together, as segments of the digital text from the 2channel forum stream pass the darkened windows (Figure 1).[12]

Concomitant to the reworking of the train encounter motif, *Densha otoko* bespeaks a transformation in the nature of the commuter and crowd that is exemplified in the authorial designation "Nakano Hitori"—"one among the group." While alluding to a modern paradigm of alienation, the phrase *nakano hitori* realigns relations to refer to a condition of being-in-connectivity. *Nakano hitori,* one among the group, announces a desire for connectivity that precedes connection. Borrowing from science fiction—in the otaku spirit—like the designation of the character from *Star Trek: Voyager,* Seven-of-Nine, it bespeaks perpetual connection to a finite unit within the framework of a larger collective (like nation, or Borg) that, although important, is less significant in one's everyday life since the unit, rather than collective, is the immediate framework of individual identity. *Nakano hitori* is connectivity to a determinate group that supplants kinship and company as well as the classic binaries of public/private, individual/social. It is why we never hear of Densha's family, although presumably he lives with them.

> THE TRAIN ENCOUNTER IN *DENSHA OTOKO,* HOWEVER, IS MERELY A VEHICLE FOR INTERNET ENCOUNTER, AND IT IS THE STORY OF THE SPONTANEOUS EMERGENCE OF A VIRTUAL COMMUNITY THAT TURNS AN OTHERWISE UNREMARKABLE ROMANCE INTO AN UNUSUAL EVENT.

FIGURE 1. Internet and train merge in the cinematic representation of *Densha otoko*.

WAR BY METAPHOR

Military metaphors begin in *Densha otoko* with the designation of the chapters as "Missions." But they do not gain momentum until after a relatively civil Mission 1, in which the 2channel group coaches Densha through phone calls to Hermès and subsequent preparations for the first date—new clothing, haircut, contact lenses. Beginning with the preface to Mission 2, the language of *Densha otoko* becomes suddenly rich with military metaphors:

> In the unbearable anticipation of waiting for Densha's return, the others' imaginations run wild and just when they are ready to burst, Densha returns. Slowly but surely he begins dropping the bombs.[13]

When Densha finally appears the alarm is sounded: "Air Raid! Air Raid! To your positions!" As Densha relays the content of his dates with Hermès—the small victories like holding her hand or the first kiss, the 2channel participants respond:

635 Name: Mr. Anonymous Submission Date: 04/04/23 23:02
Air Raid! Air Raid!

All hands evacuate!

654 Name: Mr. Anonymous Submission Date: 04/04/23 23:10

Search team what are you doing!

Lay down a barrage!

All members of unit 1, take your positions![14]

As Michael Hardt and Antonio Negri observe, the rhetoric of war is often applied to situations outside actual armed conflict. Military metaphors find their way into sports events, commerce, and politics as a means of emphasizing the associated risks, competition, and conflict.[15] Naturally, these terms are equally applicable to the tensions that accompany a budding romance. Hardt and Negri also observe that war is invoked as a "metaphorical discourse" in political or social campaigns (like "the war on poverty") for its efficacy in mobilizing society toward a common goal, which is similarly relevant to the manner in which battle metaphors in *Densha otoko* work to create a sense of community.

> READ AS METAPHOR, THE LANGUAGE OF CONFLICT IN *DENSHA OTOKO* INSISTS THAT DENSHA'S ROMANCE WITH HERMÈS *IS* AN ATTACK ON THE OTHER 2CHANNEL PARTICIPANTS.

Intent as they are on delivering their political prophecy, what Hardt and Negri fail to consider is the potential comic effect of battle metaphors and imagery when applied to the presumptive antithesis of war—love. For the most part, the military metaphors in *Densha otoko* are simply humorous, performing as otaku self-parody. When the presumably otaku 2channel participants draw on images of armed conflict to convey their sense of shock and envy over Densha's romantic adventures, it substantiates both initial comic premises behind the story, that the otaku are romantically challenged and that otaku are obsessed with depictions of weapons and war. The language, moreover, establishes a correlation between the two assumptions, suggesting that an obsession with war and weapons is decidedly fetishistic, a substitute for women, romance and sex.

The humor and sense of community invoked through metaphors of violent armed conflict in *Densha otoko* also needs to be situated in a historical context with another Internet-based practice among youths, one marked by violence and often problematized in the Japanese media: *netto shūdan jisatsu*, or "Internet [facilitated] group suicide." Like *Densha otoko*, *netto shūdan jisatsu* exploits the Internet bulletin board format to bring together complete strangers. The sociality it cultivates, however, could not appear more antithetical to that of *Densha otoko*, with the violence of the latter remaining figurative while that of the former realized in an abstruse gesture of communal bond. In *netto shūdan jisatsu* the individuals typically meet only once and rent a car to drive to some secluded location, where they seal the windows before igniting charcoal burners inside the car, causing eventual asphyxiation. Amid the anxiety concerning the mental health of the nation's youth that such practices have inevitably spurred, the seemingly innocuous banter and evocations of conflict in *Densha otoko* resounds with a cathartic effect.

THE POWER OF METAPHOR

Humor aside, what is remarkable about the military metaphors in *Densha otoko* is the mostly conventional nature of the weaponry. There are no lasers, no satellite guided missiles, and no futuristic metal battle suits. Instead, there are only simple aim-and-shoot guns, drop-and-explode bombs, and an occasional antiaircraft missile. The weaponry corresponds to the modality of modern industrial war and to the story's initial thematic device, the train, not only by virtue of the role played by the railroad in modern warfare but also via a common logic of interval. The impulse behind this logic is exemplified in the force of the weapons imagery as metaphor.

The power of metaphor lies in its capacity to establish equivalence between dissimilar things. This is of course the premise behind Hardt and Negri's observation concerning war rhetoric. Although Hardt and Negri tend to use metaphor and analogy interchangeably, there is an important difference between the terms. As Paul de Man suggests, what allows for equivalence through metaphor is a process of abstraction that involves "ceasing to think of the properties by which things are distinguished in order to think only of those qualities in which they agree."[16] Thomas Keenan expounds on de Man's definition, positing that through abstraction the semantic perimeter of a thing is ruptured, opening up the possibility of an "axis of commonality or channel of communication between different things and within different uses."[17] Keenan chooses his words carefully. A "channel of communication" denotes the creation of medium that is nevertheless obscured in the final production of equivalence. Metaphors not only suggest but rhetorically insist that something *is* something else. By contrast, analogy only suggests resemblance. Like metaphor, it opens a "channel of communication" between two things but stops short of vanishing that medium of correspondence by the addition of the preposition. Read as metaphor, the language of conflict in *Densha otoko* insists that Densha's romance with Hermès *is* an attack on the other 2channel participants. Densha's reports are literally bombs that rain down on the forum participants. As analogy, the language of conflict lacks impact, suggesting only that Densha's budding relationship *is like* an armed attack on the otaku virtual community.

The power of metaphor lies in its capacity to produce through immediacy an affect of presence, which in *Densha otoko* amounts to creating a communal *mise-en-scene* for a social intercourse that otherwise lacks a recognizable terrain. This is demonstrated clearly in one of the more remarkable instances in which the description of romance evokes images of armed conflict. The passage adopts a long soliloquy-like style and appears in Mission 6, when Densha signs off after describing a long-anticipated kiss with Hermès in a car:

> It's gotten all quiet here.
>
> It's as if the intense air strike never happened, in the silence, the surviving soldiers huddled together happy to be alive. Had the bombing begun in the early morning? That too, is now a long-lost memory. But still, looking across the field, a mountain of skeletal remains. Random body parts, hands, legs, fingers, hairs, eyeballs . . . what a destructive force. The damage sustained by the few survivors is in itself horrifying.
>
> Next to me stands an otaku soldier continuing to aim his M92 into the emptiness even though he's out of bullets. Staring into the void, he mutters to himself, "he's come." Grinning from ear to ear. Only the continuous clicks of his trigger echo hopelessly across the battlefield.
>
> The gun points in the direction where he [Densha] flew off. He [Densha] said, "We'll resume by the end of today.[18] I can't think at all. My skull is still rattled from the explosions. Surely he's going to begin attacking again in a few hours as promised. The command center has been annihilated. But . . . I . . . can still move . . . and will fight to the end . . ."[19]

The tone is poetic, evoking pathos in the desolate scene of the battlefield and its ghostly images. These are not firsthand descriptions of real battle, or even an articulation of a desire to experience real war, but rather filmic idioms borrowed intact and deployed specifically for their cinematic currency and effect in producing a virtual landscape for a context that has no other site than a screen and text. The writer exploits the vision to invoke community in the fraternity of defeat by picturing not himself but the shock and awe of his devastated/envious companions. For a moment we forget that these are most likely the words of someone sitting alone in their room in front of a monitor. We can see in our mind's eye the soldiers huddled in silence and the skeletal remains, and we can hear the sorrowful clicking of the rifle trigger as we have seen and we have heard it before in countless films and novels.

By virtue of its impulse toward instantaneity and production of presence, metaphor shares a certain spatial and temporal logic with the trajectory of modern technology and communication media. According to what has become a conventional narrative, the history of modern technological progress has been marked by a drive toward the elimination of interval, or a "logic of immediacy dictates that the medium itself should disappear and leave us in the presence of the thing represented."[20] Paul Virilio characterizes this development as a march toward the eclipse of interval by interface, of real space by real time, and the experience of departure and journey by arrival as society succumbs increasingly to the valorization of ends over means.[21] Modern war, according to Virilio, exemplifies—if not drives—this process under the principle that conflicts are determined in a field of perception whereby to see an enemy is to be able to destroy it. The corollary is that movement of images in modern war is ultimately as significant (if not more so) than the movement of troops or weapons. Cinema and war and camera and gun converge as the sights of a weapon, eye, and viewfinder line up, succumbing to the impulse to eliminate the time and space between event and representation, between the discharge of a bullet or bomb and its impact.[22]

In Virilio's and other theories of new media, digital communication technology often emerges as falling comfortably into this narrative of technological progress. Accordingly, digital technology is imagined to do what analog does but better, eliminating almost entirely the effects of mediation. In fact, digital recording and communication technology seems to perform so well, with such instantaneity and lossless efficiency, that it initiates a logic of reversal, giving rise to anxieties over the loss of substance and depth of culture and social relations.

In the following, I look at how the playful manipulation of symbols and characters in the text of *Densha otoko* suggests an alternative to the narrative of technological progress as determined by an underlying impetus to the elimination of the medium. I show that, rather than obscuring medium, the text of *Densha otoko* works to foreground it as a site of empowerment. In representations of war that exploit computer graphics, to which *Densha otoko* alludes, something similar happens. The result is a shift in focus from creating the sense of the real to producing the possibility of being there but being radically transformed at the same time and a presentation of the body as a site symbolic excess.

INDULGENCE IN THE MEDIUM

The text of *Densha otoko* presents a blend of semantic and phonetic word-plays, extensive character transpositions from *hiragana* and *kanji* into *hankaku* (*katakana*) *moji, emoji* (picture characters), and elaborate graphics in Japanese ASCII art.[23] The combination and array of textual permutations produce a range of nuance in meaning and affect while foregrounding questions of readability. To begin to understand the specificities of the different expressions would require an extensive analysis that is beyond the parameters of this article. In the following, I want to focus only on the manner in which the text draws attention to its digital medium.

Many of the wordplays in *Densha otoko* operate by means of a kind of textual disfiguring that uses homonymic or phonetically similar *kanji*. One especially prevalent example is the use of character for "poison" (*doku*) together with "man" (*otoko*) to mean "bachelor." In contrast to the standard combination for the word using the *kanji* for "single" (*doku*) with "person" (*shin*), and "man" (*otoko*), the "*doku otoko*" combination conveys an element of comic cynicism in the implication that otaku are either poisoned by their lack of a (female) partner or alone because they are poisoned. Another frequent textual occurrence uses the *kanji/hiragana* combination for "leak" (*more*) to mean "I," instead of the proper character for the familiar pronoun, *ore*.[24] As the writer and critic Suzuki Atsufumi notes in an analysis of *Densha otoko*, it is impossible to know whether such word plays were begun intentionally or were initially the result of script conversion misses (*henkan misu*)—a kind of typographical error produced when inputting Japanese phonetically via a QWERTY keyboard for a digital medium.[25] In either case, the combination foregrounds the real-time temporality of Internet communication, linking the input of text with its transmission (rather than storage) and subsequent impossibility of revision.

Hankaku moji accentuate another dimension of the digital medium. They appear as half-width characters and are technologically distinct in their use of one byte of data, rather than two bytes required for *kanji* and *hiragana*. Significantly, according to the editor in charge of *Densha otoko* at Shinchōsha, prior to the publication, *hankaku moji* were exclusive to digital media, setting them outside the domain of official publishing markets and conventional print economy.[26] In *Densha otoko*, words typically written in *hiragana* or *kanji*, like *kita*, meaning "has come," are regularly converted to *hankaku moji*. The permutation produces a certain affect of playful exuberance and is used especially when Densha returns to the forum following his dates with Hermès. It plays as well on the expression, "the train has come/arrived" (*densha ga kita*).

The creation of *emoji* with Japanese ASCII symbols, either on their own or with *hankaku moji,* further embellishes the text with affect, as in the accompanying example expressing irrepressible excitement at Densha's return from a date (Figure 2).

Companions to the emoticon, *emoji* can be input on *keitai* (third-generation [3G] Internet cell phones) or in some computer programs in the symbol format and converted to emoticons by *henkan* or the "Return" key. Infusing the text with sentiment pictorially, their superlative format is typically the animated emoticon, and in some cases in the online text of *Densha otoko* animated *emoji*. Although it seems likely that *emoji* have a significant precedent in manga, they are an unequivocal index of digital communication.

The Japanese ASCII art in *Densha otoko* is diverse and impressive, denoting a considerable investment of time and effort. Some illustrations are only loosely connected with the topic of the conversation thread, appearing more as displays of technological proficiency. A few, however, appear as graphic equivalents of the military metaphors, depicting some manner of military or war-related scene (Figure 3).

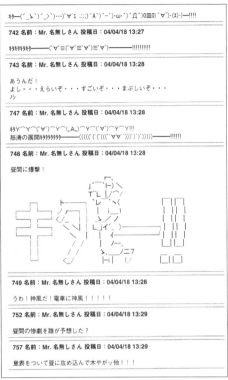

FIGURE 2. A typical section of discussion thread from the story.

Whereas the military metaphors operate via a semantic dimension once removed from the surface of the text to conjure images in the mind of the reader, the digitally specific symbol configurations perform at a graphic level. While all text functions via a graphic element, the inability in the majority of instances to align the symbols with a phonetic register or to apprehend decisively their meaning confines them as an event to the surface of interface and a visual economy that, importantly, conveys unmistakable extravagance; it is not simply that to create these combinations demands a considerable investment of time and labor but also the sense of excess relayed by seemingly unnecessary repetition. Overall, what emerges is a display of indulgence in the possibilities of the medium and its transformative powers. Such

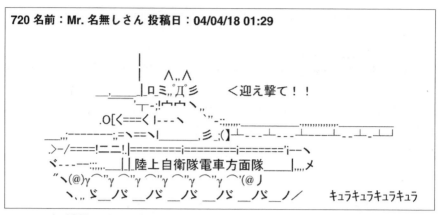

FIGURE 3. An ASCII rendition of a tank.

indulgence is precisely the object of digitally empowered representation and nothing provides a more ideal setting than the depiction of armed conflict. Through computer graphics, representations of war are events of graphic extravagance that situate the body specifically as a site of impossible excess. War figures thus not as an inevitable human tragedy but rather as a scene of symbolic extravagance.

SPECTACLES OF EXCESS

A commensurate relation between the performance of digital text in *Densha otoko* and representations of combat rendered via computer graphics is established in *Densha otoko* when Densha insists on giving Hermès *The Matrix* film trilogy (1999–2003) and then discussing the films with her at length.[27] The films are an obvious means for acquainting Hermès with the 2channel existence, which Densha cannot disclose to her for fear of revealing himself as an otaku and the possibility that she might discover that he has been discussing their dates in detail with hundreds of strangers. A reality defined by perpetual connectivity is the premise behind both the 2channel world and the construct of the world in *The Matrix*; the condition of *nakano hitori* is also the condition of *The Matrix* and an expression of simultaneous multiplicity and unity as the result of networked minds.

Where *Densha otoko* indulges in the digital medium through a textual excess, *The Matrix* films present scenes of fantastic combat. Combat is the pretext for connectivity within the story and the underlying spectacle for the audience. On a thematic level, *The Matrix* films demonstrate that the point of the digital connectivity is not simply an increased sense of immediacy and presence afforded by the better connection but rather the chance to be there and be radically transformed at the same time. There is, after all, no point to virtual reality if one is forced to be the same person as in the nonnetworked world. The "there" of virtual reality, moreover, is the medium itself such that "being there" works against the rationalizing ends-over-means trajectory associated with technological progress under capitalism.

> THROUGH COMPUTER GRAPHICS, REPRESENTATIONS OF WAR ARE EVENTS OF GRAPHIC EXTRAVAGANCE THAT SITUATE THE BODY SPECIFICALLY AS A SITE OF IMPOSSIBLE EXCESS.

As spectacle, the graphic extravagance of combat in *The Matrix* films recall the kind of symbolic excess that Georges Bataille attaches to sacrifice in a general economy. Spectacular excess, not war as a topic, is the objective of digitally rendered representations of war just as in a general economy war is a means to useless consumption embodied in the lavish sacrifice of prisoners rather then an end in itself.[28] The gratuitous violence of digitally rendered combat, like the useless consumption of sacrifice exceeds the threshold of the symbolic economy. The focus of both is the body, with computer graphics–created wars transfiguring and destroying bodies in a manner as sumptuous as the ritual of human sacrifice in ancient Mexico, which Bataille describes vividly as involving a priest who would tear out the still beating heart of a sacrificial victim and hold it up as an offering to the sun.[29] Unlike in the horror film, whose force lies in the premise of a viewer's empathy with the tortured body, in the digitally rendered conflict the body is pure spectacle, transformed into an impossible and otherworldly object like the sacrificial body, thus foreclosing the possibility of viewer identification.

....

Notes

1. Translated into English, *ni channeru* means simply "second channel." According to the site's founder, Nishimura Hiroyuki, the name is a reference to television's second channel, which in Kantō is an empty space of white noise in Japan's broadcast spectrum and an opening for other media such as videotape and game machines. Interview with Nishimura Hiroyuki at Kuwasawa Design School moderated by Ozaki Tetsuya, posted to "RealTokyo," February 10, 2005, http://www.realtokyo.co.jp/english/redesign/004_1.htm (no longer accessible). The OED defines an otaku as "a person extremely knowledgeable about the minute details of a particular hobby (esp. a solitary or minority hobby); *spec.* one who is skilled in the use of computer technology and is considered by some to be poor at interacting with others." The term "otaku" is embedded within a vast social discourse

on Japanese youth that encompasses concerns over the alienating effects of technology and perceptions of a refusal among the younger generation to submit to conventional structures of labor and production—of either capital or children. Typically male, anywhere from early teens to middle age, the otaku is seen as harboring an obsession for anime and manga, choosing its world of fantasy infused with depictions of fantastic futures and technologies, exhilarating battles, and idealized (impossibly proportioned) female heroines over reality. He commits his life labor to this world, piously collecting related paraphernalia and embellishing, translating, pirating, remixing, and circulating anime within a network among other otaku, which comprises his only ostensible link to other human beings, and remains comfortably within the parameters of his fantasy domain. It is not just that the otaku is skilled with computer technology, but moreover the perception of an inherent commensurability between the ontology of the computer and otaku practices. In the capacity it provides for manipulating, organizing, and storing vast amounts of data, its support of complex fantasy games, and its role in the creation of a seamless and perpetual distributed network for file sharing and virtual communication among discretely situated otaku, the computer seems to have emerged in direct response to the desires of otaku practices.

2. Prior to *Densha otoko* the most powerful images of otaku in the media were by Miyazaki Tsutomu, a serial killer arrested in 1989 for the gruesome murder of four young girls, and Taku Hachirō, a once popular television character whose strikingly unattractive appearance facilitated a negative stereotype of the otaku. *Densha otoko*'s success did much to rehabilitate the social status of the otaku in Japanese media. In contrast to these two images, *Densha otoko* presents the otaku as naïve but ultimately courageous, genuine, gentle, and attentive. International interest in the otaku in academia and the media has been spurred by the perceived relation between otaku and anime, and the ascension of the latter over the past two decades to the status of a recognized global commodity and item. Concurrently, this international attention has provided momentum in Japan to an otaku discourse. The Tokyo University professor Azuma Hiroki is one significant contributor to this discourse. Asserting the notion of an inherent postmodern quality to otaku practices, Azuma emphasizes the otaku's penchant for simulacra, online communication and file sharing, exploitation of a database of characters and narratives in the production of a supplemental fanzine-like body of work, and the otaku's ostensible disregard for the conventions of the mainstream profit-oriented culture industry Azuma Hiroki, *Geemu teki riarizumu no tanjō: Dōbutsuka suru posutomodan 2* (The birth of game-like realism: Animalizing postmodern 2) (Tokyo: Kōdansha, 2007).

See also Thomas Lamarre's discussion of Azuma and the otaku discourse in "An Introduction to Otaku Movement," *Entertext* 4, no. 1 (2004/2005), http://arts.brunel.ac.uk/gate/entertext/4_1/lamarre.pdf (accessed June 9, 2008).

3. This assumption was emphasized in the television miniseries of *Densha otoko* by the casting of the well-known model Itō Misaki as Hermès. Similarly, in the film version, Hermès is played by the actress/model Nakatani Miki.

4. *Densha otoko*, "Mission One 1 Emergency Operation (*kinkyū shirei*)," 2channel Web site, http://www.geocities.co.jp/Milkyway-Aquarius/7075/trainman1.html (accessed June 9, 2008).

5. An "*Akiba-kei* otaku" is an otaku who frequents the "Electric Town" neighborhood

around Tokyo's Akihabara train station, which is famous for its concentration of technology-related establishments.

6. Nakano Hitori, *Densha otoko* (Tokyo: Shinchōsha, 2004); translated by Bonnie Elliot as *Train Man: The Novel* (New York: Del Rey, 2007).

7. The editor in charge of the *Densha otoko* project was Gunji Hiroko, whom I interviewed February 2005. She explained that another editor who often checks 2channel had come across the text by accident and suggested it for publication for a niche audience of readers accustomed to the Web but unlikely to read a long text on a computer screen. The overwhelming popularity of the text was unexpected. Published in autumn 2004, it sold 260,000 copies in just three weeks and half a million copies in two months.

8. See for example, "*Densha otoko ga būmu ni*" (*Densha otoko* becomes a boom), *SPA*, December 13, 2005, 91; Tsubouchi Yūzō, "*Densha otoko wa, aru imi de shōsetsu no dentō ni nottotteru ne*" (*Densha otoko* complies to some extent to the traditional novel), *SPA*, January 25, 2005, 116–19; Uchiyama Hiroki, "*Densha otoko yomu onna no ren'aijukudo*" (The level of romantic maturity of women who read *Densha otoko*), *AERA*, November 22, 2004, 29–30.

9. Richard Coyne, *Technoromanticism: Digital Narrative, Holism, and the Romance of the Real* (Cambridge, Mass.: MIT Press, 1999).

10. Similarly, it is a space and time marked by shared sense of alienation from traditional relations. See Lynne Kirby, *Parallel Tracks: The Railroad and Silent Cinema* (Durham, N.C.: Duke University Press, 1997).

11. Okazaki Takeshi points out that if *Densha otoko* had merely been the story of one young man's struggle to confess his love to a woman, it would not have been interesting. It is the effect of the countless anonymous posters who rush to help Densha that lends the story its energy. Okazaki Takeshi, "Besutoseraa: Shinsatsushitsu" (Bestseller: Examination room), *Chūōkōron* 120, no. 2 (2005): 264–65.

12. *Keitai* are 3G cell phones with Internet access. They can access special *keitai* formatted Web pages through a *keitai* Web browser (some also reduce regular Web pages to a *keitai* format) and can be used to send and receive email.

13. Nakano, *Densha otoko,* 66. Unless otherwise noted, translations from Japanese to English are my own.

14. Ibid., 209–10.

15. Michael Hardt and Antonio Negri, *Multitude: War and Democracy in the Age of Empire* (New York: Penguin Press, 2004), 13.

16. Paul de Man, quoted in Thomas Keenan, "The Point Is to (Ex)Change It: Reading *Capital,* Rhetorically," in *Fetishism as Cultural Discourse,* ed. Emily S. Apter and William Pietz, 152–85 (Ithaca, N.Y.: Cornell University Press, 1993).

17. Ibid.

18. I have glossed over a mistype in the original where "by the end of the day" (*kyō jū*), appears as a combination of the characters for "today" (*kyō*), and "gun" (*jū*). This does not appear to be an intentional play on words, like the examples discussed in the latter part of my argument, because there is no recognizable semantic, graphic, or phonetic play from the character combination.

19. Nakano, *Densha otoko,* 305–6.

20. David Jay Bolter and Richard Grusin, *Remediations* (Cambridge, Mass.: MIT Press, 1999), 5–6.

21. Paul Virilio, *Open Sky* (London: Verso, 1997).

22. Paul Virilio, *War and Cinema: The Logistics of Perception* (London: Verso, 1989). In Virilio's theory, the corporeality of embodied vision presents the final obstacle in the pursuit of speed in televisual apparatuses, demanding ultimately that the human be displaced as a seeing subject.

23. Japanese ASCII art is distinguished from ASCII art by its use of symbols from the Shift_JIS character set.

24. The use of *more* instead of *ore* also suggests the combination of *ore to monachan*, which refers to the 2channel character *monachan* to mean "me and *monachan*."

25. Suzuki Atsufumi, *"Densha otoko" wa dare na no ka: "Netaka" suru komyunikeishon* (Who is *Densha otoko*: Neta-ization communication) (Japan: Chūōkōron Shinsha, 2005), 19–20.

26. According to the editor, when Shinchōsha initially approached their publishing section with the idea for the *Densha otoko* book they were told that it would be impossible without developing new printing technology. However, this may not be entirely accurate. It seems more likely that the difficulty arose from the slight disparity in the character display among different web browsers and operating systems. In other words, a character, symbol or spacing input on one type of web browser sometimes appears different on another type of web browser. Because of the unconventional use of characters and symbols, combined with the inability to know what web browser and system a specific poster is using, it would be impossible to determine the original text and intention. Again, this is a problem particular to the digital medium.

27. On the second date Densha gives Hermès *The Matrix* trilogy collection on DVD as required viewing, warning her that the story gets complicated. He then devotes later dates to explaining the films to her and they discuss the relations between its central characters.

28. The film *300* (2006) also comes to mind. Far more important than the narrative in this film is the extravagant spectacle of carnage empowered by computer graphic technology.

29. Georges Bataille, *The Accursed Share: An Essay on General Economy* (New York: Zone Books, 1988), 49–50.

History / Memory

DENNIS WASHBURN

• • •

Imagined History, Fading Memory: Mastering Narrative in *Final Fantasy X*

The convergence of media over the past two centuries has made access to various forms of representation and information nearly instantaneous and, at least potentially, global in reach. Participatory, interactive technologies that have been developed over the past three decades in particular have accelerated the pace of this convergence and intensified some of its most profound effects, including the compression of the experience of time and space and the disruption of older regimes of knowledge. Henry Jenkins has observed that "the power to participate within knowledge communities" now exists alongside the power of the nation-state and of corporations to control the flow of knowledge, and thus has the potential to act as a corrective to them. Jenkins, however, tempers this optimistic view somewhat by also noting that older regimes are already seeking to co-opt participatory media, and that, in any case,

> there are no guarantees that we will use our new power any more responsibly than nation-states or corporations have exercised theirs. We are trying to hammer out the ethical codes and social contracts that will determine how we will relate to one another just as we are trying to determine how this power will insert itself into the entertainment system or into the political process.[1]

The cautionary tone Jenkins adopts concerning the moral and political ramifications of the accelerated pace of media convergence is wise, but it is also of a piece with an ongoing anxiety about the effects of convergence characteristic of the culture of modernity.[2]

David Harvey has argued that this anxiety arises in part because the compression of the experience of space and time and the disruptions of traditional regimes of knowledge have contributed to a sense that modern life is fleeting, ephemeral, and contingent. The consequence is that modernity is seen to have no respect even for its own past. If history has any meaning, it can only be found in the disruptive process of change itself: "Modernity, therefore, not only entails a ruthless break with any or all preceding historical conditions, but is characterized by a never-ending process of internal ruptures and fragmentations within itself."[3] The fragmented, transitory nature of the condition of modernity renders history discontinuous, and thus the collective unity of historical time, the linearity that traditionally bound the present and the future to the past, is no longer accepted as plausible, but has to give way to heterological conceptions of historical narrative.

The disruption of a sense of historical continuity has had an especially profound impact on the hierarchical relationship between memory and history. Pierre Nora has identified this disruption as "the acceleration of history"—a concept he defines in terms that echo Harvey's description of the culture of modernity:

> An increasingly rapid slippage of the present into a historical past that is gone for good, a general perception that anything and everything may disappear—these indicate a rupture of equilibrium. The remnants of experience still lived in the warmth of tradition, in the silence of custom, in the repetition of the ancestral, have been displaced under the pressure of a fundamentally historical sensibility . . . We speak so much of memory because there is so little of it left.[4]

The collapse of memory, in Nora's view, has occurred because it operates in fundamental opposition to history. Memory atomizes the sheer data of experience and emphasizes the present as the temporal context in which individual lives may be understood. Because the acceleration of history disrupts the individual's sense of connection with the past, a sense of the collective unity of the past can be recovered only through what Nora calls "sites of memory," places where an imagined collective memory acts as a simulacrum of actual memory to resituate the present within a historical narrative of the past. In Nora's account, memory is spontaneous and absolute, "a perpetually actual phenomenon, a bond tying us to the eternal present," while history is "a representation of the past," a critical discourse that can conceive of the relative only.[5]

Nora locates the cause of the breakdown of older regimes of knowledge—whose authority derived from historical consciousness based on actual memory—in the rise of mass media and global culture. Here again his analysis overlaps with Harvey's and provides a useful starting point for considering the specific impact of interactive technologies, which, as noted above, have helped accelerate the convergence of media. The relatively recent development of videogames in particular, especially those games with complex narratives that create alternative worlds and simulated histories, provide new formats for telling stories through a synthesis of older media, both textual and cinematic, within a framework created by the conventions and practices of gameplay. Such highly narrativized games reflect, and reflect on, the disruptive effects of convergence, and, more important, make use of the rift between history and memory as a central element of narrative, theme, and game design.

> IN NARROWLY RHETORICAL TERMS THE GENRE OF FANTASY AT LEAST STRIVES TO MIMIC THE REALITY EFFECTS, ESPECIALLY THE ILLUSION OF TEMPORAL PROGRESSION, OF HISTORICAL NARRATIVES.

An example of a work that makes the relationship of memory, history, and the struggle for control of knowledge a central element of both its gameplay and its narrative is *Final Fantasy X* (hereafter, *FFX*). The *Final Fantasy* series is Square Enix's most successful franchise, and *FFX* has been one of the most popular titles in Japan since its initial release in 2001.[6] It was the first game in the series released for the PlayStation2 console and designed to take full advantage of the visual capabilities of that particular platform. *FFX* merges electronic game, written text,[7] soundtrack and music, and digital film consisting of cut scenes of varying length and production quality, to construct a long and complex story.

The unfolding of the story creates a series of intersections between the history of the fantasy world of Spira and the individual memories of the major (i.e. playable) characters. As a fantasy narrative, *FFX* establishes an alternative history—and in doing so creates a fully developed game environment—that does not necessarily have to be plausible in the sense of achieving the reality effects of historical narratives, but that must be at least internally coherent *as narrative* in order for the player to be able to understand or read the game. In narrowly rhetorical terms, then, the genre of fantasy at least strives to mimic the reality effects, especially the illusion of temporal progression, of historical narratives.

The intersections between imagined history and individual memory are apparent in the lengths to which *FFX* goes to establish the background story and thereby provide information to help the player negotiate the various tasks that must be performed in order to successfully unfold the entire narrative and complete the game. For example, the player learns that before the present time of the game there was a war between the Spiran cities of Zanarkand and Bevelle. Zanarkand's ruler, Yevon, realized his city was doomed because his *summoners*, beings with a command of special magic powers, were no match for the advanced technology, the *machina*, of Bevelle. With the physical destruction of Zanarkand assured, Yevon devised a plan to preserve his city in the form of a memory. To accomplish this, he ordered most of the city's surviving citizens to become *fayth,* beings whose souls are sealed inside statues in a kind of living death. Fayth existed before the war between Zanarkand and Bevelle, and were a source of power for the summoners, who would establish a mental and spiritual connection with these living statues in order to gain access to an individual fayth's dreams. Those dreams would then be transformed into physically real and powerful creatures, *Aeons,* that could aid the summoner in battle or in a time of need. Yevon, in order to save some vestige of his lost city, used the individual memories of all the citizens he had ordered to become fayth to conjure a collective dream projection, or memory, of Zanarkand. To protect these dreaming fayth, Yevon enclosed himself in an Aeon-like leviathan known as Sin, a monster that randomly attacked the cities and villages of Spira, and brought the threat posed by Bevelle's machina (and all subsequent technological progress) to a halt.

> THE ABILITY TO COMPLETE THE GAME REQUIRES MASTERING NOT ONLY THE INSTRUMENTAL CONTROLS NEEDED TO ACQUIRE AND PERFECT GAME SKILLS BUT ALSO THE NARRATIVE ITSELF, THE CULTURAL KNOWLEDGE OF SPIRA THAT FACILITATES THE ACQUISITION OF SKILLS AND ABILITIES.

To maintain order and to give the people hope in the face of the cyclical terror of Sin, Yevon left a series of teachings to his daughter, Lady Yunalesca, who used them as the foundation for an institutionalized religion established in the city of Bevelle. The Yevonite religion banned the use of machina and taught that Sin was a result of humanity's pride and could be vanquished only when Spirans had attained purity and been cleansed of their past sins. Until purity was achieved, the only recourse for the inhabitants of Spira was a ritual known as the Final Summoning, in which a powerful creature, the Final Aeon, would be called forth to defeat Sin and provide a temporary respite from its terror. The Final Summoning, however, never ended the spiral of destruction. For Yu Yevon's spirit would always emerge, possess the Final Aeon, and use it to give birth to a new Sin.

The preceding synopsis illustrates how an imagined history unfolds in the course of gameplay. However, it also emphasizes a linear chronology, with its illusion of temporal continuity, whereas the game itself constructs this complex history through the accumulation of fragmentary data taken from what may be described as various sites of memory—ruins, religious and social customs, video spheres that contain recordings of the past, conversations with characters met along the way, and the recurring presence of a wandering scholar named Maechen. Indeed, one of the most intriguing minor features of the game is that it allows you to purchase video spheres that contain all the full-motion cut scenes that the player has managed to open by completing various stages of the game, thus giving players the opportunity to replay, as a stand-alone animated film, their own experience of the unfolding history of the game. In this way the gameplay of *FFX* itself acts as a simulacrum of a site of memory.

Because there are numerous subplots and secondary characters, the synopsis above merely outlines some of the main narrative threads, and provides only the barest sense of how the player experiences the history of Spira. The unfolding of the narrative, and the player's reading of the game, is largely determined by the technical parameters of the console and software. The ability to complete the game requires mastering not only the instrumental controls needed to acquire and perfect game skills (e.g. the battle system or the sphere grid that allows the player to acquire new strength and abilities for the playable characters) but also the narrative itself, the cultural knowledge of Spira that facilitates the acquisition of skills and abilities. For this reason *FFX,* like so many videogames, employs the conventions of a quest narrative as a way to create a task- or goal-oriented interface between the player and the story. In *FFX* the player is both participant and spectator, and the development of a back-story for each of the characters means that the defeat of Sin is not the sole outcome. Instead, the game is also about the growth and self-realization of the characters, who achieve their own (and by implication the player's) total mastery of the fantasy environment, including the history of Spira.

FFX may be described as highly narrativized, insofar as it presents a detailed fantasy history that unfolds as a direct consequence of gameplay. However, the shifting, unstable position of the player as both participant (through an avatar) and spectator calls into question the appropriateness of analyzing a videogame *as* narrative according to the methods commonly employed in film and literary studies. The assumption that games like *FFX* can be read as a cinematic narrative, or even as a literary text, has been challenged forcefully in recent scholarship, which has reframed the subject through an alternative set of questions. Given the disruptive effects of media convergence, are not games, especially role-playing games, so different in structure that they resist analysis by the methods of established disciplines?

One way to address this question is to study games as ethnographic artifacts that reveal larger social and cultural trends. This was the method Sharon Kinsella, for example, took in her study of another popular medium, manga—an approach for which she provided a vigorous justification:

> Another way of making an enquiry into manga, other than observing its production, would be to read it . . . But on the whole, this book does not employ that approach. Rather than *taking apart* the constituent elements of manga stories on an abstract level, this book is based on research into how the different elements which make manga are *put together* in the first place. It is an ethnographic study of *cultural production*. The understanding of manga that this approach generates is quite different to the type of understanding achievable from the assessment of manga texts alone. The analysis laid out in this book is in many ways better evidenced, more precise, and more clearly situated within social history. The starting point of this book is not a defense of manga (which is already well defended) but a defense of the modernity, creativity, and complexity of society in Japan in the postwar period.[8]

While this is a productive approach to understanding the industry, it ignores the key function of manga, which is to tell a story, and thus sets aside key evidence such as the conventions and rhetoric of the form—the poetics of manga—for the description and understanding of modernity, creativity, and society. After all, narrative genres, attitudes, and style are also forms of historical and social data, every bit as "hard" as the latest industry sales figures.

In the case of electronic games and media studies, there have been a number of scholars who have sought to establish more rigorous disciplinary frameworks by taking a very different approach from Kinsella, which is to build on established paradigms for both film and literary narrative studies.[9] While recognizing the differences that electronic media platforms create in the process of narration, these approaches both analyze and defend the reading of cybertexts and videogames as narratives in a more traditional sense by placing them on an already established and recognizable continuum of interpretative conventions.

This strategy in turn has been strongly challenged by ludologists, who want to focus on the unique properties of games and who thereby stake out the disciplinary boundaries of game studies independent from film or literary studies. Markku Eskelinen, for example, has taken a rather hard line on the issue:

> It is relatively stress-free to write about computer games, as nothing too much has been said yet and almost anything goes. The situation is pretty much the same in what comes to writing about games and gaming in general. The sad fact is that they are under-theorized . . . So if there already is or soon will be a legitimate field for computer game studies, this field is also very open to intrusions and colonizations from the already organized scholarly tribes. Resisting and beating them is the goal of our first survival game in this paper, as what these emerging studies need is independence, or at least relative independence.[10]

The critical language here is almost self-parodic in that it employs the charged jargon of gameplay as a tool for resisting the perceived dangers of academic poaching.

Espen Aarseth goes even further when he examines what he sees as a controversy raging over the relevance of narratology for game aesthetics:

> Underlying the drive to reform games as "interactive narratives" . . . lies a complex web of motives, from economic ("games need narratives to become better products"), elitist and eschatological ("games are a base, low-cultural form; let's try to escape the humble origins and achieve 'literary' qualities"), to academic colonialism ("computer games *are* narratives, we only need to redefine narratives in such a way that these new narrative forms are included"). This latter motive . . . seems to me to spring out of a certain ideology, much practiced by humanists, and also well beyond our ivory towers; an ideology that we might call "narrativism." This is the notion that everything is a story, and that storytelling is our primary, perhaps only, mode of understanding, our cognitive perspective on the world.[11]

Eskelinen and Aarseth may seem militant, but they raise a point familiar to earlier debates about the relationship of the discipline of film studies to literary studies in their insistence that analysis should be grounded primarily in the formal characteristics of video games—a position that is quite different from Kinsella's approach of eschewing an analysis of formal qualities but that also resists the translation of disciplinary assumptions from film and literary studies.

Their criticism of a narrative-centered approach to understanding the poetics of video games is, prima facie, based on a number of reasonable observations. First, since not all games are narratives, or even minimally narrativized (e.g., *Tetris*), a broader account of gameplay theory is required. Second, the need to achieve competence or mastery over the game environment disrupts the normal temporal flow of a narrative—a feature of many games, including, as mentioned above, *FFX*. Third, games like *FFX* are often structured so as to include, or even emphasize, localized tasks or puzzles, a structure that can work against the expectations a player might bring to the game from film or literary narratives. Even for highly narrativized videogames of the kind that Square Enix specializes in producing, there can be prominent differences in the ways a narrative unfolds—that is, the degree of interactivity may vary depending on the number and quality of side quests or even on the technical capabilities of a particular game platform.[12] Fourth, role-playing with an avatar provides more intense identification and illusion of choice than is found with other media—though again, this is a matter of degree and of individual reaction, since readers and viewers are capable of intense identification with certain film or novelistic narratives. Finally, in the case of narrativized games, the disjuncture between participation and spectatorship affects the experience of diegetic time and space.

These observations force a reconsideration of the assumptions we may bring to looking at videogames as a medium for storytelling. As a result, a number of scholars of electronic media, including Henry Jenkins, have proposed a middle ground that tries to think of narrative in videogames in ways more appropriate to the developing convergence of media:

> Much of the writing in the ludologist tradition is unduly polemical: they are so busy trying to pull game designers out of their "cinema envy" or define a field where no hypertext theorist dares to venture that they are prematurely dismissing the use value of narrative for understanding their desired object of study. For my money, a series of conceptual blind spots prevent them from developing a full understanding of the interplay between narrative and games.[13]

Jenkins blames these blind spots on the call for stricter disciplinary guidelines for ludology, and suggests that reading games in terms of other disciplinary approaches to narratives may not be so misguided after all. For one thing, critics of "narrativism" assume a narrow model preoccupied with the rules and conventions of classical linear storytelling at the expense of considering other types of narrative that emphasize spatial exploration over causal events as a means to balance the competing demands imposed by the narrative logic of temporal continuity and by the spatiality of spectacle. The critics of narrativism also focus too much on the activities and aspirations of the storyteller and too little on the process of narrative comprehension and readership. Their all-or-nothing attitude leads them to assume either that whole games must tell a story instead of acknowledging that narratives may play a part in the game at specific points, or that narratives are self-contained rather than serving a function within the game environment established by a convergence of various types of media.

Jenkins's view provides a cogent defense of reading *FFX* as both a cinematic and a textual narrative. Perhaps a more nuanced theory of reading needs to be developed for videogames in general, but in the case of a work like *FFX*, which was designed so that the unfolding of a narrative is a central component of gameplay, the convergence of media, in which older media survive in a transformed environment, suggests that narratological approaches may be useful not just to the critical analysis of a game but also to the aesthetic experience of it.

It takes many hours of gameplay to completely explore the environment and to unfold the entire story of *FFX*. The cut scenes alone, which often contain vital information for play (as opposed to filling in the back-story), make for an extremely long film when strung together.[14] As a result, the experience of *FFX* is not shaped solely by the level of the player's gaming skills. The long interruptions in the flow of the gameplay created by the cut scenes have been a source of irritation for players who dislike being made passive spectators, while for others it is a welcome relief from the constant and occasionally monotonous task of killing fiends and other enemies. In either case, the disruptive effects produced by the convergence of media are replicated in *FFX* in the interface between the game and the conventions of a fantasy quest narrative.

The complementary regimes of skill and knowledge needed to competently play the game and master the historical narrative of Spira are focused through the main playable character, Tidus. The events of *FFX* take place one thousand years after the war between Zanarkand and Bevelle, beginning with a cut scene at the ruins of Zanarkand, where Tidus begins a flashback narration of "my story." He is a star blitzball player in the dream-memory

Zanarkand. His father, Jecht, was also a star player who disappeared ten years earlier. Tidus hates his cold, macho father, and his resentment is the key motivating element of his character. The story proper begins when Tidus's Zanarkand is attacked by Sin, and Tidus, along with his longtime mentor, Auron, is sucked into Sin's vortex and emerges alone a millennium later in the ruins of Baaj temple.

Tidus is picked up by a group of *Al Bhed,* members of an ethnic group ostracized by the Yevonites for their continued used of machina. He meets a young woman named Rikku, the daughter of the leader of the Al Bhed (a recurring *Final Fantasy* character named Cid). Rikku is able to speak Tidus's language, and when she informs him that Zanarkand was destroyed long ago Tidus is incredulous. Rikku then tells him that since he was in contact with Sin's toxin, his memory must have been affected. Tidus is brought aboard the Al Bhed ship, but after only a short time is swept out to sea in another attack by Sin.

Tidus is washed up near the small town of Besaid, where he meets Wakka, a blitzball player and captain of the local team. Tidus demonstrates a powerful kick move and Wakka, impressed by his skills, takes Tidus to the village and introduces him to most of the rest of the playable cast, including the second main character Yuna. Yuna, who is originally from Bevelle, is the daughter of the late High Summoner Braska, the last summoner to have defeated Sin. Braska, like all summoners who defeat Sin, was killed in the battle, and Yuna's memory of her father has inspired her to become a summoner as well. The moment Tidus arrives coincides with the completion of her initiation rites, during which she summons her first Aeon at the temple in Besaid. Determined to emulate her father's heroic feat, she sets out her own quest to defeat Sin, accompanied by her guardians Wakka, Lulu (also of Besaid), and Kimahri (a member of the half-beast/half-human Ronso tribe). Eventually, Tidus's guardian Auron joins the party, as does Rikku of the Al Bhed.

To become a high summoner herself, Yuna must travel to all the major Yevonite temples throughout Spira and commune with the fayth sealed in a statue at each place in order to gain control of all the Aeons, which she will need for the final battle with Sin. In the course of their quest, Tidus and Yuna fall in love, and Tidus is determined that she will not meet the fate that befell her father. He gradually learns the history of Spira, seeking information that will help him find a way to save Yuna. As the history of Spira unfolds, the hypocrisy and corruption of the Yevonite religion is exposed, and the system of belief that has sustained the cultures of Spira is radically undermined. In addition, Tidus learns a number of important facts about himself. He discovers that he is nothing more than a memory and that his Zanarkand is a projected collective dream of the surviving citizens who became fayth. He also learns the truth about his father.

The most recent Calm was achieved ten years ago through the quest of Braska, Auron, and Jecht. It turns out that Jecht, like Tidus, had been transported from the dream-memory Zanarkand to the real world of Spira and had sacrificed himself to bring forth the Final Aeon without knowing that Yu Yevon would possess him and revive the monster Sin. In the final battle of the game, Tidus reconciles with his father before he has to kill him and defeat Sin. Without a sacrificial fayth to create a new Final Aeon, Yu Yevon is destroyed at last. The fayth no longer have to continue their task of projecting a dream vision of Zanarkand out of their memories, and as their dream ends, it bursts into millions of small bubbles, each containing a single memory. One of those memories is Tidus, who fades before Yuna's eyes,[15] leaving her, along with the rest of Spira, to face a future that is uncertain, but without false hope.

As the above synopsis of Tidus's quest makes clear, *FFX* makes heavy use of cultural and narrative conventions—conventions that are, within the context of recent Japanese history, highly charged emotionally—within a game designed literally and figuratively around the goal of achieving competence or mastery. In a narrowly instrumental or pedagogical sense, mastery means acquiring the skills and knowledge dictated by the need to solve tasks or to unveil, or reconstruct, the narrative. The acquisition of competence through simulation and role-play is also equated with self-realization, with becoming an individual fully aware of the expectations of those social and cultural conventions peculiar to the game environment. This is the idea of mastery at the heart of certain narrative forms, such as the *Bildungsroman,* centered on the process of coming of age. The aim of mastery, then, provides a way to think about narrative conventions, technical platforms, and game modes as part of a continuum.

> IN THE CASE OF *FFX* MASTERY IS ONLY ACHIEVED SIMULTANEOUSLY WITH THE UNFOLDING OF THE IMAGINARY HISTORY OF SPIRA AND THE SIMULATED MEMORY OF THE CHARACTERS.

Given the importance of mastering narrative to the structure of role-playing games, one way to discuss games *as* narratives is to use the idea of competence that emerged out of reader-response theory to highlight the fluid relationship between participation and spectacle so crucial in the narrative design of *FFX*. Jonathan Culler has argued for a de-emphasis of the position of both reader and text, and proposed a poetics that focuses on a complex system of signs that readers conventionally apply to literature: "To read a text as literature is not to make one's mind a *tabula rasa* and approach it without preconceptions; one must bring to it an implicit understanding of the operations of literary discourse which tells one what to look for."[16] This implicit understanding is what he terms "literary competence"—a notion that locates the organizing principles of interpretation not in the text or reader but in institutions that teach readers to read. This notion of mastery, or competence, provides a way to read videogames on their own terms. It works as both a strategy for play and a key element of the narrative itself, thus placing discussions of the mode of gameplay, the content of the story, and the platform by which reception or consumption takes place on a more or less equal footing.

In the case of *FFX* mastery is only achieved simultaneously with the unfolding of the imaginary history of Spira and the simulated memory of the characters. The destruction of Zanarkand leads to the creation of a collective memory, the dream city, which is always absolute, always in the present, and always in a cyclical, spiraling conflict with the authoritative, relative history established by the Yevonite religion. The unfolding of this history through the various sites of memory in *FFX* evokes a number of culturally vital discourses in Japan that the designers of the game drew on: the modernist aesthetics of evanescence, the loss of faith and belief in a society where technology and religion clash, the desire for a dream realm of memories as the source of an alternative history, and the nostalgic desire for the sublime experience of the annihilation of the past and the completion of history. These discourses, every bit as much as the conventions of gameplay and the technical platform of the game system, are vital to both the structure of the *FFX* narrative itself and to the ways we read and interpret that narrative in order to gain mastery over it.

The most intriguing aspect of the narrative of *FFX* is that it serves as an analogue to Japan's experience of modernity. A linear perception of history that stressed the concept of progress through the development of technology and the rise of the corporate state led to the intense production of sites of collective memory as a way to simulate the sense of possessing a shared identity, history, and culture. *FFX* ends with a society that has wiped out its past by undermining the belief systems and the institutions that supported older regimes of knowledge, authority, and power. The twist in *Final Fantasy X*, one that mirrors the twisted dialectics of Japan's culture of modernity, is that mastering the narrative is an utterly self-enclosed historical turn, an end in itself. In disclosing and thus authoring the story, the player creates the illusion of achieving a historical consciousness that, like its avatar Tidus, is nothing more than an evanescent bubble, a passing memory doomed to fade.

....

Notes

1. Henry Jenkins, *Convergence Culture: Where Old and New Media Collide* (New York: New York University Press, 2006), 244. Jenkins draws heavily on Pierre Lévy's *Collective Intelligence: Mankind's Emerging World in Cyberspace*, trans. Robert Bononno (Cambridge, Mass.: Perseus Books, 1997).

2. The compression of our experience of space-time and the breakdown of older hierarchies of knowledge are more commonly seen as characteristics of postmodern culture. However, I am identifying these effects with the culture of modernity to stress the long history of convergence and to suggest that postmodern culture arises as the convergence of media becomes truly global in scale.

3. David Harvey, *The Condition of Postmodernity: An Enquiry into the Origins of Cultural Change* (Oxford: Basil Blackwell, 1989), 11–12. Although Harvey does not identify a fixed point of origin for the kinds of cultural changes he identifies as characteristic of modernity, he does cite the crisis of capitalism in 1847–48 as the moment when those changes first achieved a kind of critical mass and became widely felt. In terms of media convergence, the mid-nineteenth century, which witnessed the development of both telegraphy and photography, is certainly a crucial moment.

4. Pierre Nora, "Between Memory and History: Les Lieux de Mémoire," in *Representations* 26 (Spring 1989; special issue, *Memory and Counter-Memory*): 7.

5. Ibid., 8–9. Although I am focusing narrowly on Nora's claim of a rift between memory and history for the purpose of this essay, his view of contemporary modes of historical perception overlaps the work on historiography of Frank Ankersmit and Michel de Certeau. For a clear and sympathetic account of recent trends in historiography, see Jürgen Pieters, "New Historicism: Postmodern Historiography between Narrativism and Heterology" *History and Theory* 39, no. 1 (February 2000): 21–38.

6. For example, in March 2006 the videogame fan magazine *Famitsū* published a poll of its readers' favorite videogames, and *FFX* was listed as the top vote getter.

7. The convention of using subtitles, which is a holdover from earlier games that did not have voice actors, is continued in *FFX*, which means that you read text as the game unfolds. There are other sources of textual information within the game itself, but the "text" of the game also includes peripheral information found in numerous guides, fan blogs, the official Web site, and so on, all of which are in a real sense part of the game platform.

8. Sharon Kinsella, *Adult Manga: Culture and Power in Contemporary Japanese Society* (Honolulu: University of Hawai'i Press, 2000), 14–15.

9. See, for example, Janet Murray's *Hamlet on the Holodeck* (Cambridge, Mass.: MIT Press, 1997) or Marie-Laure Ryan's *Narrative as Virtual Reality* (Baltimore: The Johns Hopkins University Press, 2001).

10. Markku Eskelinen, "Toward Computer Game Studies" in *First Person*, eds. Noah Wardrip-Fruin and Pat Harrigan (Cambridge, Mass.: The MIT Press, 2004), 36.

11. Espen Aarseth, "Genre Trouble: Narrativism and the Art of Simulation," in *First Person,* eds. Noah Wardrip-Fruin and Pat Harrigan (Cambridge, Mass.: The MIT Press, 2004), 49.

12. It must be noted that even in a game where the player has a lot of options for input, the basic story is set and doesn't change. Rather, it is uncovered by gameplay. Interactivity means that a player can determine the order or even some nuances of the story. However, even a complex game like *FFX* is not truly open ended. The idea that the player can actually exercise choice is an illusion—though it is an illusion that, as noted earlier, mimics the reality effects of historical narrative through the creation of a fantasy environment, the history of Spira.

13. Henry Jenkins, "Game Design as Narrative Architecture," in *First Person*, eds. Noah Wardrip-Fruin and Pat Harrigan (Cambridge, Mass.: The MIT Press, 2004), 120–21.

14. To insert a personal observation—it took me nearly ninety hours, spread over several months, to complete the game. I mention this because it is important to note that my experience of the game may well be different from more ardent and skilled gamers who are faster "readers" than I. Nonetheless, the time it took me to complete the game is not at all unusual.

15. The image of life as an insubstantial bubble, as froth, has a long history in Japanese literature. It is a striking instance of how the creators of *FFX* situated their game-narrative within a number of culturally charged discourses. The paradox of Tidus's fading is that, even though he was part of a collective dream-memory, he was thrust into the real world of Spira by the fayth, who were exhausted and wanted Yu Yevon to be destroyed so that they might be released from their hellish existence and sleep without dreaming. This paradox that Tidus is both a dream and real, both a memory and in history, was the catalyst for a sequel, in which Yuna searches for her lost love.

16. Jonathan Culler, "Literary Competence," in *Reader-Response Criticism: From Formalism to Post-Structuralism,* ed. Jane P. Tomkins (Baltimore: The Johns Hopkins University Press), 102.

MICHAEL DYLAN FOSTER

Haunted Travelogue:
Hometowns, Ghost Towns,
and Memories of War

In late July 2007 I traveled to Sakaiminato in Tottori prefecture, hometown of Mizuki Shigeru (b. 1922), the prolific manga/anime artist famous for his graphic narratives concerning Japanese monsters and spirits known as *yōkai*. Mizuki is especially well known as the creator of *Gegege no Kitarō*, which has appeared since the 1960s as a manga and as numerous animated television series, has been adapted for video games, and most recently was produced as a 2007 live-action movie, with a sequel in 2008. In contemporary Japan, Mizuki's yōkai images are so deeply ingrained in the cultural imagination that you would be hard-pressed to find a child or adult unfamiliar with Kitarō or Mizuki's other paradigmatic creations. In addition to his creative and narrative work, Mizuki is also a yōkai researcher who has explored religious and secular traditions to illustrate and describe numerous "real" yōkai from around Japan, effectively (re)popularizing supernatural imagery and folk beliefs among a wide readership.[1]

Another facet of Mizuki's work stems from his personal experiences as a child growing up in rural Sakaiminato and as a soldier during World War II. In a series of memoirs, both prose and manga, Mizuki's war experience figures as a terrible trial by fire out of which he emerges reborn and forever altered. And Sakaiminato, where he innocently spent his childhood before the war, comes to represent an eternally premodern place in which yōkai, and the dreams they inspire, still have meaning. It is in Sakaiminato that he hears stories from an old woman called Nonnonbaa (Granny Nonnon), who teaches him about yōkai and how they interact with the human realm. Mizuki lionizes Sakaiminato as a pure *furusato* or hometown, a nostalgic space metonymic of a time all but forgotten in postwar and postindustrial Japan.

In the last volume of *Mechademia*, I contributed an essay on Mizuki that touched on this portrayal of Sakaiminato as an Edenic otherworld where the mysteries of the past are preserved. I concluded, in effect, that the construction of such an otherworld—through manga, anime, and the narrativization of memory—reflects not only a conservative longing for a time already passed but also a creative desire for a better future. In the final stages of writing that piece I visited Sakaiminato to take some pictures to accompany the essay, and began to think about how yōkai and the nostalgic sentiments they signify are embedded in the village itself. That trip inspired me to write the present essay, in which I reconsider Mizuki's brand of hopeful nostalgia with a slightly more critical eye, attempting to appreciate but also to resist the redemptive logic of the nostalgic narrative and seek instead the cracks that, ultimately, make such narratives meaningful.

TRAVELING TO SAKAIMINATO

Even today a journey to Sakaiminato is a slow passage through lush countryside, as if you are gradually shedding the bustling contemporary world. The train from Okayama into Tottori snakes through overgrown valleys and mountains spiked with cedar, and across shallow rocky rivers with water like scratched crystal refracting the sunlight. Crows perch on branches and an occasional egret sprouts like an exotic white plant from the banks of a creek. There are villages too: a cluster of houses balanced along a hillside or neatly ensconced among rice paddies or surrounded by fields of scallions and watermelons. And as the train trundles by, you might catch a glimpse of an old man peering up from his work, his eyes sheltered from the sun by a broad-brimmed straw hat.

Once you finally arrive in Sakaiminato, there is undoubtedly something otherworldly about the place, but the uncanniness does not stem from a disassociation with commercial enterprise and popular culture; rather it is quite the opposite. In the last several decades, villages throughout Japan have struggled to reenergize their economies through processes known as *mura okoshi* (village revitalization) or *furusato zukuri* (hometown making). Such revitalization efforts often exploit or develop a particular cultural resource or local industry. In the case of Sakaiminato, that resource/industry is the link with Mizuki.[2]

> IN A SENSE, THE MIZUKI NARRATIVE TELLS OF TRIAL AND REBIRTH, AND OF TRANSCENDING THE CATACLYSM OF WAR.

I will not investigate the economics of this revitalization project or explore the political and practical aspects of its implementation here. Rather, I would like to offer a professedly unscientific travelogue through the Mizuki/yōkai narrative as it is constructed in Sakaiminato and the surrounding countryside, and also recounted in Mizuki's historical and autobiographical retelling of the events of the Shōwa period (1926–1989). In a sense, the Mizuki narrative tells of trial and rebirth, and of transcending the cataclysm of war. To set this uplifting narrative in relief, I also take another brief excursion, this one to a museum dedicated to artists who, unlike Mizuki, did not survive the war, a place that provides a narrative very different from the story of redemption displayed in Sakaiminato. In exploring these two different sites of memory, I focus particularly on the function of nostalgia as a mode of both remembering and forgetting. Because nostalgia can often be seductive, it is important to recognize that the narrative it articulates is only part of the story—or, rather, that there are also many other, less satisfying, stories that should also be remembered.

THE KITARŌ TRAIN TO SAKAIMINATO: LANDSCAPE WITH MONSTERS

The journey from Okayama to the city of Yonago takes about two hours; from there, you transfer to the Sakai Line for the forty-five minute trip to Sakaiminato. For all intents and purposes, however, the Mizuki adventure begins before you even depart Yonago. A bronze statue of Kitarō, the charming yōkai boy star of *Gegege no Kitarō,* greets you on the Sakai Line platform, and many of the trains on this local line are one-car vehicles dedicated to characters in the series. I happened to arrive on a Sunday afternoon, just in time to board the Kitarō train, festooned inside and out with colorful pictures of Kitarō himself (Figure 1).[3] As I stood on the platform admiring the train, two middle-aged women asked me to take a picture of them posing in front of it. Several small children squealed with delight when they saw the train, and then clambered onto the bronze statue of the yōkai hero, their parents clicking photos. Despite the Disneyesque feel, however, not all the passengers are tourists: in particular, junior high school students in uniform board and get off at stops along the way.

Including Yonago and Sakaiminato, there are sixteen stations on the Sakai Line, each labeled with a place-name. But in addition, every station, often nothing more than a single cement platform, also has an alternate name derived from a yōkai. Yumigahama Station, for example, has a sign denoting it as Azuki arai Station (after the *Azuki arai* yōkai found in the Tōkai region). The yōkai themselves are selected from regions throughout the Japanese archipelago—including, significantly, Okinawa and Hokkaidō.

In this way, Mizuki's yōkai world is stitched into the landscape, like a doppelganger realm supplementing the immediately apparent present. Not only do the yōkai metonymically represent their particular region of origin, reproducing across the several rural miles of the Sakai Line a map of Japan in miniature, but disparate groups (Okinawans, Ainu) are also purposefully included in the construction of the (yōkai) nation. With each region and its inhabitants signified by a particular yōkai, the forty-five-minute journey is reminiscent of the traditional literary convention of the *michiyuki*, found in *nō* theater, puppet theater, and other dramatic forms, in which characters move symbolically through a constructed landscape coded with poetic or

FIGURE 1. The Kitarō train. Photograph by author.

historically significant places names. The *michiyuki* is a device that draws the readers/audience (or in this case, passengers) into, as one scholar puts it, "a world apart, where unexpected, wondrous beings and events are likely to be encountered."[4]

With this in mind, it is no coincidence that Sakaiminato Station, terminus of the Sakai Line and destination for so many Mizuki/yōkai fans, is named for Kitarō, the optimistic, good-hearted boy yōkai. It is as if the train has taken you back in time, to a forgotten rural town certainly, but also to a prelapsarian moment when, like the vision represented by Kitarō, the world was innocent, childish, and full of possibility. I walk out of the station and immediately see a small crowd of people gathered around a life-sized bronze statue of Mizuki himself, sitting at a bronze desk, writing. He is facing away from the station, as if generating with his pen and paper the town that spreads out before him (Figure 2).

ON THE ROAD

The primary tourist attraction in Sakaiminato is Mizuki Shigeru Road. At first glance, the Road is unremarkable—a typical narrow street, part of it covered with an arcade, with small shops and restaurants on either side. But every twenty or thirty feet there is a small bronze statue, anywhere between six and thirty inches high, perched atop a stone pedestal. Each neatly labeled figure represents a yōkai documented by Mizuki in his books. Around these diminutive statues you often find a cluster of tourists, posing and taking pictures. Children excitedly shout out the name of the yōkai in question, while older visitors bend down to carefully read the engraved nameplate.

Almost a kilometer long, Mizuki Shigeru Road is festooned with some 120 of these bronze figurines. The idea for the road was first proposed in 1989 by city employees who envisioned it as away to liven up the once-bustling shopping street near the station. The initial city investment (for a total of eighty statues) was approximately 440 million yen, and the road opened (with twenty-three statues) in 1993. In 2007, for the first time, the number of visitors exceeded one million.[5] For people who have grown up with the yōkai images of Mizuki, a saunter down the road can excite memories of a more innocent, carefree time; eclectic writer and scholar Aramata Hiroshi describes the sensation of seeking out the next yōkai statuette: "Even if my head has been corrupted by old books and cigarettes, my heart, it seems, is still a child's."[6]

FIGURE 2. In front of Sakaiminato (Kitarō) Station: life-sized bronze image of Mizuki at his desk. Photograph by author.

In 1993, with some twenty empty storefronts, the shopping street reflected the general economic state of small-town Japan. While these empty shops have all but disappeared, the businesses lining the street now are anything but typical for a country town.[7] They are dedicated to all things Mizuki, selling a cornucopia of Mizuki-related *omiyage* (souvenirs) and "yōkai goods," edible and otherwise. You can find books, DVDs, yōkai *manjū* (bean cakes), yōkai *sake*, yōkai beer, coffee, cookies, ice cream, *senbei* (rice crackers), playing cards, key chains, cell phone straps, figurines, T-shirts, hats, postcards, stationery, fans, handkerchiefs, scarves, and jewelry. Everything has a monstrous motif or is shaped like one of Mizuki's yōkai. You can even buy dried squid on a stick, artistically fashioned to resemble Ittanmomen, an animated, flying strip-of-cloth, and a popular member of Kitarō's yōkai gang. The theme-park quality of Sakaiminato is underscored as you stroll down the road. Here and there you find "life-sized" wooden cutouts of yōkai characters into which you can insert your face and have your photo taken. There are taxis done up with yōkai motifs and you might even bump into Kitarō himself sauntering down the street, having his picture taken with tourists young and old alike (Figure 3).

FIGURE 3. Costumed image of Kitarō posing with bronze statue of himself. Photograph by author.

About midway along the road, you come to the Yōkai Shrine (*jinja*). At first glance, this shrine opened in the year 2000 seems like an obvious idea; after all, so many of Japan's traditional shrines are dedicated to ambiguous figures, like *kappa, tengu, kitsune,* and other common yōkai creatures, whose demonic and deific aspects are not clearly distinguished. The Yōkai Shrine in Sakaiminato, however, is a refreshingly explicit invented tradition. Like many shrines, for example, you can dedicate a votive plaque (*ema*) to your prayer, but these plaques are illustrated with Mizuki's images, as if the sacred "otherworld" itself can be found in a manga (Figure 4).[8]

COMING HOME

Eventually, toward the end of the street, you arrive at the Mizuki Shigeru Memorial Hall (Kinenkan). While it is not unusual in Japan for significant cultural figures to have a memorial hall or museum dedicated to them, it does strike one as odd, and somehow indicative of Mizuki's dry sense of humor, that this particular "memorial" has been established before the individual being memorialized is actually dead. Though well into his eighties, Mizuki is still alive and not only kicking but seemingly more productive than ever. In a sense, however, the hall does indeed serve as a memorial—for the Sakaiminato of Mizuki's childhood, for the lost Japan that his work longingly invokes. As if to emphasize this veneration of the past and the transference of memories from one generation to the next, a life-sized bronze tableau in front of the museum features

FIGURE 4. *Ema* (votive plaque) for sale at the Yōkai Shrine. Photograph by author.

a version of Mizuki as a child in conversation with Nonnonbaa, the old Sakaiminato woman from whom he originally learned about yōkai.

Inside the Memorial Hall, you walk through an illustrated narrative of Mizuki's life (replete with voiceovers by Mizuki himself), starting with his childhood right there in Sakaiminato. You then follow him through his experiences as a reluctant soldier gravely wounded in Rabaul (in present-day Papua New Guinea) and learn of his affection for the natives there and the way they helped him recover from injury and illness. Then you follow him back to postwar Japan, where he struggles to make good in a burgeoning economy. And you learn of his gradual success, both critical and popular, and his eventual rise to media fame. As a coda to the story, there are also photographs of his joyful return to Rabaul to be reunited with his old friends, and of course his triumphant reemergence as a hero of Sakaiminato, his hometown, and by metonymic extension, the hometown of so many other yōkai-loving Japanese.

The narrative of Mizuki's life—his happy-go-lucky boyhood, his blundering military career, his self-deprecating rise to prominence in the manga/anime world, his emergence at the turn of the new century as a dry-witted patriarch—is well known to readers of his memoirs. It is a narrative of authenticity, trial, and triumph. Sakaiminato (and all hometowns like it) features as a sort of paradise out of which Mizuki (and Japan) is forced to leave, and to which he (and his nation) eventually returns. In this narrative, war is an important if tragic rite of passage for both nation and individual. Pen in hand, Mizuki is at once a keen observer and also a participant; his personal story unfolds against the backdrop of the Shōwa period, with its militarism, war, defeat, occupation, and miraculous economic rebirth. The Memorial Hall is a tribute not only to Mizuki and his entourage of monstrous characters but also to this national narrative.

> PEN IN HAND, MIZUKI IS AT ONCE A KEEN OBSERVER AND ALSO A PARTICIPANT; HIS PERSONAL STORY UNFOLDS AGAINST THE BACKDROP OF THE SHŌWA PERIOD, WITH ITS MILITARISM, WAR, DEFEAT, OCCUPATION, AND MIRACULOUS ECONOMIC REBIRTH.

The same narrative, articulated in much greater detail and with beautifully intricate images, is portrayed in Mizuki's award-winning *Komikku Shōwa shi*, an eight-volume manga history of the Shōwa period. "If you think about it," Mizuki notes in the afterword, "the 'history of Shōwa' is the history of myself."[9] And indeed, the text intertwines Mizuki's personal journey with the journey of the nation—complete with political, economic, social, and cultural events—to document a collective experience and a moving set of shared memories.[10] Not surprisingly, the war plays a central role in Mizuki's account: we witness not only the political movements and conflicts that led to the war itself but also Mizuki's own experiences as a soldier. Most striking are his battles with malaria, the loss of his left arm, and his gradual recovery through the kindness of the "people of the forest"[11] in the Rabaul village.

As in the Memorial Hall, *Shōwa shi* also details Mizuki's 1970 return to this native village, a pristine paradise that seems a substitute for the Sakaiminato of his childhood.[12] But in the *Shōwa shi* version, we can read a quiet, understated sadness, an intimation that the "little heaven"[13] of Mizuki's memory no longer exists (if it ever did). In his war recollections, the village is a place of abundance and healthy fresh food, nourishment that literally saves his life. But on his return, Mizuki discovers that the water used to make coffee is full of mosquito larvae.[14] He also learns that Epupe, a beautiful woman he remembers fondly and who, it is hinted, had a crush on him during the war, has led a tragic life, struggling with an alcoholic first husband, a sick second husband, and a sick child.[15] Indeed, toward the conclusion of the eight-volume history, Mizuki documents one of many later return trips to Rabaul in which he takes his friends out to eat ramen noodles. When he notices one of them carefully collecting leftovers to take home for her family, he realizes for the first time "that they are poor. They probably don't get to go to a restaurant to eat ramen even once every three years."[16]

Later, Mizuki buys his friends a used truck, and one of them comments, "I'm glad you have returned your debts from the war." Mizuki, for his part, thinks, "I was probably dazed from malaria, so I never realized it . . . but even though they were poor, they never asked for anything." It is left ambiguous as to whether this poverty is recent or something Mizuki only understands now in comparison to Japan's newfound wealth. Whatever the case, though, it is clear that his friends have not prospered economically, while Mizuki and Japan certainly have. The truck he buys them, not surprisingly, is a Datsun made in Japan.[17]

In the text of *Shōwa shi*, Mizuki's initial return to Rabaul immediately precedes another kind of homecoming, one that provides an ironic counterpoint to his own journey. These are the famous returns, several of them, of soldiers left behind during the war, soldiers who for decades did not know, or stubbornly refused to acknowledge, that the war had ended. For a quarter of a century—the same quarter of a century during which Mizuki rose to prominence as a manga artist and media star—they languished in the jungles of Southeast Asia. Of all the events from 1972, Mizuki writes, "the one that was particularly shocking to me was the homecoming of Yokoi Shōichi."[18] Yokoi was the first of three famous so-called stragglers; for some twenty-seven years he had lived in the Guam jungle, bedding down in a cave and surviving on fruits, berries, fish, and small animals, before he was finally discovered and repatriated.[19] His arrival in Japan caused a great commotion; while his antiquated sense of patriotism may have seemed honorable to some, to many it was an embarrassing reminder of a bygone age of militarism and blind devotion to the Emperor. His homecoming, as noted in his 1997 *New York Times* obituary, "stirred widespread soul-searching within Japan about whether he represented the best impulses of the national spirit or the silliest."[20]

Yokoi Shōichi's return highlighted the distance Japan had traveled in the years since the war's end. His sudden reappearance in the midst of the nation's remarkable economic revival was like that of a ghost returned from the dead, a living anachronism and the embodiment of uncomfortable, inconvenient memories. Juxtaposed with the story of Yokoi and the other "stragglers," Mizuki's own "homecoming" to Rabaul—a journey geographically and symbolically opposite Yokoi's—underscores the advances of Japan as a nation and Mizuki as an individual. Mizuki too had survived hardships in the jungle and then struggled for economic survival back in Japan but, unlike Yokoi left to languish alone in the past, he had moved (with Japan) into a bright and promising future.

Indeed, as portrayed in his museum and his manga, the narrative of Mizuki is ultimately about transcendence and rejuvenation. He poignantly describes how during the war, after he is gravely wounded and loses his left arm, he finally begins to feel his strength coming back: the odor of a newborn

> THE NARRATIVE OF MIZUKI IS ULTIMATELY ABOUT TRANSCENDENCE AND REJUVENATION.

baby emanates from the stump of his severed limb.[21] But of course the arm itself does not grow anew; rebirth is found through transcending the loss—not replacing it. Mizuki's left sleeve, in his manga as in real life, hangs empty, a constant reminder of the war that shaped him and shaped the nation.

VOICELESS/VOICE

Several weeks after my trip to the bustling fairground of Sakaiminato, I had the chance to visit another kind of memorial hall, also dedicated to visual artists, but this one strangely and purposely silent. A sober cement building in a bucolic mountain setting in Ueda, Nagano Prefecture, the Mugonkan—literally "Voiceless Hall"—provides a startling contrast to Mizuki's yōkai wonderland in Sakaiminato. Opened in 1997, the Mugonkan is a private museum dedicated to artwork by artists killed during the Pacific War. Many of them were art school students or recent graduates, mostly in their twenties or early thirties, who died either in Japan or while serving abroad. Displayed along with their paintings and sculptures are fragments of their daily lives—diaries, letters, and other personal effects. The artwork itself is varied. The common theme is not subject matter or style but the lives of the artists: personal narratives, one after another, that ended too soon.[22]

An almost religious reverence pervades the museum. People step quietly, speak in hushed voices, and children are told to behave. This is not the quiet of a conventional art museum; rather, it is as if each painting is imbued with a meaning beyond aesthetic value, a poignancy engendered by the short biography of each artist. And each narrative is eerily similar, telling the story of a young man with great artistic promise that would never be fully realized, a life ended before it could be lived.

Of course, a sustained comparison of the Mugonkan with Sakaiminato would be unreasonable. But having coincidently visited one so soon after the other, it was impossible for me not to contrast these two very different approaches to the conundrum of finding present-day meaning in the traumas of the past. Despite their differing objectives, the two sites share striking similarities: both are about the war, both celebrate visual artists, and both present their subjects as innocent men caught up in forces beyond their control. Ultimately, the Mugonkan is about regret and mourning, speaking silently but eloquently of the tragic stifling of potential, of the people left behind as the nation moved on. Visitors walk slowly and quietly through the museum encountering one brief episode after another: each short artist biography is an unfinished story, lacking a satisfying narrative arc. Visitors to Mizuki's Memorial Hall, on the other hand, experience his long biography as a tale of close calls and terrible ordeals, but ultimately of triumph and narrative completion. Mizuki is the lucky artist who fulfilled the potential of all these other artists. His world—his manga, his Memorial Hall, his revitalized Sakaiminato—incorporates the trauma of war into a satisfying circle of narrative.

Indeed, this sense of narrative completion and the outward boisterousness of Sakaiminato even work to obscure the town's own story as a victim,

> THE MUGONKAN EXPRESSES A POIGNANT REMEMBRANCE OF DEVASTATING LOSS BUT ALSO INTIMATES THE POSSIBILITY THAT THE LOSS WILL NEVER—CAN NEVER, SHOULD NEVER—BE COMPLETELY EXPRESSED OR TRANSCENDED. INVERSELY, MIZUKI'S WORLD ACTIVELY WORKS TO TRANSCEND LOSS, ENABLING HIM AND HIS HOMETOWN TO PROSPER IN THE LIVING PRESENT.

like so many other rural communities, of late twentieth-century urbanization and economic resurgence. This tale of depopulation and empty storefronts becomes but a faint, plaintive subtext amid the vigor of yōkai commercialism. Just as Mizuki himself emerges successfully from the devastation of his war experiences, so too Sakaiminato, at first glance, seems to have artfully transcended its loss of economic relevance in modern Japan by milking the popularity of its most famous native son. Although my own visit by no means represents a thorough exploration, I did soon discover that the streets just a few yards from Mizuki Shigeru Road are practically deserted. The proprietor of a small restaurant complained to me that most tourists just come for the day, visit the road and the Memorial Hall, and then return to the larger city of Yonago for dinner and lodging. For him at least, the fantastic world celebrated one street over is a colorful façade, a bandage skillfully applied to a still unhealed wound.[23]

Perhaps we can extrapolate here two distinct approaches for grappling with the traumas of the past. The Mugonkan expresses a poignant remembrance of devastating loss but also intimates the possibility that the loss will never—can never, should never—be completely expressed or transcended. Inversely, Mizuki's world actively works to transcend loss, enabling him and his hometown to prosper in the living present. To be sure, Mizuki is outspoken in his criticism of the Pacific War and of all wars. He closes *Shōwa shi* with a hopeful insignia of a peaceful future: crossed rifles with knotted barrels, and the comment that, "The history [of the Shōwa period] is a big lesson teaching us that we must not have any more war; we must never again commit the same mistakes."[24] But in Sakaiminato, the clattering commercialization of memories and the clear, satisfying narrative drowns out the silence of those crossed rifles.

POSTSCRIPT: THE LARVAE IN THE COFFEE WATER, OR REREADING NOSTALGIA

One element that links the Mugonkan with Sakaiminato is nostalgia. Both sites nostalgically commemorate a prewar Japan that is simultaneously personal and national. In its simplest form, nostalgia might be characterized as a longing for a past (time, place, self) that is impossible to (re)claim because it no longer exists or, more likely, never did. But in contemporary cultural life, the affect of nostalgia is anything but simple.[25] Literary scholar and novelist Svetlana Boym has characterized nostalgia as tending to be either "reflective" or "restorative." Within such a typology, the Mugonkan, by celebrating the art of students whose hopes for a bright future were stolen by a war beyond their control, suggests a reflective nostalgia that "does not follow a single plot line but explores ways of inhabiting many places at once and imagining different time zones."[26]

> THERE IS ALWAYS THE DANGER OF OVERLAYING HISTORY WITH WHAT HISTORY MIGHT HAVE BEEN.

The narrative—broken into dozens of fragments—provides no solace or closure. Nostalgia at the Mugonkan is an excruciating affliction; it is a longing for more than a homecoming, for an impossible reversal of the events that caused the breach between now and then. It forces the viewer to reconcile the terrible events of the past with the complacency of the present and the possibility of a more sanguine future.

In contrast, Sakaiminato articulates a restorative nostalgia that, in Boym's words, "proposes to rebuild the lost home and patch up the memory gaps."[27] We experience a set of personal memories stitched into the broader national history to represent a completed narrative, a linking of the past with the present through a happy transcendence of difficult moments. The trauma of war and irrecoverable loss is softened by an indulgence in coming home; nostalgia in Sakaiminato is not a bitter draught of insatiable longing but an ease, a kind of comfort food. Through promulgating a complete narrative, an idyllic past is neatly linked to the present. The memory of pain—and the pain of memory—along with its meaningful role in shaping the future, is bridged by a compelling story moving along energetically, inexorably, toward a happy ending. The danger is that the "fond backward gaze," as one scholar describes the nostalgic impulse, can too easily make the present seem connected to a gloriously imagined past and accordingly threaten to "foreclose the future, to reject the possibility of productive change."[28]

Nostalgia is often seen in this way as a conservative, nonproductive, even dangerous form of desire, a longing for a mythical home place/time that can be manipulated for nationalist and other ideological purposes. But as Fredric Jameson once suggested, "there is no reason why a nostalgia conscious of itself, a lucid and remorseless dissatisfaction with the present on the grounds of some remembered plenitude, cannot furnish as adequate a revolutionary stimulus as any other."[29] Indeed, several recent studies have set out to reclaim nostalgia as a creative, progressive force that, in John J. Su's words, "facilitates an exploration of ethical ideals in the face of disappointing circumstances."[30] My own view is that, if read critically, even ironically, with an eye for the cracks and inconsistencies, nostalgia can be translated from a wistful longing for an idealized past into productive stimulus toward a future that incorporates ideals without ignoring the realities of the present. Some presentations of nostalgia lend themselves more easily to this kind of productive critical reading, while others resist such narrative unpacking.

Boym's notions of reflective and restorative nostalgia are useful for contemplating the way memories are presented and experienced, but they are certainly not mutually exclusive: the individual subject's experience of one can supplement or deepen the experience of the other. Just as Mizuki's glorious return to Rabaul assumes fresh poignancy when he understands for the first time the shocking poverty of his friends, so too the lively and prosperous Mizuki Shigeru Road takes on new meaning when you also visit the Mugonkan or venture onto Sakaiminato's own lonely side streets.

The challenge of memory, I suppose, is like any experience of reading or interpretation. We must take care not to be seduced by our own longings for continuity, our desire for a satisfying narrative arc with a whole past, fully wrought characters, and a gratifying conclusion. There is always the danger of overlaying history with what history might have been, of convincing ourselves that Sakaiminato Station is really Kitarō Station. In a new century already wracked by international wars and lives cut tragically short, it is particularly easy, I think, to be seduced by hopeful, redemptive narratives of nostalgia. At times like this, then, it is fragmented, incomplete stories, like the disrupted narratives of the Mugonkan or the ragged subplots of Mizuki's world, that most powerfully convey the traumas of the past. I am not disparaging all nostalgic narratives, nor criticizing Sakaiminato's revitalization. Rather I am simply suggesting that, whether the articulation is restorative or reflective, ultimately the onus is on the reader. Even (or especially) when the presentation seems clean and smooth, we can read nostalgia critically, reflectively—so that we also see the larvae in the coffee water, the stragglers who come home too late from the war, the poverty in Rabaul, and the struggles of small shops on the side streets of Sakaiminato. Such details subvert the tyranny of the storyline, opening up the possibility of new journeys and alternative endings.

Notes

1. For more on Mizuki, including a discussion of the 2005 film *Yōkai daisensō* as well as manga, anime, and live-action versions of *Gegege no Kitarō*, see Zilia Papp's article in this volume. For additional background on Mizuki, see Michael Dylan Foster, "The Otherworlds of Mizuki Shigeru," in *Mechademia* 3 (2008): 8–28, and Frederik L. Schodt, *Dreamland Japan: Writings on Modern Manga* (Berkeley, Calif.: Stone Bridge Press, 1996), 177–82. For an extended biography and analysis, see Adachi Noriyuki, *Yōkai to aruku: Hyōden, Mizuki Shigeru* (Walking with yōkai: Critical biography, Mizuko Shigeru) (Tokyo: Bungei Shunjū, 1994). I use the word *yōkai* here as a general term for all sorts of monstrous and mysterious creatures, also sometimes referred to as *bakemono* or *obake*.

2. So-called *mura okoshi* and *machi zukuri* (town making) movements began during the 1960s in response to the depopulation of fishing and agricultural communities throughout Japan. By the early 1970s, Prime Minister Tanaka Kakuei would note: "The rapid rise in urban population has caused an increase in the number of people living in the big city—with no mountain in which to chase a rabbit, no river in which to catch small carp, and only a tiny apartment to call their hometown [*furusato*]. In such a situation, I expect it will be difficult to pass on to the next generation the excellent nature and traditions of the Japanese people." Tanaka Kakuei, *Nihon rettō kaizō ron* (Theory for rebuilding the Japanese archipelago) (Tokyo: Nikkan Kōgyō Shinbunsha, 1973), 1–2. In Tanaka's comments, we find already a desire for an untrammeled past; starting in the 1980s the federal government officially promoted *furusato zukuri* programs "designed," as anthropologist Schott Schnell notes, "to capitalize on this nostalgic sense of longing by helping rural towns and villages develop (or perhaps in some cases invent) their own unique attractions." *The Rousing Drum: Ritual Practice in a Japanese Community* (Honolulu: University of Hawai'i Press, 1999), 271. Not surprisingly, *mura okoshi, machi zukuri,* and *furusato zukuri* are often fraught with political and economic complexities on both local and national levels. See Jennifer Robertson, *Native and Newcomer: Making and Remaking a Japanese City* (Berkeley and Los Angeles: University of California Press, 1991); Marilyn Ivy, *Discourses of the Vanishing: Modernity, Phantasm, Japan* (Chicago: University of Chicago Press, 1995); John Knight, "Rural Revitalization in Japan: Spirit of the Village and Taste of the Country," *Asian Survey* 34, no. 2 (July 1994): 634–46; and Takashi Iguchi, "Depopulation and *Mura-Okoshi* (Village Revival)," in *Forestry and the Forest Industry in Japan,* ed. Iwai Yoshiya (Vancouver: University of British Columbia Press, 2002), 259–77. For a clear explanation

of the historical and political distinctions between *mura okoshi, machi zukuri,* and *furusato zukuri,* including references to Sakaiminato, see Yasui Manami, "Machi zukuri, mura oko-shi to furusato monogatari" (Town making, village revitalization, and the *furusato* story), in *Matsuri to ibento* (Festival and event), ed. Komatsu Kazuhiko (Tokyo: Shōgakukan, 1997), 201–26. See also Saitō Tsugio, *Yōkai toshi keikaku ron: Obake kara no machi zukuri* (Theories of yōkai urban planning: Town building through monsters) (Tokyo: Sairyūsha, 1996), which focuses particularly on the usage of yōkai for these purposes.

3. There are also several other trains: a *Medama oyaji* (Papa Eyeball) train, dedicated to Kitarō's faithful familiar (and father), a disembodied eyeball with arms, legs, and a high-pitched voice (the train headlights offer themselves nicely to incorporation of the eyeball theme); a *Neko musume* (Catgirl) train; and a *Nezumi otoko* (Ratman) train.

4. Anthony H. Chambers, "Introduction" to Ueda Akinari, *Tales of Moonlight and Rain,* trans. Anthony H. Chambers (New York: Columbia University Press, 2007), 25.

5. *Asahi shinbun,* August 19, 2007, 30.

6. Aramata Hiroshi, *Shin Nihon yōkai junreidan: Kaiki no kuni Nippon* (New Japan yōkai pilgrimage group: Weird nation Japan) (Tokyo: Shūeisha, 1997), 180.

7. With a population of some 37,045 people (statistics from December 2006; "Sakana to Kitarō no machi: Sakaiminato gaido mappu" [City of fish and Kitarō: Sakaiminato guide map], 2), Sakaiminato is officially considered a city (*shi*). The once prosperous fishing industry has fallen into significant decline since the depletion in the sardine (*maiwashi*) population beginning in the 1990s. Coincident with this reduction in the size of the catch has been an increase in the number of visitors to the Mizuki Shigeru Road. See *Asahi shin-bun,* August 19, 2007, 30. While the Sakaiminato tourist board promotes a range of events and attractions, many of which relate to fish and the fishing industry, the Mizuki/yōkai connection is the primary allure for tourists.

8. In one sense, the Yōkai Shrine institutionalizes an informal practice that was already occurring before it was built; Aramata notes that when he visited the road in 1996, he was intrigued by the five-yen and ten-yen coins placed around each statue, like offer-ings to a deity. See Aramata, *Shin Nihon yōkai junreidan,*182–83. During my own visit a decade later, I saw very few coins like this, with the exception of those around a figure of Medama oyaji bathing in a saucer, a shape particularly conducive, perhaps, to the place-ment of offerings.

9. See Mizuki Shigeru, *Komikku Shōwa shi* (Manga history of Shōwa), 8 vols. (Tokyo: Kōdansha Komikkusu, 1994). Subsequent citations will note specific volume and page numbers. The quotation here is from 8:274.

10. It is not just in Japan that the "framed, self-conscious, bimodal form" of comics has proven particularly conducive to the kind of interweaving of personal and histori-cal narrative Mizuki employs in *Shōwa shi.* As Hillary Chute notes, "The most important graphic narratives explore the conflicted boundaries of what can be said and what can be shown at the intersection of collective histories and life stories." Hillary Chute, "Comics as Literature? Reading Graphic Narrative" *PMLA* 123, no. 2 (March 2008): 457, 459. The paradigmatic example of this style in a Western context is Art Spiegelman's award-winning *Maus* series.

11. Mizuki, *Shōwa shi,* 6:21–40.

12. Mizuki's chapter on this journey back is entitled "The Battlefields after Thirty

Years," though based on the date he provides (December 14, 1970) for his return, he had been away for approximately twenty-five years; see Mizuki, *Shōwa shi,* 7:231–46.

13. This is how he refers to the native village in one of his memoirs: Mizuki Shigeru, *Musume ni kataru otōsan no senki* (Papa's war-diary told to his daughters) (Tokyo: Kawade Shobō Shinsha, 1995).

14. Mizuki, *Shōwa shi,* 7:257.

15. Ibid., 8:28–35.

16. Ibid., 8:253.

17. Ibid., 8:254–55.

18. Ibid., 8:40.

19. Mizuki, or the editors, mistakenly state that Yokoi had been in the jungle for "thirty-seven years" (Mizuki, *Shōwa shi,* 8:40).

20. Nicolas D. Kristof, "Shoichi Yokoi, 82, Is Dead; Japan Soldier Hid 27 Years," *New York Times,* September 26, 1997. For more on Yokoi and other so-called stragglers, see Beatrice Trefalt, *Japanese Army Stragglers and Memories of the War in Japan, 1950–1975* (London: Routledge Curzon, 2003).

21. Mizuki, *Shōwa shi,* 6:38–39; see also Mizuki, *Musume ni kataru,* 153–54.

22. For more on the Mugonkan, see Yoshikuni Igarashi, *Bodies of Memory: Narratives of War in Postwar Japanese Culture, 1945–1970* (Princeton, N.J.: Princeton University Press, 2000), 3–11; also Kuboshima Sei'ichirō, *Mugonkan: Senbotsu gagakusei 'inori no e'* (Mugonkan: 'Prayers in pictures' of art students lost in the war) (Tokyo: Kōdansha, 2006), which includes images from the museum as well as brief biographies of the artists. For a discussion of various ways in which Japanese war dead have been memorialized, see Jan van Breman, "Monuments for the Untimely Dead or the Objectification of Social Memory in Japan," in *Perspectives on Social Memory in Japan,* ed. Tsu Yun Hui, Jan van Bremen, and Eyal Ben-Ari, 23–43 (Folkstone, Kent: Global Oriental, 2005); also Nakamichi Hirochika, who invokes the term "interrupted lives" for the people being memorialized: "Memorial Monuments of Interrupted Lives in Modern Japan: From Ex Post Facto Treatment to Intensification Devices," in *Perspectives on Social Memory in Japan,* ed., Hui, van Bremen, and Ben-Ari, 44–57. For a sensitive treatment of the politically controversial Yasukuni Shrine, see John Nelson, "Social Memory as Ritual Practice: Commemorating the Spirits of the Military Dead at Yasukuni Shinto Shrine," *Journal of Asian Studies* 62, no. 2 (May 2003): 443–67.

23. This is not to deny the real and meaningful economic boost Mizuki has brought to Sakaiminato, for certainly many of the shops on the road are prosperous. Rather my point is that even in successful narratives of *mura okoshi* there are also other stories, less sanguine, that should not be forgotten.

24. Mizuki, *Shōwa shi,* 8:269.

25. "Nostalgia," coined in 1688 by Swiss physician Johannes Hofer from the Greek *nostos* (= to return home) and *algia* (= pain/grief), was originally configured as a disease of homesickness that affected both body and mind. In contemporary discourse, the concept encompasses a diverse range of feelings concerning "the juxtaposition of an idealized past with an unsatisfactory present": George K. Behlmer, "Introduction," *Singular Continuities: Tradition, Nostalgia, and Identity in Modern British Culture,* ed. George K. Behlmer and Fred M. Leventhal (Stanford, Calif.: Stanford University Press, 2000), 7. It is often still invoked as an intense longing for home—whether temporal or geographical or both.

In Japanese, a number of words are associated with this sense of longing: *nosutarujia* or *nosutarujii*, cognate with "nostalgia"; *natsukashii*, used in poetry for centuries and still commonly invoked in everyday language as an expression of bittersweet remembrance; and *mukashi*, a word that "alludes to the Good Old Days—to modes and contexts of sociability long since transcended, abandoned, or dismantled, but reconstructable and revivifiable in a selective form through nostalgia" (Robertson, *Native and Newcomer*, 15). For a discussion of recent Japanese forms of nostalgia, particularly "nostalgia products" that draw on the mass culture of the 1920s and 1930s, see Ivy, *Discourses of the Vanishing*, 54–59.

26. Svetlana Boym, *The Future of Nostalgia* (New York: Basic Books, 2001), xviii.

27. Ibid., 41. Boym's typology is more complex than my adaptation of it here. In general, restorative nostalgia tends to allow for complacency, while reflective nostalgia inspires the possibility of creative thought and progress. In the kind of restorative nostalgia that seems to operate in Sakaiminato, "Distance is compensated by intimate experience and the availability of a desired object. Displacement is cured by a return home, preferably a collective one. Never mind if it's not your home; by the time you reach it, you will already have forgotten the difference" (44). On the other hand, the Mugonkan inspires a reflective nostalgia, "a form of deep mourning that performs a labor of grief both through pondering pain and through play that points to the future" (55).

28. Behlmer, *Singular Continuities*, 7.

29. Fredric Jameson, "Walter Benjamin, or Nostalgia," in *The Legacy of German Refugee Intellectuals*, ed. Robert Boyers (New York: Schocken Books, 1972), 68.

30. John J. Su, *Ethics and Nostalgia in the Contemporary Novel* (Cambridge: Cambridge University Press, 2005), 4. Other examples of this more optimistic attitude toward nostalgia include Janelle Wilson, who maintains that as a concept/emotion, nostalgia has "gotten a bad rap." Janelle Wilson, *Nostalgia: Sanctuary of Meaning* (Cranbury, N.J.: Rosemont Publishing, 2005), 7. See also Peter Glazer, *Radical Nostalgia: Spanish Civil War Commemorations in America* (Rochester, N.Y.: University of Rochester Press, 2005), and Tamara S. Wagner, *Longing: Narratives of Nostalgia in the British Novel, 1740–1890* (Lewisburg, Pa.: Bucknell University Press, 2004).

SHENG-MEI MA

• • •

Three Views of the Rising Sun, Obliquely: Keiji Nakazawa's A-bomb, Osamu Tezuka's Adolf, and Yoshinori Kobayashi's Apologia

"The twentieth century began with a futuristic utopia and ended with nostalgia," writes Svetlana Boym in *The Future of Nostalgia*.[1] This zeitgeist of looking backwards materializes in Japanese manga and anime as a belated rendezvous with World War II, as a gaze across half a century into the Rising Sun and the invariable averting from the blinding rays of wartime history. Japanese comics' "return of the repressed" entails a coming to terms with the collective trauma that allegedly ended in 1945, yet this yearning to engage a specific past of great pain is adulterated by the human instinct for pleasure and a withdrawal from pain. After all, any gaze into the sun results in a turning away, lest blindness or madness set in. Instead of staring into the sun himself, Van Gogh lets his sunflowers do that, maintains Georges Bataille. Bataille further casts this paradox of attraction and revulsion of the sun in the image of Icarus: "the summit of elevation is in practice confused with a sudden fall of unheard-of violence. The myth of Icarus is particularly expressive from this point of view: it clearly splits the sun in two—the one that was shining at the moment of Icarus's elevation, and the other that melted the wax, causing failure and a screaming fall when Icarus got too close."[2] Drawn to the best and the worst of times of Imperial Japan, the three manga artists—Nakazawa Keiji in the 1970s, Tezuka Osamu in the 1980s, and Kobayashi Yoshinori at the turn of the century—manage to capture, in the words of Bataille, either "the preceding sun (the one not looked at) [which] is perfectly beautiful" or "the scrutinized sun [which] can be horribly ugly."[3] Rather than dwelling on Japan's historical responsibility over the war, Nakazawa's *Barefoot Gen* (1973–74, *Hadashi no gen*) represents the tragedy of the atom bomb from the lone perspective of a pacifist family, Tezuka's *Adolf* (1983–85, *Adorufu ni tsugu*) gives vent to a bizarre anti-Semitic Hitler myth, and Kobayashi's *Taiwanron* (2001, On Taiwan) peddles his right-wing apologia for Japanese militarism.[4] Either from the left or the right of the Japanese political spectrum, the wartime Rising Sun is viewed obliquely like Hokusai's famous "One Hundred Views of Fuji."

In order not to gaze unblinkingly at the sun or the Japanese wartime history, both Nakazawa and Tezuka locate their subject matter in the pacifist minority before, during, and immediately after the war. Favoring the left-wing liberal politics, the two manga artists make possible the English-speaking reader's sympathy and even identification with the antiwar position of the protagonists, who are, needless to say, victims of conservative, militaristic forces of the time. Who can argue with the tragedy of *hibakusha* (explosion-affected person[s]) in Nakazawa, except it is not balanced by any representation of Japanese aggression and atrocities? Indeed, there is no representation at all of Japanese oppression of its colonies other than one Korean character forced into hard labor in Japan. Tezuka weaves his version of the Hitler myth by means of, likewise, an antiwar protagonist. From Nakazawa's A-bomb testimony, Tezuka moves into the controversial realm of, in Alvin H. Rosenfeld's term, imagining Hitler.[5] Yet the witness and the daydreamer are replaced on the threshold of the twenty-first century by Kobayashi's virulent reactionary polemic. The antiwar position shifts into its nemesis, or Kobayashi's diatribe advocating a revival of the Japanese spirit symbolized by militarism. Composed for the Japanese domestic market as well as, strangely enough, a sizeable market in Taiwan in Chinese translation, Kobayashi's *On Taiwan* was not and will quite possibly never be translated into English. By contrast, in English translation, Nakazawa appeals to the global readership in terms of the antinuclear peace

> DRAWN TO THE BEST AND THE WORST OF TIMES OF IMPERIAL JAPAN, THE THREE MANGA ARTISTS MANAGE TO CAPTURE EITHER "THE PRECEDING SUN [WHICH] IS PERFECTLY BEAUTIFUL" OR "THE SCRUTINIZED SUN [WHICH] CAN BE HORRIBLY UGLY."

movement and Tezuka in terms of the fascination for Hitler. Not only are the three artists looking, obliquely, at the sun, but the global audience does the same in English, Chinese, and other translations.

NAKAZAWA KEIJI'S *BAREFOOT GEN*

Six years old at the time of the atomic bombing of Hiroshima, Nakazawa Keiji in his early career as a cartoonist refrained from the subject altogether, "hat[ing] the very mention of the word." Nakazawa reminisced in "Introduction: My Hope for *Barefoot Gen*" in *Barefoot Gen: Out of the Ashes*, which was the fourth and last of the series:

> But in October 1966—twenty-one years after the bomb—my mother died
> . . . When her body was cremated, I discovered something that made me
> tremble with rage: nothing was left of her bones. Usually the bones remain
> after cremation, but radioactive cesium had eaten my mother's bones away,
> and they had turned into ash. The A-bomb had taken everything from me,
> even my precious mother's bones.[6]

Nakazawa's rage over the belated incineration and total erasure of his mother propelled him to confront the bomb. A classic return of the repressed, the cartoonist might have attributed to the bomb what is possibly a case of osteoporosis, a lifetime of calcium loss that would similarly leave little physical remains after cremation. This autobiographical detail makes all the more significant the episode in *Barefoot Gen* when the protagonist Nakaoka Gen retrieves his father's and two siblings' bones from the ruins, after an extended period of denial of their deaths. After all, the survivors of the Nakaoka family do not revisit the site of their house for the remains of the dead until volume 3, *Barefoot Gen: After the Bomb*, when they have long perished at the end of volume 1, *Barefoot Gen: A Cartoon History of Hiroshima*. The entire second volume, *Barefoot Gen: The Day After*, manifests Gen and his mother Kimie in various stages of psychological denial. Contrary to Christ's advice, only the living can bury the dead. Gen's family begin their return to reality once they come to accept the fate of the loved ones.

In 1972–73, Nakazawa serialized *Barefoot Gen* in *Shūkan shōnen janpu*, the largest weekly comic magazine in Japan. Art Spiegelman describes Nakazawa's "draftsmanship [as] somewhat graceless, even homely, and without much nuance, but it gets the job done . . . The drawing's greatest virtue is its straightforward, blunt sincerity . . . It is the inexorable art of the witness."[7] Compared to Spiegelman and other graphic novelists of the same calibre,[8] Nakazawa's drawings appear to be artless, yet the simplistic, unadorned style befits the testimonial mode of bomb survivors. The story revolves around the survival of the Nakaoka family, the father's antiwar stance turning them into scapegoats for wartime misery. Indoctrinated by propaganda and patriotic jingoism, the Nakaokas' neighbors and the children's classmates and teachers label them traitors, subjecting the pariah family to discrimination and violence. The only exception seems to be the decent Korean neighbor Mr. Pak, sympathetic because he himself is an oppressed minority. The metaphor of wheat, "push[ing] its shoots up" despite "winter frost" and human trampling, as the father explains in the opening panel, becomes the key to rejuvenating the surviving Nakaokas. Gen (meaning "root") inherits this undaunted spirit, forever resourceful and of good cheer, particularly after the father, the oldest daughter Eiko, and Gen's younger brother Shinji are consumed by the conflagration in the wake of the bomb.

The motif of death and rebirth repeats itself in the manner of a fugue from the wheat imagery to numerous "reincarnations." Gen and the mother Kimie survive the blast purely by chance, protected by a concrete wall and in the attic. Having witnessed three members of her family burned to death, Kimie gives birth to Tomoko amid the rubble, yet Tomoko dies in her infancy due to either malnutrition or the radiation-caused cancer. Gen also rescues Shinji's lookalike, Ryūta, and an Eiko substitute, the novice dancer Natsue. Gen's pluck notwithstanding, Ryūta is forced to join the ruthless postwar underworld and Natsue is unlikely to realize her dream as a performer with her keloid-scarred face. Even the invalid painter Seiji is, figuratively, pulled back by Gen from the jaws of suicidal depression. Regeneration graces Gen himself in the concluding pages when he finds a fuzz of hair covering his bald head, parallel to the wheat seedlings after the bomb where the land is purportedly to stay barren for sixty years. This gallery of monstrosities, physically as in the case of hibakusha or socially as in the case of thieving orphans of Ryūta and his gang, illustrates Gen's picaresque journey through hell. These supporting characters around Gen emerge and vanish in the narrative without much logic, akin to the chaos in Hiroshima.

What remains constant is the grotesquerie and agony of survival. Numerous reports and testimonies of the atom bomb have familiarized twenty-first century readers with the nuclear horror, yet to see, page after page, the walking dead with peeled-off skin dragging behind, with the flesh torn clean off the bones, with melted faces, with maggots squirming in the wounds and flies feasting on corpses is so nauseating that the reading induces, as Robert Jay Lifton argues in *Death in Life* (1967),[9] compassion fatigue. Although John Hersey's *Hiroshima* (1946),[10] Hachiya Michihiko's *Hiroshima Diary* (1955),[11] Ibuse Masuji's

> THE MOTIF OF DEATH AND REBIRTH REPEATS ITSELF IN THE MANNER OF A FUGUE FROM THE WHEAT IMAGERY TO NUMEROUS "REINCARNATIONS."

Black Rain (1970),[12] writers collected in Ōe Kenzaburō's *The Crazy Iris* (1985),[13] Kurosawa Akira's *Dreams* (1990), and a host of others have shared their mushroom vision, either survivors' close-ups or artists' long shots, with us for decades, the rawness of Nakazawa's art still assaults our senses. Nonetheless, the cartoonist balances the nightmarish images with comic conventions of physical slapstick and humor, courtesy of the indomitable Gen, the combination of which proves to be a saving grace, sustaining not only the Nakaoka household but also the reader.

The choice of wheat as a central metaphor is intriguing. Throughout the four volumes, the Nakaoka family teeter on the verge of starvation, from wartime rationing to the postwar collapse of economy, particularly for a refugee family, to the U.S. military "foodstuffs" Gen risks his life to steal from trigger-happy American guards. Such cans turn out to contain packs of playing cards and rubber balloons, an ironic reference to condoms and the sex industry accompanying the American GIs wherever they go. The never-ending search for food focuses on the staple of the Japanese diet, rice, against which is the Nakaoka icon of wheat, as if the cartoonist deliberately chooses an atypical Japanese food to embody the antiwar, dissenting spirit of the Nakaokas. The erstwhile un-Japanese sentiment comes to be embraced wholeheartedly in postwar Japan.

IMAGING HITLER IN JAPAN

Lionized as the "God of Comics" and "God of Animation" in Japan, Tezuka Osamu's long career boasted of five hundred titles of manga and animations and about 150,000 drawn pages. His most representative works include, in chronological order from the 1950s to the 1980s, *Metropolis, Jungle Emperor, Tetsuwan Atomu* (or *Mighty Atom), Phoenix, Ribon no kishi* (or *Princess Knight), Black Jack,* and *Adorufu ni tsugu* (*Adolf,* or more precisely, "Tell Adolf").[14] Tezuka's five-volume *Adolf* (subsequent references use volume number and page number) was serialized in the Japanese magazine *Shūkan bunshun.* Though *Adolf* was the first book by Tezuka to be translated into English, perhaps on the merit of its sensational subject matter more than anything else, *Jungle Emperor* might be the one most familiar to the American public, thanks to its 1960s and '70s resurrection as the TV animations *Kimba, the White Lion*, which in turn inspired Disney's *The Lion King*. Despite Disney's denials, the resemblance of Kimba and Simba and that of a host of other characters and episodes underline the derivativeness of global cultural productions, Tezuka's *Adolf* included. As Jean Baudrillard declares of the postmodern age, "we live in a world where there is more and more information, and less and less meaning."[15] The voluminous information on the Third Reich obtained by Tezuka, evidenced in the year-by-year comparative timeline of World War II appended to many chapters, gives way to the most sensationalizing, slanderous, and anti-Semitic hoax about the mass murderer, namely, Hitler was, to borrow Sander Gilman's coinage, a self-hating Jew.[16] His artistic imagination seems captured not so much by the actual deeds of Hitler as by the large liberties promised to him by the free association of the name Adolf. Put another way, Tezuka pirates the given name of the mass murderer as a loaded "logo" to advance his "action thriller." Just as Disney plagiarizes his Kimba, Tezuka borrows from the Hitler kitsch. In so doing, the history of World War II constitutes merely the backdrop to a highly improbable plot involving three Adolfs.

In addition to Adolf Hitler, the other two Adolfs are: Adolf Kaufmann, born in Kobe of a German consular official and his Japanese wife, who is sent back to Germany and eventually becomes a ruthless German officer; and Adolf Kamil, the son of a Jewish-German refugee couple who ran a bakery in Kobe. All three Adolfs have something to hide. Hitler tries to conceal his alleged Jewish ancestry, for which he sends Kaufman on a mission back to Japan. A member of the Hitler Youth and later of the SD, Kaufman denies his Japanese, hence non-Aryan, blood. The Kamils flee the Nazis to Japan and the Jewish boy believes that he is entirely Japanese, even though his playmates call him "whitey." The two younger Adolfs are childhood friends turned deadly enemies.

Not only does racial passing occur but cultural and generic boundaries are crisscrossed as well: the five-volume story spans Japan, Germany, and the Middle East; in terms of genre, the Holocaust seems too weighty a topic for comics. The vehicle for breaching borders of race, culture, and genre proves to be the narrator, Tōge Sōhei, a former college track-and-field star turned newspaper reporter. He covered the 1936 Berlin Olympic Games for a Japanese newspaper, and his communist brother was the one who passed on to him the documents of Hitler's birth. Tōge is pivotal to *Adolf* because, unlike the three namesakes who are either murderous or angst ridden, Tōge is funny. Upright and unsophisticated, Tōge provides a great portion of the gags and laughs, central to the appeal of comics. On the other hand, Tōge offers a frame for the story befitting the grave, ponderous nature of the subject matter. The opening (1:12–14) and the conclusion (5:253) hook up like the two ends of a full circle as Tōge visits Kamil's grave at an Israeli cemetery.

Similar to the conclusion of Art Spiegelman's Pulitzer Prize–winning *Maus I* and *Maus II* (1986, 1991) with the tombstone of his Holocaust-survivor parents, Tezuka captures the dirge-like quality of the Holocaust. But Tōge's interior monologue, repeated at the beginning and the end of the story, spells the problematics of imagining Hitler or, put another way, of translating the Holocaust: "This is the story of three men named Adolf. Each Adolf lived a life that was very different from that of the other two . . . Yet the three of them were bound together by a single twist of fate" (1:12–14). In the last pages of the fifth volume, Tōge proceeds to remark that the story he is leaving behind "will be read by millions of 'Adolfs' all over the world" (5:251). Adolf becomes everyman who becomes Hitler. A chilling implication, Tezuka perpetuates Hannah Arendt's theory of the banality of evil, except that the cartoonist ups the ante of the case study from Eichmann to Hitler.[17]

> THE VOLUMINOUS INFORMATION ON THE THIRD REICH OBTAINED BY TEZUKA, EVIDENCED IN THE YEAR-BY-YEAR COMPARATIVE TIMELINE OF WORLD WAR II APPENDED TO MANY CHAPTERS, GIVES WAY TO THE MOST SENSATIONALIZING, SLANDEROUS, AND ANTI-SEMITIC HOAX ABOUT THE MASS MURDERER, NAMELY, HITLER WAS, TO BORROW SANDER GILMAN'S COINAGE, A SELF-HATING JEW.

While the hidden ideology is irresponsible and reprehensible, it is lightened considerably by Tezuka's mastery of the medium. His techniques of storytelling enable him to traverse nations and time periods with great ease, albeit with many coincidences that require suspension of disbelief. The action and mystery, which Tezuka manages to maintain well over a thousand pages, testify to his power as a comic artist, but they jar against the somber, lamentational opening and ending. The plot revolves around the struggle over possession of documents proving Hitler's racial background, including Hitler's birth certificate and letters written by his mother to his Jewish grandfather. Both the Japanese and German secret agents, Adolf Kaufman among them, attempt to rob Tōge of these documents. Tōge, on the other hand, risks everything to protect the documents, which he repeatedly claims would "bring down Hitler."

This brief sketch suffices to demonstrate the anti-Semitic drift of Tezuka's text. The Holocaust is attributed to Jewish self-loathing. In other words, by annihilating Jews from the face of the earth, Hitler denies, in effect, his own Jewishness. A viciously ahistorical interpretation of *Endlosung,* this approach finds eager advocates among modern artists trying to contain the genocide in individual psychosis, such as George Steiner's *The Portage to San Cristobal of A.H.* (1981)[18] and W. D. Snodgrass's *The Fuhrer Bunker* (1977).[19] Anti-Semitic rhetoric also rears its head in Tezuka's character of Frankenburger, Hitler's wealthy Jewish grandfather, who is said to have raped his German maid and to have sired Hitler's father. This follows the racist stereotype of lascivious Jewish males coveting Aryan women. Another stereotype of Jews surfaces in the Jewish girl Eliza's father, an opportunistic businessman. In order to survive, he not only collaborates with the Nazis but he encourages Eliza to befriend the Hitler Youth member Adolf Kaufman as an "investment" against any impending catastrophe.

The translator Yuji Oniki writes in his "Introduction: Tezuka's Twentieth Century" to *Adolf: An Exile in Japan* that "The story revolves around the secret of Adolf Hitler's Jewish ancestry. The historical validity of this premise is less important than the fact that each Adolf in Tezuka's story represents not a particular race or nationality, but a particular 'mixed' circumstance." Such a casual dismissal of the anti-Semitic thesis from a then PhD candidate in comparative literature at the University of California at Berkeley is disturbing. It is tantamount to saying that the official whitewashing in Japanese history textbooks of the Rape of Nanking in 1937 is "less important than the fact that" atrocities take place in every war due to multiple causes. The translator's fashionable discourse of universalism obfuscates historical responsibility and collective memory; his promotion of a global village of mixed races and cultures makes possible amnesia over past traumas and contributes to ever-increasing racial and ethnic strifes. The translator's sentiment is echoed by Annette Roman, who as the editor of the *Adolf* series at Cadence Books, agrees that the plot is "somewhat contrived" but adds that "I am a child of survivors, but in a sense all of us are survivors of some kind." Roman's father is a Hungarian Jew who survived forced-labor camps, but her mother is a Protestant German who acquires the survivor status, in Roman's view, as a result of having endured the Allied bombings. Though of different generations and nationalities, Tezuka, Oniki, Roman, and perhaps many of their readers share in the willful abuse of terminologies and in the revisionism of collective memory.

Conceivably, fans of manga would defend Tezuka's shift from the historical Hitler to the fictitious Adolfs on grounds that Tezuka is, after all, a

Japanese, removed from the European continent where the drama of the extermination of Jews unfolded. Such apologists would surely contend that any representation of the Holocaust is bound to be a translation. A survivor's memoir such as Elie Wiesel's *Night* (1956)[20] and Primo Levi's *Survival in Auschwitz* (1959)[21] is certainly closer to the collectivity of human tragedies we have come to call the Holocaust than a fictitious work such as William Styron's *Sophie's Choice* (1979),[22] D. M. Thomas's *The White Hotel* (1981),[23] and Sylvia Plath's various poems on her suicidal wish. The distance between *Endlosung* and its various translations—autobiographical or imaginary—may be one of degree rather than kind, though. Even Spiegelman's *Maus,* based on the life story of his survivor father Vladek, remains a representation of the Holocaust, as I argued in "Mourning with the (as a) Jew: Metaphor, Ethnicity, and the Holocaust in Art Spiegelman's *Maus*":

> What a reader holds in the hands is several removes from the actual event— from the incomprehensible totality known as the Holocaust, to the fraction experienced and then selectively recalled by Vladek, to Art Spiegelman's "doodle drawings" based on the shaky recall of that fraction, and eventually to mass-produced, market-oriented "facsimiles" of Spiegelman's originals. The contrived spelling of *Maus* exemplifies at the outset the comics' artifice and, therefore, its removal from the reality of that animal.[24]

Yet even as a Japanese artist transcribing his wartime experience onto the half a dozen pages of *Adolf* on the Japanese Royal Army's atrocities against the Chinese, Tezuka's representation is well-intentioned yet woefully inadequate. The artist's indulgence in fantasies over Hitler sharpens his failure to confronting Japan's own historical responsibility in the Chinese theater and elsewhere. The emphasis on Japan itself, furthermore, lapses into a self-congratulating reiteration of the sacrifices of dissidents in Japan, such as Tōge and his leftist friends, whose efforts, revealingly, concentrate on the outlandish scheme of exposing Hitler's Jewish ancestry rather than on sabotaging the Japanese war machine. After all, instead of *Adolf,* why did Tezuka not draw comics titled *Hiro* after the Japanese emperor Hirohito? Why does he expend so much ink—and Tezuka is meticulous in his drawings—on a foreign devil, Hitler? Perhaps the Japanese readers prefer an escape into the fantasy land of the Third Reich, hyped by the grotesque mass destruction. Even as fervent a manga critic as Frederik L. Schodt concedes that *Adolf* may have inspired the popular trend in Japan marked by "bizarre, fantastic theories about Jews . . . With subject matter ranging from recycled American and European anti-

Semitic tracts, to claims that Jews are a superior race and (guess what?) that Japanese—not Europeans—are actually the true Jews."[25] Through the English translation of *Adolf*, Tezuka extends his influence from the Pacific Rim to the United States and around the world, educating the young on the plasticity of history and the thrill of imagining Hitler.

The translation and publication of *Adolf* for the English-speaking, hence world, market are underwritten by the "colonization of the mind" already manifest in the Japanese texts. Tezuka's trademark of Japanese female characters with Caucasian facial and physical features have undoubtedly endeared his postwar readers longing for beauty and power embodied in the West. Accordingly, the geisha Kinuko (Honda Sachi) in fact resembles Rosa Lampe, a German Barbie doll with an unrealistically proportioned body and impeccable face. With exactly the same face, Kinuko has slightly darker pupils and wears a geisha's hairdo and kimono. Japanese women in the Western image have cloned themselves in manga and other forms of cultural production. The economic superpower of Japan continues to fantasize itself in terms prescribed by Western media and icons.

KOBAYASHI YOSHINORI'S *ON TAIWAN*

As manga and anime fans around the globe are enamoured by the fantastic rather than political nature of the genre, Kobayashi Yoshinori is not as well-known a figure as Tezuka Osamu and Miyazaki Hayao. Nonetheless, Kobayashi's manga enjoys a considerable domestic market, particularly among right-wing conservatives and, further afield, pro-Japan Taiwanese. When the Chinese translation of Kobayashi's *On Taiwan* was published in Taiwan in 2001, an uproar raged over its apologia for Japanese militarism during World War II, for colonization of Taiwan and other parts of Asia, and for postwar nationalism in Japanese and Taiwanese politics. Protests erupted over the representation of the "benevolent" Japanese colonization of Taiwan and, in particular, over the claim that Taiwan's aboriginal military units and comfort women "volunteered" their service to Japan. While the historical entanglement and political intricacy of the controversy escapes the attention of global fans, Kobayashi's manga has touched a raw nerve in Japan and Taiwan, unleashing furious public debate.

Undoubtedly, Kobayashi is the spokesperson for Japanese discontent over postwar liberal democracy, indulging in the golden past of Japanese colonialism, perpetuating a revisionism of the war. Along with right-wing politicians, Kobayashi has even contributed to the diluting of the history of the war in Japanese textbooks.[26] Kobayashi stands for a revolt against what he sees as "masochistic" liberal guilt over wartime aggression and atrocities. In addition, he embodies the fear of the rise of China in the twenty-first century, in reaction to which he raises the specter of Japanese nationalism. Breathing new life into the revisonist project in *On Taiwan*, the cartoonist buttresses his case by virtue of prominent pro-Japan personages in Taiwan, including ex-President Lee Teng-hui, industrialist Hsu Wen-lung, and long-time Taiwanese independence activist Jing Mei-ling. The Nipponophile chorus from Taiwan is lauded by Kobayashi as the last sanctuary of the good old Japanese spirit, preserved like a time capsule among many Taiwanese over the age of sixty who were educated and came of age during Japanese colonialism of Taiwan in 1895–1945, uncorrupted by left-leaning culture in Japan proper. The Taiwanese writer and critic Chen Ying-chen quotes the historian Dai Guojun in attributing Lee's and other Japan zealots' motives to an "accomplice structure." Chen contends that these pro-Japan Taiwanese have been so implicated in Japanese interests and their sense of identity so inextricably bound to Japan that they must idolize Japan and turn a blind eye to its historical faults.[27]

> OWING TO SUCH POLITICAL FAULTLINES IN JAPANESE AND TAIWANESE DOMESTIC POLITICS, AS WELL AS TO INTERNATIONAL TENSIONS AMONG CHINA, THE UNITED STATES, JAPAN, AND TAIWAN, *ON TAIWAN*, DESPITE ITS NARCISSISTIC KITSCHINESS AND DISTASTEFUL DIATRIBE, BURSTS OPEN TAIWAN'S SILENCE OVER JAPANESE MILITARISM.

In terms of Taiwanese history, Lee and his cohort find in Kobayashi's comics an echo of their nostalgia for the past, prior to the island's takeover by Chiang Kai-shek's Nationalist troops in 1949. In the shared pro-Japanese sentiment, Lee and like-minded Taiwanese forge a common identity against Chiang and the "mainlanders," the occupying force that brought the white terror, such as the February 28 Incident, in which Taiwanese dissidents were persecuted. The exponential growth of the Chinese economy and might across the Taiwan Strait further fuels Taiwanese paranoia over the affiliation of mainlanders in their midst. Taiwan independence becomes a rallying cry against reunification with China alleged to be the dream of Taiwan's mainlander population. Owing to such political faultlines in Japanese and Taiwanese domestic politics, as well as to international tensions among China, the United States, Japan, and Taiwan, *On Taiwan*, despite its narcissistic kitschiness and distasteful diatribe, bursts open Taiwan's silence over Japanese militarism.

Delving into topics somewhat serious for comics, Kobayashi even attempts to chronicle Taiwanese history and political struggle. But he often willfully distorts historical facts. A case in point: the Taiwanese resentment against the arrival of Chiang's nationalists is aptly captured in the Taiwanese saying at the time: "dogs leave; pigs come." "Pigs" refer, of course, to nationalists, whereas Kobayashi seems to feign ignorance over the meaning of "dogs"—Japanese colonists. In general, Kobayashi presents a simplistic version of complex social issues. He even gets basic statistics wrong: he claims that mainlanders constitute 16 percent of Taiwan's population, Taiwanese 82 percent, aborigines 2–3 percent, leaving out the Hakanese altogether, as if this large minority does not exist. With all his trouble, Kobayashi's agenda is self-serving. His sycophantic hero worship of Lee Teng-hui and the discovery of the Japanese spirit in certain Taiwanese are tautological and ultimately bestow honor on the old Japan. If Lee and Hsu Wen-lung embody the "warrior" or "samurai" tradition, then they are neither Taiwanese nor Chinese. Rather, they are the real Japanese long vanished in postwar Japan.

Working in cahoots, the cartoonist and pro-Japan Taiwanese attribute to Japanese colonialism nearly all the modern amenities on the island, from its unique species of rice, the irrigation system, the Sun-Moon Lake, the railroads, the infrastructure for electricity, the sugar industry, and whatnot. Kobayashi even compares Japanese colonization favorably with British India, with the former bent upon improving living standards on Taiwan. In his narcissistic and polemical style, Kobayashi is the protagonist in *On Taiwan*, marked by the ant-like antennae of hair overhanging his forehead. Seeking a verisimilitude of real people, Kobayashi tends to blow up the characters' faces and heads. With political idols such as Lee Teng-hui, Kobayashi invariably draws Lee as looming large, godlike, over the panel. Kobayashi also resorts to actual photographs for key moments in this loosely organized travelogue across Taiwan and memorable audiences with Taiwanese luminaries. Unlike Nakazawa and Tezuka, whose comics lend themselves to the tastes of different segments of manga fans globally and are hence translated into the global lingua franca of English, Kobayashi is translated into Chinese and marketed in Taiwan only, for the right-wing reactionary Japanese politics is not embraced elsewhere.

The look back by three manga artists casts the rising sun during World War II in varying light to perpetuate their respective artistic and ideological interpretations. Ultimately, the massive sufferings caused by the Holocaust and wartime Japanese atrocities are perhaps too weighty for comics and even for literature as a whole, resulting in gazes that are all somewhat oblique.

Notes

1. Svetlana Boym, *The Future of Nostalgia* (New York: Basic Books, 2001), xiv.

2. Georges Bataille, "Sacrificial Mutilation and the Severed Ear of Vincent Van Gogh," in *Visions of Excess: Selected Writings, 1927–1939,* ed. Allan Stoekl with C. R. Lovitt and D. M. Leslie Jr., 61–72 (Minneapolis: University of Minnesota Press, 1985).

3. Georges Bataille, "Rotten Sun," in ibid., 57–58.

4. Nakazawa Keiji, *Barefoot Gen*, vols. 1–4 (subtitled, respectively, *A Cartoon Story of Hiroshima, The Day After, Life after the Bomb,* and *Out of the Ashes*) (Philadelphia: New Society Publishers, 1987–94). Tezuka Osamu, *Adorufu ni tsugu* (Tokyo: Bungei Shunjū, 1985); trans. Yuji Oniki in 5 vols. (*Adolf: A Tale of the Twentieth Century, Adolf: An Exile in Japan, Adolf: The Half-Aryan, Adolf: Days of Infamy,* and *Adolf: 1945 and All That Remains*) (San Francisco, Calif.: Cadence, 1995–96). Kobayashi Yoshinori, *Taiwan lun* (On Taiwan), Chinese translation (Taipei, Taiwan: Avanguard, 2001). Kobayashi's Chinese translator is not named.

5. Alvin H. Rosenfeld, *Imagining Hitler* (Bloomington: Indiana University Press, 1985). When Alvin H. Rosenfeld published *Imagining Hitler* in 1985, he was well aware that much was being excluded from his purview of fictions and narratives in the United States and the West. Indeed, just as *Imagining Hitler* came out, Tezuka Osamu's *Adorufu ni tsugu* (translated as the five-volume *Adolf*) had been serialized for two years in the Japanese magazine *Shūkan Bunshun.*

6. Nakazawa Keiji, "Introduction: My Hope for *Barefoot Gen,*" in *Barefoot Gen: Out of the Ashes,* x.

7. Art Spiegelman, "Foreword: Comics after the Bomb," in *Barefoot Gen: Out of the Ashes,* vii.

8. Art Spiegelman, *Maus: A Survivor's Tale; Part I, My Father Bleeds History* (New York: Pantheon, 1986); *Maus: A Survivor's Tale; Part II, And Here My Trouble Began* (New York: Pantheon, 1991).

9. Robert Jay Lifton, *Death in Life: Survivors of Hiroshima* (New York: Basic Books, 1967).

10. John Hersey, *Hiroshima* (1946; repr. New York: Alfred A. Knopf, 1985).

11. Hachiya Michihiko, *Hiroshima Diary: The Journal of a Japanese Physician, August 6—September 30, 1945,* trans. and ed. Warner Wells (Chapel Hill: University of North Carolina Press, 1955).

12. Ibuse Masuji, *Black Rain,* trans. John Bester (Tokyo: Kodansha International, 1970).

13. Ōe Kenzaburō, ed. *The Crazy Iris and Other Stories of the Atomic Aftermath* (1984; New York: Grove, 1985).

14. See discussion of Tezuka's *Metropolis* (1949) in Lawrence Bird's "States of Emergency: Urban Space and the Robotic Body in the *Metropolis* Tales," *Mechademia* 3 (2008): 127–48.

15. Jean Baudrillard, *Simulacra and Simulation*, trans. Sheila Faria Glaser (Ann Arbor: University of Michigan Press, 1994), 79.

16. Sander L. Gilman, *Jewish Self-Hatred* (Baltimore: The Johns Hopkins University Press, 1986).

17. Hannah Arendt, *Eichmann in Jerusalem* (1963; New York: Viking, 1966).

18. George Steiner, *The Portage to San Cristobal of A.H.* (New York: Simon and Schuster, 1981).

19. W. D. Snodgrass, *The Fuhrer Bunker* (Brockport, N.Y.: Boa Editions, 1977).

20. Elie Wiesel, *Night,* trans. Stella Rodway (New York: Bantam, 1982).

21. Primo Levi, *Survival in Auschwitz* , trans. Stuart Wolf (New York: Collier, 1986).

22. William Styron, *Sophie's Choice* (New York: Random House, 1979).

23. D. M. Thomas, *The White Hotel* (New York: Viking, 1981).

24. Sheng-mei Ma, "Mourning with the (as a) Jew: Metaphor, Ethnicity, and the Holocaust in Art Spiegelman's *Maus,*" *Studies in American Jewish Literature* 16 (1997): 115–29.

25. Frederik L. Schodt, *Dreamland Japan: Writings on Modern Manga* (Berkeley, Calif.: Stone Bridge Press, 1996), 252.

26. See Mark Driscoll's "Kobayashi Yoshinori Is Dead: Imperial War / Sick Liberal Peace / Neoliberal Class War" in this volume.

27. See Chen Ying-chen, "Taiwan lun zi baoyen jiqi gungfeng gozhao" (Violent rhetoric and its accomplice structure), in *Sanjiaozai* (Three-legged thing), ed. Li Shoulin, 6–19 (Taipei, Taiwan: Haixia Shueshu, 2001).

● ● ●

CHRISTOPHER BOLTON

Virtual Creation, Simulated Destruction, and Manufactured Memory at the Art Mecho Museum in Second Life

It is not your typical art museum. The building's glass atrium is topped by a rotating tower built to resemble a giant nineteenth-century optical toy. The walls are made of translucent paper, and at night the building glows like a Japanese lantern. There is no roof. Patrons traversing the museum's catwalks and balconies sometimes lose their balance and fall crashing to the galleries below. Other visitors descend from the sky on jetpacks and make soft landings in the museum courtyard. And we have not even begun to describe the patrons themselves, or the art (Figure 1).

The museum is located in Second Life, a virtual online world in which hundreds of thousands of people each month log on from around the world and use avatars to interact with each other in a virtual, three-dimensional, user-built environment. Second Life (SL for short) bears some resemblance to massively multiplayer online video games like *World of Warcraft,* and it includes some game-like activities, but its open-ended rule base and customizable environment (everything from avatar clothing and bodies to local gravity can be adjusted by users) makes it more adapted to social, commercial, and artistic activities. For example, it is host to an enthusiastic network of artists and exhibitors who make, buy, sell, and display virtual art and architecture.

FIGURE 1. An aerial view of the Art Mecho Museum, with its rotating zoetrope tower. Photograph by author.

Compared with online war games, where players can forget themselves in a frantic rush toward annihilation, Second Life has an arguably different relationship to creation, destruction, and temporality, opening space and time for more deliberate reflection on the nature of digital art and identity.

In the middle of one of SL's oceans, on an archipelago governed by an educational consortium, stands the Art Mecho Museum. The name is borrowed from *Mechademia*'s term for the cluster of aesthetic, social, and theoretical practices surrounding Japanese anime and manga. The museum is devoted to this art.

I designed the museum in 2007 and built it in Second Life in collaboration with students and instructional technology staff at Williams College—or rather their avatars: all activity in Second Life, including construction, is conducted by or through these online agents (Figure 2).[1] The museum was intended as a kind of virtual laboratory to test or demonstrate certain ideas about how we interact with animated art. It is part of an effort to think about how criticism can be conducted not just on but within visual media. But the result is more a process or an experiment than a coherent critical statement,

FIGURE 2. A scene from the museum's construction, showing members of the build team floating in the distance. Each part must be created and shaped individually by an avatar working in Second Life, so structures come together progressively like real buildings (but there is nothing to prevent the second story from being constructed before the first). Photograph by author.

FIGURE 3. Avatar Kuri Basiat in the museum's business office. Photograph by author.

so in keeping with the open-ended or multifaceted quality of the project and the dual or multiple nature of identity in Second Life, I have chosen to describe the museum for *Mechademia* in the form of a conversation between myself and avatar Kuri Basiat, the museum's virtual director (Figure 3).

CHRISTOPHER BOLTON: Please start by telling our readers what inspired the project to build a museum like this.

KURI BASIAT: It was inspired by critical work in anime studies, especially around the experience of watching anime—how the experience of viewing anime differs from other media like prose fiction or so-called live-action film. Thinking about these questions requires the spectator not just to look carefully at anime but to step back and watch him or herself watching anime. Only by doing that can we start to think critically about how we experience this medium.

CB: Susan Napier talks about this using the idea of a "fifth look" that goes beyond other kinds of viewing. It is the power to look at yourself as you look at the film.[2]

KB: Yes, although Napier's idea, which starts from Paul Willemen's "fourth look," includes a kind of moral or ethical sense that relates to narrative content as well as the visual style.[3] Here I am thinking more specifically about the spectator's visual relationship to anime, his or her physical (bodily) and phenomenological or epistemological relation to the film. That is where Second Life can help. It forces the user to animate him or herself as an avatar, and then watch the animated self move through the museum and interact with the art. The exhibits are designed to provoke some thought about the relationship between these different layers or entities.

CB: Can you give our readers an example?

KB: Well, some critics have argued that linear perspective—with its depth and smooth recession into the distance—is not a neutral artistic device but a visual technology associated with surveillance, targeting, and power. It is something that enmeshes both the scene and the viewer in a web of control. These ideas have been applied to literature and film, but you and Thomas Lamarre have both argued that anime might offer a visual escape from these networks. Things like the combination of two- and three-dimensional elements in anime or its division of foreground and background into separate two-dimensional layers foil the logic of linear perspective and generate a sense of physical speed or freedom—Lamarre mentions Miyazaki Hayao's flying scenes. And this may generate a feeling of political freedom as well, a sense that the characters *and spectator* are trying to escape this web of control.[4]

CB: Yes, though I would add that the fantasy element often casts that freedom in an ironic light. It is only while we inhabit these fanciful, sometimes ridiculous worlds that we can fly above these webs, and the wry self-referential quality of the fantasy makes this hard to forget. Some of that has parallels in Second Life. By default the avatars mirror the abilities and constraints of human beings, except that they can fly. Avatars teleport and fly everywhere. Linden Labs, the company that created Second Life, has woven that into a metaphor for a world in which you can go anywhere, create and do anything, and this strain of naive utopianism clings to many discussions of Second Life:

the electronic frontier spirit, the altruism of online communities, the supposed freedom and equality imposed by the anonymity of your avatar, and on and on. But there is not always enough attention to the role of the virtual in all this. In Second Life I don't necessarily see the same irony or self-awareness about that fantasy that I do in anime. On a mailing list for educators in Second Life, someone suggested changing your avatar's race on January 15th in honor of Martin Luther King Day. That kind of silliness—

KB: —well, it might hold some interest in certain contexts. But yes I agree, it is easy to detect these utopian discourses surrounding SL, and hard not to pick them apart. What the museum represents is actually an attempt to refocus the discussion back on visual effects in animation and think more carefully about how specific visual tropes might function. Returning to my earlier point, Second Life is a visual regime like the one you and Lamarre have described: a mix of 3D perspectival modeling and 2D layering that alternates constantly between realism and fantasy, or between the illusionistic and the abstract.

CB: I am definitely interested in the way anime seems to oscillate back and forth between self-conscious two-dimensionality and a cinematic regime with apparent depth. That links to the oscillation you mentioned earlier, between immersion or suspension of disbelief and self-conscious spectatorship. I think there are many possibilities in that oscillation for making the viewer think about simulation itself. But in my experience these effects can be hard for the viewer to perceive and difficult for the critic to articulate . . .

KB: Exactly. So the art in the museum functions as a kind of visual metaphor for some of these operations that can help bring them to light. One of the museum's permanent installations, called "Muybridge Revisited," takes the smooth three-dimensional animation of SL and breaks it up into its component frames, to reveal the two-dimensional component. Eadweard Muybridge was the nineteenth-century photographer whose experiments in stop-motion and sequential photography arguably gave birth to cinema. His famous sequence of a running horse represents the first time a photographer had captured pictures of figures in rapid motion, pictures Muybridge and Thomas Edison eventually learned to reassemble for cinematic projection. The art in "Muybridge Revisited" decomposes the smooth motion of SL in the same way Muybridge did, to remind us not only of the history of animation but also of the gaps in our mediated vision. So in one part of the museum, when an avatar walks across the floor it leaves a trail of life-size two-dimensional figures behind it, figures that seem to capture the successive postures in its stride, like a Muybridge sequence. The cutout figures remain for a while, drifting around the gallery like blown paper before they eventually vanish.

CB: That's evocative. But are we to see those gaps as spaces of possibility or lack?

KB: That is a good question. In the eighteenth century, Friedrich Schiller identified this as a central problem of subject formation. Schiller posed the existence of a "sensuous drive" that allowed humans to move and change by recreating themselves over and over in successive instants, while the "formal drive" connected these discrete lived existences into a coherent self through reason. Like Kant and other German Idealist philosophers, Schiller believed that art could reconcile these drives and unite the realm of concrete experience with that of abstract moral reason.[5] But today, poststructuralist philosophy has been concerned precisely with breaking down these unities of spirit and exposing the gaps in those seemingly smooth surfaces of meaning, narrative, and self.

CB: So what we are talking about is a kind of video game based on the philosophy of Immanuel Kant and poststructuralism?

KB: In a way! Though relating the visual art with the underlying critical theory is a challenge in Second Life, which is almost resolutely nontextual. The interface makes it difficult to present or communicate long pieces of text to museum visitors. It's a world of enforced semiliteracy. But we've embraced that challenge to suggest the richness of these theories largely in visual terms.

CB: How?

KB: Again, the key is capitalizing on the ability of the art to interact with the avatar and making the spectator (the user) think about that interaction. The other piece of "Muybridge Revisited" is based on a zoetrope—a nineteenth-century optical toy that allowed the animation of sequential drawings and eventually Muybridge's sequential photographs as well. It consists of a spinning drum with images along the inside wall. A conventional zoetrope is small enough to fit on a table, but ours is twenty meters across and several stories high. It doubles as the main tower of the museum, and visiting avatars can fly up inside it and see Muybridge's images of the running horse become animated. But our tower does not work quite like a real-life zoetrope. There are some unexpected effects that come from the multiple levels of simulation, from trying to animate an animation device inside SL. The levels of simulation set up interference patterns with one another, patterns that allow the spectator to think again about those gaps that exist in an animated simulation, and animation's ability or inability to portray or critique itself.

CB: What do the interference patterns look like?

KB: It is easier to grasp visually than to explain in prose (that is precisely the point!) but the rapidly spinning tower rotates at a rate approaching the screen refresh rate for the SL application on your computer, which makes the tower appear to slow down and even spin backwards, while the images of the horses become animated and start to run. It's a phenomenon called aliasing, what is referred to in early cinema as the "wagon wheel effect" . . .

CB: . . . where the spoked wheels in old westerns would appear to spin slowly or backwards because the frame rate of the camera corresponded closely to the periodic motion of the wheels.

KB: Yes. That does not happen in animated film, but it reappears in real-time computer animation like SL.

CB: Though animated film has sometimes simulated aliasing to masquerade as a more cinematic medium, just like animators simulate optical distortion, lens flare, or camera shake to appear more like live-action film. It is again part of this oscillation between the cinematic and the stylized.

KB: "Muybridge Revisited" aims to expose some of these operations.

CB: But breakdowns in the smooth animation inside SL are not rare or surprising in themselves. In fact, doesn't SL have a second-class status among real-time online gamers, who prefer worlds without museums, worlds like *World of Warcraft Online* that are optimized for combat? And numberless anime have been translated into interactive video games, on platforms where the visual effects are more sophisticated than in SL. Why not look at them?

KB: There are interesting things being written about those platforms, but we are not writing about SL; the museum itself is our critical text. Unlike *World of Warcraft,* content in SL is user-generated, and that enables us to develop content that comments on the nature of animation and simulation itself, to turn the camera (the simulating machine) back on itself. I will give you an example: right now we are mounting a show by Eron Rauch called "Leveling," which consists of screenshots taken from *World of Warcraft,* images he transformed editorially and (re)exhibited in SL.

CB: Rauch may be familiar to our regular readers as the photographer behind the cosplay spread in *Mechademia 2.*

KB: This project relates to Eron's earlier work in that it deals to some extent with role playing and identity, but it is really more focused on the idea of landscape and location. One of the galleries at the museum features a series of vertical canvasses suspended in mid-air. The canvasses are insubstantial, so the avatar can walk right up to the art and pass through it to the other side, and find him or herself standing in front of the next image in the sequence. We were hoping some artist would take advantage of the format to design something around this idea of the spectator merging with the art, and Eron came up with a series of images taken from *World of Warcraft* that showed progressively more severe glitches in the rendering engine: points where whole chunks of the world disappeared or dissolved into abstract shards of color (Figure 4). The canvasses are large and occupy your whole view, and as you walk through them, you first experience a kind of simulation within the simulation—a feeling that you have been transported into *World of Warcraft* within Second Life. Then you encounter a controlled dismantling of that simulated reality that is surprisingly evocative, even disorienting. Eron calls it a "satori moment."

CB: That format for exhibiting the art reminds me of some innovative anime and manga exhibits at conventional museums that we have featured in *Mechademia.* At Vienna's Museum of Applied and Contemporary Art (MAK), a manga exhibit displayed pages of manga enlarged to life size and placed in vertical panels hung from the ceiling, giving viewers the feeling that they were walking through the panels of the manga itself (Figure 5).[6]

KB: Yes, that exhibit was among the inspirations for the Art Mecho Museum.

CB: But Rauch's "Leveling" project exists exclusively in Second Life?

FIGURE 4. A member of the museum staff (in mech armor) inspects Eron Rauch's installation "Leveling," a consideration of digital landscape based on material from another multiplayer online game *World of Warcraft*. The canvases at right recreate rendering glitches in a way that immerses avatars in a disintegrating virtual world. At left a massive collage ironically memorializes hundreds of dead avatars Rauch encountered on his online travels. Photograph by author.

KB: No, actually it is based on a gallery exhibit of his printed photographs. Eron captured the images from *World of Warcraft* sessions, then generated the photographs for his gallery show, and later at our request converted them back to online SL images for the Art Mecho Museum.

CB: Reverse importation.

KB: Or simulacra. In one of the series that make up the "Leveling" show, called "Travels," Eron took landscapes from *World of Warcraft* and processed them to appear like nineteenth-century black-and-white landscape photography of the American West by Timothy O'Sullivan or William Henry Jackson. One guesses that those prints must have a materiality and presence in the gallery that contrasts with the digital, but unfortunately they lose that in the translation into SL; but other images that might appear cartoony or abstract in a real-life gallery suddenly become "realistic" in the Art Mecho Museum because they look so similar to the surrounding reality or context. The rendering glitches I described are an example.

CB: Let me shift gears slightly, without leaving that larger point about the possibilities those layers of simulation generate for commentary or metanarrative. The theme of this volume of *Mechademia* is War/Time. You have talked a lot about time and duration in the context of the "Muybridge Revisited" exhibit, and now we're onto war, or at least *Warcraft*. The comparison with O'Sullivan and Jackson also seems to relate the frontier of *World of Warcraft* to the conquest of the American West. Does Rauch's installation comment on the violence of some of these narratives?

FIGURE 5. A 2006 manga exhibit at Vienna's Museum of Applied and Contemporary Arts (MAK). Photograph courtesy of the exhibit's curator, Johannes Wieninger.

KB: It does. The centerpiece of the "Leveling" show is a series of screenshots of hundreds of dead avatars he encountered traversing the levels of the game. These were originally exhibited in the gallery show as panels of small photographs, but for the Art Mecho installation, Eron arranged them in a huge mosaic, ten meters high and over thirty meters long in the scale of the museum. It is visually quite beautiful, but not at all poignant. It is death abstracted.

So SL can comment on things like that. But at the same time, the idea that SL is a pacifist artistic reinvention of the first-person shooter is part of the naive utopianism you referred to earlier. That FPS legacy is never far beneath the surface. Many avatars in SL are armed to the teeth, and even the scripting language used to program the museum's interactive exhibits bears traces of being optimized for virtual warfare, with code examples and function calls that often refer to guns, impacts, and explosions. At a genetic level that informs the art.

CB: And of course SL has its own cultures of virtual violence. It is possible to hack buildings and other avatars in various ways. But while the victims take these virtual attacks pretty seriously, some of the perpetrators seem to regard them as a kind of performance, no more or less dangerous than subversive art.[7]

KB: Yes, the museum has been hacked before, sometimes by its own builders. We originally had an automatic door that was supposed to rise out of the way when an avatar approached, but a programming error caused the door to stay in place and the rest of the building to leap six feet into the air whenever someone got near the entrance. Sometimes the designers and builders introduced those kinds of things deliberately for effect. The text of the building itself has a quality of instability and literary play to it. There is also more destructive vandalism and harassment in SL, and as you hint, that also makes a fascinating study. But again my interest is in elements of control and surveillance that inhere in less obvious aspects of the interface itself. For example, the "camera" that gives the user his or her view of the world is not strictly tied to his or her avatar, so the user's viewpoint can separate itself from the avatar's body. That division has interesting implications for how the avatar looks at the art, but it is also inherently voyeuristic. You never know where people are looking. You can spy on what Jack's avatar is doing in an upstairs room while your avatar remains downstairs talking to Jane's. I think it would be interesting to leverage that power in a future installation.

CB: What other work do you now have on display?

KB: Yasmin Saaka did a custom installation for us of a series of floating canvasses the avatar walks through. These are the same kinds of canvasses Eron Rauch used for the glitchy landscapes series, but Yasmin took a completely different approach and produced an autobiographical piece. Let me back up a little: most of the two-dimensional art in typical Second Life galleries and museums hangs on the virtual walls in virtual frames just like in real life. We developed the idea for those floating canvasses before we had any art to go on them, but our thought was that viewing them would be a little like reading a manga, looking at each page, zooming in, then walking into the art and through it to "arrive" at the next page. Yasmin is an up-and-coming American manga artist: she debuted a few years ago as runner-up in TOKYOPOP's Rising Stars competition. She produced a manga sequence for us called "4me," which represents her own trajectory as an artist. It consists of a series of self-portraits, all in the shōjo idiom, but each in the style of a different artist who has influenced her: Tanemura Arina, Watase Yuu, CLAMP, and finally a fourth canvass in her own style (Figure 6).

CB: I'm looking at the photos, and the first three look virtually identical to me. And they all look like Japanese schoolgirls.

KB: There are subtle differences in the styles, but Yasmin is also playing with the homogeneity of shōjo manga. It's a piece about the changing versus the

FIGURE 6. Museum patron Frenchy Prudhomme looks at images from Yasmin Saaka's "4me" series. Photograph by author.

essential elements of manga style, and how you find your own voice within that, especially as an American manga artist. Saaka says some readers seem to want her work to be more Japanese, others more American, and some more African American. She also talks about trying to develop conventions for portraying African American features in an idiom that seems to lack any good precedents for it.

CB: So as your avatar walks through the canvasses and merges with Saaka's successive avatars in the drawings, you are supposed to think about the status of duplication and originality vis-à-vis your own digital identity.

KB: Potentially, yes. The piece connects questions about the status of race and gender in virtual communities back to ideas about style and genre that are also relevant to the discussion.

CB: How do you plan to incorporate this interaction between art and avatar in future exhibitions?

KB: We are working on plans for a show called "Shadow Box" that would feature wall-size manga pages with a limited 3D quality, so that avatars could climb up into the panels and pose with the drawn characters. The idea is that you could change the narrative by acting in the story.

CB: And how can readers see more of these exhibits or find out more about the museum?

KB: Our Web site, http://artmecho.org, has additional information. Those who would like to visit us in Second Life can get a free account and follow the directions to the museum that are on the Web site.

....

Notes

1. Mitch Brooks produced the initial blueprints and elevations for the museum based on my design. The building was constructed in *Second Life* by a team of colorful avatars manipulated by instructional technology interns at Williams College: Jonathan Berch, Isaac Bernstein, Alda Chan, Teia Fanciullo, Marcus Freeman, Allegra Hyde, Benjamin Kolesar, Kefei Lei, Moaj Musthag, Theresa Ong, Peter Schmidt, and James Sweeney. The project received help and support from the Faculty Center for Media Technologies at Williams and Williams Instructional Technology staff, including Gayle Barton, Mika Hirai, Trevor Murphy, Adam Wang, and particularly Jonathan Leamon, our virtual foreman on the build. I also owe a considerable debt to Bryan Campen, Jen Caruso, Aaron Collins, John Craig Freeman, and Christian Hudak, who advised me at various points in the project.

2. Susan J. Napier, *Anime from "Akira" to "Princess Mononoke"* (New York: Palgrave, 1997), 242.

3. Paul Willemen "The Fourth Look," *Looks and Frictions: Essays in Cultural Studies and Film Theory* (Bloomington and London: Indiana University Press and The British Film Institute, 1994), 99–110.

4. Thomas Lamarre, "The Multiplanar Image," *Mechademia* 1 (2006): 120–43; Christopher Bolton, "Visual and Political Dynamics in *Blood: The Last Vampire*," *Mechademia* 2 (2007): 125–42.

5. Friedrich Schiller, *On the Aesthetic Education of Man in a Series of Letters,* ed. and trans. Elizabeth M. Wilkinson and L. A. Willoughby (Oxford: Clarendon, 1982).

6. Christopher Bolton, "UAAAAAA! Trashkultur! An Interview with MAK's Wieninger," *Mechademia* 2 (2007): 298–300.

7. For an introduction to these cultures, see Julian Dibbell, "Mutilated Furries, Flying Phalluses: Put the Blame on Griefers, the Sociopaths of the Virtual World," *Wired* 16, no. 2 (February 2008): 90–97.

Genre Violence

TAKAYUKI TATSUMI

Translated by Seth Jacobowitz

● ● ●

Ninja, Hidden Christians, and the Two Ferreiras: On Endō Shūsaku and Yamada Fūtarō

Thomas Pynchon's alternately fun and melancholic West Coast romance *Vineland* (1990), the fourth novel by the master of American postmodern literature, probes the essence of eighties culture from the perspective of sixties radicals. Yet we should not overlook the host of Japanese signifiers playing beneath the surface of the simple narrative. In addition to the ninja master Inoshiro-sensei and his student DL Chastain, who belongs to the Caucasian female ninja corps called "Kunoichi Attentives," over-the-top ninja signifiers are deployed one after another—from the *Fist of the North Star*–like "Vibrating Palm" that dooms its victims to eventual death one year later, to the high-tech Oriental regenerative machine called the Puncutron that can save them.[1]

THE DESIRE FOR A BLACK COSTUME

The average American reader of *Vineland* will see the influence of stereotypically "Japanesque" ninja novels and Hollywood films that rose to sudden popularity in the wake of eighties-era go-go capitalism and Pax Japonica. Shimura Masao points out that Eric Van Lustbader's 1980 novel *The Ninja* was followed by the hit films *Enter the Ninja* (1981), *Revenge of the Ninja* (1983), and *Ninja III: The Domination* (1984), starring the Japanese actor Shō Kosugi. Also riding the ninja boom were the Caucasian ninja series *American Ninja* (1985), starring Michael Dudikoff, and then, starting in the late eighties, the various *Teenage Mutant Ninja Turtles* films and TV series, about turtles from New York raised by an Oriental rat who is accomplished in the ninja arts.[2]

Each of these works was popular in its own way, so it is by no means a co-incidence that cyberpunk texts like William Gibson's *Neuromancer* (1984) and Bruce Sterling's *Schismatrix* (1985), which triggered the boom in cyberpunk science fiction, were so keenly aware of ninja culture and so easily integrated it into the hacker's culture of jacking into cyberspace to steal information and sell it off bit by bit. While Pynchon's taste for the Japanesque dates back to the kamikaze combo in *Gravity's Rainbow* (1973), what is new and important here is that cyberpunk writers, whose development was tremendously impacted by Pynchon, mixed in the figure of the ninja when they created the postmodern Luddite saboteur called the "hacker" in the eighties; then at the start of the nineties, Pynchon himself took this and made it the basis of an impressively comical series of reciprocal literary-historical negotiations in *Vineland*, with its cadre of Caucasian *kunoichi* female ninja.[3]

Consider American films like *Ninja III: The Domination* (1984)—which establishes the potential of the white female ninja in the way it depicts a Caucasian woman possessed by the spirit of a ninja—and 1987's *American Ninja 2: The Confrontation*, which advances the preposterous idea that a ninja's genes could be reused to mass-produce killer replicants. These works insisted that not only is the ninja no longer confined to an extinct Japanese culture of the past but that, through a process of self-mastery, non-Japanese may also be initiated into what are now transhistorical and multinational traditional arts. Without a doubt, Pynchon's *Vineland* is a further extension of this way of thinking. In American postmodern culture the ninja was chosen and cultivated as the figure that could most strikingly represent humans' dual nature as both cyborg (man-machine interface) and creole (multicultural intermixing).

However, the average reader in Japan might respond very differently to the same ninja-based context of *Vineland*. Instead of running on about Pynchon's Japanesque interests, he or she would more likely point out that the book was "like something out of Yamada Fūtarō," whose *Ninpōchō* (Ninja Scrolls) series first appeared in 1958 and became a bestseller in 1963.[4] As Kasai Kiyoshi and others have indicated, Fūtarō's novels have influenced later Japanese ninja manga like Shirato Sampei's *Ninja bugeichō* (1959–62, Ninja martial arts scroll), Yokoyama Mitsuteru's *Iga no Kagemaru* (1961–66, Kagemaru of Iga), and Hisamatsu Fumio's *Kaze no Fujimaru* (1964–65, Fujimaru of the wind). Through their influence on Ishinomori Shōtarō's manga *Cyborg 009* (which started in 1964), Fūtarō's novels have also shaped the special-effects-driven television superhero shows in Japan now known as "*sentai series.*" This is clear from looking at the

> IN AMERICAN POSTMODERN CULTURE THE NINJA WAS CHOSEN AND CULTIVATED AS THE FIGURE THAT COULD MOST STRIKINGLY REPRESENT HUMANS' DUAL NATURE AS BOTH CYBORG (MAN-MACHINE INTERFACE) AND CREOLE (MULTICULTURAL INTERMIXING).

television genealogy that extends from *Ninja butai gekkō* (1964–66, *Phantom Agents*) to *Ninja sentai kakurenjaa* (1994–95, Ninja squadron hidden ranger), and the American show that incorporated the latter, *Power Rangers* (1993).[5] The history of Japanese television films, which began in 1953, has given rise to innumerable superheroes based on the ninja template.

With this context in mind, a Japanese reader of *Vineland* might look at the importation into English of Fūtarō's trademark term "*kunoichi*" and other elements—the blending of sexual relations with ninja killing techniques, the creation of a fantastic machine for bringing people back to life, or tricks for brainwashing minorities that make free use of feminist theology—and wrongly assume that Pynchon (resurrected by cyberpunk), had set out to write a sequel to Yamada Fūtarō's *Kunoichi ninpōchō* (1961, Kunoichi ninja scrolls).[6] Of course Pynchon was unable to read Japanese. Rather, what is fascinating is that the ninja culture that proliferated through a web of cultural misreadings in Hollywood films and American paperbacks went round and round and incredibly—without anyone being aware of it—converged again with the Yamada Fūtarō narrative elements that constituted the origin and orthodoxy of the genre in Japan. If African-American author Toni Morrison once made her heroine a black girl who yearned for blue eyes, now protagonists are increasingly Japanophilic Caucasian-outlaw-technologists longing to dress in black ninja garb. In this way, those who draw near to the cyborg dimension also approach creolization at the exact same time.

THE NINJA'S SORCERY, THE HIDDEN CHRISTIAN'S TECHNOLOGY

To reexamine these issues, it is worth considering a text that has been called one of Yamada Fūtarō's biggest flops, but also numbers among his most beloved works: *Gedō ninpōchō* (1962, Heretical doctrine of the ninja scrolls).[7]

The extraordinarily far-fetched plot revolves around a vast treasure hoard brought back from Rome by the late sixteenth-century Japanese youth and Catholic emissary Julian Nakaura. The treasure was scattered and its location concealed, incredibly, in the very vaginas of fifteen virgins with ninja powers. Ninja from the Iga and Koga clans join forces to seek it out. Referring to *Kunoichi ninpōchō,* upon which this work is based, we see a similar group of heroines on a holy quest: the female ninja in that story carries the unborn child of the warlord Hideyori and keeps it from the evil clutches of the Tokugawa government. Among the most Fūtarō-esque ninja techniques is the *"kunoichi yadokari"* (literally "borrowed house") described in that novel: when a pregnant female ninja finds herself in physical danger she can transfer her fetus to the body of another woman. Moreover, the woman who carries the baby as the "borrowed womb" in the story ironically turns out to be none other than Kasuga no Tsubone (Ofuku), who should be the enemy of the pregnant ninja. As the child moves from one womb to another, the irresistible story has the renowned Kasuga no Tsubone, an exceptionally loyal follower of the Tokugawa family, carrying Toyotomi Hideyori's illegitimate child by the female ninja Omayu. While hardly as miraculous as the Virgin Mary's immaculate conception or the technology of the surrogate mothers depicted in Margaret Atwood's *The Handmaid's Tale* (1985), this represents a shocking form of "birth control" (ninpō).

> GEDŌ NINPŌCHŌ DESERVES PRAISE AS AN EXPERIMENT THAT SEEKS TO BRING TOGETHER THE SORCERY OF THE NINJA WITH THE CONCEALED ESOTERICISM OF JAPAN'S HIDDEN CHRISTIANS.

This sensibility might be easier to understand today translated into our own electronic culture, as the theft of the Holy Grail of top-secret information by cyberspace cowboys, who shift and graft the information from one file to another. Conversely, we may also say that the post-cyberpunk spate of Hollywood films that feature zombie-like transmigration and genetically engineered mass production of ninja have always already been set in the mold of Yamada Fūtarō's ninja stories.

In terms of the period background that enabled Fūtarō to convert the legend of the Holy Grail into a gold rush narrative, we should, of course, bear in mind his own historical context: the postwar ruins of the 1950s, with black marketeers and scrap-metal thieves hustling to survive. But Fūtarō continued to probe these themes in a work from the 1960s, *Ginga ninpōchō* (1968, Milky Way ninja scrolls), which foregrounds the structural tensions and internal contradictions between high-tech and low-tech, between a "big science" supported by the "white arts" versus the "black arts" of outlaw technology.[8] While it appears in that story that the ancient black arts represented by ninja techniques are overtaken by the new white arts of Western science, nevertheless the Tokugawa technocrat Ōkubo Nagayasu ironically suffers defeat at the hands of the villain Rokumonsen no Tetsu. And there is the added irony that even Nagayasu's white arts retain a faint connection to the machinery of the Inquisition and other modes of thought originally tied to the black arts.

Precisely because of its connections to Fūtarō's later work, and in spite of its obvious narratological shortcomings, *Gedō ninpōchō* deserves praise as an experiment that seeks to bring together the sorcery of the ninja with the concealed esotericism of Japan's hidden Christians, who practiced their religion in secret after it was outlawed by the shogunal government in the seventeenth century. Like the ninjas, hidden Christians were a closeted group who concealed themselves stealthily in the darkness, and their isolation from Western missionaries as well as the need to disguise their religion eventually transformed their Christian practices into something like esoteric hybrid ceremonies. The Kunoichi art of womb transfer suggests that ninja techniques are black arts that seek out and protect a signifier that might be compared to gold or currency, then transfer it from one vessel to another, preserving it even as they alter its form (in this respect these arts constitute a self-referential figure for the cultural history of the ninja themselves). In this case it seems inevitable that the hidden Christians should manifest themselves as the ninja's virtual twins, transforming, disguising, and preserving their Christianity in the same way. So the ninja's transformation into a multicultural symbol actually begins much earlier than the late twentieth century: since the sixteenth- and seventeenth-century persecution of Christians in Japan, the ninja has been the mediator who secretly grafts one culture onto another, the closest analog to the hidden early Christians in the way it embodies the cyborg/creole hybrid subject.

FŪTARŌ'S FERREIRA AND ENDŌ'S FERREIRA

Let us explore the way *Gedō ninpōchō* incorporates the story of the seventeenth-century apostate priest Padre Cristóvão Ferreira. According to historical record, Ferreira was born in Portugal in 1580, entered the Jesuit order at age sixteen, and set off for the East at twenty-one. He was ordained a priest in Macao and gave his first mass there. In 1609, at the age of twenty-nine, he headed to Japan to spread the faith. But in 1614 the Tokugawa government announced severe edicts against the Christian faith, and among the hardships visited on the Christians, many priests were expelled from the country. It was a time of difficult circumstances when only those like Ferreira, who were resolved to face martyrdom, remained secretly in Japan.

Almost twenty years later, in 1633, Ferreira was captured by Inoue, the magistrate of Chikugo. Although no one predicted Ferreira would ever turn apostate, the priest did the unthinkable and tragically renounced his faith after being tied up and suspended upside down in an offal pit for five hours. His renunciation may trace to the fact that he survived and suffered long past the point where most died, and this experience had the psychological effect of stripping from him altogether the unique heroism of a martyr. Thereafter Ferreira received the name and former wife of an executed prisoner, and henceforth was known as Sawano Chūan. He became the magistrate's right-hand man in the pursuit of missionaries, earning his infamy as the author of the anti-Christian tract *Kengiroku* (1636, The deceit disclosed), and the inventor of the *fumie,* a small image of Christ that suspected Christians were forced to step on to prove they were not believers.

Of course, given the circumstances of Ferreira's death from illness in 1650, there is convincing evidence that he was remartyred, and the most persuasive reading, especially in Japan, has been that for the rest of his life Ferreira cursed himself for his apostasy rather than sincerely embracing Buddhism. Particularly in the context of post–World War II discussions about the wartime collaboration or "conversion" of prewar progressives (*tenkōron*), there has been a tendency to see a Christianity that justified the weak and the betrayer—the Christianity of the compassionate mother Mary rather than of a strict father—as somehow appropriate for Japan. For example, this is the central theme of Endō Shūsaku's novel *Silence* (*Chinmoku*), which won the Tanizaki Jun'ichiro Award in 1966. The novel depicts not only Ferreira but also his disciple, Padre Sebastian Rodriguez, who journeys to Japan hunting for Ferreira and becomes the hunted: he tries to convince Ferreira of the error of his ways only to end up treading on the *fumie* himself. In Endō's novel, Ferreira's apostasy is actually premised on a deeper Christian faith, which cannot escape the paradoxical conclusion that Christ, too, would likely have trampled on the *fumie*. It is Endō's interpretation that Ferreira renounces the faith to stave off the unbearable suffering and death of countless Christian believers. It is this philosophy that Endō's Ferreira imparts to Rodriguez:

> "I did not apostatize because I was suspended in the pit. . . . The reason I apostatized . . . are you ready? Listen! I was put in here and heard the voices

of those people for whom God did nothing. God did not do a single thing. . . . A priest ought to live in imitation of Christ. . . . Certainly Christ would have apostatized for them. . . . You are now going to perform the most painful act of love that has ever been performed," said Ferreira, taking the priest gently by the shoulder.[9]

Yamada Fūtarō was virtually the same age as Endō (the former was born in 1922, the latter in 1923), and he published *Gedō ninpōchō* in 1962, just four years before *Silence*. In Fūtarō's work, Ferreira regards those who relinquish their faith as lower than animals and plots a way to make them apostatize. Here he explains himself to Monica Okyō, one of the fifteen virgins hiding the secret treasure:

> You want to know why I renounced the faith? . . . How can I put it in words? Was it the sickness of emotional perversity (*kanjō tōsakushō*)? . . . Well, in the end I convinced myself that the thing I feared the most is what would make me happiest: I began to love and delight in evil, ugliness, and suffering, and to despise honor, peace, wealth, and epicurean delights. I didn't surrender to the pain of torture; I was converted by the pleasure of torture. . . . I know only too well what a sinner I am. I am worse than you think, believe me, a thousand times worse. That's why every day I am happy, so happy I can scarcely bear it![10]

On one hand, Endō's Ferreira sees no contradiction between the despair of the colonizer and the morality of the apostate, and thus makes his disciple Rodriguez into a copy of himself. On the other hand, Fūtarō's Ferreira retrieves the secret treasure from Monica Okyō's body using a magical sexual technique to control a finger that is virtually an artificial cyborg organ. But what is most notable is the fact that Fūtarō had his own Rodriguez: in the 1950 short story that formed the model for *Gedō ninpōchō,* "Yama yashiki hizu" (Secret map to the mountain mansion), the Sicilian priest Giuseppe Chiara (Endō's model for Rodriguez) is already connected with Ferreira.[11] *Gedō ninpōchō* carries this association even further, boldly merging Ferreira's and Chiara's apostate personalities into one. It is unclear whether Endō himself read "Yama yashiki hizu," but regardless, what is striking about this juxtaposition is the way the cyborg-like figure of Ferreira in Fūtarō's early popular novel and the creolized figure of Ferreira in Endō's belles-lettres (*jun bungaku*) novel both parody and complement one another.

Both of these authors used the apostate priest as a central figure of their narratives. Moreover, not only did they endorse the Japanese sixties discourse of conversion (*tenkōron*), but, within different literary frames of reference, each expressed the perverse logic of a period when differing cultures were grafted together. Within the postwar discourse of conversion theory, Fujii Shōzō associates conversion less with submissiveness to power than with things premised on freedom, like "breakthrough," "disillusionment," "frustration," and "change of heart" (*kaishin*).[12] Yet what the representations of Ferreira in Japanese literature signify is a conversion technology that transcends the narrowly framed political disputes of the postwar period (disputes surrounding the U.S.–Japan Joint Security Treaty and Japan's international responsibilities)

> WHAT THE REPRESENTATIONS OF FERREIRA IN JAPANESE LITERATURE SIGNIFY IS A CONVERSION TECHNOLOGY THAT TRANSCENDS THE NARROWLY FRAMED POLITICAL DISPUTES OF THE POSTWAR PERIOD AND INSTEAD TREATS CONVERSION IN A BROADER POSTCOLONIAL CONTEXT.

and instead treats conversion in a broader postcolonial context. What Endō Shūsaku realized was the paradox that the Jesuit missionaries did not Christianize the Japanese; rather, the Christian faith taught by the missionaries was Japanized to conform with the Japanese mother complex or perhaps the structure of dependency called *amae no kōzō*. At the same time Yamada Fūtarō came up with the corresponding notion that Ferreira is reconverted by the Christian female ninja Monica Okyō, who uses her ninja powers to brand on his retinas the image of a cross written in blood.

This point brings us back to the conversionary context of Pynchon's *Vineland*, in which the Japanese man Takeshi Fumimota is brought back to life by the Puncutron resurrection machine, then brainwashed by something like feminist theology. Of course, the Puncutron is conceived as a kind of Oriental medical technology, a Westernized version of an acupuncture technique based on yin-yang and the five elements. Piling up one form of pseudoscience on another like this may seem to be overkill. Yokoyama Kuninori points out that yin-yang philosophy did not necessarily precede and produce the superior results of Chinese acupuncture; it would be more accurate to say conversely that it was only because this supremely effective *practical* technology existed that an intellectual pretext was invented to explain it.[13] Today Western medicine has been grafted onto these Eastern medical practices, by combining the needles with electric stimulation to produce electro-acupuncture and laser acupuncture devices. These kinds of high-tech results force us to consider the possibility that already in the age of the hidden Christians and ninja, it was not so much that these techniques were produced from a philosophy (*shisō*) but that the products of technology led to a philosophical conversion.

JAPAN'S HEART OF DARKNESS

As suggested by narratives of colonialism from Joseph Conrad's *Heart of Darkness* (1899) to Francis Ford Coppola's film adaptation *Apocalypse Now* (1979) and the 1995 movie *Congo* (based on Michael Crichton's 1980 novel), Christian missionaries traveled from the darkness of the West to the darkness of Japan, and were lured deeper and deeper into the heart of that blackness.

All this casts new light on the almost eerie coincidences between Fūtarō's popular novel *Gedō ninpōchō* and Endō's literary one, *Silence,* and the way these two books that were originally from very different literary contexts bear mutual testimony to the schema of the hunter becoming the hunted (*miira tori ga miira to kasu*). These coincidences must be examined from a postcolonial position that goes beyond ideas of faith or conversion, to arrive at a horizon where cyborg and creole are no longer contradictions. What lies in store for us is a point where the strange figure of Marlon Brando's Kurtz, the colonizer who becomes a god to the jungle natives in *Apocalypse Now,* melds not just with the images of science fiction, like H. G. Wells's genetic engineer Dr. Moreau, but with the apostate priest Cristóvão Ferreira, or even the French missionary Bernard Petitjean, who encountered the hidden Christians after Japan was reopened in the nineteenth century: their completely distorted religious customs shocked him, but also allowed him to reconfirm his own beliefs.[14]

This is a colonizing journey not only in space—from West to East, from the Christian world to the Buddhist one—but a trip we take from our own late-capitalist present into the history of Japan's seventeenth century. Slipstream literature, with its affinity for alternate history novels, may be part of this great exploration, a virtual Orientalist experience open to everyone. If so, then Yamada Fūtarō's ninja stories are an unmatched expression of that literature, shot through with the fantasy that if you but set out, you may never return from the heart of darkness, and yet also the illusion that there is nothing greater than these forbidden pleasures.

···

Notes

1. Thomas Pynchon, *Vineland* (Boston: Little, Brown, 1990). Pynchon's novel was translated by Satō Yoshiaki, and published by Shinchōsha in 1998.

2. Shimura Masao provided some insight into the negotiations between ninja fiction and ninja movies as a panelist on an "Exploring *Vineland*" panel at the Sixty-third Conference of the English Literary Society of Japan, held in May 1991 at Meiji University. The novel's translator, Satō Yoshiaki, also appeared on the panel. Incidentally, I believe the resonance between *Vineland*'s Don Quixote–style anachronism and Yahagi Toshihiko's *Suzuki-san no kyūsoku to henreki*, originally published the same year as Pynchon's novel, is more than mere happenstance. Yahagi Toshihiko, *Suzuki-san no kyūsoku to henreki: Mata wa kakumo hokoraka-naru dōshiibō no kikō* (Suzuki's rest and pilgrimage) (Tokyo: Shinchō Bunko, 1994).

3. The Japanese word *kunoichi* (くノ一) is a graphic word play on the Chinese character for woman (女), which appears to be made up of two conjoined *kana* syllables—*hiragana ku* (く)and *katakana no* (ノ)—bisected by the Chinese character for one, *ichi* (一). For general information on ninja, see "Ketteiban: Ninja no subete" (The authoritative edition: All about the ninja), special issue of *Rekishi dokuhon* (December 1991). In English, see Tomiki Kenji, "Ninjutsu," *Kōdansha Encyclopedia of Japan* (Tokyo: Kōdansha, 1983), 6–7.

4. For information on Yamada Fūtarō, see these special magazine and journal issues devoted to the author: *Tōkyōjin* (December 1996), *Bessatsu shinhyō* 12, no. 2 (Summer 1979), and *GQ* (March 1995). For a science-fictional reading of Fūtarō, see Sui Kyoshi, *Midare sappō SF hikae* (Osaka: Seishinsha, 1991). In English, see the first novel in the *Ninja Scrolls* series, *Kōga ninpōchō,* which was translated by Geoff Sant as *The Koga Ninja Scrolls* (New York: Del Rey, 2006) and was the basis for the 2005 film *Shinobi: Heart under Blade,* dir. Shimoyama Ten, subtitled DVD (Funimation, 2007).

5. Kasai Kiyoshi, *Kaisetsu* (Afterword) to *Kenki Ramabutsu* (The great Lamaist swordman), by Yamada Fūtarō (Tokyo: Kōdansha, 1994), 362–67. Saitō Minako points out that the lone woman in these later series is a "'a solitary flower' among the team members," making her a descendant of Yamada Fūtarō's female ninja. Saitō Minako, "Kurenai no senshi: Hiirō dorama no hiaintachi" (Scarlet warriors: The heroines of heroic dramas) in *Haipaa voisu,* ed. Arimitsu Mamiko et al. (Tokyo: Just System, 1966), 94–117.

6. Yamada Fūtarō, *Kunoichi ninpōchō* (Kunoichi ninja scrolls) (Tokyo: Kōdansha, 1960).

7. Yamada Fūtarō, *Gedō ninpōchō* (Heretical doctrine of the ninja scrolls) (Tokyo: Kōdansha, 1962).

8. Yamada Fūtarō, *Ginga ninpōchō* (Milky Way ninja scrolls) (Tokyo: Kōdansha, 1968). The original title was *Amanogawa o kiru* (Slashing the Milky Way).

9. Endō Shūsaku, *Chinmoku* (Tokyo: Shinchōsha, 1966); translated by William Johnston as *Silence* (Tokyo: Sophia University and Tuttle, 1969), 265–69. See also Endō's novel *Kirishitan no sato* (Christian village) (Tokyo: Chūōkōronsha), 1964. It is worth noting in spite of the criticism Arai Sasagu leveled at Endō's view of Jesus on historiographic grounds, later authors have conclusively sided with Endō's vision regarding the strong emphasis on maternal love in Christian doctrine, especially since Endō's *Iesu Kirisuto* (Jesus Christ) (Tokyo: Kōdansha, 1979). Arai Sasagu, *Iesu to sono jidai* (Jesus and his times) (Tokyo: Iwanami Shoten, 1974); Endō Shūsaku et al., *Endō Shūsaku to Shusaku Endo: Amerika "chinmoku to koe" Endō Shūsaku bungaku kenkyū gakkai hōkoku* (Endō Shūsaku and Shusaku Endo: A report from the American Endō research group "Voices of silence") (Tokyo: Shunjūsha, 1994).

10. Yamada, *Gedō ninpōchō,* chapter 1, section 3.

11. Yamada Fūtarō, "Yama yashiki hizu" (Secret map to the mountain mansion), in

Baishoku shito gyōden (Journey of the prostitute apostles), vol. 5 of *Yamada Fūtarō sōsaku taizen* (Works of Yamada Fūtarō) (Tokyo: Kōsaidō Bunko, 1996); originally published in *Omoshiro kurabu* (November 1950). In the short story, the character's name is Joseph Chiara.

12. Fujii Shōzō, *Tenkō no shisōshiteki kenkyū* (The intellectual history of *tenkō*), vol. 2 of *Fujii Shōzō chosaku shū* (Works of Fujii Shōzō) (Tokyo: Misuzu Shobō, 1997).

13. Yokoyama Kuninori, introduction to *Tōyō igaku o manabu hito no tame ni* (An introduction to Eastern medicine), ed. Yamashita Kumio et al. (Tokyo: Igaku Shoin, 1984).

14. See Yamada Fūtarō's 1956 short story "Himegimi doko ni orasu ka" (Where is the princess?) in *Baishoku shito gyōden*.

ZÍLIA PAPP

• • •

Monsters at War: The Great Yōkai Wars, 1968–2005

Miike Takashi, the Japanese director of infamous films such as *Koroshiya Ichi* (2001, *Ichi the Killer*) and *Zeburaaman* (2004, *Zebraman*), surprised audiences by directing the 2005 remake of the 1968 horror/fantasy film, *Yōkai daisensō* (*The Great Yōkai War*).[1] With its cast of cute folkloric monsters (generically referred to in Japanese as *yōkai*), this was the first child-friendly movie produced by Miike, whose work is better known for excessive Tarantino-like violence, gangster stories, and blood spilled on screen. But, despite their association with simple and straightforward horror tales and family entertainment, both the 1968 classic and Miike's 2005 remake use yōkai to communicate strong, if also strongly differing, political messages. This essay compares the two films and also traces the evolution of the *Yōkai daisensō* story through several manga, anime, and live-action versions produced over the past forty years.

The emergence of yōkai-themed films in Japan dates from the 1960s and coincides with the television broadcast of Mizuki Shigeru's 1968–69 *Gegege no Kitarō* animation series, based in turn on Mizuki's hugely popular manga. The series traced the adventures of the yōkai boy Kitarō and his monster companions, particularly their battles with various other malevolent yōkai entities. Following the success of the television series, the film production company

Daiei pioneered the Japanese yōkai film genre in the late sixties, producing *Yōkai hyaku monogatari* (1968, One hundred monster stories), *Tōkaidō obake dōchū* (1969, Journey with monsters along the eastern sea road), and *Yōkai daisensō* (1968).

There has been a revival of these films in the twenty-first century, not only Miike's remake of *Yōkai daisensō* but also the film version of *Gegege no Kitarō* (2007) and its sequel in 2008, and film adaptations of other yōkai manga classics: *Dororo* (2007), based on Tezuka Osamu's 1967–68 manga, and *Nekome kozō* (2006, Cat-eye boy), based on the 1967–68 manga by Umezu Kazuo. The latter two films equate yōkai with sublime, subconscious emotions in a way that suits postmodern sensibilities, but the sequential art these films were based on did not manage to capture the art history of yōkai in a convincing way, so it has been Mizuki Shigeru's work that has carried the legacy of centuries of yōkai art into twentieth- and twenty-first century popular culture.

The *Yōkai daisensō* story spans the entire evolution of yōkai in popular media as described above: it began as an episode in Mizuki's *Gegege no Kitarō* manga, published in *Weekly Shōnen Magazine* in April 1966.[2] It was later adapted for two episodes of the *Gegege no Kitarō* television anime in 1968. A live-action film version followed in the same year, produced by Daiei and directed by Kuroda Yoshiyuki. And then there is Miike's 2005 live-action remake, produced by Kadokawa Film.

What follows examines the evolution of narrative patterns and character design in these four versions of *Yōkai daisensō*—the manga, the TV animation, and the two live-action films—to point out how the seemingly apolitical yōkai are positioned in twentieth- and twenty-first-century visual media to communicate different political messages.

THE *YŌKAI DAISENSŌ* MANGA (1966)

Whether in the manga, animation, or live-action film versions, the *Yōkai daisensō* narratives center on a war fought between two groups of yōkai, a set of aggressors and defenders. The visual depiction of yōkai and yōkai wars goes back hundreds of years; for example, the Muromachi-period (1392–1573) *Tsukumogami emaki* (Utensil wars picture scroll) and Utagawa Yoshiiku's 1895 print *Kokkei Yamatoshiki* (Comical records of Japanese history) both depict wars between humans and yōkai. In the latter, each yōkai is designed to represent and ridicule soldiers from the Chinese army conquered in the Sino-Japanese War (1894–95), Meiji Japan's first important military victory.[3] By the time of the Pacific war, yōkai (mainly oni or demons) were routinely used in wartime cartoons to represent the Allied forces.[4] But the *Yōkai daisensō* narrative is the first work where two groups of yōkai fight each other in combat: in the 1960s manga, animation, and film, two sets of yōkai—one distinctly Japanese and one distinctly "Western"—reenact the traumas of the Second World War and the Cold War.

> IN THE 1960s MANGA, ANIMATION, AND FILM, TWO SETS OF YŌKAI—ONE DISTINCTLY JAPANESE AND ONE DISTINCTLY "WESTERN"—REENACT THE TRAUMAS OF THE SECOND WORLD WAR AND THE COLD WAR.

The *Yōkai daisensō* story in Mizuki's original manga is based on the Japanese folktale of Momotarō, a young boy who leads a band of animal allies to rescue the island of Kikaigashima from the demons that infest it. The Momotarō story was repeatedly adapted for propaganda animation during WWII, in a process John Dower identifies as the "Momotaro paradigm," where simplified quasi-folkloristic characters are equated with aspects of a perceived patriotism in an effort to justify acts of aggression.[5] In Mizuki's updated manga narrative, an exotically dressed boy, wearing a Vietnamese leaf hat (*nón lá*) asks for the help of Japanese yōkai to liberate his remote Okinawan island from "Western" invading monsters. Despite the warning "Western monsters are cruel," Kitarō gathers "pure-blooded" Japanese yōkai to go into war against the Westerners in Okinawa, to answer this Vietnamese child's call for liberation from Western aggression.[6] The aggressors include a series of stereotypically Western monsters: a generic witch and werewolf as well as a Dracula figure derived from Béla Lugosi's character in the 1931 film *Dracula* and a monster based on Boris Karloff's monster from the 1931 film *Frankenstein*.

Analogies to the Pacific War (1942–45), the Battle of Okinawa (1945), and the Vietnam War (1959–75) are articulated early within the manga narrative, while visual references to the Korean War (1950–53) and the hydrogen bomb experiments on Bikini Atoll (1954) appear later in the episode. When the villagers hide in a cave waiting for death, the visual rendering of the cave is a close copy of the *kamekōbaka* (turtle-back tombs), ancient Okinawan tombs built on cave openings that Japanese defensive forces and local Okinawans used for cave warfare during the Battle of Okinawa. Caves were also put to similar use during the Vietnam War, which is explicitly mentioned within the narrative.[7] The Western monsters, trying to trick Kitarō into creating a demilitarized zone that alludes to the outcome of the Korean War, claim: "Hey Kitarō, we don't want to fight a meaningless war, like Vietnam."[8] The war ends when the Western monsters are blown up in a fireball in the middle of the ocean, a scene that evokes images of the Bikini atomic tests carried out by the United States military.[9]

One of the central nationalist tropes of the narrative is Kitarō's magical vest, Chanchanko, which is taken hostage by the Western forces. According to the manga, Chanchanko is woven from the hair of the deceased ancestors of the Hakaba no Kitarō lineage, as articulated by Kitarō's father:

> Our kind, when we die, we leave one thread of spirit hair that keeps on living. Your vest is woven from those hairs. Your superpowers . . . are all thanks to the power of the spirit hair of your ancestors . . . If we cannot get back your vest, it will be a great insult to your ancestors.[10]

This aspect of the vest is reinforced on several occasions within the narrative. Without his vest, Kitarō is naked, injured, and powerless. He soon succumbs to sickness in the middle of the jungle, after losing his trademark long hair in one final, desperate fight. This echoes images of the manga-Mizuki character in Mizuki's autobiographical manga, who falls ill with malaria while stationed in Rabaul during World War II, and loses his hair.[11] However, in the midst of this desperate situation, the vest comes to the rescue of the Japanese troops:

> The vest started to emit a tremendous power to aid its descendants. At the moment when the final member of the Japanese ghost lineage was about to die, the Chanchanko turned a stark shade of red, the color of the anger it felt against the Western monsters![12]

In the closing credits, where insects sing the final theme songs, Kitarō again proclaims: "This time, sing the Gegege song for the Chanchanko, made of the spirit hair of my ancestors. I have never felt more grateful to them."[13]

Finally, the story comes full circle when the Vietnamese boy expresses his gratitude to his Japanese liberators.[14] In the figure of the helpless Southeast Asian subjects awaiting rescue by pure-hearted Japanese heroes, the Momotarō paradigm that appears in the wartime Momotarō animation trilogy is now transplanted to a postwar popular visual narrative.[15]

YŌKAI DAISENSŌ ON TELEVISION AND ON FILM (1968)

The animated version of Yōkai daisensō aired on Fuji Television as part of the Gegege no Kitarō series on March 6 and 13, 1968 (two years after the manga version), and toned down the manga original somewhat. The notions that Western monsters smell different and are cruel, aggressive, and dangerous were re-stated several times in the animation, and the discourse of pure-bloodedness remained. But references to the Vietnam War were cautiously cleared away, and the little boy asking for Kitarō's help was pictured as strictly Okinawan.

The cave fight scenes in the animated version no longer resemble his-torical images from the Battle of Okinawa as readily as in the manga version, but at one point the Western monsters pull out a map and plot their landing on Kyūshū, the southern main island of Japan. They thus reenact Operation Downfall, the Allied plan for the invasion of the Japanese mainland in 1945, with added references to a kind of "biological warfare" that will use a local monster to spread disease (Figure 1). The central message of the story is also unaltered. Chanchanko, the vest woven from the hair of Kitarō's ancestors, is still the symbol of ancestral lineage, and without the help of the ancestors the Japanese fight cannot be won.

The live-action film of *Yōkai daisensō*, directed by Kuroda Yoshiyuki, also appeared in 1968, though it did not feature the *Gegege no Kitarō* character. It was the second in a trilogy of yōkai films produced by Daiei Motion Pic-tures between 1968 and 1969. The two other films, *Yōkai hyaku monogatari*

FIGURE 1. A reenactment of Operation Downfall, the planned Allied invasion of Kyūshu, in an epi-sode of the animated TV series *Yōkai daisensō*, 1968.

and *Tōkaidō obake dōchū,* followed story lines borrowed from period dramas (*jidaigeki*) and their narratives romanticizing Edo-period samurai virtue. The monsters in these two films have minimal dialogue and appear only as a supporting cast that allegorizes human weaknesses and fallacies.

In Daiei's *Yōkai daisensō,* on the other hand, yōkai take center stage, fighting a war with an invading monster from "the West" (*seiyō*). Perhaps because this genre was more accessible internationally than manga or Japanese television animation were in the late 1960s, the film toned down both visual and verbal references to the Pacific and Vietnam Wars and distilled the theme of the monster war as a metaphor for Japanese patriotism down to its most politically correct and nonconfrontational form. In this version the "Western" invader is an ancient Babylonian monster, Daimon, who arrives in Japan to take over the souls of humans and threatens the habitat of native monsters based on Japanese folklore—the yōkai. The film is set in the Edo period (1603–1867), and accordingly neither the invader nor the occupied land invites comparisons with world conflicts in 1968.

The character design and iconography of Daimon emphasize its Babylonian origins: it is partly based on the Burney relief, a Babylonian terra cotta wall carving (ca. 2000 BCE) from southern Iraq, often associated with Lilitu, the Babylonian female demon depicted with bird wings and claws.[16] Lilitu, mentioned in the Gilgamesh Epic (ca. 2000–2150 BCE), is a vampiric night demon that, like Daimon, lives on the blood of women and children. Daimon's ability to enter the bodies of its victims can be related to another Babylonian mythical being, Ekimmu, a vampire-like spirit that lives off the life force of its human victims. In the film, Daimon's body structure is based on the late Assyrian (ca. 1800 BCE) monumental sculptures and on reliefs found in Babylonia and Assyria, in the area where Iraq stands today. Those sculptures depict anthropomorphic demon beings with upright winged torsos and the hindquarters of birds of prey, wearing pointed caps on their horned, human heads.[17]

In the film, the giant Daimon has lain dormant as a statue since approximately 2000 BCE in the ancient Mesopotamian city of Ur, until it is awakened by treasure hunters. Once disturbed, it flies to Edo-period Japan and enters the body of a local feudal lord. Daimon lives off the blood and life energy of children and women, takes over the bodies of its victims, and can multiply itself into an army of demons or grow to huge size like the giant reptile Godzilla, popular in *kaijū* monster films since the mid-1950s.[18] Daimon's first battle with native Japanese spirit beings occurs when he tears down the Shintō shrine and the Buddhist altar at the feudal lord's home. These atrocities soon wake the Kappa water spirit, who is the first Japanese yōkai to be defeated by Daimon.

Following that, local monsters gather to protect their homeland and after several encounters they finally defeat the invader by stabbing it in the eye, its weak point. The monster is not killed, but it does fly away from Japan.

The film painstakingly attempts to avoid offending postwar and Cold War sensibilities by portraying the fight as one between Edo-period Japanese and Babylonian monsters, but the film's structure nevertheless repeats the Momotarō paradigm established by the animated Momotarō films produced during the Second World War and repeated in the *Yōkai daisensō* manga and anime. The Western monster is a tall, thin figure with sharp bodily features and a long face and nose: a lonesome figure against the cavalcade of Japanese monsters (Figure 2). It is dark, scary, and monochromatic, a generic monster without many features, and its cold temperament more closely matches the *kaijū* reptile entities of the Godzilla and Gamera films. The Japanese monsters, on the other hand, repeat the Momotarō motif of a youthful savior leading a team of endearing native heroes: they lack an adult, male leader figure, as they consist of comical creatures with childlike features such as big round heads, small bodies, and weak voices.

Accentuating the youth, humor, and colorfulness of the Japanese yōkai is the contrasting Daimon, who only enters the bodies of male authority figures. It remains a serious male adult character throughout the story, like the *oni* devil characters in the wartime animation *Momotarō: Umi no shinpei* (1945, Momotarō: Divine troops of the ocean). And following the Momotarō paradigm, Daimon is not killed but expelled from the islands. The monster also repeats motifs from ancient chronicles that could be said to constitute founding texts of the Japanese state: stabbed in the eye, it is defeated in the same way as the chief deity of Japanese folklore, the *Yama no kami* (mountain god) described in *Kojiki* (680 CE, Records of ancient matters) and *Nihon shoki* (720 CE, Chronicles of Japan).

In sum, then, the manga, animation, and film versions of the *Yōkai daisensō* produced in the late 1960s all center on the idea of a Western invasion of Asian regions, exoticized by geographical or temporal distance: Vietnam and Okinawa in manga and animation, and Edo Japan in the film version. In all cases, the adult-like foreign forces are defeated through the cooperation of childlike local monsters. In the manga and animated versions, the importance of ancestor reverence is also accentuated, in alignment with the Momotarō paradigm.

This reflects the economic and political atmosphere of 1960s Japan: in 1968, Japan's Gross National Product became the second largest in the world. In an era when Japanese postwar economic recovery was at its turning point,

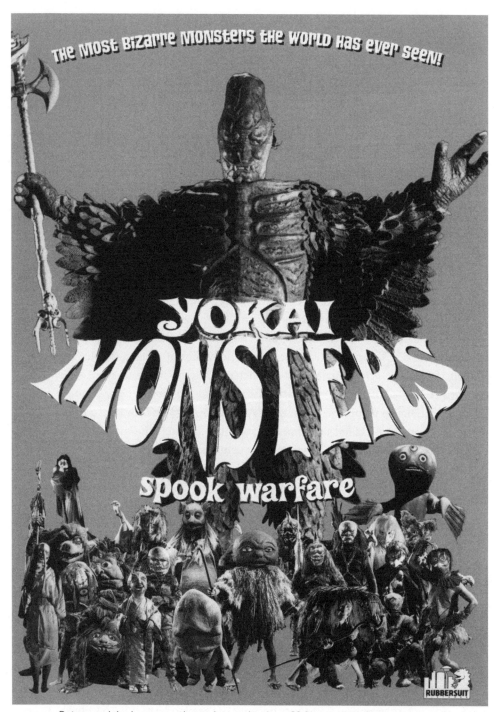

FIGURE 2. Daimon and the Japanese yōkai as depicted in the 1968 film version of *Yōkai daisensō*. The image is from the cover of the English-language DVD.

the Japanese monsters that reappeared in popular family-oriented media may have appeared guileless or innocent, but they reinforced the idea of a demarcation and rivalry between "Western" interests and Japanese ones. Simultaneously, the portrayal of Japan as protecting Asian cultures against Western occupation unmasks the ambivalent relationship of Japan toward the United States during the Cold War.

But a notable deviation from the Momotarō paradigm lies in the fact that until the end of the Second World War, yōkai were used as metaphors for foreigners and outsiders in popular visual media, while the yōkai in the *Yōkai daisensō* narratives represent "Japaneseness." This important change can be attributed to the effect of the yōkai-themed sequential art produced by Mizuki, of which *Gegege no Kitarō* was just a part: Mizuki's work contributed to the mascotization of these monsters, changing their roles from outsiders to representatives of an imagined, shared nostalgic Japanese past.[19]

YŌKAI DAISENSŌ IN THE TWENTY-FIRST CENTURY

As noted above, Miike Takashi, the director of the 2005 *Yōkai daisensō* remake, is noted for his visually exaggerated use of sexual and violent content as well as frequent application of surreal narrative and character development patterns, and, true to form, Miike delivered a relatively complex reworking of the simply structured fantasy story that constituted the 1968 classic. Miike's version is situated in futuristic Tokyo, where yōkai fight the embodiment of pollution and alienation: mecha (mechanical objects) created from discarded rubbish and yōkai souls, brought to life by ancient yin–yang sorcery in the form of *onmyōdō* wizard Katō Yasunori, a villain based a character in *Teito Monogatari* (1971, Tale of the capitol), a novel by historian and yōkai researcher Aramata Hiroshi.

In Aramata's novel, Katō is the descendant of native tribes that lived on the Japanese islands and who were annihilated by the Yamato court that constitute the ancestors of today's Japanese. Katō's parents were killed by the tenth-century Onmyōdō court wizard Abe no Seimei, and Katō was born from a dying mother. Katō, the human manifestation of the wrath of the annihilated tribes,[20] was raised in the Onmyōdō wizardry tradition and has returned to Japan throughout history to cause disasters, including the Great Kantō Earthquake of 1923.[21]

In Miike's film, Katō combines the supernatural powers of yōkai with the wrath of used tools that have been thrown away, to create *kikai,* a play on words meaning "machine-monsters."[22] (Here Miike draws on an older yōkai visual tradition: the wrath of discarded utensils is the central theme of the Muromachi-period *Utensil wars picture scroll* mentioned earlier.) The manga and animation series *Gegege no Kitarō* also frequently used yōkai characters as metaphors of environmental pollution, but Miike's 2005 film is the first instance of yōkai and mecha being combined to achieve this effect. There is no mention of Western foreigners in the story; instead, modern Japanese have themselves become foreigners or invaders in their own land, given that Katō represents the wrath of the native tribes that once inhabited Japan. The scope of the narrative has also changed: the fight takes place in the psyche of the combatants. With this intricate story line and characters, Miike has harnessed his cynical genius as a director to create a surreal setting and downplay the melodrama that fantasy films often risk.

> MIZUKI APPEARS IN THE FINAL SCENES AS THE YŌKAI DAIŌ (GREAT YŌKAI ELDER), WHO MAINTAINS THE BALANCE BETWEEN MONSTERS AND HUMANS. HIS FINAL MESSAGE IN THE FILM IS "WAR IS MEANINGLESS. YOU ONLY GET HUNGRY."

If yōkai in the Meiji period (1868–1911) were often equated with outsiders and were feared for their harmful powers over humans, those in the 1960s retained their power but were often transformed into native heroes. But in the narrative of the 2005 film they are treated as a fragile and vulnerable endangered species, the symbols of a nostalgic, rural Japanese communal life. They do not fight but simply gather for a festival in the capital. (This is a reference to the "one hundred demons night parade" that appears in one of the earliest yōkai picture scrolls, the Muromachi period *Hyakki yagyō*, but the parade is now transported to a contemporary and distinctly alienated urban setting.)

Produced during the consolidation phase of the invasion of Iraq by the United States military (2003–2006), the 2005 film does not display monsters from Babylonia/ancient Iraq; in fact, Miike instructed Muroi Shigeru, the actress playing yōkai character Sunakake Babaa (Sand Throwing Witch), to throw sand toward the imagined direction of Iraq as a tribute to the casualties of war. In contrast to the texts or subtexts of the 1960s narratives, this film emphasizes a strong antiwar message, delivered by Mizuki Shigeru himself in a final sequence (Figure 3). A production consultant on the film, the eighty-three-year-old Mizuki appears in the final scenes as the Yōkai Daiō (Great Yōkai Elder), who maintains the balance between monsters and humans. His final message in the film is "War is meaningless. You only get hungry."[23]

FIGURE 3. Mizuki Shigeru on the set of the film *Yōkai daisensō,* 2005. Photograph by author.

Despite Mizuki's cameo, the 2005 *Yōkai daisensō* was not linked to Mizuki's production company, Mizuki Pro, and consequently yōkai characters based on Mizuki's designs were omitted from the film in order to avoid copyright infringement. Instead, the film's producers, Kadokawa Eiga Film Corporation, created more than five hundred yōkai characters based on art historical yōkai depictions as well as on original ideas of the filmmakers.

Mizuki's yōkai do appear in the 2007 film *Gegege no Kitarō,* a live-action adaptation of the *Gegege no Kitarō* animation, produced by Shōchiku Film Production Company. Shōchiku purchased the copyrights to the yōkai characters that appear in the *Gegege no Kitarō* manga and animation series, so the film's yōkai design adheres closely to Mizuki's style. Therefore, this film did not produce new innovations in yōkai representation, but it did update Mizuki's character design to cross over to the live-action film genre, and some details of that transition offer an interesting final perspective on the changing identification of yōkai as foreign, native, or liminal figures.

The 2007 *Gegege no Kitarō* film showcased the efforts of a cast of eminent designers. Set designer Inagaki Hisao (*Narayama bushikō* [1983, *The Ballad of Narayma*]; *Kuroi ame* [1989, *Black Rain*]; *Tokyo Zombie* [2005]), special effects artist Egawa Etsuko (*Teito Monogatari* [1988, A tale of the capitol]; *Kogitsune*

Helen [2006, Little fox Helen]), and costume designer Hibino Kozue (who designed advertising campaigns for Shiseidō and Comme des Garçons in the 1990s) were teamed with a distinguished cast of actors including Katō Koyuki (*The Last Samurai*, 2003) and Kabuki actor Nakamura Shidō (*Letters from Iwo Jima*, 2006). The film was a tribute to the *Gegege no Kitarō* manga and animation series, and an attempt to remake the image of the Kitarō franchise for a new generation of adolescents.

FIGURE 4. Wentz Eiji in the role of Kitarō, on a flyer for the film *Gegege no Kitarō*, 2007.

Kitarō's character was updated by casting the television celebrity, model, and boy-band member Wentz Eiji in the role. Casting Wentz to play the all-Japanese boy hero was a risky and perhaps risqué choice: the young actor appeared in black leather shorts, wearing a Chanchanko vest made of a skunk pelt, with long silver hair falling into his face (Figure 4). But the choice proved a success, attracting enough fans to lead to a sequel film in 2008. Yet Wentz's popularity with young people was not the sole reason for casting him in the role of Kitarō: Shōchiku said that he was chosen based on his "otherworldly looks."[24] Similarly, an interview with Tsujimoto Tamako, casting coordinator and associate producer for Tōhō's 2007 yōkai film *Dororo*, reveals that the actress Tsuchiya Anna was cast as *Dororo*'s main yōkai character Mai Mai Onba because she combined "beauty with eerie otherworldly looks."[25] What makes these comments significant is that Wentz and Tsuchiya are both half Japanese: Wentz's father is German American, while Tsuchiya's father is Russian American.

Yōkai, as visual symbols, traditionally occupy a niche on the borderline between the familiar (*uchi*) and the outside world (*soto*) in Japanese visual narratives. This is why some texts can cast them as the foreign threat, others as the native Japanese heroes, and still others—including several versions of *Yōkai daisensō*—as both. Half-Japanese, half-Western actors like Wentz and Tsuchiya have been cast as yōkai because, according to the filmmakers, their facial features are attractive but at the same time unfamiliar. If Westerners are decisively part of the Other (*soto*), then "halfs" (the colloquial Japanese expression used for persons of mixed ethnicity, mostly with one Japanese and one Caucasian parent) occupy a niche in Japanese society that can be paralleled with the traditional role of yōkai: on the borderline between insiders and outsiders, like us, but not quite.

> IN THE GUISE OF INNOCENT FANTASY, VISUAL REPRESENTATIONS OF YŌKAI HAVE ALWAYS SERVED AN AGENDA PERTAINING TO THE SPECIFIC HISTORICAL PERIODS IN WHICH THEY HAVE APPEARED AND REAPPEARED.

This twist in yōkai representation represents a new role for yōkai that corresponds to changing social dynamics in Japan. With attributes perceived as desirable but at the same time upsetting, half-Japanese represent a social stratum that emerged largely in the postwar period. At one end of the spectrum are half-Japanese entertainers like Wentz and Tsuchiya whose "exotic" physical and facial features have added to their popularity and who have became increasingly visible in popular media toward the end of the millennium; at the other end are the estimated four thousand Amerasian offspring of local Okinawans and temporarily stationed U.S. military personnel, who often become social outsiders from an early age.[26]

CONCLUSION

In the guise of innocent fantasy, visual representations of yōkai have always served an agenda pertaining to the specific historical periods in which they have appeared and reappeared. From Yoshiiku's post-Sino-Japanese war print *Kokkei Yamatoshiki* (1895), ridiculing the Chinese army, to the *Momotarō* animation trilogy produced in the final stages of World War II, visual representations of yōkai have served the needs of militarist propaganda since the Meiji period, and the *Yōkai daisensō* narratives in manga, animation, and cinema follow in this tradition.

The role of yōkai could be manipulated in postwar visual media because of the yōkai's inherent ambivalence. In the postwar manga, animation, and cinema versions of *Yōkai daisensō*, yōkai were transformed to represent a nostalgic Japanese past. This was the era of the Cold War and of Japan's economic recovery, and what emerged in popular visual media was the narrative of a West versus Japan power struggle, in which yōkai served as righteous patriotic entities, legitimized by ancestral lineage, who guarded Japan from outside forces.

But in the case of Miike Takashi's surreal contemporary vision of *Yōkai daisensō,* one set of yōkai are equated with environmental pollution and metropolitan alienation. Like the process of gradual degradation of local minor deities theorized by Yanagita Kunio, the yōkai of *Yōkai daisensō* have become less and less powerful with each remake.[27] While yōkai fought off the enemy in Okinawa in the 1966 manga and 1968 animated versions, they become timid and vulnerable in the 1968 film version, and by the 2005 remake, they are rendered useless, cowardly, and childish or senile; in Miike's film it is ultimately only their utter incompetence that leads them to victory. Finally in films like *Dororo* and the 2007 version of *Gegege no Kitarō,* yōkai regain a heroic quality, but their "celebrity" status is created or regained by equating them with liminal ethnic or racial categories that are viewed ambivalently in postwar Japan.

Their fluidity as visual symbols permits yōkai to be adapted to new roles in contemporary media, including manga, film, animation, and computer games, and these roles change with each new patriotic war they undertake to protect the Japanese homeland from invaders. Nonetheless, their core feature remains unaltered: they live in a no-man's-land between right and wrong, which readily lends them to new interpretations in their constant visual evolution within Japanese popular visual culture.

....

Notes

1. *Yōkai daisensō,* dir. Kuroda Yoshiyuki (1968); translated as *Yōkai Monsters: Spook Warfare,* DVD (ADV, 2004); *Yōkai daisensō,* dir. Miike Takashi (2005); translated as *The Great Yōkai War,* DVD (Tokyo Shock, 2006).

2. Mizuki Shigeru, *Gegege no Kitarō* (Tokyo: Chūō Kōronsha, 1988), 1:918.

3. Stephen Addiss, ed., *Japanese Ghosts and Demons: Art of the Supernatural* (New York: George Braziller, 1985), 18.

4. Noriko T. Reider, "Transformation of the Oni: From the Frightening and Diabolical to the Cute and Sexy," *Asian Folklore Studies* 62, no. 2 (2003): 147.

5. John W. Dower, *War without Mercy: Race and Power in the Pacific War* (New York: Pantheon Books, 1986), 255. On wartime Momotarō animation, see the chapters by Thomas Lamarre and Ōtsuka Eiji in this volume.

6. Mizuki, *Gegege no Kitarō,* 1:154, 157.

7. Ibid., 1:175, 179.

8. Ibid., 1:187. In 1969, Mizuki published a six-volume manga in which Kitarō joins the Vietnam War. Kitarō's yōkai army goes to Vietnam to help the local people there, joining the National Liberation Front against the American forces. At one point Konaki Jijī (Old Crybaby monster) fights a Scorpion submarine. The story, which appeared in mainstream children's comic magazines, also narrates the history of Vietnam. Mizuki, *Kitarō no Betonamu senki* (Kitarō's Vietnam war diary) (Tokyo: Bungei Shunjū, 2000), 12, 40.

9. Mizuki, *Gegege no Kitarō*, 1:198.

10. Ibid., 1:174.

11. Mizuki Shigeru, *Manga Mizuki Shigeru den* (Tokyo: Kōdansha, 2004), 2:280.

12. Mizuki, *Gegege no Kitarō*, 1:188.

13. Ibid., 1:202.

14. Ibid., 1:203.

15. Dower, *War without Mercy*, 255.

16. Thorkild Jacobsen, "Pictures and Pictorial Language (the Burney Relief)," in *Figurative Language in the Ancient Near East,* ed. M. Mindlin, M. J. Geller, and J. E. Wansbrough (London: University of London School of Oriental and African Studies, 1987), 1–11.

17. Anthony Green, "A Note on the 'Scorpion Man' and Papazu," *Iraq* 47 (1985): 75–83.

18. Ion, ed. *Gamera gahō: Daiei hizō eiga gojūgo nen no ayumi* [The Gamera chronicles: The history of DAIEI fantastic movies 1942–1996] (Tokyo: Take Shobō, 1996), 101.

19. Michael Dylan Foster, "The Otherworlds of Mizuki Shigeru," *Mechademia* 3 (2008): 8–28.

20. Iwasa Yōichi, ed., *Yomigaere! Yōkai eiga daishūgō!!* (Resurrect! Great yōkai movie collection) (Tokyo: Take Shobō, 2005), 28.

21. *Kwai* 19 (2005): 7.

22. Nashimoto Takanori, ed., *Yōkai eiga natsu no jin: Kyōgoku Natsuhiko "Ubume no natsu" vs. "Yōkai daisensō"* (Yōkai movies summer edition: Kyōgoku Natsuhiko's "The summer of the Ubume" vs. "Great yōkai wars") (Tokyo: Yōsensha, 2005), 53.

23. Zen Nihon Yōkai Suishin Iinkai, ed., *Shashin de miru Nihon yōkai daizukan* (Great Japanese yōkai illustrated photographic reference book) (Tokyo: Kadokawa, 2005), 84.

24. *Gegege no Kitarō* (Tokyo: Shōchiku, 2007), 27.

25. Yuhara Hiroki and Gushiken Haruka, eds., *Dororo kanzen zue* (Dororo complete picture book) (Tokyo: Media Factory, 2007), 61.

26. Sean J. Curtin, "International Marriages in Japan: Part Three—Amerasian Children in Okinawa," Social Trends 15, *Global Communications Platform* (November 8, 2002), http://www.glocom.org/special_topics/social_trends/20021108_trends_s15/index.html (accessed June 2, 2008).

27. Yanagita Kunio, *Yōkai dangi* (Discussions about yōkai) (Tokyo: Kōdansha, 2004).

REBECCA SUTER

• • •

From Jusuheru to Jannu: Girl Knights and Christian Witches in the Work of Miuchi Suzue

In the vast and diverse world of manga, war is traditionally considered to be the domain of *shōnen* manga, or boys' comics, while *shōjo* manga, or manga for girls, are perceived as primarily concerned with romance. As Kotani Mari and Saitō Tamaki note, love and war merge in the *sentō bishōjo* or "battling beauty" motif, in which these traditionally separate themes are combined, allowing identification on the part of different readers and making it a particularly popular and increasingly visible figure in contemporary Japanese popular culture.[1] The *sentō bishōjo* is a productive trope that spans different genres and appears in boys' and girls' manga alike, as well as in their animated versions and related merchandising.

In this article, I want to look at the uses and implications of another figure that, by contrast, appears almost exclusively in *shōjo* works: the "girl knight." While battling beauties and girl knights share a number of traits, including their challenge to traditional notions of femininity, they differ in some significant aspects, most importantly, as I will try to demonstrate, in their epistemological approach to, and use of, war/time. I therefore propose to study the peculiar combination of themes of war, time, and cultural and gender identity in the girl knight trope as a means to reflect more broadly on the uses of history in *shōjo* manga.

In the first part of the article, I will look at the development of the girl knight figure in modern girls' manga and analyze the way it combines history, parody, and fantasy to subvert conventional notions of reality. In the second part, I will analyze one specific case of subversion of Western history and war/time through the use of the girl-knight figure, specifically Miuchi Suzue's creative misreading of the legend of Joan of Arc. A canonical author of girls' manga and very popular among fans in Japan, Miuchi is seldom studied in the West.[2] Looking at her works will thus allow me to look at the treatment of history and gender in mainstream *shōjo* manga, a topic that is generally overlooked by critics on both sides of the Pacific, who tend to focus on more radical and experimental (and, undoubtedly, more pleasant-to-read) authors.

POWER LEOTARDS AND KNIGHTS WITH RIBBONS

If in boys' manga from the late 1950s to the early 1970s casting children in the role of pilots of fighter planes and giant robots functions as a form of empowerment for young readers, girls in these stories generally maintain a passive role, in line with the conventional representation of women and children as symbolic civilian victims of war. From the torments of an adolescent woman hit by atomic radiation in Shirato Sanpei's *Kieyuku shōjo* (1957, The vanishing girl) to the death by starvation of little Setsuko in Takahata Isao's *Grave of the Fireflies* (1988, *Hotaru no haka*), in Japanese popular culture, and particularly in boys' manga, girls are almost invariably portrayed as victims rather than agents of war.

With the evolution from robot manga to the so-called "power suit" stories, where, rather than piloting a giant machine, characters don robot armor that gives them various kinds of powers, the encroachment of technology on the body, among other things, begins to undermine gender differences, and female characters increasingly gain access to active warrior roles. Interestingly, however, compared to their sturdy, armor-like male counterparts, girls' power suits tend to be tight-fitting, flimsy garments that appear designed to reveal the body rather than shield it, as epitomized by the power leotards worn by the Knight Sabers in *Bubblegum Crisis* (1987, *Baburugamu kuraishisu*). As Kotani notes, while being a warrior-like figure, "aggressive as any boy," a battling girl must also be "a beauty, which configures her in relation to boys' desires."[3] Accordingly, empowered girls usually have either hyperfeminine, Wonder Woman–like bodies or *lolikon*-oriented schoolgirl looks. In either case, the subversion of gender roles is accompanied by a high degree of sexualization of the characters according to traditional stereotypes of femininity, adult or adolescent. In both *shōnen* and *shōjo* manga, battling girls are constructed according to male standards and objectified through a male gaze.

Very different in this respect is another recurring battling female of manga, the "princess knight." Launched by Tezuka Osamu's *Ribon no kishi* (1953, The knight with the ribbon; also known in English as *The Princess Knight*) and consolidated in Ikeda Riyoko's *Berusaiyu no bara* (1972, *The Rose of Versailles*), this trope does not involve physical transformations but relies instead on a combination of cross-dressing and historical settings. The two are fused in an aestheticization of European war tales that focuses on fashion, in the form of exotic-looking, elegant uniforms and/or a combination of shiny armor and lace frills. The uniforms worn by Oscar and Sapphire, the respective protagonists of Ikeda's and Tezuka's manga, are radically different from power suits, in that they do not alter biological identity; rather, they expose its constructed and performative nature. Cross-dressing thus becomes a critique of conventional, rigid notions of gender: its initial inversion of the male/female binary ultimately leads to an undermining of the categories themselves, which are shown to be not natural and grounded in the physical body but arbitrary and acquired.

The historical settings, revisited through a fantastical filter, perform a similar function. *Berusaiyu no bara* is a good example of such strategies; the background of the French Revolution is both an occasion to display exotic landscapes and romanticizing clichés about Europe, and a way to address social and political concerns in a displaced, allegorical mode. The protagonist of the manga, Oscar François de Jarjayes, is a girl raised as a boy, who pursues a military career in prerevolutionary France and eventually becomes captain of the Royal Guard. In the course of the story Oscar becomes romantically involved both with queen Marie Antoinette and André, the son of Oscar's housemaid and one of the few people to know her female identity, as well as with other characters from the aristocracy and from the underclass. A nobleman and an army official in the service of the aristocracy, Oscar is led by her love for André to sympathize with the cause of the people. Her inability to side with the aristocracy and to fulfill her role as protector of constituted order intertwines with her personal identity conflict; both class and gender categories are presented as obstacles to self-realization, obstacles that ultimately prove insurmountable, as shown by Oscar's tragic death on the barricades after failing to convince Marie Antoinette to withdraw the troops from the streets of Paris.

Such rewriting of historical battles as allegories for personal and social struggles is not new to manga; it was a common feature in the *gekiga*[4] of the 1950s and 1960s, traditionally considered the two great seasons of political commitment of Japanese comics. While children's comics tend to depict war through fantastic tales of adolescent pilots, from the numerous Pacific War manga of the 1960s and Nagai Gō's giant robots of the 1970s all the way to contemporary mecha anime; *gekiga*, targeted mostly at an adolescent and young adult audience, used medieval wars and samurai stories to stand for current social and political fights. Renowned examples are Shirato Sanpei's *Ninja bugeichō* (1959–62, Chronicle of a ninja's martial achievements), which symbolizes the student and worker revolts of the 1960s through the portrayal of peasant uprisings of the Edo period, and his *Kamuiden* (1964–71, The legend of *kamui*), which performs a similar operation but using the story of a *buraku* boy fighting against discrimination and oppression.

> THE CREATIVE ANACHRONISMS OF *SHŌJO* MANGA, LIKE THOSE OF *GEKIGA*, ARE A MEANS OF APPROPRIATING HISTORY AS A WEAPON.

While *gekiga* relies mainly on Japanese history, *shōjo* manga displays a marked preference for foreign settings.[5] This adds a further layer to the rewriting of history as parody, creating a romanticized and displaced version of the West that duplicates, and exposes, Western mechanisms of stereotyping the Orient, in their peculiar combination of exoticization and domestication. If in Hollywood movies all the characters speak English regardless of their nationality, here everybody speaks Japanese, and revolutionary France becomes a repertoire of exotica and stylized images, performing the same function as *geisha* and *samurai* in American and European popular fiction. While catering to their readers' taste for all things foreign, *shōjo* authors also exhibit a remarkable boldness in appropriating Western history for their own purposes, a fact that problematizes the common image of Japanese awe toward Western culture. *Shōjo* manga's rewriting of Western history is thus a particularly ambiguous and interesting operation.

In her analysis of the evolution of manga from an "art of the people" with radical political content to an increasingly conservative medium, Sharon Kinsella sees the boom of girls' manga in the 1970s as the sign of a shift toward sentimentalism and disengagement, echoing the view of Japanese critics who describe it as "a form of petty individualism and a reactionary retreat from more important political and social issues."[6] In this essay, I would like to attempt a reassessment of mainstream *shōjo* manga, suggesting that, while it remains a form of mass culture that often serves to convey conservative messages and contain dissent, in rewriting Western history it introduces elements of social and political critique that prompt, or at least permit, reflection on the part of the readers.

Through a blend of historical faithfulness and fantastical fiction, and a juxtaposition of modern and premodern elements, "girl knight" stories produce creative misreadings of history that allow the authors, the characters, and the readers to reflect critically on the conventions of culture and society, while making them aware of the pervasiveness of such conventions. The creative anachronisms of *shōjo* manga, like those of *gekiga*, are a means of appropriating history as a weapon.

In this article, I want to explore one case of imaginative reinterpretation of history: Miuchi Suzue's rewriting of the legend of Joan of Arc as a "girl knight" story, which also becomes a reinterpretation of the Hundred Years' War as a conflict between the Christian god and devil, both represented through a fantastical framework as exotic supernatural creatures. Through the combination of these two elements, the girl knight trope and Christian imagery, this manga portrays war as a binary opposition of good against evil, us against them, and women against men: an opposition that is ultimately subverted, revealing the very categories it is based upon to be arbitrary and constructed.

In order to highlight the specific articulation of this mechanism, I propose my own anachronism as a critical tool to uncover the strategies at play in the work. To explain Miuchi's use of girl knights and Christianity, I will read her story against an apparently completely unrelated, yet intriguingly similar text: the sacred book of the early Christians, *Tenchi hajimari no koto* (*The Beginning of Heaven and Earth*; hereafter *Tenchi*).[7] The two texts, as we will see, have much more in common than we could think, and juxtaposing them will allow us to shed light on Miuchi's rewriting of Western history.

MAYA, MARUYA, AND JUSUHERU

In many respects, Miuchi's works read as paradigmatic *shōjo* manga, and follow all the genre's visual and thematic conventions, including floral and art deco motifs, shining eyes and flowing hair, cute unthreatening male protagonists, fashion-conscious female characters dressed in frilly skirts or trendy pantsuits, and romantic stories often featuring a rags-to-riches dynamic.

In this sense, her works are a far cry from the experiments of the so-called *24nengumi,* and belong more to the tradition of Tezuka Osamu's mainstream comics than to the movement for the appropriation of manga by female writers of the 1970s.[8] Miuchi's manga are rather tame both in style and in content when compared to those of some of her contemporaries such as Hagio Moto and Takemiya Keiko, and more radical authors who border on the world of *dōjinshi.*[9]

Miuchi's most famous work is *Garasu no kamen* (1976–present, The glass mask), a long series tracing the adventures of teenage Kitajima Maya in her quest to become an actress at the Tsukikage school. While the story reads as a fairly conventional *bildungsroman,* the choice of an actress as a protagonist allows Miuchi to reflect on the performative nature of identity in general, and more specifically of gender roles. Like the "glass mask" of the title, female identity is presented as something that needs to be learned, and even once acquired, is constantly in danger of shattering.

Her shorter works, too, often revolve around the struggles of female teenage protagonists in their socialization as women.[10] Her protagonists are for the most part tomboys, physically fit and with a strong character. Often they are either obsessed with sports or overachievers in school, and both types attract criticism from their family and society at large for the resulting lack of femininity. In story after story, Miuchi's girls struggle with their inability to fit into gender roles. Besides coming-of-age tales, the other main register of Miuchi's stories is horror, with a specific focus on ghosts, creatures from the past that allow her to introduce history into the manga in a highly fantastical mode. Her girl knight stories are arguably the most interesting combination of these two elements, the concern with gender roles and the rewriting of history through fantasy.

The concern with the arbitrariness of gender roles and the interest in horror also provide an important background to her interpretation of Christianity. Two of the most intriguing cultural adaptations performed by early Christians are the reinterpretations of the figures of Mary and of Lucifer; both resonate with contemporary manga's revisiting of Christian legends.

Early interpretations of Christianity in Japan are in themselves a fascinating example of cultural adaptation. This adaptation is partly related to the work of cultural negotiation undertaken by the Jesuits in the sixteenth century, when the religion was first introduced to Japan. Alessandro Valignano, the main evangelizer in Japan after the departure of Xavier for China in 1551, was one of the strongest advocates of the idea of cultural adaptation in missionary work.

As in China, where missionaries had rendered the word *God* as *Shang Di* (Emperor) or *Tian* (Heaven), in Japan, in an effort to make Christian doctrine comprehensible in local terms, the Jesuits translated a number of key terms into Buddhist equivalents. As a result, Christianity was

EARLY INTERPRETATIONS OF CHRISTIANITY IN JAPAN ARE IN THEMSELVES A FASCINATING EXAMPLE OF CULTURAL ADAPTATION.

initially interpreted as a form of Buddhism, yet another Buddhist sect that had been imported from China. The most controversial term was the word *God* itself, which was initially translated as *Dainichi* (*Mahavairocana*, the Buddha revered by the Shingon sect). Later on Francisco Xavier, realizing that this led the Japanese to think that they were converting to a form of Buddhism and not to Christianity, forbid the cult of *Dainichi*, declaring it "the devil's invention," and the Christian god was renamed *Deusu*.[11] This initial confusion, coupled with the myth of Lucifer as a fallen angel, resulted in a strong concern among early Japanese Christians with the ambiguity of the Devil/God binary, which is clearly reflected in their reinterpretation of the figure of Lucifer.

Interestingly, this intrinsic ambiguity of the Devil/God binary is addressed by a number of modern authors of fiction and in popular culture. I should make a caveat here: I am not trying to prove a historical continuity between these interpretations or imply that there was an uninterrupted tradition of questioning of Christianity that goes from the *Tenchi* to modern manga. Rather, my working hypothesis is that the early Christians' misreading of religion informed popular perceptions of Christianity that are still alive today, and, more importantly, that this phenomenon shows an active appropriation of Western culture in Japan, which ultimately undermines Western categories of thought by presenting them from an estranged perspective.

A first instance of such similarities between *kirishitan* and modern interpretations of Christianity can be seen in the representation of the figure of Mary. In the *Tenchi*, the Biruzen Maruya (Virgin Mary) is portrayed as a gifted and bookish teenage girl, who becomes endowed with magical powers after her encounter with God. When read against Miuchi's stories, Maruya appears to be the perfect *shōjo* heroine, yet another girl knight endowed with supernatural powers. Here is how she makes her first appearance in the book:

> In the country of Roson [Luçon, in the Philippines] where King Sanzen Zejusu [three thousand Jesuses] reigned, a girl of humble birth by the name of Maruya also lived. Since her seventh year, she had set her heart and soul on the pursuit of learning. By age twelve she had made great strides and reflected thus: "When I consider the state of our world, I wonder how I can be

saved in the world to come now that I have been born into the world of humans." As she thought relentlessly about this, how mysterious it was when she received this heavenly oracle: IF YOU MARUYA WILL REMAIN SINGLE FOR YOUR ENTIRE LIFE LIVING THE ASCETIC LIFE OF A BIRUZEN, I WILL QUICKLY GRANT YOU THE SALVATION YOU SEEK. Much amazed and rejoicing, the girl Maruya threw herself to the ground and worshiped.[12]

Shortly afterward, the Biruzen Maruya is asked to marry the king of Roson. The king offers her worldly goods, but she refuses, claiming that, despite her low rank in this world, she his superior because of her "secret arts." She is depicted as a shaman or magician, summoning supernatural beings, even concentrating the force in her *hara* in the best martial arts tradition:

> Without so much as a glance at the king's treasures Maruya responded, "Your treasures are temporary and pertain to an ephemeral present. Once you have used them up, they are useless. But now I will show you my secret arts." Turning her face to the heavens above, pressing her palms together and gathering all her force to the center of her being in prayer, the girl Maruya worshiped and invoked while these words flooded from her: "Reveal to us your mystery and power in this instant."[13]

After summoning a table laden with food and a snowfall in the middle of summer, Maruya ascends to Heaven on a flower wagon. She then returns to Earth and receives the visit of San Gamuriya Arikanjo (The Archangel Gabriel), who asks her to "use her young and fresh body" to give birth to the Son of God. From that point on, the text focuses on the life of Jesus, but Maruya accompanies him in most of his travels and is an active participant in his adventures. No mention of a husband is made; Santa Maruya remains a powerful, shaman-like virgin mother throughout the story, a squire, more than a mother, to the Son of God.

Another departure of the *Tenchi* from the biblical tradition can be found in the portrayal of Lucifer, called Jusuheru in the text. While Jusuheru fulfills the same role of tempter that he has in the Bible, the actual dynamic of the temptation is quite different. He first appears on the scene as a rival deity, trying to convince Ewa and Adan to worship him, reenacting the Dainichi/Deusu mechanism:

> One day while Deusu was away, Jusuheru seized the opportunity to deceive the anjo and said: "As I am also like Deusu, worship me from now on."

Hearing this, the anjo worshiped him saying, "Ah, behold, behold!" Ewa and Adan then asked, "Isn't Deusu here?" But Jusuheru replied swiftly by saying, "The Lord is in Heaven, but because I am like Deusu, tens of thousands of anjo revere me. Therefore, Ewa and Adan, you too worship me, Jusuheru."[14]

Deusu promptly arrives and chases Jusuheru away, but he does not seem particularly concerned with the danger of idolatry. On the contrary, he appears to be rather accepting toward the possibility of polytheism, and only warns Ewa and Adan: "even if you should worship Jusuheru, don't eat the fruit of the masan."[15]

When Jusuheru comes back and lures Ewa into eating the fruit, he claims: "it is forbidden because whoever eats it will obtain the same rank as Deusu,"[16] and when she hesitates he insists, "eat this, and obtain the same rank as I, Jusuheru."[17] He is then expelled from Paraiso shortly after Adan and Ewa and transformed into the God of Thunder.[18]

The focus on rank, part of the localization of religion, allows the text to present identity as intrinsically ambiguous and constantly shifting: if godliness is a rank rather than an essence, it can be gained and lost, and easily reversed. While the Lucifer of the biblical tradition is a fallen angel who loses his divine status as a result of sin, Jusuheru retains his ambiguous status (he still has the same rank as God) and thus embodies the fundamental ambivalence of the God/Devil, or Dainichi/Deusu, binary in the vision of the early *kirishitan*. This operation is strikingly similar to that performed in girl knight stories: divine nature is represented here as an accessory and arbitrary factor, just as girl knight characters' gender identity is determined by their armor, uniforms, and military training, rather than by any biological essence.

Interestingly, in her manga Miuchi shows a similar fascination precisely with the ambiguity of Lucifer, which she combines with gender-bending elements to further destabilize both male/female and good/evil, God/Devil binaries. How then do we get from Jusuheru to Jannu, and who is Jannu anyway?

JANNU, JIRU, AND THE MAGIC POWER OF CULTURAL TRANSLATION

Jannu is the protagonist of *Shirayuri no kishi* (1975, The knight of white lily), a story based on the legend of Joan of Arc (Figure 1). The title, while focusing on Joan of Arc's role as a warrior, is also an obvious reference to Tezuka

Osamu's *Ribon no kishi,* thus situating the story in the "princess knight" tradition of mainstream *shōjo* manga.

The story begins with a metatextual moment, portraying Jannu reading stories about Telesia, a queen who dressed as a warrior to defend her country.[19] Joan of Arc's legend is thus framed as a tale of female empowerment—she is a girl who wants to be a boy and a soldier—and as a story of formation of identity through identification with literary figures. The scene is a *mise en abyme* of the text's own appropriation of Western history, hinting at the position of girls as readers, interiorizing the roles they are presented with, but also at the possibility of their appropriating this mechanism by choosing which figures to identify with, and rewriting them on their own terms.

While she ostensibly declares herself to be an instrument in God's hands, Jannu in fact uses God's call to realize her long-held dream of becoming a knight, like the protagonist of her fairy tales. Her mission to save France in God's name is most of all an occasion to gain agency, to defy social conventions and construct her identity beyond conventional gender roles.

After introducing Jannu, the manga shifts to the other main thread of the plot: the plan of a group of worshipers of Lucifer, led by a shady figure named Guillaume, to prevent Charles VII from regaining the throne.[20] Alerted by Lucifer to the imminent arrival of a White Knight who will hinder their plans to conquer France, they decide to bid the Black Knight, Renard Edmontes (alias William George Stempleton), an English nobleman who has come to France as a spy, to find him. Or, rather, *her*: the White Knight is, of course, none other than Jannu.

The stories of the White and the Black Knight run parallel throughout the manga; they repeatedly meet, and there is even a hint at a possible romantic involvement, which is never realized. This both pays homage to and subverts the conventions of *shōjo* manga, as the love story is very marginal to the plot. The two are presented as mirror figures, one the negative of the other—Jannu has short hair and silver armor, William/Renard has long flowing hair and black armor, and both have crosses on their chests.

The ambivalence of this binary couple mirrors the ambiguity of the war between God and Lucifer, which in the manga is the real conflict underlying the Hundred Years' War. In the final part of the story, the mastermind behind the whole war is revealed to be Guillaume, who, with the help of one general La Treuil, fomented the hostilities in order to weaken both countries and ultimately establish the reign of Satan in Europe.

The manga thus rewrites the story of the siege of Orléans as a war between the forces of the Christian God and Devil, who are portrayed as uncanny supernatural beings, fundamentally equivalent. This is particularly evident on the visual plane. While the cult of Lucifer is performed with all the stereotypical devices of black magic, such as horns, capes, magic circles, five-pointed stars, rising smoke, and dark caves, the angel Michael, who brings Jeanne God's request to devote herself to the cause of France, appears in the middle of a thunderstorm, in a similar horror/gothic mode, and crosses and angels carry similar ominous resonances throughout the comic.

Even more ambivalent is the portrayal of the figure of Gilles de Rais, protagonist of the second half of the story. When Jannu finally manages to speak to the Dauphin and offer him her services, the King's evil counselor assigns her the impossible task of obtaining financial help from De Rais, in the conviction that she will fail and possibly be murdered. The characters of Jiru do Re and Jannu mirror each other on multiple levels, as do the respective historical figures. Like Jeanne d'Arc, de Rais was also tried and condemned for witchcraft, and like her, he later became the object of a posthumous semi-canonization (there are churches devoted to him and his effigies are said to perform miracles).[21]

In the comic book, he is portrayed as a solitary and dark figure, living alone in a castle peopled by wax dolls, which we later discover to be the embalmed cadavers of the friends and relatives who have died around him, gaining him the nickname *shinigami*, "God of death". Besides the nickname, his association with rival creation is reinforced by his activity as an alchemist, desperately trying to find a way to create gold so that he can become the richest man on earth, and by the fact that his castle is surrounded by a cemetery, which once again allows the manga to dwell on gothic imagery of crosses and tombs.

Jannu befriends Jiru and redeems him, in typical Beauty-and-the-Beast fashion, obtaining his support in the war against the English. The evil power of de Rais is thus turned into "good magic" in the service of God and France. In his choice to put his supernatural powers at the service of good, Jiru do Re mirrors the actions of Jeanne and her ability to perform miracles, for which she will later be condemned to death as a witch. Significantly, Jannu's power is often referred to as magic in the story.[22]

Gilles de Rais's sorcery, the schemes of the worshippers of Lucifer, and the miracles of Jannu are presented as different manifestations of occult power, facets of a Christian religion that is ultimately identified with magic. The manga ends with the death of the Black Knight among the flames, which cannot but remind the readers that Jannu, too, will soon be burned on the stake by her fellow countrymen, once again pointing to the overlap of witchcraft and religion, and at the arbitrariness of the good/evil, God/Devil binaries.

CONCLUSION

By retelling the legend of Joan of Arc as a "girl knight" story, *Shirayuri no kishi* performs two simultaneous inversions, which ultimately reinforce one another. On one hand it inverts and undermines the male/female binary, pointing at the constructed nature of gender roles; on the other, in rewriting the Hundred Years' War as a conflict between a God and a Devil that express their power on humans through almost identical forms of witchcraft, it blurs the divine/demonic opposition and ultimately reveals it to be meaningless, thus exposing a fundamental contradiction of Christian religion and of Western culture (Figure 2). Just as gender roles are based on an arbitrary distinction, the saintly and the demonic are shown to be ultimately one and the same, and to elicit the same kind of reaction in believers. In this sense, the combination of accurately researched foreign setting and fantastic rewriting of history assumes further significance: we should not see this creative misreading as born of ignorance or lack of understanding but rather as a playful yet pointed critique, showing us that God worship is, ultimately, superstition, just as Devil worship is.[23]

Through creative appropriation of this specific war/time, the manga questions conventional notions of femininity and religion, and more broadly of culture and identity. It does so through a rewriting of history that differs greatly, however, from that performed by revisionist comics that have recently become popular in adult male manga, epitomized by the works of Kobayashi Yoshinori. Crucial in this respect is its reliance on the fantastic, fairy-tale mode that is typical of *shōjo* manga.

As noted by Sharon Kinsella in her pioneering work on adult manga, neo-conservative *seinen* comics offer a supposedly objective alternative to official history relying on a realistic and objectifying narrative and visual style. The content is presented from an apparently neutral perspective, effacing the authorial function; this strategy de-individualizes the works, presenting them as reality showing itself directly, and thus makes their message pass for a neutral statement of fact, downplaying its ideological content.[24]

In contrast, *shōjo* manga are for the most part clearly antirealistic and replete with metatextual references that make the authorial presence felt throughout. They are obviously fictions, to be perceived as such, without any pretense of objectivity. This combination of historical accuracy and thoroughgoing fantasy suggests a possible

FIGURE 2. Cover of *Jūsangatsu no higeki,* a story by Miuchi centering on the subversion of the God/Devil binary. Republished in 1996 by Hakusensha in *Miuchi Suzue's Best Works.*

new interpretation of the personal focus in *shōjo* manga, which contrasts with the generally accepted notion that it constitutes a retreat into interiority and a renunciation of political engagement. While this escapist element is undoubtedly present in the genre, works such as Miuchi's point to a more complex social function of girls' manga, which is acted out on the level of form. *Shōjo* manga's antirealistic and self-reflexive style can at times prove a more effective tool for social criticism than a realism that, through the use of a supposedly "transparent" visual and narrative mode, ultimately endorses existing power structures through a naturalization of the arbitrary.

In girl knight stories, employing the tension between historical content and fantastic form as a background for the female protagonists' self-realization allows the texts to address the constructed nature of identity, which is presented as something that is acquired through the performance of precon-stituted roles but also as something that can be changed and rewritten. In saying this, however, I do not mean to imply that girls' manga are necessarily radical or subversive, either. This very act of rewriting is also the most ambiguous feature of this genre. In fact, the stories generally focus on the socialization of the individual and on how to come to terms with imposed paradigms on a personal level, rather than looking at the formation of the system as a whole, let alone suggesting the possibility of changing it. Thus they function as an instrument of containment of the same dissent they produce. Such a blend of subversive and conservative strategies is arguably what makes girls' manga such popular items of consumption; it is also what makes them a productive subject of study, one worthy of further scholarly attention.

Notes

1. Kotani Mari, "Metamorphosis of the Japanese Girl: The Girl, the Hyper-Girl, and the Battling Beauty," in *Mechademia 1* (2006): 167; for a discussion of the battling beauty trope, see also Saitō Tamaki, *Sentō bishōjo no seishin bunseki* (Psychoanalysis of the battling beauty) (Tokyo: Ōta Shuppan, 2001).

2. In her analysis of adult male manga, on the other hand, Sharon Kinsella writes briefly about Miuchi Suzue, whom she calls "Kakue," when discussing the growth of mainstream girls' manga in the 1970s, describing her as an example of conservative and shallow girl manga, in the "less politically controversial tradition of child-oriented, cute *manga* pioneered by Tezuka Osamu and his ex-assistants." Sharon Kinsella, *Adult Manga: Culture and Power in Contemporary Japanese Society* (Honolulu: University of Hawaii Press, 2000), 112–13.

3. Kotani, "Metamorphosis of the Japanese Girl," 166.

4. *Gekiga*, literally "dramatic images," generally refers to manga of the postwar period, written mainly by and for working-class teenagers and young adults, mostly with radical political content and a fairly experimental, expressionist graphic style. It was revived in the 1960s, when it became connected with the *Zengakuren* (All-Japan Student Federation) and the *shinsayoku* (New Left). For a discussion of the evolution of the genre, see Kinsella, *Adult Manga*, 24–36; Frederick Schodt, *Manga! Manga! The World of Japanese Comics* (Tokyo: Kodansha International, 1986), 68–79; and John Lent, "Japanese Comics," in *The Handbook of Japanese Popular Culture*, ed. Richard Gid Powers and Hidetoshi Kato, 229–30 (New York: Greenwood Press, 1989).

5. There are significant exceptions to this pattern; Miuchi herself wrote about Japanese history in *Nihon rettō ichimannen* (1971, A thousand years of the Japanese archipelago), in *Niji no ikusa* (1976, The battle of the rainbow), which rewrites the life of Oda Nobunaga from the perspective of his teenage wife, Nōhime, and in her most recent series, *Amaterasu* (1986–94), devoted to the story of the Sun Goddess, mythical ancestor of the Japanese people.

6. Kinsella, *Adult Manga*, 37.

7. I will be quoting from the translation by Christal Whelan, *The Beginning of Heaven and Earth: The Sacred Book of Japan's Hidden Christians* (Honolulu: University of Hawaii Press, 1996).

8. *24nengumi*, or, as it is sometimes called in English, the 49 group, refers to a group

of female *mangaka* who were all born in or around the year 24 of the Shōwa era (1949 in the Western calendar). The origins of the *24nengumi* are traced to the Ōizumi, the apartment where Hagio Moto and Takemiya Keiko were living and working together, in Ōizumi Nerima-ku, in the years 1970–73. The group was thus from the beginning openly referencing Tezuka Osamu's famous experiment with the Tokiwa-sō, the school where he trained his disciples while also giving them room and board; the *24nengumi* authors' ostensible goal was to reappropriate the production of *shōjo* manga, which was still in their opinion dominated by male authors, while also claiming the right for women to write in different genres, e.g., *shōnen* manga and science fiction. Born in 1951, Shōwa 26, Miuchi belongs to the same generation, but was never associated with the group, which criticized her work as too conventional.

9. The term *dōjinshi* refers to amateur manga, circulated and distributed along informal channels such as the *comiketto* (comic market) conventions. They are generally associated with experimental and avant-garde content and drawing style, and have a close relationship with the world of published manga: many artists begin their career by writing *dōjinshi*, and published authors occasionally draw *dōjinshi*. For a discussion of the evolution of the phenomenon and its implications for the history of manga, see Kinsella, *Adult Manga*, 102–38.

10. One of the most interesting examples is *Dainamaito miruku pai* (1982, Dynamite milk pie), where the protagonist has to undergo special training in girlishness when she is hired by the family of a rich teenager, to whom she bears an uncanny resemblance and who has recently fled from home, to play the part of their daughter in order to defer the scandal for as long as possible. While the training also involves learning everything about the girl's past, her allergies and favorite foods, Miruku also needs to become a proper *"ojōsan,"* who can play the piano, laugh softly, and display the appropriate ladylike behavior. This gives Miuchi a chance to deride standards of femininity while at the same time stressing its performative nature.

11. For a discussion of the Early Christians of Japan, see Carlo Caldarola, *Christianity: The Japanese Way* (Leiden: Brill, 1979); George Elison, *Deus Destroyed: The Image of Christianity in Early Modern Japan* (Cambridge, Mass.: Harvard University Press, 1973); J. F. Moran, *The Japanese and the Jesuits: Alessandro Valignano in Sixteenth-Century Japan* (London: Routledge, 1993); and Mark Mullins, *Christianity Made in Japan: A Study of Indigenous Movements* (Honolulu: University of Hawaii Press, 1998).

12. Whelan, *"The Beginning of Heaven and Earth,"* 45.

13. Ibid., 47.

14. Ibid., 40.

15. Ibid.

16. Ibid., 41.

17. Ibid.

18. In another intriguing anachronism, at this point Ewa and Adan, realizing that their sin has been discovered, kneel down and recite the *Salve Regina*, praying for the intercession of the Virgin Mary!

19. Miuchi Suzue, *Shirayuri no kishi* [The knight of the white lily] (Tokyo: Hakusensha, 1975), 5.

20. While this element is not part of most Joan of Arc legends, it is in fact historically

accurate and refers to the diffusion of cults of Satan in medieval France, although the manga transforms it into a crucial factor in the Hundred Years' War.

21. Rais was charged with kidnapping about one hundred and fifty women and children in order to sacrifice them to Satan, and the history of his life contributed to the formation of the legend of Bluebeard. In Japan, he also appears in Endō Shūsaku's *Scandal* (1986, *Sukyandaru*); he is a minor character in the series *S & M no Sekai* (2002, The world of S&M) by Saitō Chiho and Be-Papas, and appears as a vampire in videogames.

22. For instance, to convince the count of Vaudricourt to give her an army of a thousand men, Jannu makes all the roses in his garden wither and all the cutlery in his kitchens fall to pieces, miraculously restoring them to their previous state once her request is granted. Vaudricourt then watches her leave and comments: "Jannu do Aruku . . . kami no tsukai ka dō ka wakaran ga . . . maru de washi made mahō ni kakerarete shimatta yō da . . . nani ka ano . . . ano shōjo ni wa fushigina chikara ga aru . . ." [Jeanne d'Arc . . . I don't know if you are a helper of God or what, but it looks as though you have bewitched me . . . that girl . . . that girl has a strange power . . .]. Miuchi, *Shirayuri no kishi*, 53.

23. This focus on the ambiguity of Christianity and its relation to Devil worship is at the center of another story, *13gatsu no higeki*, (1973, The tragedy of the thirteenth month). The title references one of the most famous and groundbreaking works by Hagio Moto, *11gatsu no gimunajiumu* (1971, The gymnasium of November). Both explore the theme of life in a foreign boarding school, but in very different ways. Hagio's work, the story of the troubled relationship between Eric and Thoma, two beautiful boys at a German collegium, is generally acknowledged to mark the birth to the genre of *shōnen ai*, or boys' love manga, whose main features will be popularized by Takemiya Keiko's *Kaze to ki no uta* (1976, A song of wind and trees).

Miuchi's comic, on the other hand, involves no romance, homosexual or otherwise. Instead, it focuses once again on Christianity in a horror/fantasy mode. It tells the story of Marii (Mary), a young girl in a fictional European country who enters in mid-semester a religious school called Sei Barajūji (Saint Rose-Cross), founded by Christian Rosenkreutz, the leader of a seventeenth-century secret brotherhood of alchemists and sages that aspired to conquer Europe with the help of the Devil while wars of politics and religion ravaged the continent. The sisters who run the school, too, regularly conduct black masses and summon Lucifer with the ultimate goal of conquering the world, and the story constantly juxtaposes images of nuns and images of devils, magic circles, monsters, and beheaded young girls in sailor suits. At the end of the story, Mary is almost burned at the stake by the sisters, together with a male protagonist who makes a brief appearance, in yet another reversal of the witchcraft/religious fanaticism trope.

24. For a discussion of the tendency to photographic realism in neoconservative adult male manga, see Kinsella, *Adult Manga,* 70–101 and 162–201, particularly 172–78.

Mobilization / Domestication

CHRISTINE MARRAN

● ● ●

Empire through the Eyes of a *Yapoo*: Male Abjection in the Cult Classic *Beast Yapoo*

MALE ABJECTION IN EARLY POSTWAR JAPAN

The celebrated cult classic *Beast Yapoo* (1956–58, *Kachikujin yapū*) by Numa Shōzō and the four-volume manga version created by writer Ishinomori Shōtarō and artist Sugar Satō (1983–84, 1993) prominently feature the abjection of the Japanese male.[1] Based heavily on the novel, the manga series describes the galactic travel of Japanese student Rin'ichirō to a white matriarchal empire in space. In this technologically advanced matriarchy, "yellow men" are considered nonhuman "simian sapiens" and surgically altered to serve specific purposes such as animate toilets, living scooters, and tiny replicas of Japanese cultural heroes who wipe their faces with white women's saliva to win in battle. *Beast Yapoo* portrays a Japanese man who suffers a cultural trauma not so different from Jonathan Swift's Gulliver, whose similarly humiliating ordeals of enslavement on a global imperialist stage result from his subjection to other species and races.

The antiheroic Japanese male has been a central figure for writers and artists in depicting Japan's position in postwar global politics. Kobayashi Yoshinori is one manga artist who has provocatively used the image of the abject Japanese man to critique in nationalist terms a postwar politics in which Japan is the "whipping boy" of America. For example, in his manga *A Theory of War* (1998, *Sensōron*), Kobayashi included a depiction of Japanese government leaders "naked on hands and knees, faces pressed against a mirror into which they panted apologies to a foreign power who was violating them from behind."[2] This image in Kobayashi's work resides alongside caricatures of idealized imperial heroes—kamikaze pilots flying over round suns and snowcapped Fujis. In this satirical juxtaposition, Kobayashi leaves no question that there can be an *unabjected* Japanese sensibility that is not subservient to U.S. power.[3] Another conservative, now Tokyo governor (mayor), Ishihara Shintarō, in a youthful self-portrait drew himself as an abject figure "who had come apart, a head with one skeletal arm attached by hinges and the other limbs akimbo and out of reach. It was as if Ishihara were expressing the disequilibrium he had experienced as a thirteen-year-old when the war ended in 1945 and the world turned on its ear."[4]

> ANTIHERO RIN'ICHIRŌ DOES NOT EMBRACE DEFEAT. RATHER, HE EXPERIENCES A COLLAPSE OF BOUNDARIES IN THIS TRAVEL NARRATIVE IN WHICH A LOST PILGRIM WHO CANNOT RETURN HOME CONFUSEDLY ASSESSES HIS NEW LIMITS.

Ōe Kenzaburō, winner of the Nobel Prize for Literature, pointed to the symbolic castration of the postwar Japanese male that produced ironically "a nation of sexual men, indulging in peace and comfort by being dominated and subordinated to a mighty America." Arguing implicitly for a masochistic vision of the Japanese male, he wrote, "I see difficulties and anxieties burdening the progressive political activists in this nation; an overpowering wall stands against them. In a country of sexual men, political men can be nothing but outsiders, not only powerless but also funny and tragic."[5] In this case Ōe points to a symbolic castration of the Japanese male in wartime who readily submits to that castration in the postwar. Takayuki Tatsumi has argued that sado-masochistic (SM) metaphorics are always lurking within international politics generally and especially within the Japan–U.S. relationship, and that a discourse of "creative masochism" abounds in postwar Japan in which the humiliating experience of defeat is "turned into a techno-utopian principle of construction."[6] He refers to other writers who have similarly described the postwar mentality of defeat as masochistic in terms like "creative defeat" (Tsuru Shigo) and the "strategy of being radically fragile" (Matsuoka Seigo). In writing about *Beast Yapoo,* Takayuki suggests that "Numa's biological degradation of the Japanese foresaw the self-referential, metastructural logic of consumerist masochism, in which the subject consuming new technology enjoys being disciplined, whipped, and finally consumed by technocracy itself."[7] Here Takayuki seems especially to gesture toward a practice of *reading* masochistically.

It is not uncommon to suggest that the male masochistic figure within a text can introduce a disrupting and critical perspective—of patriarchal society, of imperialist history, of dominant gender codes.[8] In postwar Japan, the male who performs submission has often been used to symbolize (for example, in the postwar stories and films about the lover of famous sadistic mistress Abe Sada by Ōshima Nagisa) a romanticized rejection of patriarchal privilege. On the other hand, in the satirical plays of Satō Makoto, the male masochist's humiliating submission is deemed not countercultural but required by fascistic totalitarianism.[9] So what about the protagonist of *Beast Yapoo* (a novel often described as an SM/SF), who is chained, naked, and subservient to his white mistress throughout the story? The novel and manga do reflect the metaphorics of creative masochism that Takayuki suggests, in the sense that they are about the total destruction of Japan and the dispersion and consequent erasure of Japanese culture (into a new, white empire). Further, the great popularity of a novel and manga that depict relentless scenes of mutated Japanese bodies certainly suggests a metastructural logic of *consumerist* masochism.

The *Yapoo* texts, however, do not feature a masochistic psychology but a psychology of abjection. Antihero Rin'ichirō does not embrace defeat. Rather, he experiences a collapse of boundaries in this travel narrative in which a lost pilgrim who cannot return home confusedly assesses his new limits. In other words, the novel and manga suggest a doomed psychic space from which the Japanese male is expected to operate in the postwar. At the same time, the manga and novel prove to be an odd critique of the past Japanese imperial system in that the imperial history of the galactic empire that abjects Rin'ichirō is strikingly similar to his own.

READING *BEAST YAPOO*

The manga *Beast Yapoo* is unusually faithful to the original novel. The novel was first serialized from 1956 in the SM magazine *Strange Club* (*Kitan Kurabu*), which accounts for the common description of it as an SM novel. This essay focuses on the manga version but both the novel and manga begin with a time traveler named Pauline Jansen making a forced landing on Earth from her future into postwar Germany, where she encounters a white woman named Clara and her Japanese fiancé, Rin'ichirō. As the novel progresses, Germany and Japan are shown to have divergent postwar trajectories. Pauline is from the Empire of a Hundred Suns (EHS)—a galactic empire that considers "yellow men" as beasts. She is disgusted to see Clara treat Rin'ichirō as a human. Pauline decides to take Clara and Rin'ichirō to EHS in order to transform Rin'ichirō into a *yapoo*—a personal domestic slave who would serve white woman Clara's every need. Stunned by a bite from Pauline's man-dog, Rin'ichirō is unable to resist his abduction to EHS. He is taken centuries into the future, around the year 4000, where he has no bearings. Unable to speak the language of EHS, he is reliant upon his Germanic betrothed who strangely can communicate with other EHS women over space and time. Rin'ichirō is in exile in this nostalgic complaint in which the loss of an imperial masculine sensibility is articulated through endless scenes of abjection showing the Japanese man as unable to find his place in the new galactic-political history.[10]

How the Japanese man comes to be enslaved beast in the EHS is explained in detail in the second volume of the manga. Subtitled "Japan's Nightmare History" (*Akumu no Nihonshi*), the volume's early chapters describe the global warfare that turned the thriving nation into a breeding ground for primitives at the turn of the twentieth-century. This historical tale of Japan's destruction begins with the simple detail that Japan had "put its fate" in the hands of the American military. When the United States chose to attack communist-bloc countries in the postwar, along with the Central and South Americas and the Middle East, Japan too suffered tremendous radiation sickness along with most other "yellow peoples" (*ōshoku jinshu*).[11] America suffered Soviet germ warfare that disabled and killed 99 percent of its white population, while those who were "pure-blood blacks" (*junketsu kokujin*) survived and even thrived. In Japan, the birth rate somehow increased, but 60 percent were "born dim-witted and with birth defects."[12] Asia dried up from the radiation, and so healthy Japanese in their twenties and thirties sought to emigrate. (At this point in the story, Japanese become stand-ins for all Asians throughout the text, which uncritically eliminates other Asian national identities).[13] The Japanese workers were allowed into Brazil but only with blue collar work permits. Those remaining in Japan were unable to run their government, and an ineffective police force led to the strong prevailing over the weak. Children didn't take care of their parents and many people died of hunger, were killed for food, committed suicide, went insane, or died of plagues. The chapter concludes, "'Japan' perished."[14]

A few decades later in this detailed minihistory of the decline of the Japanese empire, the remaining people in Japan are discovered by a galactic "General Mac," who returns to the Earth in 2067 after building the space colony "Terra Nova." In order to save the remaining white people on the polluted globe, he builds a space ship that can carry the remaining whites to the colony. Blacks are abducted to be slaves, with the the remaining blacks on Earth killed with lasers. Upon discovering people living in caves on the Japanese archipelago, "Colonel Rosenberg" determines that they are not human but animals, in order to make it easier for the colony to use them in experiments and labor without the need to take responsibility for their lives or deaths. If they were "apes," he argued, there would be no reason to recognize their rights as humans. "General Mac" accepts this "policy," as it made it easier for whites to assert their power. It is decided that Japan will become a breeding ground for these "apes"—a "monkey island." They are referred to as *simian sapiens*—a likely reference to the sorts of names Americans used in propaganda wars against the Japanese during World War II. Historian John Dower has documented at length the common use of "monkey" and "simian" in wartime efforts to frame Japanese as nonhuman or subhuman, to humiliate but also to make killing Japanese justifiable:

> Among the Allied war leaders, Admiral Halsey was the most notorious for making outrageous and virulently racist remarks about the Japanese enemy in public . . . Simian metaphors described the Japanese as "stupid animals" and referred to them as "monkeymen." During the war he spoke of the "yellow monkeys," and in one outburst declared that he was "rarin' to go" on a new naval operation "to get some more Monkey meat."[15]

The metaphor of the simian was common in wartime in Britain and American media: "*Collier's* featured several full-color covers by the British artist Lawson Wood portraying Japanese airmen as apes, and *Time* ran a cover portrait pertaining to the Dutch East Indies in which a Japanese apeman dangled from a tree in the background."[16] These are only a few examples of the simian epithets cast at the Japanese. In Numa's story, white militaries have gone a step further. A third of the people in the camps created by "Mac" are to be allowed to return to Japan to be raised as a supply of animals upon which the Empire can perpetually draw. They will be given the impression that they are under control of their own destiny, but in reality the country would be a *protectorate* called "Jaban" (combining "yaban" meaning "primitive" and Japan).

This history of the destruction of Japan invokes the American-induced radiation sickness, Cold War struggles, and advanced military technologies that negatively impacted Asian nations during and after World War II. The idea that Japanese have no right to their own destiny and must become a protectorate of Western powers led by General Mac recalls occupied Japan. Japanese bodies are considered contaminated, mutant, defective; and while Britain and the United States are named as those that used nuclear weapons, it is noted that Japan went along with these two global powers, thereby showing Japan to have participated in its own demise. The EHS is hierarchical and that hierarchy is based on nineteenth-century evolutionary notions of race and power. In the empire, black slaves do the intellectual labor, while scientifically altered "yellow people" provide sexual pleasure and entertainment, as well as do household chores. The empire requires this kind of hierarchical treatment of individuals to maintain control, extend its base, and generally conduct the work of the empire. So far are the *yapoo* at the bottom rung of the social (and evolutionary) ladder that their white mistresses do not even recognize them as part of the human race as initially articulated by the policy set by "Rosenberg." EHS scientists have, in nineteenth-century fashion, *proven* scientifically that these so-called *simian sapiens* are inferior to the human race. Since they are considered animals, the white women have no qualms about physically altering the *yapoo* to use for human purposes.[17] In this sense, Numa creates a dystopic universe in which Japan is completely destroyed and the Japanese reduced to "apes" in the eyes of the West. It is a depraved world that is the source of profound confusion and pain for the new arrival, Rin'ichirō.

THEORIZING ABJECTION

The protagonist of *Beast Yapoo*, Rin'ichirō, is captured, surrounded, and eventually defined by another culture. He is manipulated and then carried off to become chattel for an Aryan matriarchy. Once abducted to EHS, he is made into a perversion of himself and a projection of the Other. The projection by the other of him as beastly is successful enough that he grows to have an ambiguous, decreasingly solidified sense of self. He becomes an *abjected* figure in Julia Kristeva's sense that the abject confronts us "with those fragile states where man strays on the territories of animal,"[18] unable to remain within the boundaries created as pure and clean and undefiled. In *Beast Yapoo*, the Japanese man becomes an irrational subject who fails systematically to produce a pure "I" that does *not* reside in the "Other" by virtue of a slow loss of a sense of being a unique self from a discrete culture.

The abjected Rin'ichirō cannot understand the religion, morality, or law of the new empire—he wonders why he must follow it—and yet he consistently notes its similarity to his own homeland. The "Law" in EHS is similar to that discussed by Kristeva in reference to Dostoyevsky who, she argues, displays the Law as sexual and moral abjection. In *Beast Yapoo*, the Law is displayed as a world of fathers

> IN *BEAST YAPOO*, THE JAPANESE MAN BECOMES AN IRRATIONAL SUBJECT WHO FAILS SYSTEMATICALLY TO PRODUCE A PURE "I" THAT DOES *NOT* RESIDE IN THE "OTHER" BY VIRTUE OF A SLOW LOSS OF A SENSE OF BEING A UNIQUE SELF FROM A DISCRETE CULTURE.

who are repudiated, bogus, or dead, and of debauched matriarchs who hold sway. The perpetrators of the Law, the imperial matriarchy of EHS, have ferocious fetishes that are marked as *normal* and that are *internal* to the Law. This is the horrific context in which abjected Rin'ichirō finds himself.[19] So, the story is not about Rin'ichirō's embrace of a masochistic position but rather about *transformation*—his confused resistance and reluctant capitulation to a new Law whose history seems uncannily based on his own. Rin'ichirō, with his guts examined by black lab assistants, is throughout the novel and manga in the process of becoming an other within EHS at the expense of his own death, but he is always within that state of *becoming* . . . a monster, a tumor, cancer, a beast.[20] He is no longer the benign, internationally traveling Japanese subject. He, amid his own anguish and cries of regret, first realizes his state of exile when he attempts to grab the shoulders of Clara to convince her to return home with him. His reaching out to her is greeted with alarm. Other EHS women gather round to see if she is alright, to see whether she has been defiled by the bestial *yapoo* who would touch her without permission.

Kristeva also describes the abject self as one who jettisons phenomena that both threaten and create the self's borders: "I expel myself, I spit myself out, I abject myself within the same motion through which 'I' claim to establish myself."[21] Rin'ichirō is disgusted by the other *yapoo* he sees. They disgust him for their self-abasement. They become symbolic of his own future psychic and spiritual death, or the "corpse" in Kristeva that is the abject reminder that we will cease to be and whose presence violates one's own border. Just as the corpse is an "infection" into one's being, the other *yapoo* infect Rin'ichirō's psychic life. Their abjection is a mirror of his impending fate. They remain on the periphery of his conscious as his imminent future. The figure of the defiled Asian at the hands of the imperial Japanese has encroached upon the Japanese man in the postwar, post-imperial landscape of the occupation. Wartime experiments, science, and imperial law collapse into a visual reminder of vivisection now perpetrated on a *yapoo* in EHS. This image of abjection must be repudiated but it haunts.

The psychological experience of Rin'ichirō revolves around his sense of being part of a country familiar yet distant.[22] This *yapoo* is reformed physically and mentally to suit the interests of the EHS. According to its history, one of the three great inventions of the EHS was the invention of telepathy such that the *yapoo* would always know his mistress's desires. This created an extreme permeability of the body and mind. The *yapoo* is given a shot of the body fluid of its master and then through a "telehormone" can understand the mistress's thoughts. And in keeping with another aspect of abjection, lives are not sustained by desire but by exclusion. In the case of the telepathic *yapoo,* he is excluded except as a telepathic medium of white female *desires.* In Rin'ichirō's confused wish to return home and to pleasure Clara, whose desires have started to become his own, the boundary of the external and internal has become unclear. In this science fiction manga, Rin'ichirō is a creature that does not know what it wants, or vaguely knows what it wants but cannot repudiate others' desires.

Beast Yapoo, like so many postwar works, addresses loss. But how to interpret the endless scenes of sadism in which imperial loss is embraced in all its unbearableness? How should we understand this psychology of (male) abjection? Murakami Takashi has argued that the infantilized male in the postwar, in body and image—the "little boys"—are a product of U.S. paternalism; an unsurprising product of the infantilization of Japan after the war with its forced removal of a military army and so on. But Murakami's "little boys" are still intriguing, motorbike-riding, counterculture heroes. Rin'ichirō is no longer able to articulate a distinct coherent self, invoking an aspect of mourning and loss that such a figure in postimperial Japan inevitably produces. From this perspective, the man undergoing a sense of loss and abjection is not yet the countercultural masochist who "acts out in an insistent and exaggerated way the basic conditions of cultural subjectivity, conditions that are normally disavowed . . . [or] loudly proclaims that his meaning comes to him from the Other, prostrates himself before the gaze even as he solicits it, exhibits his castration for all to see, and revels in the sacrificial basis of the social contract . . . [and] radiates a negativity inimical to the social order."[23] Rin'ichirō barely tolerates his abjected state; Numa shows it inescapable. This is a lament of the loss of the imperial blood relation and not a performative, masochistic embrace of a weakened position. The Japanese male is submissive, but his original parent has been replaced by an imposter. He tolerates abjection, but under a sovereign mistress.

THE ROLE OF MYTHOLOGY AND LANGUAGE IN
BEAST YAPOO'S DESCRIPTION OF EMPIRE

In this story of Japan's nationalist, imperialist past and a galactic Aryan future, an abject male becomes a critical presence for playing out the logical consequences to masculine subjectivity of the new geopolitical position in which he finds himself. The novel and manga are about place and displacement.[24] The context in which the novel was first serialized was one in which Japan had experienced a collapse of imperial paternal laws and even a welcoming of democratic ones, but an ambivalence still existed regarding the casting out of imperial nationalism. Some scholars feared a return to imperial totalitarianism: Ishimoda Shō, in the postwar, argued for "national emancipation and the struggle against imperialism" to break the spell of the system under which his citizens were held. He specifically wrote about the primary mythical texts that had been celebrated as those founding the Japanese empire, the *Kojiki* (680, Record of ancient matters) and *Nihonshoki* (720, Chronicles of Japan).[25] Such discussions were part of what was called the "Heroic Age Debate" of the 1950s, which sought to reinterpret the imperial system through analysis of these "founding" texts. Both the novel and manga *Beast Yapoo* are saturated with references to the *Kojiki* and *Nihonshoki,* suggesting the important role they have played in articulating arguments for and against imperialism in Japan. In other words, Numa critiques Western imperialism and its racism in *Beast Yapoo,* but his empire is strikingly similar to the Japanese empire, which suggests a critique of Japanese imperialism as a similarly unfair, abusive hierarchy. The very name of the galactic empire, Empire of a Hundred Suns, throws a twist into what might otherwise be a straightforward critique of white colonialist empire building. Since the foundational myths of this sadistic matriarchy that abjects, scapegoats, and dominates Rin'ichirō are so strikingly similar to imperial Japan's own, the heroism of Japan's imperial history is undermined in this highly ideological story.

Myths of progeny and etymological tracings of language in the style of Motoori Norinaga are important to asserting the EHS imperial power structure. Naming represents the will to grasp and own the world. In empire building, the essence and hierarchal position of the object is determined by the name bestowed on the object, and this point is a core feature of the novel, replicated in the manga. Numa created for EHS an entire vocabulary consisting of *kanji* or *katakana* glossed with English or German as a way of emphasizing the importance of naming in EHS—the inevitable link between naming, origins, or words and imperial lineage—i.e. the placement of bodies physically and hierarchically. The language of *Beast Yapoo* is regularly doubled with a Japanese word glossed with a foreign reading. The imperial community is etymologically grounded in Japanese and a western language. Further, through detailed references to the *Kojiki* and *Nihonshoki* and the academic essays of *kokugaku* scholar and founder of national language studies Motoori Norinaga, Numa rewrites Japan's origin myths in a new galactic space to expose the close relationship between empire building and language use. Lengthy etymological descriptions of the EHS vocabulary for objects and the founding myths of the empire parody the style of Motoori's *Kojikiden* (1764–98, Treatise on the *Kojiki*). For example, in the novel, a philological explication of the term *oshink*—the name for the creature who absorbs through his mouth the urine of the mistresses of EHS—extends for pages and quotes various seemingly real sources in delineating the history of the word, its current meaning, and its current usage. As with Motoori's *Kojikiden,* historical fact is created from archaic word.

The complicated lexicon and processes of naming in the novel and manga reflect naming practices as portrayed in the *Kojiki* and *Nihonshoki* themselves. According to Isomae Jun'ichi, these texts relate how, during the solidification of an imperial lineage, the conquered were given a special name by the emperor, which became an index of identity that revealed one's position and duties within the sovereign order. Everything within Japan's national territory— both nature and people—was named by the emperor and placed within his order, and through this process subjects saw themselves differently:

> Conquest takes place in the contact between two epistemological systems and involves political conflict as well as discord at the level of worldviews. The position that one gives to things is negated by a different epistemological system, such that a reversal takes place in which one's own status as seer is changed by the other into that of the seen. As a result, the conqueror expands his own epistemological system by appropriating the other, whereas the conquered undergoes a repositioning from seer to seen. In this sense, myth or historical narrative must be described as a conceptual act of violence.[26]

Numa shows eloquently the way in which language and naming consolidates the sense of national bond and fraternity and how the idea of racial homogeneity is used to perpetuate a sense of national belonging. Rin'ichirō's nostalgic desire to be part of such a bonded culture is revealed most when he recalls how the myths of EHS were once part of his own. The novel illustrates how the language of imperial myth weaves an illusion of natural belonging, which enables imperialist interventions. At the same time, the use of both Japanese and German or English words creates an odd double-layered history of imperial authority. The history of the protectorate "Jaban" works its way into the language of the colonizers, but the Japanese language is not associated with power. The unproblematized relationship of language to national history in *kokugaku* studies, which attempts to "recover and regenerate" origins to produce a national consciousness, is mimicked when the narrative of the history of EHS contains a footnote that cites Motoori's interpretation of the term *muchi* in the *Kojiki* as a "misinterpretation." In the satirical, darkly comic novel and manga, Numa's complex etymologies suggest that the spell of empire is deeply grounded in the myth of an original and unique language.

So, in a parody of Motoori, who constructed with painstaking detail an ethnic and nationalist history for early modern Japan, Numa creates a complicated ancient history for EHS out of the fabric of Japan's imperial myths. And in this new order created through language and mythmaking the Japanese man has no name. Rin'ichirō is lost because he finds that his country's history has been rewritten in such compelling fashion that he must consider the notion that the historiographic narrative of imperial lineage in his beloved "Kiki" (for *Kojiki* and *Nihonshoki*) may have been wrong. For example, the most beautiful woman in EHS history is explorer Anna Terasu who, in traveling to old Japan to look for her abducted little sister, was worshipped by the Japanese as "Amaterasu Oomikami." In catching a glimpse of her, Rin'ichirō is amazed to find how much she looks like the people from that era as they are described in the *Kojiki,* and he cannot but help think that it is their version that is true:[27]

> He would have been happy to believe these things to be an illusion, a dream
> . . . At the root of the pride of his people was the love for the gods of the
> beautiful lore about how they had given birth to a single imperial line of emperors. He had not forgotten to take the *Kojiki, Nihonshoki,* and *Manyōshū*
> with him on his trip to study in a foreign country. But in learning the truth
> [*shinsō*] of the Japan myth, he knew that the last thing he had pride in and
> that supported his very personality was in danger of crumbling.[28]

Rin'ichirō, who comes to believe that the ancient Japanese had seen women's dress from EHS and copied it, is without self and nation.[29] Primal narcissistic identification with the imperial paternal Japan cannot take place. To rephrase Kristeva, an unshakable adherence to Law is necessary if that perverse interspace of abjection is to be hemmed in and thrust aside, and Rin'ichirō can no longer do this.

The manga (and novel) in this way writes an interference or denial of narcissistic fullness or identification with the religious nation of Japan. Rin'ichirō is abjected by the same kind of imperial nationalist structure he nostalgically wants to return to. He becomes ambivalent. The abject male figure of the *yapoo* embodies a cultural trauma similar to Gulliver's as described by John Kucich, who argues that Gulliver's "ordeals of enslavement and humiliation culminate in his subjection to an unquestionably superior race. This subjection compels Gulliver to disavow the sense of legitimacy he had once vested in his nation and in himself, making melancholic abjection, in his case, a vehicle for social transformation."[30] The title of Numa's book is reminiscent of the term "yahoo" from Jonathan Swift's *Gulliver's Travels*. Yahoos are savage, filthy creatures who possess unpleasant habits but resemble human beings. Just as Swift's yahoos appear barbaric and unclean to Lemuel Gulliver, Numa's *yapoo* appear barbaric and unclean to EHS women, until the former are transformed into useful instruments for work, pleasure, and entertainment. *Gulliver's Travels* fully explores the limits of English economic power and morality; and one of Swift's primary contributions was to turn on its head the facile dichotomy in which Europe embodied enlightenment, progress, technological advancement, and ethics, whereas Asia the barbaric and the crude with regard to technology and ethics. Robert Markley argues, "In their combination of fantasy and realism, Gulliver's encounters with the Japanese register profound anxieties about the limitations of English economic power, national identity, and morality in a world that until 1800 was dominated economically by the empires of South Asia and the Far East."[31] Swift's decision to send Gulliver to Japan itself represents an inversion of Eurocentric discourses of colonialism, imperialism, and barbarism. Japan is used to critique the English empire of the eighteenth century and its orientalist ways. Numa's imagined hierarchy similarly satirizes imperialist values through an abjected figure. In developing accelerated technology, Japanese men are surgically altered; in the pursuit of heroism, tiny replicas of Japanese cultural heroes commit seppuku in dioramic boxes while white women look on; high art is listening to an orchestra of tiny yellow men wildly drawing to and fro their violin bows while Aryan women roll around in onanistic pleasure on live couches in this Empire of a Hundred Suns.

Rin'ichirō's psychological transformation into a *yapoo* is a gradual process that shifts to a masochistic sensibility only in the last pages of the story. This newly emergent psychology is framed in geopolitical and racial terms in the manga when Rin'ichirō recalls a story his father told him about being humiliated by an American soldier and his *"pan pan"* escort. Rin'ichirō has now come to believe that the *pan pan* prostitute was right to say that all Japanese men are useless [*darashinai*].[32] The same night that Rin'ichirō recalls his father lying beaten and humiliated on the ground after being pummeled by an American soldier, his mistress Clara gives him the freedom to return to

> IN FINALLY ACCEPTING HIS "PROTECTORATE STATUS," RIN'ICHIRŌ FULLY TRANSITIONS TO BEING A *YAPOO.*

Japan. Rin'ichirō refuses her offer, choosing to remain her *yapoo*, a dog-slave at her feet. He desperately wants to explain to her that he can't go home because he has fully assimilated the EHS's discriminatory view of the Japanese as ugly in body and spirit. When Clara suggests that he be brainwashed before he goes back so that he won't remember all he has seen, Rin'ichirō replies that he can't live without her, so Clara (wondering if he isn't "genetically suited to this humble position") declares to baptize him anew: "You will be like the country that has unconditionally surrendered and will not desert the occupying military," to which Rin'ichirō replies, "Yes, I am not an independent country but your protectorate." Clara continues: "You want to be my pet right? And so you don't care how you are treated, right?" Rin'ichirō replies: "Yes! Absolutely!"[33] In these final pages, Rin'ichirō no longer feels an abject sense of loss, anger, or frustration. Rather, he revels in his passionate sense of devotion.[34] In finally accepting his "protectorate status," Rin'ichirō fully transitions to being a *yapoo*. No longer an ambiguous self, he embraces this new humiliated position. The conclusions to both the novel and manga may reject Rin'ichirō's earlier sense of homelessness that he retained for most of the story, but it is the stark suddenness of this transformation in the final pages that makes it somehow strained. Nevertheless, Numa concludes with a masochistic man who rejects any troubled self-identity and sees himself through Western imperialist eyes as—a *yapoo*.

Kristeva treats the psychic life of the individual prior to his subjection to the symbolic order as the space where abjection occurs. But abjection facilitates the defining of broader imaginaries, especially imperialist imaginaries. Curiously, Kristeva's examples of the connections between the abject and society-building focus on primitive societies, such as the following: "The abject confronts us, on the one hand, with those fragile states where man strays on the territory of animal. Thus, by way of abjection, primitive societies have marked out a precise area of their culture in order to remove it from the threatening world of animals or animalism."[35] But it is not just the primitive that incorporates abjection; we might suggestively look to the case of French imperialism in the postwar to suggest that Kristeva has unwittingly responded with her theory of abjection to the collapse of an imperial society closer to her in time and space. The cult classic *Beast Yapoo,* and especially the manga created not long after Kristeva's *Powers of Horror,* uncannily insists that empire operates through the logic of abjection and the logic of abjection through empire.

....

Notes

1. The manga volumes based on the novel by Numa Shōzō used for this paper, scripted by Ishinomori Shōtarō and illustrated by Satō Sugar, are *Kachikujin yapū: Uchū teikoku e no shōtai* (Beast yapoo: Invitation to a galactic empire) (Tokyo: Tatsumi Shuppan, 1983; *(Zoku) Kachikujin yapū: Akumu no Nihonshi hen* (Beast yapoo continued: The nightmare history of Japan) (Tokyo: Tatsumi Shuppan, 1984); and *Kachikujin yapū: Mujōken kōfuku hen* (Beast yapoo: Unconditional surrender) (Tokyo: Tatsumi Shuppan, 1993). All translations from these texts are by the author. There are no published English translations available for these texts.

2. John Nathan, *Japan Unbound* (New York: Houghton Mifflin, 2004), 129.

3. Ibid., 151. Nathan also writes that in a related case, in a heated public debate about the depiction of the Nanking Massacre, "the Sankei media group" led a media campaign deploring textbook histories that were "anti-Japanese" or "masochistic" histories.

4. Ibid., 173.

5. Ōe Kenzaburō, "Warera no sei no sekai" (Our world of sex) in *Shuppatsuten* (Starting point) (Tokyo: Iwanami Shoten, 1980), 145; quoted in Yumiko Iida, *Rethinking Identity in Modern Japan: Nationalism as Aesthetics* (New York: Routledge, 2001), 131.

6. Takayuki Tatsumi, *Full Metal Apache: Transactions between Cyberpunk Japan and Avant-Pop* (Durham, N.C.: Duke University Press, 2006), 168.

7. Ibid., 57.

8. See Kaja Silverman, *Male Subjectivity at the Margins* (New York: Routledge, 1992), and Gilles Deleuze, *Masochism: Coldness and Cruelty and Venus in Furs* (Cambridge, Mass.: Zone Books, 1991), among others.

9. See chapter 5 of Christine Marran, *Poison Woman: Figuring Female Transgression in Modern Japanese Culture* (Minneapolis: University of Minnesota Press, 2007).

10. It is possible to read *Beast Yapoo* as an inversion of Mori Ōgai's short story "Dancing Girl" (1890), in which Toyotarō, a Japanese student in Germany, abandons a German dancing girl, Elise, to become a Japanese state bureaucrat. Just as Elise cannot believe her abandonment and suffers a lifelong state of shock and distress, Rin'ichirō similarly agonizes over his abandonment by a German woman who puts affairs of state and pleasure before his welfare.

11. Numa, Ishinomori, and Satō, *(Zoku) Kachikujin yapū: Akumu no Nihonshi hen,* 23.

12. Ibid., 30.

13. Japanese women are also relatively absent in *Beast Yapoo* texts. *(Zoku) Kachikujin*

yapū: Akumu no Nihonshi hen shows how especially "caucasian-looking" Japanese women function as borrowed wombs. They are raised in "Jaban" and then chosen to live at the "nunnery" on EHS. It is there they first learn about EHS and that blacks have become slaves and other Japanese have been reduced to being "yapoo." However, once they are told that they enjoy special privileges, "they feel a certain amount of pride," according to the text.

14. Ibid., 31.

15. John Dower, *War without Mercy: Race and Power in the Pacific War* (New York: Pantheon Books, 1986), 85.

16. Ibid., 87.

17. The manga suggests here the way that our current society for the most part has no qualms about submitting animals to vivisection and other physically and mentally destructive treatment.

18. Julia Kristeva, *Powers of Horror: An Essay on Abjection,* trans. Leon Roudiez (New York: Columbia University Press, 1982), 12.

19. Ibid., 20.

20. Ibid., 5.

21. Ibid., 3.

22. Kristeva writes that abjection is what disturbs identity, system, order, and what "dissembles," and what does not respect borders, positions, rules. It is the "in-between," the "ambiguous," and the "composite."

23. Kaja Silverman, *Male Subjectivity at the Margins,* 52.

24. Kristeva has argued, the abject is an exile who asks "Where am I?" instead of "Who am I?" "A deviser of territories, languages, works, the dejected never stops demarcating his universe whose fluid confines . . . constantly question his solidity and impel him to start afresh . . . The abject 'is simply a frontier' and 'sublime alienation'" (*Powers of Horror,* 8).

25. Isomae, Jun'ichi, "The Space of Historical Discourse: Ishimoda Shō's Theory of the Heroic Age," trans Richard Calichman, *positions* 10, no. 3 (Winter 2002): 631–68.

26. Ibid., 660.

27. Numa, Ishinomori, and Satō, *(Zoku) Kachikujin yapū: Akumu no Nihonshi hen,* 53.

28. Ibid., 61.

29. Ibid., 68.

30. John Kucich, *Imperial Masochism: British Fiction, Fantasy, and Social Class* (Princeton, N.J.: Princeton University Press, 2006), 4.

31. Robert Markley, "Gulliver and the Japanese: The Limit of the Postcolonial Past," *Modern Language Quarterly* 65, no. 3 (September 2004), 458–59.

32. Numa, Ishinomori, and Satō, *Kachikujin yapū: Mujōken kōfuku hen,* 121.

33. Ibid., 226.

34. Kristeva in *Powers of Horror* writes: "The abjection of self would be the culminating form of that experience of the subject to which it is revealed that all its objects are based merely on the inaugural loss that laid the foundations of its own being. There is nothing like the abjection of self to show that all abjection is in fact recognition of the want [the lack] on which any being, meaning, language, or desire is founded" (5).

35. Ibid., 12.

MARCO PELLITTERI

• • •

Nippon ex Machina: Japanese Postwar Identity in Robot Anime and the Case of *UFO Robo Grendizer*

What seems like a radical contradiction—that a Japanese anime with giant robots as alien characters might represent *both* the totalitarian invaders *and* the good old American defenders of freedom and justice—is actually evident in more than one anime series of the 1970s. In this essay I will analyze Japanese postwar identity in the 1970s, especially as it emerged in the context of Japan's complex relationship with the United States, through anime dealing with adventure, technology, and war. I focus on one representative series, *UFO Robo Grendizer,* which features a giant robot who is a defender of humanity and within which we can see a symbol of Japan's relationship to the United States and to other countries.[1] I will not address the formal elements of the anime but only focus on the structural, narrative, and symbolic elements.[2]

I argue that in *Grendizer* the protagonist and his robot are, in the context of Japan's geopolitical position, an allegory of the relationship between Japan and the United States, in that both its American and Japanese characters are united against totalitarian invaders. The presumed political aspect of the Vegans, the enemies of the protagonist, are not specified as either fascist or communist, because the Japanese in the postwar period have repudiated both totalitarianisms. Yet in the graphic style and character

> IN *GRENDIZER* THE PROTAGONIST AND HIS ROBOT ARE, IN THE CONTEXT OF JAPAN'S GEOPOLITICAL POSITION, AN ALLEGORY OF THE RELATIONSHIP BETWEEN JAPAN AND THE UNITED STATES, IN THAT BOTH ITS AMERICAN AND JAPANESE CHARACTERS ARE UNITED AGAINST TOTALITARIAN INVADERS.

illustrations of the evil alien, whose countenance merges both pseudo-fascist/Nazi and quasi-Soviet traits, it is possible to imagine that the reference—surely slight and probably unconscious—is rather to the communists. This is due in part to the political situation in East Asia in the 1970s and to the relationship between Japan and the United States.

Understanding the plot will make it possible to see the relation between the Japanese zeitgeist in the 1970s, the ideas professed by Nagai, the director of the anime, and the Tōei producers in that period. The film focuses primarily on the role of Japan in Asia, which is—and has been—a delicate geopolitical situation. In *UFO Robo Grendizer,* the wisdom of Earth assumes a central value as the only place where it is possible to war against and, this time, defeat a foe whose power is seemingly invincible.

The plot of *UFO Robo Grendizer* acts, in a way, as a third chapter to two previous series by Nagai and Tōei: *Mazinger Z* and *Great Mazinger.* The resulting trilogy has been baptized *Mazinsaga.*[3] The story of *Grendizer* begins with the Vega Nebula's Reign and their critical situation: due to the irresponsible use of atomic energy, the Reign's main planet is going to explode and shortly will become uninhabitable because of the resulting deadly *vegatron* radiation. King Vega, who with his army dedicates his very existence to attacking other planetary systems, has shortly before this occupied a pacifist planet known as the *Reign of the Fleed,* and that planet's survivors are very few.

Among them is the prince, Duke Fleed, who escapes by stealing the mighty Grendizer vehicle, a powerful Vegan weapon improved with Fleedian technology, but not before witnessing the death of his parents and the (provisional) death of his planet as it is contaminated by vegatron. After an interstellar voyage, Duke Fleed finds Earth and lands in Japan, in a green valley not far from Tokyo. Here he is detected by the Institute of Astronomic Researches, directed by Doctor Umon Genzō, who becomes his friend and hides the Grendizer vehicle in the Institute's secret underground hangars. In order to cover up Duke Fleed's identity, Umon gives him the name Daisuke, and presents him as his son. The Vegan fleet, meanwhile, is looking for a world to settle in: since the Reign's destruction, caused by radioactivity, is impending.

The Vegans reach Earth and prepare an attack with their *enbanjū* (monsters-flying saucers) by establishing a secret base on the dark side of the Moon.

Shortly thereafter, young Kabuto Kōji is returning to Japan in a TFO (terrestrial flying object) flying saucer of his own design after one year at NASA, where he has led research on UFOs and their flight technologies. He is going to the Shirakaba (white birch) farm, owned by Makiba Danbei, father of the pretty Hikaru and little Gorō. Umon and his three assistants are waiting for him. Duke Fleed pretends to be a simple guy, a lover of the country life, but Kōji notices something weird about him. Duke Fleed tries to hide his real identity, but Kōji soon discovers it. Later, a strong friendship will link them.

Meanwhile, Vega launches its first attack. Duke Fleed, a pacifist, is obliged to resume his control of Grendizer in order to protect his adoptive homeland. After many fights, Duke Fleed finds out that his sister, Maria Grace, was not dead on Fleed but has also escaped, thanks to a brave old Fleedian who, by taking her to Earth and pretending to be her grandfather, has hidden the horrible truth of her planet from her. But before dying, the old man reveals it to her, and the two Fleedian aristocrats acknowledge their relationship and shared responsiblity.

FIGURE 1. The *UFO Robo Grendizer*'s "good guys." From the left, facing away: Kabuto Kōji; Makiba Goro; his father, Makiba Danbei. From left, facing front: Doctor Umon Genzō; Duke Fleed in his Terrestrial clothes as Umon Daisuke; his sister, Maria Grace Fleed; Danbei's daughter, Makiba Hikari. The Terrestrial characters are all Japanese, but their apparel echoes movies from the West, which was among the reasons the series was acquired by American producer Jim Terry in 1979. *UFO Robo Grendizer,* copyright Nagai Gō / Dynamic Production / Tōei Dōga. Images provided thanks to the help of Francesco Anteri (www.tanadelletigri.info).

From now on Grendizer is no longer assisted by Kōji's flying saucer—wrecked during a fight—but by three powerful vehicles built by the Japanese and driven by Kōji, Hikaru, and Maria Grace. Called "Double Spacer," "Marine Spacer," and "Drill Spacer," these vehicles can hook up to Grendizer for combat in the sky, under the sea, and under the earth. After another long series of conflicts, which clearly reveals the Vegans' perfidy, the war enters its last phase. King Vega and his few last lackeys decide not to surrender to their adversary's strength nor find an agreement with Earth's governments, and instead try to contaminate Earth through a suicide action. Grendizer's team, aided by a spatial superweapon that is assembled by uniting the four heroes' vehicles, counterattacks the Vegan fleet before King Vega's spaceship can reach the atmosphere and destroys it. Earth is safe and Duke Fleed and Maria Grace can go back to Fleed, which is reviving thanks to the progressive disappearance of vegatron and to the efforts of the survivors who, after exile in the space, are coming back to their homeland.

THE VILLAIN AS TOTALITARIAN INVADER

The most revealing visual aspects about the invaders are to be found in the design of the Vegan objects, which resemble something organic, and a sense of déjà vu provoked by the UFO robots. The images of the evil robots and other characters bring to mind—as does the Grendizer—the *oni*'s iconography in that the structure and decor of the lunar Vegan base resembles vegetable anatomy. The base tower looks like a plant, and the florescences oozing from the main body are locules for "death flowers." The design of the fleet's motherships are reminiscent of those biomorphic shapes seen in the movie *The War of the Worlds*.[4] The rooms are decorated with elements recalling a leaf's cellular apparatus when seen through a microscope, and all objects, even the soldiers' armor, seem like vegetable creatures from 1950s science fiction movies.[5]

> IN *UFO ROBO GRENDIZER* THE COUNTERPOSITION BETWEEN HEROES AND FOES IS MANICHAEAN. THE ENEMY REPRESENTS AN ALMOST ABSOLUTE EVIL.

In *UFO Robo Grendizer,* but also in Nagai's other anime, the key contrast is clear: alien technology's melting, fleshy, and cybernetic forms versus the clean, rational, Japanese technology that is separate from, but implicates, humanity. The "evil science," coming from subjects outside Japan, takes the form of an invader who is deaf to all civil confrontation. However, whereas in other

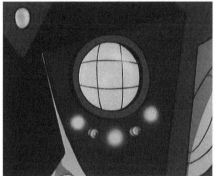

FIGURE 2. Closeup and detail of Zuril's left eye. The bionic eye shows the fusion of flesh and metal, of organic and technologic, with a monstrous rather than harmonious effect. Zuril and *UFO Robo Grendizer*, copyright Nagai Gō / Dynamic Production / Tōei Dōga.

of Nagai's series the aggressors are not really aliens (because they come from underearth or from Japan's past), in the Grendizer's story, the antagonists are actually extraterrestrial. This condition produces a different approach to the problem of the conflict and to the possible interpretations of the enemy.

Vega is a military hierarchy. As a classic cliché of adventure comics and animation—either Japanese or American—in *UFO Robot Grendizer*, the relationships between the evil officers and their soldiers are cool and inhuman. Soldiers are represented as deprived of individuality. The generals' aggressive behavior toward the lower officers and soldiers, and that of King Vega toward his lackeys, reveal the enemies' narrow range of attitudes. The narrative effect for the viewer is a dehumanization of the villains. The aggressors, except in their frightened veneration of King Vega, do not nourish any actual positive feelings for other group members, and their negative emotions are all aimed toward the beings outside their group.

Among the few exceptions to this narrative rule, created by the authors precisely to avoid creating too narrow a portrait of the enemies, are examples of the paternal love of a high officer, Zuril, for his son and that of King Vega himself toward his young daughter, a love that, according to the Vegan military compulsion, is broken by the parents' ideologies.

In *UFO Robo Grendizer* the counterposition between heroes and foes is Manichaean. The enemy represents an almost absolute evil. At work here are two symbolic mechanisms that both European and Japanese audiences recognize at once: the pseudo-Roman salutation and, in the boot snap by high officers Gandal, Zuril, and Blacky, the citation of Nazi/fascist gestures.

The aim is to push the representation of evil beyond the possibility of Japanese indications. The second mechanism is the moral simplification of

FIGURE 3. Gandal performing a sort of Roman salute. Gandal and *UFO Robo Grendizer,* copyright Nagai Gō / Dynamic Production / Tōei Dōga.

the foe, a common tactic used in all war propaganda to reify the adversary. This psychosocial dynamic is used not only in war contexts, but also has been studied in intergroup dialectics/conflicts.[6] That such a means is used in *Grendizer*, however, does not indicate a deliberate intent to dehumanize the enemy with the goal of absolving the protagonists' actions. In Nagai's series, the individuation of a foe sets in play a series of events that results in the suggestion that the robot exists as a toy.

But we can perceive in this narrative architecture the shadow of three other significations. The first concerns the remembrance, historically still unresolved, of Japan's violent imperialist past. In many anime, it is "exorcized" through assigning to Japan the role of the victim of bloody aggression: by turning upside down the roles of the invader/invaded, there is a sort of symbolic absolution, even if just in the TV fiction.[7] The second signification lies in the metaphorical figure of the invader who attacks the Japanese soil with mysterious weapons, but in this anime, Japan can now react, for it too has technologically sophisticated weaponry. The third signification is perhaps the most interesting, for it might explain some unresolved issues concerning the political position of postwar Japan.

SYMBOLIC BALANCES BETWEEN INVADED AND INVADERS: EARTH–FLEED COOPERATION AS A METAPHOR OF THE JAPAN–UNITED STATES AXIS

Duke Fleed and his sophisticated robot, as foreigners wielding more advanced science and bigger firepower, are an allegory of the United States in an imprecise future—or in an alternative present—succeeding in the democratization of Japan, in the real world, by the real Americans. In *UFO Robo Grendizer*, the menace is not the U.S. military apparatus, exorcized as foe and transformed into ally through the cultural reform put in action during the occupation right after the 1945 armistice; instead, the menace is quite different, and the enemy must be sought elsewhere.

As in other fictions where a small taskforce of heroes must resist a massive alien invader, *Grendizer*, too, tells of a small group banded together to fight against a formally hierarchized and numerically larger group. After the initial surprise of the cruel Vegan aggression, the heroes must accept as ineluctable the fact they have to fight for their very survival and—some epithets against the foes apart—they try to focus on the positive feelings between the members of their own group.

The adult figures who lead the strategy against the enemy in Nagai's robot anime are always biologic and putative fathers. The young people (Duke Fleed, Kōji, Hikaru, and Maria Grace) contrast with Doctor Umon's adult figure. Kōji's irruptive character—deeply involving him in the war—and Duke Fleed's pacifist reluctance to use Grendizer are both in contrast to the Doctor Umon's directives, for whom war is ineluctable but must be managed with prudence. Umon's decisions are presumed wise and never really discussed by the two young pilots. Despite the

> AS IN OTHER FICTIONS WHERE A SMALL TASKFORCE OF HEROES MUST RESIST A MASSIVE ALIEN INVADER, *GRENDIZER,* TOO, TELLS OF A SMALL GROUP BANDED TOGETHER TO FIGHT AGAINST A FORMALLY HIERARCHIZED AND NUMERICALLY LARGER GROUP.

youth movements, which in the real world had had their peak in 1970, this Nagaian anime proposes Japan as a simple, virtuous society still strictly based on a Confucian, or even neo-Confucian, linearity: the sons respect the father and, in general, the parental figure.

UFO Robo Grendizer, like other animated series for children—be they Japanese or not—tends to simplify the setting as mere background for the main story. The war between humans and Vegans is very local: it takes place in

Japan, on Honshu island, which hosts Tokyo, Mount Fuji, and, in the fiction, the farm where Daisuke/Duke Fleed works, and in whose neighborhoods lies Doctor Umon's scientific institute. The Shirakaba farm, close to the institute under which Grendizer is hidden, is a hundred kilometers west of Tokyo, deep in a birch forest, which corresponds, in the real world, with the Yamanashi prefecture, whose landscapes are accurately represented in the anime.[8]

As the Vegans know, in order to conquer Earth, they must first destroy or, better yet, take possession of the mighty Grendizer. Consequently, they focus their efforts to seeking out the place where they presume the robot is hidden. In *UFO Robo Grendizer,* the reason given in the narrative for the absence of a more complex world-system made of other countries and land forces to oppose the invaders is that only Grendizer and the Japanese allies represent a suitable resistance to the extreme scientific advancement of the enemies. A deeper narratological reason, however, is that the series is founded on this spontaneously mixed group of Earthlings and Fleedians who have joined together to passionately fight for their joint survival against a formalized group where relationships are arid and nonemotional.

Theirs is a coherent group sharing a territory that is represented as *heimat* (home-like), resisting an invader who does not recognize the sacrality of the soil under attack. Historically, Honshu is the mythic Yamato nucleus, where it is thought the imperial dynasty was founded in the third century CE. The repeated representation of the same places in each episode projects the audience into landscapes that become a familiar "home." For spectators in general, but more so for Japanese, this imagined home where the heroes live assumes a tremendous sacral value precisely due to the repeated visual symbols and, above all, to those symbols directly linked to the Yamato myth from a naturalistic point of view: the red sun at dawn or at sunset, portrayed on an agrestic landscape typical of Japan.

Finally, a note on the protagonists' presumed ethic superiority: in anime such as *Grendizer,* the pacifist ethics of the heroes are not a way to indicate their intrinsic superiority to their foes. Of course, the affirmation of Japanese nationalist purposes and imperialist actions during the colonial period, as well as a Nippon-centric philosophy of history, reveal a strong solidification of a national identity: the presumed status of Japan's superiority in comparison to the Western civilizations and to the other Asian nations.[9] Instead, in the conflicts in *UFO Robot Grendizer* and other seventies robot/SF anime, the distinction between heroes and villains is not on an ontological level; the anime stresses, rather, how the protagonists act rationally and choose between good and evil.

JAPAN, THE UNITED STATES, AND THE POSTWAR GEOPOLITICAL SCENARIO

In 1970s Japan, the postwar period was over, and the first energy crisis (1973) had shown the definite end of the industrial era and the beginning of the postindustrial one (and of postmodernity).[10] Japan was managing a complex relationship with the United States and, at the same time, managing difficult stances toward other Asian countries.

In order to better understand how Japan, war, and the geopolitical situation of the country were seen by Nagai Gō and the series' producers in the mid-seventies, we have to remember that *UFO Robo Grendizer* is the third chapter of a trilogy begun with the *Mazinger Z* and *Great Mazinger* TV shows. In the first two series the monstrous fusion of the animality and the artificiality of the invaders represents the degenerative use of technology in the West. This is especially true in contrast to the historically proposed equilibrium of the Japanese spirit with the Western science—hence, the motto *wakon yōsai*.[11] And in *UFO Robo Grendizer,* the parade of symbols is even more explicit: both the foes and the hero are aliens and fight on Japanese ground. Japan would be immobilized, as it occurred in real history, by a far superior power if once again the equilibrating system did not enter the game: even if Grendizer and its pilot are alien and technically superior to Japanese science as represented by Doctor Umon and his institute, they will be able to ensure survival to the new homeland only if guided by a moral and spiritual order rather than a military strategy.

William Gibson remarked that after the fast technologization ordered by the government in the second half of nineteenth century and the first part of the twentieth, and after the imperialist megalomania at the end of the Pacific War, Japanese found themselves in front of

> an enemy wielding a technology that might . . . have come *from a distant galaxy.* And then that enemy, their conquerors, the Americans, turned up in person, smilingly intent on an astonishingly ambitious program of *cultural re-engineering.* . . . And then [they] left, their grand project hanging fire, and went off to fight Communism instead. [Emphasis added][12]

In the first two series of this trilogy, the enemies are born from Western mythology. In the first series, they come from the ancient civilization of the Greek island Bardos (Rhodes in the Italian version of the anime) and in the second, from the mythic Mycenae. It would seem, then, that Japan fights against an allegory of the West. The first two chapters of the *Mazinsaga* imply a Japan assaulted by the vestiges of a glorious cultural tradition that is, at first, superior, but that is finally overcome in the series by an elementary and rude form of patriotism.

The once-glorious Western civilization has decayed in comparison to its ancient splendor, by generating, in its turn, such horrors as mutated and hybrid monsters. It is only thanks to the specific capabilities of the Japanese spirit that first Mazinger Z and then Great Mazinger defeat their monstrous enemies from the West's past. An auto-orientalist discourse seems to answer the Western one: according to it, Japanese knowledge merges with knowledge from cultural elsewheres (*yūgō*), and unites its autochtone spiritual values to European-American science (*wakon yōsai*).

Whereas *Great Mazinger* sounds an alarm to Japan as a victim of an identity crisis partially formed by the growing distance from America; in *UFO Robo Grendizer*, this crisis seems to be resolved. Japan becomes an Asian leader and a global superpower and is finally freed from its old sense of inferiority.[13]

CONCLUSIONS: JAPANESE UNEASINESS FOR THE TOTALITARIAN ENCLOSURE

In *UFO Robo Grendizer,* through a metaphor of totalitarianisms, it is possible to see an elementary version of the presumed philosophy of history in contemporary Japan. Presented are two alien "factions," Vegans and Fleedians, between which there is Japan, an ally of Fleed. If the Grendizer, as Earth's friend, is a metaphor of the United States in a period of distension—in that, since the 1945 armistice, the United States has played the role of unconditional protector and ally for Japan—one might wonder who the Vegans represent.

The answer is anticipated by the final sentence in Gibson's quotation. Gibson noted that the United States, after having dramatically contributed to Japan's democratic modernization after World War II, in 1952 quickly abandoned the occupation because they were committed on other fronts. Specifically, they were concerned with Cold War containment strategies against the expansion of the Communist bloc. During Japan's occupation, and even more so in following years, Japan found itself in territorial proximity with countries that had embraced Communism in a total—and totalitarian—way: the Chinese Popular Republic of Mao's Cultural Revolution and other countries of the Asian philo-Soviet bloc such as North Korea and Vietnam. For a long time, Japan perceived itself as surrounded by nations that were living political experiences full of deep transformation and disorder. Therefore Japan began again to nourish the sensation of being a political *unicum* in Eastern Asia, closer to the West than to the continent closest to its soil.[14]

The result was that the national political culture—which for internal reasons had always been based on those values that later would merge with a more modern center-right ideology—since the war had mostly oscillated between an enlightened liberalism and an American-style neoconservatism. It is not the case that the political power has been concentrated mostly in the moderate coalitions: the Liberal, Democratic, and Liberal-Democratic parties. The left-wing parties, very often bothered by internal dissent, have reached the electorate's trust only occasionally.

> JAPAN PERCEIVED ITSELF AS SURROUNDED BY NATIONS THAT WERE LIVING POLITICAL EXPERIENCES FULL OF DEEP TRANSFORMATION AND DISORDER.

In his classic historical study, Edwin Reischauer describes the four basic psychological and intellectual factors of postwar Japan. The first was the loss of self-confidence caused by the defeat, the demilitarization, and the occupation itself.[15] Nationalism and patriotism became awkward values, due to the negative effects that professing them for decades had caused. The economy and culture became more international—especially for younger generations. The Japanese attitude has been typified as a lack of self-belief and with an unconscious snobbishness toward the rest of Asia. Japan, since the great scientific and industrial outcomes at the end of the nineteenth century, has tended to compare itself only to the Western powers.[16]

The second tendency was a strong pacifism as a reaction to the war's disaster. In Japan, it was clear that the militarists had been wrong and that the country would need to absolutely avoid entering other wars; the general feeling was radically opposed to the possession of atomic weapons and to nuclear experimentation at home or in other countries, namely in the United States.[17] Article 9 of the Constitution establishes Japan's renouncement of war as a sovereign right and the promise to stay without an offensive military force. For these reasons, the country had a diffused idea that it would need protection against the rising communist forces in the Asian region; this led to the alliance treaties with the United States. Political attitude and the public opinion have for decades insisted that Japan pursue a strict conduct of international neutrality.

The third factor was the penetration into Japanese society of Marxist doctrine. In a period where right-wing thought was declining, communist

and socialist ideas found fertile soil as a natural counter to traditional thinking, which used to put the emperor at its center.[18] Although moderate or conservative thought prevails in Japan, Marxism in its different versions has put
its roots down more deeply than previously thought. However, political representatives espousing these beliefs have been so divided and polemic among
themselves, as happens in many other democratic countries, that it has never
broadly permeated Japanese political life. Even more important, Japan is officially politically distant from communist and socialist countries and, over
the years, the government and a large part of public opinion have not nour-
ished much leftist sympathy, not during the periods of delusion caused by the
political inadequacies of the Liberal-Democratic party or in those moments
of vivid international or internal terrorism. In the latter case, moreover, despite the nonviolent approach by the police, the State's target has primarily
been left-wing terrorism. This has been due to the national collective identity, which on this matter is uncontested.[19]

The fourth tendency is the "American fixation":[20] the wide cultural-
economic alliance with United States, which continues at present. Of course,
the United States has influenced Japan for decades in its economic development and in such sectors as mass and pop culture, mass media, entertainment, fashion, and commodities.

In the 1970s, the cultural and political climate was influenced by the
aforementioned tendencies. Pacifism was deeply felt across generations; Japan was acquiring a more balanced self-confidence with respect to its position on the international chessboard and more specifically, in reference to the
United States. This relationship reached a dramatic point during key political
crises in Eastern Asia: the withdrawal of the American army from Vietnam
(1975); the rise of the Red Khmers and Pol Pot in Cambodia (1975–76); the
last phase of Mao's rule (and his death in 1976). This means that Japan was
in a geopolitical area and in a historical period in which great attention was
necessary to the ungovernable fermentation of the communist and socialist
political-military forces and in which the internal pacifism, felt as a fundamental national value, was sustained by the solid military protection by the
United States. It was evident that the world had been divided into a totalitarian bloc and a democratic bloc, as during the Cold War and in the local conflicts after 1945, from Korea onward.[21] Therefore it is difficult not to see in
Japanese science fiction animated tales of those years—or at least in some of
them—manifestations of those fears that were common to many Japanese,
articulated with the cultural symbols of those countries, those times, and
those fears and desires.

Notes

1. *UFO Robo Grendizer,* from a manga by Nagai Gō (other versions of the manga are by Ōta Gosaku, Nagai's assistant), 74 episodes, Tōei Animation, 1975–77; better known in Italy as *Atlas UFO Robot* (where Grendizer is "Goldrake"); in France, Canada, and in other French/Arab-speaking countries, as *Goldorak*; in the United States and other countries, as *Grandizer.* Main teleplays authors: Uehara Sozō, Fujikawa Keisuke. Animation: Ketsuta Toshio. Character design: Komatsubara Kazuo, Araki Shingō (from episode 49 on). Music: Kikuchi Shunsuke. Main directors: Katsumata Tomoharu, Ochiai Masamune.

2. For a longer analysis of the whole series and of those aspects I am here neglecting, see Marco Pellitteri, *Il Drago e la Saetta: Modelli, strategie e identità dell'immaginario giapponese* (The dragon and the dazzle: Models, strategies, and identities of Japanese imagination) (Latina: Tunué, 2008), 251–83, and Alessandro Montosi, *Ufo Robot Goldrake: Storia di un eroe nell'Italia degli anni Ottanta* (*UFO Robot Goldrake*: Story of a eighties hero in Italy) (Roma: Coniglio, 2007).

3. *Mazinger Z,* various directors (1972), 92 episodes; *Great Mazinger,* various directors (1974), 56 episodes; both produced by Tōei Animation and taken from the related Nagai Gō's manga.

4. *The War of the Worlds* (USA, 1953, dir. Byron Haskin), from the 1898 novel by H. G. Wells.

5. Think of movies such as *The Thing from Another World* (USA, 1951, dir. Christian Nyby) and *Invasion of the Body Snatchers* (USA, 1956, dir. Don Siegel).

6. In the cases of intergroup tension or conflict, the ingroup, by dehumanizing the outgroup, can more easily act against them. Among the many possible sources on this issue, see at least Henry Tajfel, *Human Groups and Social Categories: Studies in Social Psychology* (Cambridge: Cambridge University Press, 1981); John C. Turner, Michael A. Hogg, Penelope J. Oakes, Stephen D. Reicher, Margareth S. Wetherell, *Rediscovering the Social Group: A Self-Categorization Theory* (Oxford: Blackwell, 1987); and Maria Paola Paladino and Jeroen Vaes, "L'umanità negata: I nuovi processi di de-umanizzazione" (Humanity denied: The new processes of dehumanization), *Psicologia contemporanea* 191 (2005): 73–79.

7. This is directed more to the authors themselves than to the very young watchers, who could hardly be expected to understand the nuances hidden in such symbols, but who would be able to recognize them years later.

8. Giovanni Villella (under pseud. Alcor), "Goldrake: Locations," in *Il Fantastico Mondo di Go Nagai* (The fantastic world of Go Nagai) Web site: http://www.nagaifans.it/goldrake/locations/locations.htm (accessed February 2007).

9. On Japan's history during colonialism/imperialism, see John W. Dower, *War without Mercy: Race and Power in the Pacific War* (New York: Pantheon Books, 1986), and Michael Weiner, *Race and Migration in Imperial Japan* (London: Routledge, 1994).

10. See David Harvey, *The Condition of Postmodernity: An Enquiry into the Origins of Cultural Change* (London: Basil Blackwell, 1989).

11. This motto is the modern adaptation of a more ancient one, *wakon kansai,* "Japanese spirit, Chinese techniques," famous in mid-nineteenth century to indicate the Japanese debt towards Chinese culture. See Michael Carr, "Yamato-Damashii 'Japanese Spirit' Definitions," *International Journal of Lexicography* 7, no. 4 (1994), 279–306.

12. William Gibson, "Modern Boys and Mobile Girls," *The Observer* Web site (April 1, 2001), http://observer.guardian.co.uk/life/story/0,6903,46639100.html#article_continue (accessed May 2007).

13. Cf. at least Tessa Morris-Suzuki, *Re-Inventing Japan: Time, Space, Nation* (New York: M. E. Sharpe, 1998).

14. Umesao Tadao, "Bunmei no seitai shikan yosetsu" (Civilization in ecologic history perspective), *Chūō Kōron,* February 1957; cited in Iwabuchi Koichi, *Recentering Globalization: Popular Culture and Asian Transnationalism* (Durham, N.C.: Duke University Press, 2002), 63.

15. Edwin O. Reischauer, *Japan, Past and Present,* 2nd ed. (Tokyo: Charles E. Tuttle Company, 1952), 250–51.

16. Ibid., 251.

17. Ibid., 251–52.

18. Ibid., 253–54.

19. Peter J. Katzenstein, *Cultural Norms and National Security: Police and Military in Postwar Japan* (Ithaca, N.Y.: Cornell University Press, 1996), 96.

20. Reischauer, *Japan, Past and Present,* 256–57.

21. Reischauer published the third edition of his book in 1964, and even then he stated that these four attitudes are not static. In fact, they have changed much during the decades. Japan today is not as pacifist as before; its self-confidence is high; left-wing ideas seem to be more in the minority than they were at the end of the seventies; and the relationship with the United States is no longer a psychological-cultural vassalage but instead a more balanced dialog. Moreover, one can see some fatigue with the presence of American forces in Japanese territories. But of course it is clear to all in Japan that the United States is the best possible ally, especially in the face of possible friction with Beijing and Pyongyang. Besides, today the Cold War's containment has vanished, since the countries of the philo-Soviet bloc—with the exception of North Korea—have undergone a quasi-total adoption of capitalism in an international market system and are accordingly experiencing economic growth.

Kobayashi Yoshinori Is Dead: Imperial War / Sick Liberal Peace / Neoliberal Class War

BULLET #1: THE FALL OF ABE SHINZŌ

A young "freeter" named Akamatsu Tomohiro shocked liberal pundits in Japan with his short piece published in the *Asahi Shinbun*'s journal of ideas *Ronza* in January 2007. Called "*Kibō wa sensō*" (My only hope is war), Akamatsu's challenge to informed readers warned that if Japanese youth continue to be robbed of an economic future, they just might turn to the military out of desperation. He darkly suggested that the disappearance of anything resembling equality in neoliberalized Japanese society could very easily be replaced by the leveling effect of a militarized and mobilized Japan. Akamatsu's challenge was that war stands a better chance of making Japanese society more equitable than any other social force and, for that reason, is more attractive for Japanese young men than out-of-date promises pitched by an increasingly irrelevant trade-unionism.

After ten years of startling commercial success that he has leveraged into a central place among political commentators in the Japanese media (and the starring role among contemporary ultranationalists), the manga artist Kobayashi Yoshinori doubtless read Akamatsu's article with glee. "My only hope is war" crystallized the central ideologemes of Kobayashi's work since his *Sensōron* (A theory of war) was published in 1998 by Gentōsha: an appeal to return to the collectivism of a militarist 1930s Japan, a refusal of what Kobayashi denigrated as the consumerist individualism imposed on Japan by the United States during the Occupation of Japan, and a recommendation to up-rooted youth that they transcend that U.S.-style alienation by participating in a remasculinized Japanese nationalism. Akamatsu provides the counter to the well-known scene at the beginning of *Sensōron,* when the author gets into a conversation with a young taxi driver who tells Kobayashi that he wants to join Japan's Self-Defense Forces to fulfill a dream of becoming a pilot. Kobayashi is immediately drawn to this seemingly nationalist sentiment until the driver stuns Kobayashi by confessing that his ability to fly a plane will allow him to jet out of Japan and save himself the next time the Japanese nation goes to war.

The overturning of the cab driver's 1998 sentiment in Akamatsu's 2007 piece had its political correlative in the victory of the ultranationalist wing of the Liberal Democratic Party (LDP) when Abe Shinzō became Japan's prime minister in August 2006. When Koizumi Jun'ichiro stepped down after a rare five-year-long stint as prime minister, his designated successors hailed from the most assertively conservative wing of the ruling Liberal Democratic Party, the Nihon Kaigi (Japan Conference). Abe was the head of this group for several years in the 1990s; the former rightist foreign minister Asō Tarō and the powerful Tokyo governor Ishihara Shintaro are also major players in the Conference. Although not a member, Kobayashi has been very close to several of group's members for several years.

The sudden hegemony of the Japan Conference should be configured as the victory of a group of politicians, academics, and, yes, cartoonists, who since the mid-1990s have been calling for a rollback against what they call the dominant "masochistic view of history" perpetrated by liberals in Japan. These liberal masochists are said to derive pleasure in obsessively punishing Japan and themselves as Japanese by reiterating specious, foreign-born narratives about the purported carnage inflicted on Asians during the period spanning Japan's victory over China in 1895 until the collapse of Japan's Empire in 1945. In concert with other elements of the far right, the Japan Conference is committed to whitewashing the already whited-out historical record of this period of Japanese Empire by substituting the masochistic and "politically correct" account with what we might think of as a wholesome and "patriotically correct" one. Therefore "rape" as a designation for something that Japanese inflicted on Chinese in Nanjing in December 1937 or for the coerced sex that happened ten or twenty times a day to individual "comfort women" at the hands of Japanese soldiers in World War II is scrupulously denied. This denial is salient in all of Kobayashi's works but is especially prominent in *Sensōron* and the 2001 *Taiwanron* (On Taiwan).

But much more than functioning as a negative critique, his main texts work primarily as affirmative mnemological utopias. While abjecting the fashion-victimed and self-absorbed Japanese youth, Kobayashi counterposes them to the projected valor and self-sacrifice of male Japanese soldiers of the 1930s and '40s. The opening scene of *Sensōron* lambasts Japan's liberal capitalist "sick peace"[1] because Kobayashi holds it accountable for producing both masses of superficial youth and the correlative loss of Japanese national pride. While radically severed from Japan's history and its organic *kyōdōtai*, consumerist individualist Japanese "have been living hassle-free in a wealthy society."[2] This lament is generated through the projected memory of all wartime Japanese living with full confidence and unthinking faith in the virtue of their national community. Repeating one of his interventions into contemporary intellectual debate, Kobayashi opines that it was impossible to be a relativist or cynical nihilist in 1930s Japan. Wartime Japanese normatively experienced a full suturing with their birthplace, family, and national community. The desire to return to this seamless suturing of Japanese fascism is what links the disparate positions of contemporary ultranationalism, a symptom particularly salient in the Japan Conference. Informed North American readers have doubtless heard of the U.S. think tank called the Project for a New American Century, whose members scripted the 2003 U.S. invasion of Iraq in the 1990s. As the Japan Conference might be rendered as the "Project for a New Imperial Japanese Half-Century," I want to discuss some of the internal workings of this group, as it will flesh out some of Kobayashi's political positions.

The Japan Conference formed officially in 1997 as an amalgam of the Conference to Defend Japan (whose members include veterans of Japan's Imperial Army and Navy) and the Society to Defend Japan, a group made up of Shintō and new religious sects.[3] Its internal think-tank is the Japan Policy Institute. However, there are several important financial and political supporters who complicate this predictable profile of ultranationalist groups. One of these groups is more familiar to Anglophone readers as the Unification Church led by Reverend Moon Sun-myung. Known by their Japanese name of Tōitsu Kyōkai, they can be seen in the streets of Tokyo preaching their "chastity preservation movement" and hawking Moon's Japanese-language newspaper *Sekai Nippō*.[4]

Before his disgraceful resignation in August 2007, Abe's platform called for swift revision of the Japanese constitution in particular and a trashing of the post–World War II order in general—what he called in Japanese *sengo rejiimu kara no dakkyaku,* or "breaking away from the old regime." He promised to overturn not only the famous Article 9, pledging Japan to pacifism, but also parts of Article 24 (which guarantees equal rights between married men and women) and Article 25, committing the

> ABE'S FALL FROM 82 PERCENT APPROVAL AT THE BEGINNING OF HIS TERM TO UNDER 30 PERCENT AT THE END ALLEGORIZES A FALL OF SORTS FOR THE ULTRANATIONALIST POSITIONS ESPOUSED BY ABE, KOBAYASHI, AND THE JAPAN CONFERENCE.

state to provide welfare to all its citizens. Abe and his cabinet have been criticized for reactionary statements on gender and sexuality (his friend and education minister Ibuki declared in February 2007 that women are fundamentally "baby-making machines"), but these views are ideological common sense inside the Japan Conference. Abe also draws on the patriarchal thought of his grandfather, the suspected war criminal Kishi Nobusuke who was the number two man in Japan's fascist colony of Manchukuo in the 1930s before going on to become vice-minister of commerce in his close friend Tōjō Hideki's war cabinet before being resurrected as two-term prime minister of Japan after World War II.

According to the leftist journalist Tahara Maki, beginning around 1998 Japan Conference followers were advised by the Policy Institute and the Unification Church to be on the lookout for Japan-based survivors of the "1968 World Revolution." As posted at that time on their Web site, the Policy Institute identified the most dangerous elements of the 1968 Revolution as feminists and queers calling for changes in the ways in which sex education is taught in Japan's schools. The Japan Conference has largely agreed with Moon's insistence that Japan in general, and Tokyo in particular, is where the free love and gender radicalism of the countercultural "'68 Revolution" has penetrated the furthest. Japan is now seen, in the words of an executive director of the Japan Conference, as the main battleground where feminists and free-lovers are trying to "disintegrate Japanese society," through inciting "violent revolution" by other means.[5] This combination of cultish rhetoric, Japanese fascist ideology, and more recognizable ultranationalism preached by the likes of Jean-Marie le Pen in France and Pat Buchanan in the United States represents the political habitus of Abe and Kobayashi.

It is crucial that while analyzing the shifting hegemony in contemporary Japan we recognize the importance of Prime Minister Abe's resignation in September 2007, after only one year in power. As the assumption of Abe the year before provided Kobayashi with unprecedented access to the top echelons of political power in Japan, Abe's defeat should be recognized as a lesser defeat for Kobayashi. Although not directly linked to Kobayashi's writings, Abe's fall from 82 percent approval at the beginning of his term to under 30 percent at the end allegorizes a fall of sorts for the ultranationalist positions espoused by Abe, Kobayashi, and the Japan Conference. This was the first check to the decade-long meteoric rise of Kobayashi, what I'm calling "bullet #1."

BULLET #2: OKINAWA

Kobayashi's four-hundred-page, 2005 *Okinawaron* (On Okinawa) claims on its front cover to form a kind of triptych with his 1998 *Sensōron* and the 2001 *Taiwanron*. The most salient aspect of Kobayashi's reading of Okinawan history is what I have called his unbridled "reverse postcolonial" take, first evidenced in his *Taiwanron*.[6] What I mean by this is that, rather than honestly interrogating the colonial past of an imperial power—whether it be British, French, Japanese, or U.S.—reverse postcolonialism eliminates almost all aspects of historical investigation in the name of affirming the heroism and honor of colonial-imperial endeavors. Similar to the reactionary revisions of the Scottish historian of British imperialism Niall Ferguson, Kobayashi manages to whitewash almost all of the central aspects of Japanese colonialism, leaving him only to congratulate Japan on the stunning modernizing successes achieved by valorous Japanese colonizers in Asia. In paradigmatic reverse postcolonial fashion, Kobayashi writes as if nothing about the ravages of colonial war and imperial excess are known, throwing himself into a schizoid temporality anachronistically shared by Japanese imperial elites circa 1935.

This plays itself out in *Okinawaron* as a ventriloquizing of the positions taken by Yanagita Kunio and other imperial *minzokugakusha* (nativist scholars) in the 1920s and '30s: Okinawa embodies the Japanese past and visiting it has the potential to remind Japanese and rewind them to a time before their country became blindly obsessed with Euroamerican modernization. Kobayashi claims that "Okinawa is Japan purified," the correlative of which is "the modernized homeland (*kindaikasareta hondo*) is the polluted (*fujun*) Japan."[7] Despite this critique of Japan's adoption of the central forms of Euroamerican modernization, Kobayashi nevertheless salutes the successful "modernization" project carried out by Japanese in underdeveloped Okinawa. This is the most extreme of Kobayashi's antinomies, with others occurring every ten pages or so.

The second appears in his insistence that Okinawa and Japan enjoyed a "latent unity" throughout the pre- and early modern periods, something that naturally led to a complete "assimilation" after the Meiji restoration. This underlying unity of Okinawa and Japan contradicts almost all the scholarship on Okinawan cultural practice and language, which locates a wealth of indigenous practices that were gradually overlayed by Chinese, then Japanese, imperial interests. Furthermore, Japanese economic historians like Hamashita Takeshi have been arguing for two decades now that Okinawa enjoyed an independent and privileged place in the China-dominated early modern world economy.[8] As a maritime trading power from the fourteenth to the seventeenth century, Japanese military interests based in Kyūshū gradually overwhelmed the peaceful trading kingdom, forcibly turning it into a part of Japan in the 1870s. This history of the violent deterritorializing of Okinawa by Japanese warrior-military concerns beginning in the mid-1600s is completely elided in Kobayashi's account. In its place is the ahistorical projection of an ethno-racial condensing of Okinawa into Japan.

Kobayashi's racialization of specific ethnicities contravenes the standard ethnological and geopolitical scholarship on Okinawa. But it is absolutely essential for him to advance his two central points in this text. The first is that the invasion of Okinawa by Kyūshū militarists was undertaken primarily to prevent the European powers doing to Okinawa what they did to China in the first Opium War of 1839–1842. This first defense of Okinawa necessitated a second, and here *Okinawaron* features the standard revisionist argument of Kobayashi's in particular and Japanese ultranationalists in general: in its self-sacrificing desire to rid Asia of Euroamerican colonizers, it was compelled to fight to the last man in defending Okinawa against the U.S. Army's "typhoon of steel." The defense of Okinawa featured Okinawans and Japanese soldiers fighting side-by-side with a shared vision. Here, Okinawa was permanently consolidated as the homeland's "*seimeisen*" (lifeline), the true southern border of Japan.

In the hands of Kobayashi, this heroic endeavor to protect Japan's southern border against the North American onslaught featured the willing participation of Okinawans—what amounted to a suicide mission in the face of the high-tech military machine of the United States. Kobayashi does not stop to interrogate the ultranationalist assumption that Okinawans were sincere in their willingness to die for imperial Japan; as he argued four years earlier in the case of Taiwan, he assumes that this is the natural response from an Okinawan people barely distinguishable from mainland Japanese who were saved from savage Europeans in the 1840s by Southern Japanese militarists from Kyūshū and who were thankful for the selfless modernizing efforts on the part of homeland Japanese beginning in the mid-1870s.

Kobayashi knows he cannot completely ignore the well-documented atrocities inflicted on Okinawan civilians by the Japanese military before and during the Battle for Okinawa. Prefacing his explanation with the reminder that the United States was the "only cause of tragedy on the Japanese mainland," he writes, "it was most unfortunate that there were isolated cases of Japanese soldiers victimizing (*kagaisha*) Okinawans."[9] While leaving out any details related to actual incidents, Kobayashi then proceeds to rationalize these unspecified Japanese atrocities. First, they need to be seen as only having occurred under the most extreme conditions (*kyokugen jōtai*) of the U.S.-inflicted "typhoon of steel." Second, he claims that atrocities were committed only *after* military discipline had broken down and soldiers were forced to flee alone or with one or two others. Kobayashi provides us with a drawing of just such a situation: three Japanese soldiers are pointing guns at five or six Okinawan civilians hiding in a cave. Approximately fifty meters from the entrance to the cave is a huge U.S. gunner tank patrolling ominously. The strongest worded critique of these actions states: "this was a serious act of betrayal against Japanese national citizens."[10]

Every year, women activists are discovering more "comfort stations" constructed by the Japanese military in Okinawa, where local women were kidnapped and forced to work as sex slaves for Japanese soldiers.[11] Naturally, Kobayashi says nothing about this and other atrocities. Even in this brief mention of isolated acts committed against Okinawan civilians by stray Japanese soldiers acting under extreme duress, the drawn image seems to justify the soldiers' actions. Crying and screaming women or children would jeopardize the location of the group in the cave, leading to a certain slaughter of everyone by the U.S. tank lurking just outside. Although the text explicitly condemns isolated actions against Okinawan civilians, it also firmly rationalizes the atrocities. But this pales in comparison to the one image we are provided with of an apparent war crime committed by a Japanese soldier: the potential act (I say potential because we are never shown a Japanese soldier actually committing a war crime; the most we get is a drawing of a solider thrusting a gun in the face of an Okinawan woman reasonably threatening to shoot her if she cannot keep silent) is justified in that it will keep the larger group alive and hidden from the U.S. tank.

These minor and ultimately excusable actions on the part of individual Japanese soldiers are contrasted against the group behavior of American soldiers. In two places in the text, after the closure of what he calls the "indiscriminate murder unleashed by the typhoon of steel,"[12] he claims that white and black U.S. soldiers went on nightly rape hunts, committing commonplace acts of sexual violence against Japanese women immediately following the end of the war. After Japan's surrender and during the early period of occupation, Kobayashi further claims that there were *daily* reports of sexual violence against Okinawan women committed by U.S. soldiers.[13]

There is no doubt that rape was a widespread phenomenon at the end of the war and continuing right up to the present, when approximately 22,000 U.S. troops remain stationed in Okinawa. However, the function of this in Kobayashi's text is to confirm the propaganda disseminated by the Japanese military during the last years of World War II to civilian women: it is far better to suicide than to face certain rape by U.S. barbarians. Although Kobayashi says nothing about the controversy raging about the Japanese military ordering civilians to suicide through *gyokusai*—either by forcing them off cliffs or ordering civilians to blow themselves up with grenades issued by soldiers—his clear message here is that it was better to have committed suicide honorably than to face nonstop rape by the black soldiers depicted raciologically as baboon-like by Kobayashi.[14] Although Kobayashi is nowhere explicit about this, the text clearly allows readers to blame both animalistic U.S. soldiers and Okinawan women, who should have taken the opportunity to kill themselves heroically— as they were ordered to do by the Japanese Army in Okinawa—rather than expose themselves to the rape hunts conducted by the savage United States.

For Kobayashi, this cowardly refusal on the part of many Okinawans to commit ritual suicide is one element in the assemblage established just after World War II that coded them as childish and immature. Immediately after the occupation of Okinawa, the United States set up huge military camps to house refugees. Many Okinawans came to rely exclusively on handouts from the U.S. Army, which led to Okinawans becoming known as the "give me" tribe. Kobayashi sees this legacy continuing in Okinawa today, where the once proud Japanized Okinawans have regressed into childlike cowards. While continuing to rely on the U.S. bases for economic support, they are seen as hypocritically obsessed with peaceful existence, summed up in what Kobayashi calls the juvenile Okinawan slogan *nuchidōtama*—"the preciousness of life."[15] Koyabashi's consistent critique of the peace and antibase movements characteristic of post–World War II Okinawan civil society is that these are naïvely dangerous as long as Okinawa continues to rely on the U.S. military for its security and economic sustainability. This immature dependence on the Unite States has, for Kobayashi, corroded Okinawan society from the top of Okinawan financial elites and rich landlords (the ones profiting from renting the land the bases lie on) all the way down to the infantile and ridiculous peace and antibase activists.[16]

The solution to this hollow Okinawan adolescence is provided in typical Kobayashi fashion through the negative example of the leftist, antiwar Japanese schoolteacher. Kobayashi eavesdrops on a Hokkaido high school teacher leading his students around Okinawa. According to Kobayashi, the teacher is indoctrinating the students with the false leftist rhetoric that passes for common sense about Okinawa among educated mainland Japanese: Okinawans love peace and tranquil "life"; Okinawa was an independent kingdom before its gradual military takeover by Japanese from Kyūshū; and the Japanese Army treated the Okinawans much worse in 1944 and 1945 than the U.S. military has since the beginning of the Okinawan campaign. The last point is what draws the wrath of Kobayashi. Anxious to erase the history of forced suicides of Okinawans by Japanese soldiers and repress the documented evidence of a vast network of comfort stations, Kobayashi's encyclopedic effort to identify the crimes committed against Okinawan women by U.S. soldiers attempts to demonstrate the absurdity of the Hokkaido leftist. Rather than mainland Japanese contributing to the extended childhood of Okinawans, they should be emphasizing the shared ethno-racial identity and homogeneous culture. The crucial first step in this Japanese nationalist endeavor is for Okinawans and mainland Japanese to delink from the U.S.-Japan security structure. Rather than emphasizing an empty "life" under continuing U.S. military occupation in Okinawa, and a life sustained by superficial consumerism in the Japanese cities, "Japanese" citizens should realize that "life is a means, not an end."[17] Kobayashi is clear that the end is always a nonnegotiable national identity, the only thing worth sacrificing one's life for.

OKINAWA RESPONDS TO JAPANESE ULTRANATIONALISTS

The publication of Kobayashi's *Okinawaron* was not as controversial as his previous celebration of Japan's colonial project in Taiwan. However, it did elicit extensive criticism in Okinawa. It is hard to tell what kind of impact Kobayashi's text had in the largest single demonstration against mainland Japanese nationalism on Okinawa in late September 2007. However, there is no doubting the fact that Kobayashi's bestselling *Okinawaron* is the most influential whitewashing of Japanese military atrocities committed against Okinawan citizens in World War II. As I pointed out above, in the huge four-hundred-page manga there is less than one page dedicated to the question of Japanese war crimes.

Emboldened by Abe Shinzō's rise to power, in March 2007 Abe's Education Ministry instructed publishers of high school history textbooks to take out the words *"Nihongun"* (Japanese military) in any context connected to the *gyokusai* Okinawan suicides, "out of concern that it might lead to misunderstandings about conditions during the Battle of Okinawa."[18] What Abe's Education Ministry wanted to do was to eliminate any suggestion that the mass suicides were ordered and carried out by Japanese soldiers. With this censoring of military involvement, young Japanese readers would be left with the idea that the Okinawans had willingly committed suicide rather than offer themselves to the slimy paws of African Americans and other sex machines in the U.S. Armed Forces. It is easy to imagine Kobayashi's sense of satisfaction when Education Ministry textbook reviewers ordered history textbook publishers to censor all references to atrocities committed by Japanese soldiers in Okinawa. As one of the Education Ministry's stated justifications for censoring is respecting "public opinion," *Okinawaron* arguably did more to contribute to the construction of public opinion about Okinawa than any one text published after World War II.

THERE IS NO DOUBTING THE FACT THAT KOBAYASHI'S BESTSELLING *OKINAWARON* IS THE MOST INFLUENTIAL WHITEWASHING OF JAPANESE MILITARY ATROCITIES COMMITTED AGAINST OKINAWAN CITIZENS IN WORLD WAR II.

To give readers some idea of what Abe's Ministry was asking for, the first paragraph in the chapter on the war in Okinawa in Sanseidō's current textbook reads: "The greatest tragedy of the Battle of Okinawa was that so many people were forced by the Japanese military to commit group suicide."[19] When the Sanseidō editors were instructed by the Education Ministry to excise "Japanese military" from this accurate description, the effect was to imply that Okinawan civilians committed suicide willfully—without the grenades, threats, and orders from the Japanese military, which we know was actually the case.

Immediately after the Education Ministry ordered the censoring, a resolution was passed in all forty-one of Okinawa's city, town, and village councils condemning Tokyo. When it became clear that Abe's Ministry was not going to give any ground on the Okinawan denunciations—going so far as to call all the eyewitness testimony of Japanese soldiers' forcing Okinawans to suicide "fabrications," impossible to document—a huge demonstration was planned, which took place at the Ginowan Seashore Park. Attended by 110,000 people, the "Okinawa Citizens' Protest Demanding Cancellation of Textbook Revisions" adopted a resolution unanimously approved by the protesters:

Textbooks play a vital role in conveying truth to the children responsible for our future. Therefore, the indisputable fact that so-called group suicides during the Battle of Okinawa would not have occurred without the involvement of the Japanese military must be communicated to them. It is our solemn duty to teach the lessons learned from the truth about the battle, to hope for peace, and to seek ways of avoiding another tragic war.

This collective "No!" addressed to Japanese ultranationalist hegemony by the Okinawan people should be seen as the second major attack on Kobayashi, what I am calling bullet #2.

BULLET #3: MARXIST-LOLITA FASHION

This last bullet will be the fatal one for Kobayashi Yoshinori. The rise of Kobayashi-inspired ultranationalism has taken place under the sign of widespread neoliberal restructuring, which intensified when Koizumi Jun'ichiro became Prime Minister in 2001. One of the most dramatic effects of this has been the hollowing out of the labor market for young Japanese and the exacerbation of social disparity. Gini coefficients that measure material disparity widened significantly from 1990 to 2005. For example, as of 2004 the top 20 percent of Japanese society appropriates 51 percent of national income, while the bottom 20 percent gets 0.3 percent and only 6 percent going to the second lowest 20 percent.[20] United Nations poverty indexes are revealing as well when we apply them to Japan. Poverty, defined by the UN as household earning half or less of the national average, has expanded from 13 percent in 1994 to 17 percent in 2004, the second highest among developed countries after the United States.[21]

Often referred to as the *freeter phenomenon*, since Koizumi the number of full-time permanent workers is dropping precipitously as the number of part-time or full-time temporary workers expands dramatically. What is worse is the pay disparity between these reserve armies of contingent workers and the shrinking pool of permanent full-time workers. Organization for Economic Cooperation and Development (OECD) figures for the ratio between permanent and nonpermanent wages is 100 to 48 in Japan, 100 to 92 in Sweden, 88 in Germany, and 63 in the United States. Koizumi pushed through a bill expanding the use of dispatch, nonpermanent (*haken*) workers in manufacturing in 2004 against huge opposition. Other changes in the labor market have occurred with less fanfare and debate.[22]

It is important that we pause here to reflect on the two fundamental axioms in nationalistic, neoliberal discourse in Japan. The first is that social class *not* be factored into any analytic of social subjectivity. For Kobayashi and his allies like Nishio Kanji, identity is a priori nationality. Although Kobayashi reluctantly talks about gender, his thoughts on ethnicity and race are limited to the racialization of the different ethnicities in the archipelago (Yamato, Ainu, Okinawan, etc.) as unproblematically Japanese. This remainders nation as the sole determinant of socio-political identity.

The second axiom is that the rampant consumerism and superficiality that absorbs the thought and affect of young urban Japanese make them by definition incapable of critical thought. There is much more that could be said about this, but in Kobayashi's three major works he never assumes that anyone under thirty-five or so is worth arguing with. For the most part, his attacks are directed at the Japanese political center and left. However, unnoticed by Kobayashi and the ultranationalists, several leftist *and* fashion-conscious youth voices have emerged as the main critics of neoliberal nationalism since Koizumi's rise to power in 2001.

The most visible in terms of book sales and appearances in the mass media is the singer, writer and Gothic-Lolita Amamiya Karin. In several well-selling books and in appearances on television (to say nothing of her ubiquitous presence at labor and left demonstrations), more than any other presence on the left in contemporary Japan, Amamiya has thoroughly repudiated Kobayashi's absurd conflation of pop culture sensibility with intellectual bankruptcy. After (barely) graduating from high school, Amamiya drifted into far-right circles and nationalistic punk scenes. She gained instant fame in subculture circles when her rightist band The Revolutionary Truth was the subject of an acclaimed 1999 documentary film done by Tsuchiya Yutaka called *Atarashii kamisama* (The new gods).

Never one to shy away from the media spotlight, Amamiya was a fan of Kobayashi until the beginning of her political awakening around 2003, a rapid reverse *tenkō* from right to left that raised the eyebrows of suspicious pundits. Whether her shift was driven by sheer careerism or motivated by a sincere change in political consciousness, she now enthusiastically sponsors events at clubs and citizens halls dealing with issues of youth poverty and neoliberalism. Moreover, in 2006 she started her own advocacy group against poverty known as the Anti-Poverty Network. With the far-right following Kobayashi, Ishihara Shintarō, and the Japan Conference in continuing to push for the glorification of imperial war, Amamiya and the freeter left have started talking about another kind of war—class war. Beginning with her latest book,

> IN SEVERAL WELL-SELLING BOOKS AND IN APPEARANCES ON TELEVISION, MORE THAN ANY OTHER PRESENCE ON THE LEFT IN CONTEMPORARY JAPAN, AMAMIYA HAS THOROUGHLY REPUDIATED KOBAYASHI'S ABSURD CONFLATION OF POP CULTURE SENSIBILITY WITH INTELLECTUAL BANKRUPTCY.

the April 2007 *Ikisasero! Nanminkasuru wakamonotachi* (Live on! Refugeed youth), which had sold sixty thousand copies as of New Year 2008, Amamiya has turned recently to the thematization and advocacy of class war.

At the annual leftist gathering held in Tokyo around December 1, Amamiya led a panel on the theme of death. With two activists from freeter unions, she twice wondered what would happen to Japanese political hegemony if young leftists were able to shift the Japanese obsession with death from that of dying in imperial war to a responsibility to incite class war.[23] Only with this shift from nationalistic war to class war, Amamiya sloganed, could neoliberalism be overthrown. A mere seven months prior to this November 30, 2007, event, she was the main attraction at the first "precariat" May Day rally in Tokyo, which drew five hundred people. The English-language poster for the event called "Mondo Mayday for the Precariat 007" stated that the rally would call for

- Value everyone's right to life!

- End wage slavery! We demand decent wages for decent lives!

- We won't let society shut us out!

- War is murder. End all wars NOW![24]

Absolutely opposed to Kobayashi Yoshinori's insistence that "life is just a means, not an end," here Amamiya and the hip Tokyo leftists were reversing Kobayashi's ultranationalist implication that life is just a means to be offered up in deathly sacrifice to the nation. By December 2007, Amamiya not only wanted to prevent further imperial wars conducted for the pleasure and profit of the Japanese bourgeoisie, but she was affirmatively advocating *class* war as the means toward the end of a life with dignity. The final and fatal bullet is fired fittingly by Amamiya, the former Kobayashi fan.

....

Notes

1. Kobayashi Yoshinori, *Sensōron* (A theory of war) (Tokyo: Gentōsha, 1998), 9.
2. Ibid., 355.
3. This information was from the Nihon Kaigi's Web site, www.nihonkaigi.org.jp.

(accessed March 11 2007). See also Muto Ichiyo's August 2006 essay called "Restore the Constitution, Glory to Empire" at www.ppjaponesia.org/modules/tinycontent/index (accessed February 9, 2008).

4. I want to thank an anonymous reader of this essay for pointing out that Kobayashi has been publicly critical of the Unification Church. However, this seems to me to be like Freud's narcissism of minor differences; Kobayashi and the Unification Church are indistinguishable in their shared opposition to the empty consumer lifestyles of contemporary Japanese; their shared disgust with the waning of paternal authority; and the way they mirror each other in denouncing Japanese women as self-centered, narcissistic, and unwilling to stay in the patriarchal home raising children.

5. Tahara Maki, "Japanese Neo-Cons Infest Gender Discourse," *Japonesia*, no. 2 (December 2006): 61.

6. See my conclusion to *Kannani and Document of Flames: Two Japanese Colonial Novels* (Durham, N.C.: Duke University Press, 2005).

7. Kobayashi Yoshinori, *Okinawaron* (On Okinawa) (Tokyo: Shōgakkan, 2005).

8. Hamashita Takeshi, *Okinawa nyūmon: Ajia o tsunagu kaiiki kōsō* (Introduction to Okinawa: A Framework of the maritime connections with Asia) (Tokyo: Chikuma Shobō, 2000).

9. Kobayashi, *Okinawaron*, 361.

10. Ibid.

11. According to the most authoritative source on the numbers of stations, the Women's Active Museum on War and Peace at the Waseda Hōshien of Waseda University in Tokyo documents close to one hundred stations in Okinawa alone on their huge wall map of the East Asia region pinpointing exactly where comfort stations operated. See www.wam-peace.org.

12. Kobayashi, *Okinawaron*, 243.

13. Ibid.

14. Ibid., 245.

15. Ibid., 107.

16. Ibid., 232.

17. Ibid., 234.

18. I'm quoting from Steve Rabson's translation of Kamata Satoshi's "Shattering Jewels: 110,000 Okinawans Protest Japanese State Censorship of Compulsory Group Suicides" posted on *Japan Focus*'s Web site on January 8, 2008, at www. japanfocus.org/articles.

19. Ibid.

20. See Takenobu Mieko, "Japan's Deteriorating Labor Market—Workers Are Degraded as Dispensables," *Japonesia*, no. 2 (September 2005).

21. See Randall S. Jones, "Income Inequality, Poverty, and Social Spending in Japan" OECD Working Paper number 556, www.olis.oecd.org. (accessed February 8, 2008).

22. On the ways in which political hegemony has attempted to manage these contradictions, see my "Debt and Denunciation in Post-Bubble Japan," in *Cultural Critique* 65 (Winter 2007): 164–87.

23. I was present at this event, which took place in Harajuku, Tokyo.

24. This is from the Tokyo Indymedia Web site, http://japan.indymedia.org/newswire (accessed February 10, 2008).

Two Phases of Japanese Illustrated Fiction

CHARLES SHIRO INOUYE

Adam Kern. *Manga from the Floating World: Comicbook Culture and the Kibyoshi of Edo Japan.* Cambridge, Mass.: Harvard University Press, 2006. ISBN 978-0674022669.

Manga from the Floating World is a welcome addition to scholarship in English on the literary culture of Japan's Edo period (1600–1868). Painted in the broadest strokes, this era is marked by three peaks of notable artistic activity: the ebullient Genroku period (1688–1704) of Ihara Saikaku, Matsuo Basho, and Chikamatsu Monzaemon; the sophisticated An'ei-Tenmei period (1772–89) of Santo Kyoden, Hiraga Gennai, and Ueda Akinari; and the decadent Bunka-Bunsei (Kasei) period (1804–29) of Jippensha Ikku, Tsuruya Nanboku, and Takizawa Bakin. Of these three, the second has been the least studied. Consequently, Adam Kern's thorough consideration of the illustrated texts that were the dominant genre of popular literature (*gesaku*) at the time is an important contribution. In addition to a solid introduction to the genre and to its era, Kern also provides translations of three of Santo Kyoden's *kibyoshi,* giving us both academic and artistic exposure to the "visual-verbal" imagination that made these works possible.

The term "visual-verbal" is Kern's. It applies to the illustration-text combination that characterizes the *kibyoshi* page. Its hyphenated inclusiveness raises a number of enduring epistemological questions that those who study visual culture must consider. Is the thought process one of seeing images? And how is a verbally produced mental image different from one

produced by pictures, figures, and other material objects? *Manga of the Floating World* chooses not to engage these questions directly. But it does deal with a third evaluative issue that follows from these fundamental considerations, namely whether or not illustrated literature is adolescent or childish. Kern convincingly shows us that a genre like *kibyoshi* is both sophisticated in its methods of expression and mature in its interests. The ostensible bias against the broader category of *kusazoshi* (illustrated writings) to which *kibyoshi* belong, often labeled even by their creators to be "for women and children," is yet another element of a growing phonocentrism that by the An'ei-Tenmei period had gathered considerable strength.

Kibyoshi are the manga and the comic books referred to in the book's title. Presented with this nomenclature, we might expect the author to portray *kibyoshi* as a progenitor of the manga with which we are familiar today. This, I believe, is a natural expectation. Yet Kern actually argues against any easy linkage between contemporary manga and this older, floating-world type. For one thing, as a genre, *kibyoshi* rose up and died away during the last two decades of the eighteenth and the first decade of the nineteenth centuries. *Kibyoshi* belong specifically to the world of Edo letters. Consequently, any reader who does not understand the specific thrust of the "floating world" descriptor runs the risk of misunderstanding this book.

Kern's argument against continuity from old to contemporary follows from his interest in honoring the actual specifics of the *kibyoshi* experience. The details that Kern provides tell us that *kibyoshi* died away and were succeeded by the more lengthy *gokan,* which lasted into the Meiji period but did not have a direct impact on early manga artists such as Kawanabe

Kyosai and Kobayashi Kiyochika. Kern's genealogy indicates that what we know as contemporary manga can be traced back to the caricatures of Charles Wirgman and *Japan Punch,* not to the work of Santo Kyoden, Torai Sanna, and others. Many others have noted that it was Hokusai who popularized the word "manga." But, according to Kern, that was a different kind of manga. Confronted with these careful distinctions, we have to wonder why Kern risked using the term "manga" in his title at all. Why argue for the nonrelationship between *kibyoshi* and manga, while calling them both manga? Perhaps the intent was to encourage comparisons.

In fact, Kern recognizes the general relatedness of illustrated texts of various kinds. He notes the linkages to anime, on the one hand, and to Muromachi- and early Edo-period illustrated texts, the so-called Nara *ehon,* on the other. Yet it is still true that this study is decidedly less interested in showing the theoretical commonality of these various illustrated forms than in the scholarly accuracy that necessarily makes these two phases of Japanese illustrated fiction look less and less alike.

Manga from the Floating World is a thorough book. We learn about the authors, illustrators, and titles. We are given plot summaries and copious annotations to help us appreciate the cultural specifics of the works being considered. Of course, Kern provides some useful interpretation of these details as well. We are presented with summaries of Japanese scholarship on the development and demise of the genre, for instance. We are also given an exciting look at the rich cultural context of the An'ei-Tenmei period, along with a thoughtful analysis of the very tricky "visual-verbal" imagination, as grounded in actual examples.

In sum, Kern's treatment of the "visual-verbal" provides us with a chunky soup rather than with a theoretical purée. After all, both the genre and the Japanese intelligence that created these illustrated texts were playful and not always stringently totalizing forces. This is

a world of mixing (*naimaze*) and tossing things together (*fukiyose*). *Gesaku* writers employed various takes (*shuko*) on established chunks of formal reality (*sekai*). Their almost manic use of in-group allusion renders deep thoughts into parodic embellishments and impressive visual performances.

Meeting the humor of *kibyoshi* with humor of his own, Kern moves us toward a conclusion about why this sometimes stunning display of literary talent died away. "The genre inevitably fizzled out . . . not because of the Kansei Reforms, but because the commercial pressure of reaching a larger, more common audience meant that writers eventually had to dispose of the very sort of in-group jokes and specialized puzzles that had characterized *kibyoshi* to begin with" (245). As I have argued elsewhere, this commercialism also has as much to do with the larger issues of semiotic development that engulfed the particulars of personalities and politics. For instance, the death of *kibyoshi* might be understood in the context of the remarkable influence that the Chinese colloquial novel *The Water Margin* (*Shuihuzhuan*) had on Japanese letters generally and on the market for reading specifically. What this very long and very colorful Chinese novel taught Japan's *gesakusha* can be summed up in a word: length. This, too, is a matter of "commercial pressure." If a narrative could be extended, à la *Shuihuzhuan*, then an established readership could be kept. It is no accident, therefore, that the birth of *yomihon* (reading books) and the transition from *kibyoshi* to *gokan,* a more extended and plot-oriented form of illustrated literature, occurred at roughly the same time.

In other words, the lengthiness of Bakin's less-illustrated "reading books" (or *yomihon*), such as *Eight Dogs* (*Hakkenden*), and an equally lengthy work such as Mantei Oga's *Eight Aspects of the Buddha: A Japanese Library* (*Shaka hasso Yamato bunko*), are a consequence of the same forces that made the *kibyoshi* unsustainable. Similarly corrosive to Tokugawa Japan's "visual-verbal" imagination was the seriousness of the Meiji-period novel (kindai *shosetsu*), which became an almost entirely a words-only endeavor. Perhaps only now, with the success of *Akira* and *Sailor Moon,* are we ready to understand the picture-phobic nature of the modern Japanese novel for what it was: a modern suppression of the grapheme in order to support a wide-ranging conceptualization of mass society that was better accomplished without too many pictures. Only now that we have recovered the sophistication of pictured reality are we ready to give the brilliance of *kibyoshi, this* early *flowering of* "*manga,*" its just due.

Whether a direct progenitor to contemporary manga or not, *kibyoshi* are good to know. To recognize the extraordinary burst of creativity that brought the genre to fruition is to gain an important perspective on the creative precedents for Japan's manga and anime artists today. The lacuna between these two phases is a crucial piece of Japanese cultural history that needs to be addressed. Thanks to *Manga from the Floating World,* we can now better understand this puzzling break and the highly illustrated work that lies on both sides of it. Appreciating both old and new manga (choosing to stay with Kern's terms), we can grasp the power of the phonocentrism that aided the development of modern consciousness and made the belittling of illustrated texts necessary.

One thing is clear from reading Kern's painstakingly researched book. Modern consciousness did not welcome the graphemic richness of manga, whether indicated by the transition to *gokan* in the eighteenth century or the transition from *gokan* to the *shosetsu* in the nineteenth. With the return of manga and the flourishing of other forms of visual media during the twentieth century, modern consciousness finally came unglued. As told by Adam Kern, the life and death of *kibyoshi* is an important chapter of the modern story. Knowing the Edo past helps us appreciate the visual splendor of contemporary Japanese culture as a come-from-behind sort of victory. In

the ongoing battle between image and text that W. T. J. Mitchell calls culture, the score in recent innings is Image 7 and Word 6. For the foreseeable future (until the electricity goes off), I would bet on the team with the most pictures.

Review Editors' Note

More information about *kibyoshi*, plus detailed summaries and illustrations, are available in the symposium edited by Adam Kern, "*Kibyoshi*: The World's First Comicbook?" *International Journal of Comic Art* 9, no. 1 (Spring 2007): 1–486.

Paradise Lost . . . and Found?

PAUL JACKSON

Ergo Proxy. 2006. Murase Shūkō (Director). Geneon Entertainment USA. Long Beach, Calif. 6 volumes. ASIN B000I2JSVM, B000KB48MA, B000MKXEM4, B000NVIGK2, B000N2HD5U, B000P296B2.

Much has been made of *Ergo Proxy*'s superficial similarities to *Ghost in the Shell*. In truth, these amount to little more than reflections of a shared genre lineage, which, although significant, belies *Ergo Proxy*'s true scope and ambition. Here, cyberpunk themes and imagery, still very much present and intact, are used only as a point of departure. From there, *Ergo Proxy* uses intertextuality and recurring motifs of awakening and death to explore very different facets of the human experience. This essay will specifically explore how the series incorporates biblical allusions in its construction of character and meaning.

The story opens in the domed city of Romdo, on the surface a gleaming utopia of individual and collective prosperity, a shining bastion of civilization amid a world of frozen oceans and barren continents. In an anonymous lab, however, a humanoid monster (or Proxy) writhes on an examination table. As onlooking AutoReivs (subservient robots) and scientists try to sedate it, the creature pulsates violently, eventually frees itself, and escapes. Additionally, Romdo's reliance on AutoRievs is threatened by the Cogito Virus that is thought to imbue infected artificial intelligences with self-awareness. Similarly, immigrants from other domes have created a new underclass that threatens to unbalance Romdo's elaborately maintained approach to population control. Good citizens are grown in artificial wombs, not welcomed from other cities.

Re-l Mayer, one of the two principal protagonists, is an inspector employed by the Civilian Intelligence Office. During a routine job she comes face to face with the escaped Proxy and mounts a personal investigation into its origin and purpose. Under Re-l's supervision is Vincent Law, a brooding young immigrant working toward becoming a citizen of Romdo. He too finds himself tangled in the creature's wake, which sets in motion a series of events that culminate in Vincent's unwitting expulsion from the city. Far from the sanctuary he sought, Vincent finds himself outside the dome.

As a term, cyberpunk originated in a short story of the same name written by Bruce Bethke. Published as part of the *Amazing Stories* anthology in 1983, the tale of school truants running amok in the Net was, by Bethke's own admission, "unremarkable."[1] It did, however, provide a label both vague and evocative enough to represent the literary style and thematic concerns of a collective of authors whose novels depicted near-future landscapes of rapid technological advancement, typically seen through the eyes of characters marginalized within their social infrastructures: hookers, bums, and con men.

Ergo Proxy shares numerous themes and stylistic flourishes with the canonized cyberpunk works but elsewhere diverges greatly. Cyberpunk futures have commonly presented societies so intrinsically connected to technology that boundaries between man and machine become blurred: where does one end and the other begin? *Ergo Proxy* offers a much less homogenous future. Body modifications and cyborgs don't exist; technology and humanity are very much separate entities. As such, the existential search at the heart of the series avoids secular questions of what makes us human and instead probes issues of faith in a technology-dependent future.

In his essay "Notes toward a Postcyberpunk Manifesto," Lawrence Person states that "cyberpunk's lasting impact came from the immersive world-building technique that gave it such a revelatory quality."[2] True to this tradition, *Ergo Proxy* presents a fully realized if intentionally opaque worldview. An anachronistic design aesthetic presides throughout, juxtaposing dandy fashions with future technologies, and later incorporating surreal remnants of our present. The series' attention to detail is staggering. With a few telling exceptions, a predominantly dark and subdued color palette casts the world of *Ergo Proxy* in shadow, concealing the mechanisms of a thoroughly convincing future.

The series incorporates two major intertextual allusions, both important to understanding its construction of meaning. In episode 1, tellingly titled "Awakening," the series establishes numerous threads that run throughout its twenty-three episodes. In addition to the awakening of the laboratory Proxy, the spread of the Cogito Virus, and the formative steps of Re-l and Vincent's eventual discoveries, the episode's title more broadly alludes to the biblical awakening of life: Genesis.

Like other anime features and series before it (e.g., *Neon Genesis Evangelion*), *Ergo Proxy* incorporates religious imagery freely but adheres to no one prescribed ideology. In an early scene Re-l laments Romdo as a "boring utopia," establishing the city as an Edenic paradise (shattered by the series' climax). The notion of original sin has no direct equivalent in *Ergo Proxy*, but Vincent and Re-l's awakening shares certain characteristics with Adam and Eve's expulsion from paradise. Like Eve, Re-l is driven by the temptation that her "eyes will be opened . . . knowing good and evil" (Gen. 3:5), visualized quite literally throughout the first episode. Vincent, at least initially, is content to live true to Romdo's instruction—"Never doubt the system, obey all the rules." But he, like Adam, is banished through circumstances beyond his control before eventually choosing Re-l as a lover.

However, despite its biblical allusions, *Ergo Proxy* isn't simply a religious parable. Again building upon themes of awakening, the series also draws specific parallels between the character of Vincent and the Russian folktale and hero *Ivan the Fool*.[3] Various interpretations of Ivan's story exist, but certain constants remain throughout. Ivan is one of three sons born to peasant parents. His brothers are unsatisfied living off the land and endeavor to seek something more: one yearns for power as a soldier, while the other pursues fortune as a merchant. Ivan, however, is too simple to long for such things and toils day and night in his father's fields, farming what is needed and desiring little else. In social stature, Vincent, an immigrant, is immediately placed alongside Ivan. Both also share the same unquestioning devotion to their designated tasks, Ivan to provide for his family and Vincent to become a good citizen. Also of note, Ivan, like Vincent, embarks on a journey to Moscow aboard a flying ship.

Of further note, in Leo Tolstoy's *A Tale About Ivan The Fool*,[4] Ivan and his brothers become rulers of their own kingdoms. Ivan's siblings rule by taxation and military might, eventually succumbing to greed and losing their wealth as a consequence. During Vincent's journey to Moscow, he finds himself in an abandoned dome, a shattered reflection of Romdo's utopia. High in an imposing tower set amid the barren expanse of urban decay, the city's sole occupant and Proxy, Kazkis Hauer, enjoys copious bottles of wine as his AutoReivs wage war on a nearby settlement. Like Ivan's brothers, this particular kingdom has been lost through greed and military maneuvers. As Proxies, Hauer and Vincent are representatives of the same Creator, suggesting an obtuse sibling relationship that further recalls Ivan and his brothers and hints at Vincent's eventual destiny.

Ergo Proxy's biblical connotations are further developed outside of Romdo. Expulsion from Eden isn't the only consequence of eating the forbidden fruit: with the knowledge of good and evil comes mortality. Throughout the series, Re-l and Vincent's journey of self-discovery pushes them to the same realization, albeit in a very different manner. Episode 11 finds Vincent lost in a suffocating fog, wandering aimlessly before stumbling upon a bookstore. Inside, hundreds of volumes litter the floor and weigh heavily on towering shelves. Their pages are blank. All, however, share the same title: Vincent Law. Like Adam, Vincent has no memories. Significantly, it is here, while confronting the riddle of his missing past (and unwritten future), that Vincent realizes his true identity. He is Ergo Proxy, the proxy of death and representative of an omnipotent creator.

"Awakening" also refers to the natural cycle of life and death to which Vincent, as Ergo Proxy, is irrevocably bound. Inside the bookstore, the first in a sequence of scenes that operate figuratively rather than literally, Ergo Proxy remarks: "Nature halted the circle of life . . . [but] cannot escape the existence of the circle." For the world to exist, man is required to recognize it as such and, as in Adam and Eve's awakening, for life to flourish, so must death. When Vincent and his comrades return to Romdo, the situation has dramatically deteriorated. Man and machine riot in the burning streets. Elsewhere, in a darkened corridor, Cogito-infected AutoReivs are kneeling in prayer. Again, with self-awareness comes fear of mortality. Paradise is crumbling.

Above the disintegrating city, Vincent climactically confronts a doppelgänger who embodies the Creator and the sadness of his rejection. As Romdo's citizens accept the end of paradise, so too must the Proxies accept that the Creator has also deserted his representatives. Empowered by his love for Re-l, when confronted with the choice between his lover and the immortality of an Angelic counterpart, Vincent forsakes the Creator's wishes, choosing human life and the natural cycle of destruction and regeneration.

By doing so Vincent sheds any associations with Ivan the Fool and for the first time takes control of his destiny. In the final scene, standing amid the devastation as sunlight breaks through oppressive black clouds, Vincent (now an amalgamation of his two previous identities) states: "[here] the real battle begins, for I am Ergo Proxy, the emissary of death." As life returns to Earth, inevitably so must death. Like the consumption of the forbidden fruit, Vincent's (re)awakening ensures that mortality again enters the world. Here, the destruction of paradise isn't so much the end of humanity as its rebirth: "Evening came, and morning came; it was the first day" (Gen. 1:5).

A testament to *Ergo Proxy*'s scope and ambition, many intertextual references remain unremarked upon. Some are purely superficial, amounting to little more than acknowledgment of works admired by the creative staff. Others, however, like those discussed above, add significant depth and meaning to both character and setting. *Ergo Proxy* represents the kind of intelligent and informed storytelling that can be achieved within genre confines and, more generally, by serialized anime as a whole. The possibilities the series projects onto a seemingly familiar canvas offers welcome respite from genre pieces that willingly repackage and resell all-too-familiar stories and ideas.

Notes

1. Bruce Bethke, "The Etymology of Cyberpunk," 2000; http://www.brucebethke.com.nf_cp.html (accessed February 20, 2007).

2. Lawrence Person, "Notes toward a Postcyberpunk Manifesto," http://slashdot.org/features/99/10/08/2123255.shtml (accessed February 20, 2007).

3. Arthur Ransome, ed., *Old Peter's Russian Tales: The Fool of the World and the Flying Ship*; http://www.surlalunefairytales.com/russian/oldpetersrussiantales/fooloftheworld.html (accessed May 16, 2007).

4. Leo Tolstoy, "Ivan the Fool," in *"Ivan the Fool," "A Lost Opportunity," and "Polikushka": Three Short Stories of Count Leo Tolstoy*, 9–80 (1885; repr., Amsterdam: Fredonia, 2001).

Molten Hot: Japanese Gal Subcultures and Fashions

THERESA M. WINGE

Patrick Macias, Izumi Evers, and Kazumi Nonaka (illustrator). *Japanese Schoolgirl Inferno: Tokyo Teen Fashion Subculture Handbook*. San Francisco, Calif.: Chronicle Books, 2004. ISBN 978-0-8118-5690-4.

Patrick Macias and Izumi Evers have packed a clever combination of historical overview, ethnographic study, subculture field guide, and fashion magazine into *Japanese Schoolgirl Inferno*. This book takes a chronological look at the chaotic and fashionable lifeworlds of teenage "gal" subcultures in Japan from the late 1960s to the present. While some of the gal subcultures highlighted in this book no longer exist, most have been immortalized in manga, anime, live-action television series, and movies. For example, the authors indicate the characters in the film *Kamikaze Girls*[1] were members of gal subcultures—the Lolita subculture and the Yanki subculture (which descended from the Lady's subculture).

The Introduction sets the context for the Tokyo teenage gal-fashion subcultural scene by sharing a narrative about a visit to a Japanese nightclub. Macias and Evers suggest that many Japanese fashion trends can be traced back to single teenage girls or groups of girls. In the Introduction, the authors describe meeting and interacting with some gal-subculture members who are savvy young women and not merely fashion statements. This point is further established throughout the book's interviews with individual subculture members. The Introduction concludes with a foldout gal-relationship chart, which presents the chronological progression and interrelated natures of the Japanese teenage gal-fashion subcultures. This chart illustrates the direct and indirect connections between Bad Gals, Sexy Gals, and Artsy Gals, from the late 1960s to present, with highly stylized illustrations of representative subculture members.

The body of *Japanese Schoolgirl Inferno* is organized chronologically, providing historic overviews of Japanese female subcultures divided into decades from the late 1960s to the present. Each female subculture highlighted includes a description of the subculture, quotes, photographs of actual members, illustrations, profiles with a diagrammed illustration of fashion details, must-have items, and the ideal boyfriend. In addition, there is supplemental information, such as how to recreate the Manba makeup, the day in the life of an Ogal and a Gothloli, and interviews with individual subculture members.

The "Bad Gals" section discusses the Sukeban, Takenokozoku, and Lady's gal subcultures. It concludes by discussing Japanese schoolgirl uniforms. These subcultures are first seen in Japan during the late 1960s and some groups continue through present day. The bad gal subcultures seem be a response to male subcultures and activities center around motorcycles (or scooters).

Macias and Evers credit the Sukeban (female boss) with being the first Japanese all-girl gang, in the late 1960s. The preferred fashions for the Sukeban is the schoolgirl uniform, especially the Sailor Fuku style, with accessories including white school shoes, razors, and chains. The Sukeban were the female counterparts to their "ideal boyfriend" the Yakuza, violent male gangs.

The Takenokozoku (bamboo sprout tribe) were street dancers who gathered in large numbers. The authors credit the Takenokozoku with reinventing and bringing youth back to the Harajuku neighborhood in the late 1970s and early 1980s. The preferred fashion for the Takenokozoku was brightly colored, baggy clothing inspired by traditional kimonos, with garish ribbons, necklaces, hats, bows, and whistles

as accessories. The ideal boyfriend for the Takenokozoku was a good dancer who shared her fashion sense.

The Ladies were all-girl biker gangs from the mid-1980s to the mid-1990s who most likely descended from the Sukeban. The preferred fashions for the Ladies were Tokku Fuku robes with *kanji* embroidery and net sandals, along with motorcycle helmets, cigarettes, and scooters or motorcycles as accessories. The Ladies were the female counterparts to the Bosozoku (speed tribe), male motorcycle gangs.

The "Bad Gals" section concludes with a discussion of schoolgirl uniforms. Macias and Evers trace the history of the Japanese schoolgirl uniform and its connections to the Gal subcultures highlighted in *Japanese Schoolgirl Inferno*. Most notably, the Kogal subculture popularized schoolgirl uniforms by exaggerating aspects of it. Japanese schools also encouraged the popularity of school uniforms by contracting designer brands, such as Benetton, Hiromichi Nakano, and ELLE, to design and update school uniforms.

The "Sexy Gals" section includes the following gal subcultures: Kogal, Gonguro, Manba, Kigurumin, and Gal, along with a "How-to Manba Make-up" and a "Day in the Life: Ogal" supplemental information. These subcultures were first seen in Japan during the mid-1990s and some groups continue today. The sexy gal subcultures commonly adopted Western styles, such as tan skin, designer brands, and blonde hair, in exaggerated ways.

According to the authors, Kogals emerged in the mid-1990s and disappeared in the late 1990s. The Kogal took its name from the words *kodomo* (child) and *gal* (for a fashionable young woman). The Kogal subculture may be the most identifiable and controversial of the gal subcultures discussed in *Japanese Schoolgirl Inferno* because of their overtly sexualized schoolgirl uniforms and (rumors of) dating older men for money. Kogal fashion consisted of shortened plaid skirts; oversized, loose socks (requiring sock glue to stay up); very tan skin; brown contact lenses; and designer clothing. The ideal boyfriend for a Kogal was a wealthy adult male, although she most likely thinks of him as an accessory. The Go-Go Yubari character in Quentin Tarantino's film *Kill Bill Vol. 1* (2003) is a Kogal.

Gonguro (blackface) was originally known as Ganguro, and the media named these women *Yamanba* (mountain witch hag). This gal subculture surfaced in the late 1990s and disappeared by the early 2000s. Their preferred fashion was extremely dark tan skin, white accented eyes and lips, bleached hair, gold jewelry, platform shoes, and short dresses. The controversy around the Gonguro was that they were rumored to be "dirty girls," lacking good hygiene habits. There is not an ideal boyfriend for the Gonguro, because this look was more repellent than attractive.

Manba surfaced as the descendants of Gonguro in the early 2000s and still exists today. As a result, many Gonguro characteristics, such as the hygiene controversy, similar make-up, and colored contact lenses, extended to the Manba. The Manba fashion includes Alba Rosa clothing (floral motifs), colored hair extensions, and facial decals. The ideal boyfriend for the Manba is a Center guy, who shares her fashion sense.

According to Macias and Evers, the Kigurumin (ethnic mascot) subculture existed only from 2002 through 2003 (but note the continuation of the animal-human fashion within the Decora subculture). The Kigurumin's preferred fashion was animal costumes and Manba make-up. There is not an ideal boyfriend for the Kigurumin because no one wants to date an animal-human character.

Gal refers to a young woman drawn to the Gal circles in certain areas of Tokyo, but in this section, Macias and Evers primarily discuss the Gals who have returned to these areas and formed a new, older Gal subculture, such as the Onee Gal (older sister). The preferred fashion for the Gal is curled hair, perfect make-up, expensive and sparkling jewelry, and high heels. The ideal boyfriend for a Gal is a wealthy, attractive young man.

The "Arty Gals" section describes Nagomu Gal, Gothloli, and Decora subcultures, and includes a "Day in the Life: Gothloli" supplement. These subcultures were first seen in Japan during the 1980s and some groups continue to the present.

The Nagomu Gal subculture was thought to reign in the streets of Tokyo during the 1980s. This subculture gathered around a common interest in Japanese subcultural music, and their name was based on an indie record label—Nagomu. The Nagomu Gal's preferred fashion was sunglasses, long-sleeved tee shirts, and rubber-soled shoes. The Nagomu Gal's ideal boyfriend was an indie band member.

According to Macias and Evers, the Gothloli subculture began in the late 1990s and continues now. However, other sources suggest this subculture has roots as early as the mid-1980s (e.g., the formation of brands such as Milk in 1989 and Metamorphose in 1993 establish the commercial success of the subculture's fashions as early as the late 1980s). The preferred fashions for the Gothloli is the black lacy dress, frilly knee-high socks, head dress, and goth-style accessories, with pale face makeup and dark eyeliner and lipstick. The ideal boyfriend for a Gothloli is a member of a Visual Kei band. *Rozen Maiden,* for example, is an anime, manga, and video game that have Gothloli characters.

The Decora is an eclectic subculture seen in Tokyo during the mid-1990s through the present day, and primarily don costumes from the pages of *Fruits* and *Fresh Fruits.*[2] The Decora are considered to be ultracute and prefer fashions of brightly colored clothing, cute character goods, and novelty accessories. The ideal boyfriend is a boy who hangs out in Harajuku and appreciates the eclectic Decora style.

The book concludes with "What Kind of Gal are You?" and a yes–no flowchart that allows the reader to determine if she (or he) is a Bad Gal, Sexy Gal, or Arty Gal. By answering questions such as "Do you like cute things?" and "Are you partial to gorgeous things?" a reader moves along a path specific to her or his fashion preferences to an end at a gal subculture destination.

Patrick Macias and Izumi Evers have presented an informative, humorous, and timely take on the global pop culture phenomenon of Japanese gal subcultures and fashions in this book. Kazumi Nonaka's illustrations complement the text and photographs to create a beneficial field guide to gal subcultures and emerging fashions in Tokyo. This book will be appreciated by a wide and varied audience for its novel and easily accessible presentation of Japanese gal subcultures and related fashions.

Notes

1. *Kamikaze Girls,* dir. Nakashima Tetsuya (Viz Video, 2006).

2. Aoki Shoichi, *Fruits* (New York: Phaidon Press, 2001), and *Fresh Fruits* (New York: Phaidon Press, 2005).

Monstrous Toys of Capitalism

BRENT ALLISON

Anne Allison. *Millennial Monsters: Japanese Toys and the Global Imagination.* Los Angeles: University of California Press, 2006. ISBN 0520245652

Anne Allison's latest book examines Japan's powerful toy manufacturing industry, a rapidly growing influence on the global toy market. Allison (no relation to the reviewer) introduces her book with its main point—she attributes the global success of Japanese toys to the sense of mastery that they offer children. While this point is not new, children's ability to disassemble and recombine disparate parts of these toys speak to children who crave "commodity animism" (86) as a result and corrective of life governed by fluctuating postmodern capital. This monstrous political economy of endless consumption results in similarly monstrous arrangements of living and subjectivities that are shifting, porous, and fragmented (30). This review will offer a brief summary of the book and interrogate issues that Allison discusses.

Japan found its industry and militarist ideology vanquished by the destruction from World War II. Ironically it was from the waste tin left by the occupying American victors that ingenious Japanese restarted an export market of toys, like model U.S. Army jeeps, to circulate back to American children (39). A new nationalist ideology bolstered by hard work and optimism for industrial and consumer technologies manifested itself in two major postwar cultural products. The monstrous reptilian Gojira and the childlike robot Tetsuwan Atomu served as different models of Japan(ese) rebuilt with technology, respectively imbued with anxiety and promise (40–65). Gojira, becoming Godzilla in the United States, had, due to failures of cultural translation and appreciation, also modeled perceived Japanese filmmaking cheesiness for Americans for decades (47).

Japan's impressive economic recovery was equaled by its thirst for high-tech consumer products and the rise of a fragmented subjectivity wherein the only commonality was the shared reality of an atomized lifestyle (70). This is in large part Allison's explanation for the social dysfunctions of general stress, *hikikomori* (or reclusive "shut-ins"), and incidents of violence well publicized in a country that perceives itself as lacking in crime. To Allison, this monstrous state of living is one side of the same capitalist coin with the monsters that pervade the Japanese toy market. It is not that toys cause these problems, Allison suggests, but that both are birthed from the same political economy.

This condition prompts Allison to treat the *Mighty Morphin Power Rangers* less forgivingly than the other artifacts of Japanese popular culture she discusses. For her, *Power Rangers* is "the embodiment of post-Fordism and a postmodern aesthetics in the realm of children's mass culture" (97) without being much else.

("Post-Fordism" is another name for a postindustrial economic condition dominated by service industries.) The superheroes are but a model of Japanese (team) workers imbued with "Weberian animist spirits" that combine Shinto cosmological sensibilities with a devoted work ethic and high-tech tools serving the state in new flexible capitalist configurations writ in spandex. *Power Rangers* requires few plausible plot devices and little audience investment in the stories and human characters; information about the tools is much more extensive. As such, it lends itself less to an in-depth examination of its fantasy world and audience reception, and more to classic macroeconomic and macrosexual analyses that she uses here. Allison compares the transnational production of *Power Rangers* with a hybridized U.S.–Japanese auto plant and the camera's gaze on tools, warriors, and robots with the "money shot" found in hardcore pornography. From her observations, the reader may infer that the franchise has all the soul of either.

Sailor Moon is treated somewhat more kindly, but it does not escape some intense criticism. A common complaint about the sexiness of the Sailor Scouts registers with Allison as an overt appeal to older men who fetishize female school students wearing traditional sailor suits. She uses this criticism as an opportunity to segue into an attack on salaryman–student *enjo kousai* ("compensated dating"), a practice on the relative decline. However, given that they are superheroes, Allison acknowledges that it is difficult to categorize the franchise as either wholly sexist or feminist (142). What seems to bother Allison more is the show's idealization of transformational practices (which she codes as consumptive) as a marker of power and femininity desired both by female and even male fans envying the status of the *shōjo* as a cavalier consumer. Less convincing is her sharp dichotomy between boy- and girl-oriented shows in general (e.g. "science, technology, and nationalism" vs. "magic, dreams, and relationships"

[137]). But there are counterexamples: *shōnen* megahits like *Bleach* and *One Piece* have lots of magic, *Gundam Wing* rebukes nationalism, and *Hikaro no Go* is very dreamlike. In these shows, as also in *Dragon Ball* and *Fullmetal Alchemist,* loyal friendship is valued above all else, and those who reject it usually meet a harsh end.

Allison brings up an important general point about *Sailor Moon,* anime, and manga that is disputed by Susan Napier:[1] most of the characters look or at least can pass as Caucasian (146). This notion was critical to Bandai and the U.S. DIC network when the latter imported the show for U.S. broadcast (150). These importers asked themselves how much should the show be Americanized, given that the characters can visually pass as European American? Bandai apparently did not think that the *Sailor Moon* dolls looked "American" enough, so it altered them to look more like Barbie (152). According to Allison, the Japaneseness of the characters did not register on the radar of fans at all, despite her assertion that the dolls carried the "smell" of cultural difference that subverted their ability to build interest in the show (155). However, from my own conversations with fans, it was *because* the U.S. dolls were made to look more Barbie-ish and less like the original Japanese anime characters that fans continue to seek out and buy the original Japanese-made dolls.

The *tamagotchi* as an electronic device shares much with its forerunners, the karaoke machine and Walkman, in reconfiguring body, space, and subjectivity (164). However, it does so through replicating a very mundane activity: the user takes care of a virtual pet. In noting this shift from identifying with heroes to reliving the everyday via prosthetic, dependent, and cybernetic life, Allison takes the reader back to the classical sociology of Émile Durkheim. If the imagination inherent in specialized and stationary rituals and ceremonies reifies the everyday, then using imagination in the everyday with a portable, queer *tomagotchi*—that is, queer in the sense of challenging the traditional paradigm of keeping animals—is both unstable but also comforting in a lifestyle that is itself in a state of shift and fluctuation (180).

Allison positions *Pokémon* as allowing the consumer both to raise imaginative creatures and to achieve a heroic status (à la *Power Rangers* and *Sailor Moon)* by becoming a Pokémon master. She uses the Foucauldian theorization of knowledge (and, by extension, power) to promote *Pokémon*'s emphasis on knowledge acquisition and creature care over the eye candy fetishization (in the Freudian and Marxist sense) of the *Power Rangers'* and *Sailor Moon*'s "money shot" (103). For Allison, it isn't that *Pokémon* is devoid of fetish but rather that the interactivity inhering in *Pokémon* bequeaths a more empowering, or at least less exploitive, fetishization in children's play. Here Allison makes her boldest franchise-specific assertion: "*Pokémon* capitalism" allows commodities to "double as gifts and companions" (197) by referencing a milieu of premodern animist spiritualism in "New Age" aesthetics. The pocket monsters promote capitalist Japan's ascendancy, but act as the accomplice and corrective of its monstrous exploitation of its people. Curiously, Allison never defines what "New Age" means exactly, nor where this age is taking Japan and North America in terms of capitalist cycles of accumulation, alienation, and healing. The answer, by implication, is not much of anywhere.

Anecdotes of violent incidents perpetuated by persons connected to these pop culture products dot the book, but because Allison stresses the lack of causality between the two, it is unclear what the references accomplish. While she rightly avoids the antifan sentiments of older academic research in this area, Allison assumes that U.S. fans equate Japaneseness with coolness and lack interest in their products' authentic Japaneseness for its own sake. This drives home her point about fan fetishization. However, it overlooks fans' need for authentically Japanese *narratives* behind the products that can speak to their identities as fans, many of whom participate in an active pedagogy of Japanese culture to make sense of both of them.

Nevertheless, Allison researched her theoretical tools and her subject matter very well. She makes especially keen insights on hybridity, mutability, and perfomativity in unexplored contexts of character identity. While postmodern in much of her approach, Allison remains steadfastly critical, even Marxist in her sensibilities toward the likes of Usagi and Pikachu. However, even those who do not occupy any of these critical camps should nonetheless make room on their shelves and in their reading schedules if they are at all interested in these new configurations of production and play.

Note

1. Susan Napier, *Anime: From "Akira" to "Howl's Moving Castle"* (New York: Palgrave, 2005)

If Casshern Doesn't Do It, Who Will?

DEBORAH SHAMOON

Kiriya Kazuaki (director). *Casshern*. 2004. Momentum Pictures. ASIN B0007Q6RZ4.

Japan may produce more science fiction epic films and television shows than any other country, but except for the Godzilla franchise, nearly all of them are animated; the United States still corners the market on live-action sci-fi. The reason, obviously, is money: the two-hour-plus special-effects extravaganza is prohibitively expensive to produce. But perhaps advances in CGI could change that. Behold, *Casshern*: Kiriya Kazuaki's massive, visually stunning epic. It features live actors performing in front of a green screen, with all the effects and nearly all the backgrounds added digitally. According to its IMDb entry,[1] its budget was a paltry $6 million, compared to $200 million for *Spider-Man 2,* released the same year. With a visual aesthetic much closer to anime and Hong Kong action films than *tokusatsu* ("special effects" films and TV shows such as *Ultraman*), *Casshern* could indicate a new direction for the genre, away from rubber-suited monsters and campy effects. But while the look is new, the story remains deeply indebted to classic 1970s anime and suggests that lingering memories of World War II have not lost their grip on the Japanese artistic psyche, even in the twenty-first century.

The film *Casshern* is a remake of a 1973 anime TV show called *Jinzo ningen Kyasshan* (Artificial human Casshern), directed by Sasagawa Hiroshi and produced by Tatsunoko, briefly revived in a straight-to-video series in 1993.[2] The new film version has a shiny CGI gloss and serious tone meant to appeal to the thirty-somethings who grew up watching it. Upon its release in Japan, the film did fairly well at the box office (although it never reached number one).[3] DreamWorks bought the rights soon after, but never provided a U.S. theatrical release. In October 2007, Paramount Home Entertainment released a DVD labeled a "director's cut," but in fact the runtime was cut by nearly thirty minutes, obscuring the political message of the film. It seems unlikely the director himself made those cuts.

Casshern offers a nightmare vision of an alternative future, in which Japan was not defeated in World War II but has colonized most of Asia and Russia, destroying both the natural environment and the native people. The visuals are lush and astonishing, packed with hulking, decaying machinery, monumental architecture, and an evocative mixture of *kanji* and Cyrillic text. *Casshern* looks like a 1930s Soviet propaganda poster come to life—with robots. It's a golden twilight and deep red–tinted fusion of retro-fascist, goth, and steampunk aesthetics that looks refreshingly original in a sea of green-and-black-toned *Matrix* rip-offs (including the latest *Appleseed* movie). It's probably not going too far to say that *Casshern* is the most visually inventive sci-fi film since the first *Matrix*. *Casshern* is not so much a live-action film as a computer-animated film with occasional close-ups of live actors. Furthermore, Kiriya (the writer, director, and cinematographer) makes it work because, rather than trying to make it all look real, he revels in an anime-type fakeness appropriate to the operatic storyline. He makes the human actors move like anime characters and in the fight scenes uses quick cuts, point-of-view shots, and extreme close-ups so you never have time to wonder how it's done. Even in the static dialog scenes, he arranges the actors in beautifully staged, CGI-embellished tableaux, like the layered panels of a manga page. Many scenes with the live actors are filmed to look deliberately blurred, distorted, or overexposed, and shot in grainy black and white for daringly long segments. It's the only way to make this hybrid of CGI and live action work and to give the convoluted story gravitas by foreclosing any questions of logic and believability.

The Nazi- and Soviet-inspired aesthetics of the backgrounds establish the ominous tone of the story. In this alternative-future Greater East Asia, ruled by a decaying, corrupt Imperial Japan, a group of Frankenstein-like clones called the Neoroids (or Neo-Humans, depending on the translation) attempt to destroy all humans with their robot army. Humanity's last best hope is Tetsuya (Iseya Yusuke), a reanimated corpse with posttraumatic stress disorder and a stretchy vinyl exoskeleton that prevents his superstrong body from exploding. Although Kiriya has eliminated some of the more childish aspects of the TV version (notably the robot dog Friender), the characters are mostly stock types from 1970s anime: Tatsuya's unloving scientist father Dr. Azuma (Terao Akira); his sickly, sainted mother archetypically named Midori (Higuchi Kanako); his innocent, childlike girlfriend Luna (Aso Kumiko); and the evil council of wrinkly old politicos. The team of Neoroids is equally stereotypical: the charismatic psychopath Burai (Karasawa Toshiaki) as the leader, the bitchy fighting girl (Sada Mayumi), the vain handsome guy (Kaname Jun), and the irritating hunchback (Miyasako Hiroyuki). As with so much anime, there are long soliloquies on what it means to be human, the evils of war, vague mysticism, and rampant oedipal conflict, all ending of course with the obligatory image of Tetsuya and Luna as children, running together in an idyllic green field.

Although there are occasional mentions of cloning and terrorism inserted to give the plot a veneer of currency, like many anime of the 1970s the real context of *Casshern* is World War II and the expression of collective guilt over Japanese wartime atrocities, in this case, vivisection and the slaughter of civilians. When the film begins, Dr. Azuma receives funding from a smarmy government lackey named Naito (Oikawa Mitsuhiro) to grow spare body parts in a lab. While the government hopes to extend the life of its aging leader General Kamijo (Nishijima Hidetoshi), Dr. Azuma primarily wants to cure his wife, who has gone blind from exposure to environmental pollution. A mysterious accident in the lab causes the parts to assemble into full bodies. Thus the Neoroids are born, and Azuma is able to revive his dead son Tetsuya. But the secret truth of Azuma's lab, revealed at the end of the film, is that the body parts were harvested from an ethnic group in a colonized region of central Asia called Zone 7. This population, called Original Humans, have cells that are capable of regeneration; they have been systematically slaughtered and harvested by Japanese soldiers, of whom Tetsuya was one. The name Zone 7 is a reference to the notorious Unit 731 in Manchuria, where during the war Japanese scientists carried out vivisection and other experiments on thousands of men, women, and children. Among the experiments were attempts to amputate and reattach limbs and internal organs.[4] The name of the official who funds Azuma's lab, Naito, is also a reference to the second-in-command at Unit 731, Lieutenant Colonel Naito Ryoichi, who after the war testified to the Americans and later went on to found the controversial Green Cross blood bank, accused of unethical practices in the late 1980s.[5] The Original Humans literally embody the lands and cultures of the Greater East Asia Co-Prosperity Sphere, which Imperial Japan intended to use as raw materials to sustain itself.

Both the Neoroids and Tetsuya are haunted by the violence of their shared past, which in the trauma of being revived they have repressed and partially forgotten. Throughout the film, Tetsuya suffers disturbing flashbacks to his time as a soldier in Zone 7 when he shot a civilian, but the full significance of this murder comes at the end of the film, when the Neoroids' identity as the Original Humans of Zone 7 is revealed. Burai and Tetsuya share several moments of intense recognition but, tragically, are unable to realize their shared humanity and work together to end the war, and so the film lurches toward its inevitable apocalyptic end.

Tetsuya as Casshern is in the end not much of a hero, but there aren't really any "good guys" in the film, only more-or-less sympathetic bad guys, reflecting Japan's own wartime past. Tetsuya's personal war crime, half repressed, has left him spiritually dead, even after his body is reanimated, and only complete destruction of the world can offer him the slightest hope of redemption. This is a sober reflection on the lingering effects of the war on the Japanese spirit. In *Bodies of Memory*, Igarashi Yoshikuni writes that the repressed memories of World War II return in Japanese popular culture in monstrous, horrifying form.[6] The monstrous bodies of *Casshern* are a reminder of Japanese war crimes, both individual and national, which have still not been adequately examined or atoned for.

As the war between the humans and the Neoroids escalates, Tetsuya's mother begs him to stop it. But as he fails to prevent Burai from detonating an enormous bomb, I am reminded of the tagline of the original TV show: "*Kyasshan ga yaraneba, dare ga yaru?*" ("If Casshern doesn't do it, who will?"). When it comes to transcending human nature and ending warfare, perhaps no one. This is a bleak ending indeed, but as

Japan begins to flirt with a return to militarism, it is one that is still relevant.

Notes

1. http://imdb.com/title/tt0405821/

2. Jonathan Clements and Helen McCarthy, *The Anime Encyclopedia: A Guide to Japanese Animation Since 1917*, revised and expanded edition (Berkeley, Calif.: Stone Bridge Press, 2006), 90.

3. http://www.animenewsnetwork.com/encyclopedia/anime.php?id=3439

4. Peter Williams and David Wallace, *Unit 731: Japan's Secret Biological Warfare in World War II* (New York: The Free Press, 1989), 48–49; Sheldon Harris, *Factories of Death: Japanese Biological Warfare, 1932–1945, and the American Cover-Up* (New York: Routledge, 2005), 81–82.

5. Williams and Wallace, *Unit 731*, 241.

6. Igarashi Yoshikuni, *Bodies of Memory: Narratives of War in Postwar Japanese Culture, 1945–1970* (Princeton, N.J.: Princeton University Press, 2000).

Psychoanalytic Cyberpunk Midsummer-Night's Dreamtime: Kon Satoshi's *Paprika*

TIMOTHY PERPER AND MARTHA CORNOG

Kon Satoshi (director). *Paprika*. 2007.
Tokyo: Sony Pictures. ASIN B000058V80.
Translated as *Paprika*. Columbia-Tristar.
ASIN B000PFU8SO.

Paprika is a delicious animated version of a science fiction novel by Yasutaka Tsutsui about a device that allows psychologists to enter people's dreams.[1] Although much lighter in tone than Kon's previous films, *Paprika* is deeper than it seems. Three of the most illuminating allusions in *Paprika* are to Ryutaro Nakamura's 1998 *Serial Experiments Lain,* Mamoru Oshii's 1984 *Beautiful Dreamer,* and Oshii's 2004 *Innosenzu.* These three create a map for locating *Paprika*'s psychoanalytic cyberpunk exploration of fantasy and reality.

Paprika is not a difficult anime the way *Lain* and *Innosenzu* are. Its images draw from avant-garde anime but Kon's earlier *Millennium Actress* is a more adventurous challenge to filmic continuity and separation of frame, background, and action. *Paprika* reinvents some well-known concepts—that dreams are windows into other realities and have great power, that the boundaries of self are not set by consensus reality, that troubles stew in the worlds revealed by dreams, and that dreams can be accessed like playing a DVD with the bio-psycho-electronic DC-Mini machine in the film. Such ideas go back to Lum in *Beautiful Dreamer* and the 1945 British film *Dead of Night,* and to Freud, *Alice in Wonderland,* and Australian aboriginal ideas about the Dreamtime as that great place of gods, totems, and origins that lives with us forever in eternal synchronicity.[2] So *Paprika* invites a middlebrow audience to see familiar mysteries in vivid, primary-color life.

But *Paprika* can bewilder certain viewers. Something *is* difficult in *Paprika*—the nature of dreams, of the *kami,* and of art itself.

Take an example of what *Paprika* is not. In the classic *Wizard of Oz* film, Dorothy travels from a black-and-white, Depression-era America to a Technicolor Land of Oz located in a dream-like Somewhere Else, and, when Dorothy finally returns to Kansas, the film becomes a trip There and Back. But the DC-Mini machine in *Paprika* is not a magical cyclone bringing us to a Slumberland where fantasy comes true. Yes, one can enter dreams through the DC-Mini, but the machine opens a two-way gate. The DC-Mini lets the dream world escape from our minds and materialize in concrete solidity right here in *our* world. Then its power becomes contagious. Because it lets dreams emerge into reality, dreams coalesce into ever more complex dreams—and then *those* dreams become real. So anyone using the machine can infect other people's dreams. When three DC-Mini machines are stolen at the start of *Paprika,* a quickly escalating mass of intersecting dreams becomes real for everyone collectively. And in the hands of a psychopath, the machine is deadly.

In *Paprika,* the Dreamtime—a place of origins, totems, and *kami*—is not a private, alternate mental-psychological-cognitive state but becomes the interpenetrating registers of a unified collective reality. The Dreamtime opened by the DC-Mini is therefore close kin to the Wired in *Serial Experiments Lain.* So the DC-Mini machine is not simply a psychological passport for entering a hallucinatory Slumberland. It is a *reification* machine and is familiar from Shakespeare:

> The poet's eye, in a fine frenzy rolling,
> Doth glance from heaven to earth,
> from earth to heaven,
> And as imagination bodies forth
> The forms of things unknown, the poet's pen
> Turns them to shape, and gives to airy nothing
> A local habitation and a name.[3]

The DC-Mini machine is precisely such a pen.

One person, Paprika herself, stands outside these processes.[4] Even middlebrow reviewers have noticed that Paprika is not simply psychologist Dr. Atsuko Chiba's alter-ego for entering patient's dreams but is a flirty, standalone goddess of dreams in her own right.[5] In fact, Paprika runs away with the film: its detective-story frame (who stole the DC-Mini?) and its *Beautiful Dreamer/Innosenzu*–style dream imagery are no match for Paprika skipping down a street or popping up on some random otaku's T-shirt or fluttering through a marvelous sequence with little fairy wings while giant tree roots chase her. The cyberpunk frame induces us to see Paprika only as part of Dr. Chiba's personality, someone younger and sexier hidden under the psychologist's austere Professional Female Scientist manner and costume. But that view is too narrow: Dr. Chiba is also *Paprika's* alter ego. Paprika is playing, flying, laughing, flirting, having a wonderful time in *her* world. Paprika is the main reality of this film.

Proof? Not hard. Dreams are a playground of primal needs, emotions, fears, and desires. Of these, what the Freudians call "oral needs" are basic, and who does Paprika/Dr. Chiba like the most? Dr. Tokita, partly because he is immensely fat but also because he is the closest to the Dreamtime: his are the *appetites* of dreaming. Paprika/Dr. Chiba knows about appetites: in the crucial scene of the film, she/they cheerfully devours the now immense bad guy, Chairman—all of him—in one hugely hungry moment of pure *incorporative* appetite. *Shlurp.*

And Paprika—and Dr. Chiba, when she gets into it—can be very sexy. We see Paprika's flirtatiousness more often and more openly than we see Dr. Chiba's sexuality, but Dr. Chiba *likes* the way Dr. Tokita feels, and Paprika thinks it's just fine that a huge, dream-enhanced Dr. Tokita (he is now a robot) picks up Dr. Chiba and pops her into his mouth. If there is any single image of desire in the film, it is this. One might think that devouring the heroine is a quick ticket to a bad end, but that is not the logic of *Paprika*—or of dreams. Dr. Chiba will soon rematerialize to pull Dr. Tokita out of a wall where his newly dream-enhanced but clumsy giant robot body got stuck when he collided with a building. And with that, we encounter two additional mysteries: the nature of the Dreamtime and the origin of Paprika.

The dreams in *Paprika* are not solely individual inventions come to life. Instead, the Dreamtime also embodies a *collective* unconscious, where myths, legends, and beings of folklore all reside. Viewers can decide if such legends existed first only in imagination and later were brought to physical reality by the DC-Mini or if the legends always inhabited a Dreamtime and merely pop through to visit us whenever the machine is used. Either way, they're real *now*—robots, walking mailboxes and refrigerators, beckoning cats, Buddhas, dolls European and Japanese, tiny airplanes—all on living parade with great and noisy enthusiasm in the streets of Tokyo. Fortunately for civic order and sanity, Paprika is among them.

One of Paprika's origins is as the tapir (*baku*) who eats nightmares, most notably from Rumiko Takahashi's *Lum Urusei*Yatsura* and from Oshii's second film version of *Lum, Beautiful Dreamer*. Apparently, this tapir was originally Chinese folklore,[6] but Takahashi adopted him. Paprika is not a tapir, and she is not exactly eating a dream, but she is eating monsters from a dream world, so she counts as an honorary, if symbolic, tapir: someone who, against Western logic, controls dreams by turning their most basic mechanism (the appetites) against them. Lain would understand perfectly.

The second origin figure is *Mahoutsukai Sally* (Magical girl Sally), from the 1966 manga by Yokoyama Mitsuteru.[7] Paprika, too, is a *mahou tsukai,* someone who can use and control magic. In fact, even if Paprika is older, she looks a good deal like Sally, and both are quite playful. And both can fly.

So, does any of this help us understand the film? Well, yes.

Take two early scenes. The first is a quite straightforward dream sequence. In it, the dreamer-protagonist Detective Konakawa lacks volition, and places and shapes morph fluidly into things they are not. So if *Paprika*'s primary colors, movement, and events make no conscious sense, they still reveal a palette for portraying dreams.

Then Konakawa awakens, and we return to neo-futurist sci-fi machines, shadows, and ominous metallic-blue corridors, all from *Bubblegum Crisis* and *Neon Genesis Evangelion*. These cross-references to *Beautiful Dreamer* and *Bubblegum Crisis* elicit a repertorial menu based on our familiarity with anime. When we try comprehend *Paprika* using this repertoire of cinematic cross-talk, we enter into certain viewing relationships to the film. One is the middlebrow vision mentioned above. Then *Paprika* becomes merely a sci-fi detective story about the mysteries of the mind set into the quasi-realism of one of Kon's favorite animation styles.

But when we meet the bad guy, Chairman, he is a dead ringer for Kim, the hacker in Oshii's *Innosenzu*. He's more than a trendy visitor from another anime; he's a warning that the mise en scene we've seen is not the real background of *this* film. And Paprika herself is not from *Innosenzu* at all—for example, she bounces about skipping and (multiplied into *four* Paprikas) disdainfully sneering at two harmless young men who try to meet her and then taking off on a motorbike that becomes a car. Realism, even the quasi-realism of the opening dream sequence, simply evaporates: we have entered the Dreamtime—not the *dream* of an anxious psychiatric patient, but the *Dreamtime* itself.

And now the film is home. It is about the Dreamtime and isn't a detective story at all. It's about those portions of the cosmos where dreams and totems live, and where—it turns out—so do bubbly *mahou tsukai* like Paprika. Kon's film is a delightful fantasy/allegory about consensus reality versus freedom and creativity. In the end art and freedom win, and the film feels like springtime.

It isn't clear how come Dr. Chiba knows Paprika. The two are good friends, and Paprika pops up whenever Dr. Chiba needs her. But one conclusion *is* clear. Dr. Chiba and Paprika do not merge with each other so much as enhance each other. They are dwellers not on the threshold but, like Lain, are inhabitants of multiple worlds. The result is that both Paprika and Dr. Chiba are perfectly happy that Konakawa rescues Dr. Chiba, now become a semi-naked Jane to his Tarzan in a Tarzan movie (plus a talking chimpanzee in a movie poster) that Konakawa has dreamed up for himself and Dr. Chiba. In the Dreamtime, appetite-laden narratives stand as archetypes for the lesser realities of everyday life.

Throughout the film, as the participants' dreams fuse and interact, the viewer is invited to disentangle different dream fabrics. Paprika herself does not have her own dream figurations, as befits her role as *kami* of the Dreamtime, but everyone else's dreams, sometimes malign, sometimes benign, are vivid and complex. From Dr. Shima comes a vibrantly loud totemic procession; a repeated nightmare plus Tarzan from Detective Konokawa; decayed dolls, corpses, and graffiti from Himuro; paranoid butterflies and rape from Osanai; power-maddened tree roots from the Chairman; a cheerful, if large, robot from Dr. Tokita; and, from Dr. Chiba, a charming, low-key romance. Against them are the dull tones of waking reality and cityscape ferroconcrete, which cannot compete with dancing umbrellas, frog bands, or even the abandoned theme parks of the Dreamtime, more accurately, the immensely rich graphic imagination of Japanese art itself. There is no question where Kon stands on *that* issue. In *Paprika,* art wins.

So, unlike *Innosenzu,* where entry into the decadent parallel universes of cyberspace implies profound danger and loss, *Paprika* ends happily. The evil Chairman has been devoured, Konakawa is free of his anxieties, and Dr. Chiba has happily latched onto Dr. Tokita, who does not seem to mind at all. By implication, the DC-Mini machine—with some new access controls!—will be approved by the government, and people will be happier with their dreams. And behind the dreams, the Dreamtime itself beckons.

Notes

1. Yasutaka Tsutsui, *Paprika* (Tokyo: Shinchosha, 1993). The novel was first serialized in 1991. The Sony DVD is in Japanese only, but the Columbia-Tristar DVD is French-made and has French, English, and Arabic subtitles. Both are region 2 DVDs.

2. And goes back to British science fiction writer Peter Philips's 1948–49 *Dreams Are Sacred,* in which psychiatrists invent a machine allowing the therapist to enter a patient's dreams. Like the DC-Mini, their contraption also causes untold problems. Philips's story was translated into Japanese in 1980 as *Yume ha shinsei,* in *Worldwide humor SF masterpiece selection 1,* ed. Asakura Hisashi, (Tokyo: Kodansha).

3. Shakespeare, *A Midsummer-Night's Dream,* Act 5, sc. 1.

4. She is actually not the only one. In another allusion to *Serial Experiments Lain,* in *Paprika's* "www.radioclub.jp" bar—where she's a regular and even runs a tab!—the two bartenders are also external to the dream machine. But their voice actors are Satoshi Kon and Yasutaka Tsutsui, the director and the author, so they're allowed to stand outside the dream frame. If you ask where this bar is, the answer is the Dreamtime.

5. Justin Sevąkis, "Beyond My Mind: Paprika," *Protoculture Addicts* 92 (May–June 2007): 20–25.

6. For traditional Japanese dreameaters (*baku*), see Hori Tadao, "Cultural Note on Dreaming and Dream Study in the Future: Release from Nightmare and Development of Dream Control Technique," *Sleep and Biological Rhythms,* 3 (2005): 49–55; Adam L. Kern, *Manga from the Floating World: Comicbook Culture and the Kibyoshi of Edo Japan* (Cambridge, Mass.: Harvard University Asian Center, 2007), 236, figure 4.26. For a modern example of the tapir as dreameater, see Takahashi Rumiko, "Waking to a Nightmare," in *The Return of Lum: Urusei Yatsura,* 141–56 (San Francisco: Viz, 1995).

7. Yokoyama Mitsuteru, *Mahoutsuki Sarii* (Tokyo: Kodansha, 2007).

トレンド
Torendo
Interview with Murase Shūkō and Satō Dai

DEBORAH SCALLY, ANGELA DRUMMOND-MATHEWS, AND MARC HAIRSTON

Murase Shūkō and Satō Dai have worked together on some of the most notable anime of the past decade. Murase was an animator or director on numerous *Gundam* series and directed *Witch Hunter Robin* (2002, *Witchi hantaa robin*). Satō has written the screenplays or scripts for *Cowboy Bebop* (1998–99, *Kaubōi bibappu*), *Eureka Seven* (2005–6, *Kōkyōshihen Eureka sebun*), *Wolf's Rain* (2003, *Urufuzu rein*), and *Ghost in the Shell: Stand Alone Complex* (2002–3, *Kōkaku kidōtai STAND ALONE COMPLEX*). They worked together on *Samurai Champloo* (2004–5, *Samurai chanpurū*) and in 2005 collaborated on developing and making *Ergo Proxy* (2006, *Erugo Purakushii*). This interview took place at *AnimeFest* in Dallas, Texas, on September 3, 2007.

DEBORAH SCALLY AND ANGELA DUMMOND-MATHEWS: *Ergo Proxy* was one of the most unique and original anime released in the United States in 2007. We would like to know the origin of this narrative. Did you already have an idea for the series or were you approached by someone else with the idea?

MURASE SŪKŌ: I think I can say that *Ergo Proxy* is almost all my idea. Manglobe, the company that produced it, approached me and just told me, "Make something." They gave me the freedom to come up with any idea I chose for an anime. So the idea I created became the basis for *Ergo Proxy*. In the process of creation, Mr. Satō and I collaborated, along with many other young writers, and produced the final version of the anime.

DS/AD-M: Why did you choose to reference René Descartes in *Ergo Proxy*? Were either of you interested in Western philosophy before you started on the show?

MURASE: At first I wanted to do something about the concept of everyone having another *self* inside of themselves: the idea that there are two personalities inside a person. My main theme for the show was to do something based

on that concept. Descartes' phrase *cogito ergo sum* sort of triggered the idea.

DS/AD-M: We got the sense that the main theme of the series focused on taking responsibility for what you create in the world. But Vincent seemed to be always trying to run away from what was inside him, to run away from what he had created. Is that correct?

MURASE: Yes, Vincent was definitely trying to get away from that other existence inside of himself.

DS/AD-M: In general, do you think anime is strengthened or weakened by incorporating these Western philosophical concepts into the story?

MURASE: Superficially at least, I don't think the Japanese are particularly influenced by these philosophical themes. Essentially, the Japanese do not seem to understand or have the nerve to look directly at their own inner selves, and that is why there are so many problems in Japanese society right now. In that sense, the entire population of Japan is in some way trying to run away from their problems, just like Vincent was running away from those aspects inside of himself. I made *Ergo Proxy* in the hope of representing this problem.

DS/AD-M: We were fascinated by the heavy influence of gnostic philosophy we noticed in the narrative, and we were wondering why you chose to do so?

MURASE: Are you asking about the philosophical question "are human beings born bad (*seiakusetsu*)"? I answer that question by referencing my own inner self. I think I am not perfect: I might even say I am essentially a bit abnormal (*abu*). On one hand, there is the theory that human beings are good when they are born, but they do bad things because of the outside influences as they live (*seizensetsu*). On the other hand, there is a theory that says human beings are born with both a good side and a bad side (*seiakusetsu*). I personally believe in the latter concept, and think if people only did whatever they wanted to do, then society would collapse. I think the former idea has some flaws. These ideas and views are always in my work.

What I am trying to say is that some people think: "I am not the one to blame for my actions, society is." But I think the ideal society would be where people accept that "I am partially responsible for the fact that I am in such a bad situation." Sometimes, when a person is in a bad situation, that person tends to think that his or her environment is to blame. But every person has some bad aspects inside themselves, and if they are not aware of that, then something will go wrong.

But that didn't really answer your question, did it?

DS/AD-M: We were asking because what stands out in the anime was how much the *language* of gnosticism was used: terms like "monad" and "demiurge" were used along with the concept of the "blind creator."

SATŌ DAI: We didn't explicitly want to express the concepts of gnosticism in the show. It was just that our personal beliefs ended up reflecting the ideas of gnosticism, so *after* the fact, we realized how well these terms fit and used them. For example, the creator forgets the fact that he or she is responsible for what he or she created and consequently becomes a "blind creator." Vince and the others were born with these issues and were running away from them. Although they ran away, they could not escape what they had created and ended up having to face up to their own responsibility.

MURASE: Philosophy and sociology are related to what's in our hearts . . .

SATŌ: . . . something like a mirror that reflects what is in our minds. But we were not making *Ergo Proxy* in order to express that notion. Philosophy is a mirror that reflects the society it comes from, and maybe the same thing could be said about anime.

DS/AD-M: The contrast between Re-l and Vincent in the story is very intriguing. It seems as if Re-l was supposed to be a witness to the transformations in society around her, while Vincent rarely opened his eyes.

MURASE: There are two ways to approach character design. We can start with the aspects of the character and then go on to make the physical design. Or, we can start from the design itself and then add the elements of the character. We tend to go either way in our work. In the case of Vincent, we wanted him to have different facial expressions from the others, so we started out with his eyes closed. The fact that his eyes are closed implies that he is not facing the reality, implying that he is not seeing all the things that have happened so far in a metaphoric way. In the case of Re-l, she is a strong character but we did not intentionally or logically make her design to counter the blindness of Vincent. But at a subconscious level, I think we had the idea of contrasting the eyes of these two characters.

DS/AD-M: The name "Re-l" sounds like the English word "real." Was that done deliberately to be symbolic or was that just an accident between the two languages?

SATŌ: No, that was deliberate. She and her name are supposed to represent reality. Her code number is "1-2-4-c" or "one to foresee." There are multiple versions of Re-l because they represent the multiple versions of reality.

DS/AD-M: So the final version of Re-l, the final reality, comprises the Daedelus and Icarus motif with the "monad" flying away?

FIGURE 1. In *Ergo Proxy*, Re-l was a witness to the transformations in society around her, while Vincent rarely opened his eyes.

SATŌ: Exactly. No one pointed that out in Japan.

DS/AD-M: So you put in that point *just* for the American audience?

SATŌ: (laughs loudly)

DS/AD-M: Were you frustrated that the Japanese audience did not get the allusion, or were you doing it to try and expose them to these Western myths?

MURASE: Most Japanese people do know the term "the wings of Icarus," but most of them probably do not know the story behind the phrase. They just know the superficial part of it. But the wings of Icarus story is part of larger Minotaur myth, and I wanted to include the Minotaur story in the *Ergo Proxy*.

DS/AD-M: So most Japanese do not know the story of the Minotaur?

SATŌ: That's right.

DS/AD-M: So was *Ergo Proxy* better received in the United States than in Japan because of all these elements with which the American audience would be more familiar?

MURASE: In general, the Japanese missed most of the elements of symbolism we incorporated in our work.

SATŌ: They cannot perceive them.

MURASE: I put many elements of those symbols in the design in hope that they would understand them, but the Japanese audiences could not see them. When I read something like the English-language Wikipedia entries on *Ergo Proxy,* I find Americans are a lot more interested in those elements, and they recognize the symbolism.

SATŌ: The Japanese-language Wikipedia article about *Ergo Proxy* is very short. The Italian and French Wikipedia articles are huge! (laughs) One thing that comes to my mind is that folklore around the world had been passed on orally from person to person, but today people do not communicate that way. So in my view, anime is a box where we can put this folklore and these mythologies for people to see them and hopefully think about those stories. I think we tried to structure a narrative similar to the Greek myths of the past.

DS/AD-M: Do you have any plans to work together on anything in the future?

MURASE: I am working on several projects and I want Satō to work with me for one of them, but Satō is pretty busy right now. So the timing is the issue.

SATŌ: We met each other for the first time in half a year at this convention, and we have been talking. We have been able to do some research and information gathering on possible projects.

DS/AD-M: Moving on to *Ghost in the Shell: Stand Alone Complex,* in the episodes where Section 9 deals with the terrorist group known as the "Individual Eleven," the basis for this group's actions is explained by an essay or manifesto in the show. Was there an actual philosophy or series of events on which you based that idea?

SATŌ: Initially, we were going to concentrate on how Japan was going to participate in war after 9/11. But by the time we were working on those episodes, the Iraq war had already started and our Self-Defense Force was sent to Iraq. So it was a fiction intended to portray the future and then the war started. During this time we also had an election. Many Japanese voted for the politicians without realizing that the politicians planned to send our troops to Iraq and Afghanistan. They did not realize the consequences of their votes until they saw the online videos of a Japanese man being captured as hostage and then decapitated. So that part of it started out as a fiction and then became a documentary. I created the episodes of "Individual 11" in order to express the irresponsibility of the Japanese people when they voted for these politicians.[1]

MURASE: So when we started making it, it was meant to be a science-fiction future but became reality when the war started.

DS/AD-M: In one of your panels, you talked about a blending of American and Japanese cultures in animation. For example, I don't know if you have seen *Afro-Samurai* or *The Boondocks* . . .

SATŌ: (breaking into English) . . . I *really* like *Boondocks*! *Boondocks* did one episode that was like *Samurai Champloo*!

DS/AD-M: Yes!

SATŌ: (laughs) I wrote that! [referring to *Samurai Champloo*]

DS/AD-M: So perhaps the Western influences on *Ergo Proxy* and *Samurai Champloo* are quite strong. Can you tell us about your philosophy concerning how the two cultures interact, particularly looking at the racial issues?

SATŌ: People asked me why we portrayed a "black" culture rather than samurai (in *Samurai Champloo*), and I said that it is a story about a minority culture. "Hip-hop" is minority culture and the members of Champloos were a counter- or minority culture in the perspective of that time as well. So connecting them created some cultural meaning. On the other hand, *Afro-Samurai* and *The Boondocks* are influenced by Japanese anime, but *Afro-Samurai* focuses on a black character and shows its Western influences. So the exchange is happening in both ways between Japanese and American cultures. I am not sure if I am going to commit myself to following that flow, but we need to know what we think about the trend and what we want to do about it.

FIGURE 2. Murase Shūkō *(center)* and Satō Dai *(right)* during their interview.

MURASE: This is a complicated question.

SATŌ: Is race an issue here? Does the fact that the Japanese are also "colored" people have anything to do with anime as a form of pop culture that merges both Western and Japanese culture? Do we have some inferiority complex about our "color"?

MURASE: I think we do have some amount of inferiority complex. It is certainly not nonexistent. But we are not making anime to express a sense of inferiority. Rather, I think anime is something that can go beyond all that. Until a few years ago, there was no way any Japanese anime characters could be accepted overseas. But now people just love them. The nationality of the character is not an issue anymore. In live-action films, a character is always recognized as having a racial background. But in anime, unless we intentionally put it forward, we do not have to worry about the race of the characters. I think this is why we can create stories that have global appeal. And that is why I take anime very seriously. It seems like many Americans now love

anything that is very Japanese. But I cannot clearly understand (or analyze) that trend.

SATŌ: I realized after coming here that anime has the power to erase racial awareness. And I am sure this realization will affect my later work.

Notes

The authors wish to thank the AnimeFest staff, particularly Jonathan Nawrocki and Robert Jenks, for their assistance in arranging this interview.

1. Editor's note: Satō is referring to an incident in October 2004 when a group linked to Al-Qaeda in Iraq captured a Japanese civilian, Kōda Shōsei, in Iraq. The group issued a video demanding Japanese troops be withdrawn. When the Japanese government refused, Kōda was beheaded and the video of his death was posted online. While this incident received only scant coverage in the United States, it was widely publicized in the Japanese media, leading to a public debate about the deployment of the Japanese troops in Iraq.

CONTRIBUTORS

BRENT ALLISON recently received a PhD in the Social Foundations of Education program at the University of Georgia.

MARK ANDERSON is the author of *Japan and the Specter of Imperialism.*

CHRISTOPHER BOLTON is associate professor of Comparative and Japanese Literature at Williams College. He is author of *Sublime Voices: The Fictional Science and Scientific Fiction of Abe Kōbō* and coeditor of *Robot Ghosts and Wired Dreams: Japanese Science Fiction from Origins to Anime* (University of Minnesota Press, 2007).

MARTHA CORNOG, MA, MS, has written articles on manga and anime for the sexological and library literature, and writes the graphic novel column for *Library Journal.* Together with Timothy Perper, she is editor of *Graphic Novels beyond the Basics* (forthcoming) and is currently editing an anthology of essays on manga and anime.

MARK DRISCOLL is assistant professor of Japanese and international studies at the University of North Carolina–Chapel Hill.

ANGELA DRUMMOND-MATHEWS is professor of English at Paul Quinn College.

MICHAEL FISCH received his PhD in anthropology from Columbia University. He is currently a postdoctoral fellow at the Harvard University Reischauer Institute of Japanese Studies, where he is working on a book concerning the intersection between new communication media and the commuter train network in contemporary Japan. He has published work on the animation of Oshii Mamoru, the fiction of Murakami Haruki, and the phenomenon of chapel weddings in Japan.

MICHAEL DYLAN FOSTER is assistant professor of folklore and East Asian languages and cultures at Indiana University. He is author of *Pandemonium and Parade: Japanese Monsters and the Culture of Yōkai.*

WENDY GOLDBERG is a PhD student in English at the University of Connecticut and an instructor at the U.S. Coast Guard Academy.

MARC HAIRSTON is a professional space physicist at the University of Texas at Dallas, where he coteaches a literature course about anime with Pamela Gossin. He is a speaker at the Schoolgirls and Mobilesuits workshop at the Minneapolis College of Art and Design and cocreator of *Cindi in Space,* the first online manga funded by NASA.

CHARLES SHIRO INOUYE is professor of Japanese at Tufts University. He is a translator of Izumi Kyōka's work. His recent publications include *Evanescence and Form: An Introduction to Japanese Culture* (2008) and "Promoting Virtue and Punishing Vice: Tarantino's *Kill Bill* and the Return of *Bakumatsu* Aesthetics" in *Postscript.* He is writing a book-length critique of modernity entitled "Figurality and the Development of Modern Consciousness."

REI OKAMOTO INOUYE is associate academic specialist in Japanese at Northeastern University. She teaches Japanese pop culture, film, and language, and she researches wartime manga.

PAUL JACKSON is a freelance writer based in England. He has written anime reviews for *Midnight Eye* and contributed to *Senses of Cinema* and *Film International.*

SETH JACOBOWITZ is assistant professor in the Humanities Department at San Francisco State

University, where he specializes in modern Japanese literature and visual culture. He recently completed *The Edogawa Rampo Reader.*

THOMAS LAMARRE is professor of East Asian studies, art history, and communication studies at McGill University. He is author of *Shadows on the Screen: Tanizaki Juni'ichiro on Cinema and Oriental Aesthetics, Uncovering Heian Japan: An Archaeology of Sensation and Inscription,* and *The Anime Machine: A Media Theory of Animation* (Minnesota, 2009)

TOM LOOSER is associate professor of Japanese studies at New York University. He is author of *Visioning Eternity: Aesthetics, Politics, and History in the Early Modern Noh Theater.*

FRENCHY LUNNING is professor at the Minneapolis College of Art and Design and codirector of SGMS: Schoolgirls and Mobilesuits, a weekend workshop there.

SHENG-MEI MA is professor of English at Michigan State University, where he specializes in Asian diaspora and Asian American studies and East–West comparative studies. His publications include *East–West Montage: Reflections on Asian Bodies in Diaspora* (2007), *The Deathly Embrace: Orientalism and Asian American Identity* (University of Minnesota Press, 2000), *Immigrant Subjectivities in Asian American and Asian Diaspora Literatures* (1998), *Chenmo de shanhen* (2005, Silent scars), and *Sanshi zuoyou* (1989, Thirty, left and right). His *Asian Diaspora and East–West Modernity* is forthcoming.

CHRISTINE MARRAN is associate professor of Japanese literature and cultural studies at the University of Minnesota. She is author of *Poison Woman: Figuring Female Transgression in Modern Japanese Culture* (University of Minnesota Press, 2007).

ZÍLIA PAPP is assistant professor in media studies in the Department of Global and Interdisciplinary Studies at Hosei University, Tokyo.

MARCO PELLITTERI is a sociologist. His most recent book is *Il Drago e la Saetta. Modelli, strategie e identità dell'immaginario giapponese* (The dragon and the dazzle: Models, strategies, and identities of Japanese imagination).

TIMOTHY PERPER, PhD, has written on manga and anime for sexological and scholarly literature. Together with Martha Cornog, he is editor of *Graphic Novels beyond the Basics* (forthcoming) and is currently editing an anthology of essays on manga and anime.

YOJI SAKATE is recognized as one of Japan's most socially conscious and politically active artists. He founded Rinkogun Theater Company in 1983, and his play *Yaneura* (The attic) was produced by The Play Company in New York City in 2007.

CHINAMI SANGO is an avant-pop artist whose major works include *Nonai Kareshi* and *Soulless Pop.*

DEBORAH SCALLY is a PhD candidate at the University of Texas at Dallas. She teaches composition, rhetoric, and literature at the Art Institute of Dallas and at community colleges.

DEBORAH SHAMOON is assistant professor of Japanese literature and popular culture at the University of Notre Dame.

MANAMI SHIMA was an actress, interpreter, and translator. She had a long involvement with the theatrical company Seinendan, directed by Oriza Hirata. She passed away in 2003.

REBECCA SUTER is lecturer in Japanese studies at the University of Sydney. She is author of *The Japanization of Modernity: Murakami Haruki between Japan and the United States.*

TAKAYUKI TATSUMI is professor of English at Keio University in Tokyo and a science fiction critic. He is author of *Cyberpunk America* and *Full Metal Apache.*

CHRISTOPHE THOUNY is a PhD candidate in East Asian studies at New York University.

GAVIN WALKER is a doctoral candidate in East Asian literature at Cornell University. He is currently translating a volume of the selected writings of Uno Kōzō.

DENNIS WASHBURN is professor of Japanese and comparative literature at Dartmouth College. His recent publications include *Translating Mount Fuji, Converting Cultures,* and translations of two novellas by Mizukami Tsutomu.

THERESA M. WINGE is assistant professor of fashion design and theory at Indiana University, Bloomington.

CALL FOR PAPERS

 The goal of *Mechademia* is to promote critical thinking, writing, and creative activity to bridge the current gap between professional, academic, and fan communities and discourses. This series recognizes the increasing and enriching merger in the artistic and cultural exchange between Asian and Western cultures. We seek contributions to *Mechademia* by artists and authors from a wide range of backgrounds. Contributors endeavor to write across disciplinary boundaries, presenting unique knowledge in all its sophistication but with a broad audience in mind.

The focus of *Mechademia* is manga and anime, but we do not see these just as objects. Rather, their production, distribution, and reception continue to generate connective networks manifest in an expanding spiral of art, aesthetics, history, culture, and society. Our subject area extends from anime and manga into game design, fan/subcultural/conspicuous fashion, graphic design, commercial packaging, and character design as well as fan-based global practices influenced by and influencing contemporary Asian popular cultures. This list in no way exhausts the potential subjects for this series.

Manga and anime are catalysts for the emergence of networks, fan groups, and communities of knowledge fascinated by and extending the depth and influence of these works. This series intends to create new links between these different communities, to challenge the hegemonic flows of information, and to acknowledge the broader range of professional, academic, and fan communities of knowledge rather than accept their current isolation.

Our most essential goal is to produce and promote new possibilities for critical thinking: forms of writing and graphic design inside as well as outside the anime and manga communities of knowledge. We encourage authors not only to write across disciplinary boundaries but also to address readers in allied communities of knowledge. All writers must present cogent and rigorous work to a broader audience, which will allow *Mechademia* to connect wider interdisciplinary interests and reinforce them with stronger theoretical grounding.

Due dates for submissions for future *Mechademia* issues

January 1, 2011: User Enhancement
January 1, 2012: Lines of Sight

Each essay should be no longer than five thousand words and may include up to five black-and-white images. Color illustrations may be possible but require special permission from the publisher. Use the documentation style of The Chicago Manual of Style, 15th edition. Copyright permissions will be sought by the editorial staff of *Mechademia*.

Submissions should be in the form of a Word document attached to an e-mail message sent to Frenchy Lunning, editor of *Mechademia*, at frenchy_lunning@mcad.edu. Mechademia is published annually in the fall.

Visit http://www.mechademia.org for more information.